The

BEECHERS

The BEECHERS

America's Most Influential Family

OBBIE TYLER TODD

LOUISIANA STATE UNIVERSITY PRESS

BATON ROUGE

Published by Louisiana State University Press
lsupress.org

Manufactured in the United States of America
First printing

Designer: Michelle A. Neustrom
Typeface: Miller Text
Printer and binder: Sheridan Books, Inc.

Jacket photograph: The final reunion of the Beecher family in New York, photographed by
Matthew Brady in 1859. Courtesy Schlesinger Library, Harvard Radcliffe Institute.

Library of Congress Cataloging-in-Publication Data

Names: Todd, Obbie Tyler, author.
Title: The Beechers : America's most influential family / Obbie Tyler Todd.
Description: Baton Rouge : Louisiana State University Press, 2024. |
    Includes bibliographical references and index.
Identifiers: LCCN 2024012762 (print) | LCCN 2024012763 (ebook) |
    ISBN 978-0-8071-8275-8 (cloth) | ISBN 978-0-8071-8338-0 (epub) |
    ISBN 978-0-8071-8339-7 (pdf)
Subjects: LCSH: Beecher family. | Beecher, Lyman, 1775–1863—Family. |
    Families of clergy—United States—Biography. | Clergy—United States—
    Biography. | Social reformers—United States—Biography. | United
    States—Moral conditions—History—19th century. | Intellectuals—
    United States—Biography.
Classification: LCC BX7260.B33 T63 2024 (print) | LCC BX7260.B33
    (ebook) | DDC 285.092/2—dc23/eng/20240711
LC record available at https://lccn.loc.gov/2024012762
LC ebook record available at https://lccn.loc.gov/2024012763

To my grandmother, Ann Lynette Gay

Contents

Illustrations follow page 92.

Foreword

EVERYBODY KNOWS about at least one of the Beechers. Immediately after the publication of *Uncle Tom's Cabin* in 1852, Harriet Beecher Stowe was celebrated by readers who were convinced by her account of the evils of slavery and just as roundly reviled by readers who perceived the book as nothing but slander of an entire society. Later, as the book was dismissed, rehabilitated, critiqued, or championed, its author remained in the forefront of American consciousness because of how widely it continued to be read.

Those with a little more historical grounding also know that Lyman Beecher, Harriet's father, was one of the nation's most renowned clergymen, moral reformers, and educators. They are aware that Harriet's younger brother, Henry Ward, was New York's best-known celebrity across the middle decades of the nineteenth century as the immensely popular pastor of Brooklyn's Plymouth Church, a widely read author, and a much-noticed weather vane of popular opinion. And they know that Harriet's older sister Catharine was a pioneering promoter of education for women as well as an author who all but invented the singularly American industry of home economics.

Alongside knowledge of these figures has existed the concomitant awareness that the Beechers were distinctive *as a family*. But no one for more than a generation has tried to do what Obbie Tyler Todd does in this book by writing about that family as a unit. And among those who have attempted this daunting feat, no one has done so with such wit and wisdom, such mastery of the Beechers' mountainous literary remains, and such perceptive use of the scholarship devoted to the nineteenth-century worlds in which they played such leading parts.

Readers will find here an unusually comprehensive account of an impressive family tree. At the root is Lyman Beecher, born nine months before the declaration of American independence and dying nine days after Abraham Lincoln issued the Emancipation Proclamation. The trunk is the three wives he married in succession: Roxana Foote, Harriet Porter, and, as a late-life consort, Lydia Jackson. The branches are Lyman's eleven children who survived into adulthood (eight from Roxana Foote and three from Harriet Porter) with a host of significant spouses grafted on (Calvin Stowe, as one example, contributed significantly to the origin of public education in Ohio and was one of the nation's premier students of the Christian Bible). Twigs are Lyman's grandchildren and great-grandchildren, many of whom Todd somehow manages to incorporate into his story.

And what a story! The family's history did not reflect the nation's history perfectly or completely, but no other American clan even came close. Following the Beechers' sprawling careers takes readers to Boston, Hartford, and Brooklyn (before it was consolidated with Manhattan), but also significant towns on the frontier (Cincinnati, Indianapolis, Milwaukee, and Jacksonville, Illinois) as well as far-flung locations like Hong Kong and Mandarin, Florida.

Various members of the family had firsthand contact with presidents William Henry Harrison, Abraham Lincoln (also Mary Todd Lincoln), Andrew Johnson, and Grover Cleveland. Harriet was not the only one in a literary circle that included Oliver Wendell Holmes Sr., Julia Ward Howe, Mark Twain, and John Greenleaf Whittier. Henry Ward was well known for what he wrote and preached about the Mexican War, the Fugitive Slave Law of 1850, John Brown's raid on Harpers Ferry, the Civil War, and subsequent political campaigns, but other Beechers also interacted with a full roster of influential public figures that numbered Lincoln's Secretary of War Edwin Stanton, Liberty Party presidential candidate James G. Birney, cabinet secretary and then Chief Justice of the Supreme Court Salmon P. Chase, Senator Charles Sumner, newspaper editor (and 1872 presidential nominee) Horace Greeley, U.S. ambassador to Great Britain Charles Francis Adams, and educational reformer Horace Mann. British luminaries Charles Dickens and Charles Darwin also drifted into the family orbit. It should go without saying that a family where all seven sons became preachers, while Harriet and Catharine published works of more theological insight than any of their brothers, knew personally a huge range of the era's noteworthy Christian ministers.

In their self-appointed role as national reformers, different Beechers at different times championed phrenology, temperance, spiritualism, Darwinism, abolitionism (some reluctant, some cautious, some radical), and women's suffrage. These commitments led them to partner, again at different times and in different ways, with Frederick Douglass and other abolitionists (the martyred Elisha Lovejoy, the Grimké sisters and Theodore Dwight Weld, William Lloyd Garrison), and then after the Civil War sister Isabella with the notorious breaker of sexual norms Victoria Woodhull.

Not surprisingly, Beechers were present at many of the nation's most crucial events. Three younger Beechers fought with the Union army at Gettysburg, and one of the physicians who tended Abraham Lincoln after John Wilkes Booth's fatal attack was named Lyman Beecher Todd in honor of the patriarch.

The family's unfolding story is full of arresting reversals. Catharine Beecher defended the Cherokee when President Andrew Jackson drove them out of the Southeast onto "the trail of tears," and other members of the family also campaigned for the rights of Native America—but one of Lyman's grandsons was killed as a soldier in a skirmish with the Cherokee shortly after the Civil War. Lyman became a national figure when he supported the nation's nascent temperance movement by publishing *Six Sermons on the Nature, Occasions, Signs, Evils, and Remedy of Intemperance*—but several of the clan battled alcoholism, not always with success. Lyman first came to wider public attention when he spoke out vehemently against dueling after Aaron Burr fatally shot Alexander Hamilton—but two of Lyman's sons killed themselves with gunshot wounds to the head. The Beechers were America's most renowned promoters of New England's Puritan virtues, as adapted to Victorian standards—but Henry Ward was at the center of the most publicized sex scandal of his age.

The enduring contribution of this book, however, goes well beyond merely recording the extraordinary doings of an extraordinary cast of characters. That contribution comes from Obbie Tyler Todd's skill in showing how Lyman's paternal influence ("maneuvering" as well as "motivating" his children and their children), combined with the hyperkinetic activism of his children, exerted an enduring national influence. A key in the background is the movement of the clan's religious commitments from modified Calvinism to anti-Calvinism or post-Calvinistic Unitarianism. In the foreground, however, remains the Puritan impulse (again modified by Lyman's embrace of a "New School" adjustment) to do good. Although "Beecherism" truly was, as Todd indicates, "less of an idea than a bravado," the story holds together because Lyman's sons and daughters were each in their own way committed to "the family business of moral influence." That influence could be conservative or progressive, often both at the same time, even in the same individual. Yet for an extended family marked almost as much by deep disagreements as shared agreements, almost all of the Beechers almost all of the time shared a belief that individuals acting freely could change the world, that the family unit was the fundamental driver of human progress, and that American Christian republicanism supplied the best ideology for guiding the human community.

Those who pick up this book will read a story fascinating in itself. They should also recognize that the story is big with implications for an American present that is both far distant from and yet still in touch with the world in which this remarkable family exerted its remarkable influence.

Mark A. Noll

Acknowledgments

I OWE A SPECIAL THANKS to many people who inspired, encouraged, and assisted me during this writing project. Although I have long been fascinated with the figure of Rev. Lyman Beecher, two Pulitzer Prize–winning historians helped introduce me to Lyman's extraordinary children: Daniel Walker Howe and Debby Applegate. In Howe's *The Political Culture of the American Whigs* (1979), I first noticed the sheer number of accomplishments of the Beechers as well as their diversity. Howe called the Beechers "one of the truly great families in American history," and he was right. However, it was not until I read Debby Applegate's biography of Henry Ward Beecher that I realized just how much personality was jam-packed into this eccentric group of people. In one of the best-written (and humorous) history books I have ever read, Applegate presents Henry Ward Beecher as an admirable *and* deeply flawed individual at the very same time. This is, in my opinion, the best way to chronicle a family such as the Beechers. I have attempted to write this book with a similar frame of mind because I believe the Beechers are, at the risk of cliché, America in microcosm.

As I was getting the project off the ground, I visited Doug Sweeney at Beeson Divinity School (Samford University) in Birmingham, and he confirmed my intuitions about what a proper telling of the Beecher story would entail. Without the encouragement of that meeting, I might not have mustered the will to compose a book about such a large family. I owe many thanks to Dr. Sweeney for the good conversation. My friend Daniel Gullotta also urged me to consider the project and showed me the need that existed for such a book. I contacted Daniel many times over several months with questions about historiography. During my research, I paid a visit to the Harriet Beecher Stowe Center in Harford, Connecticut. Their staff, particularly Elizabeth Burgess, were incredibly helpful in providing everything

I needed to investigate the lesser-known Beechers like William and James and Thomas and Charles. I'd also like to extend my deepest appreciation to the staff at Beinecke Library at Yale University for assisting me with digital copies from the Beecher Family Papers. A good portion of this book was written at the Crown Brew coffee shop in Marion, Illinois, and I owe many thanks to the fantastic people there. Above all, my wife, Kelly, was my engine for such a long and sometimes grueling project. Although she probably tired of hearing about the Beechers over the course of months, she at least feigned interest and for that I am grateful.

The Beecher Family

Lyman Beecher (1775–1863)

Famous revivalist; pastored churches in New York, Connecticut, Massachusetts, Ohio; served as president of Lane Seminary in Cincinnati (1832–50)

m. Roxana Foote 1799

Granddaughter of Rev. War gen. Andrew Ward; from a refined, highly educated Episcopalian family in Nut Plains, CT

CHILDREN:

Catharine E. Beecher (1800–1878)
- Pioneer of women's education in Hartford, CT, and in the Midwest
- Advocate for Native American rights
- Founder of home economics

William H. Beecher (1802–1889)
- Pastored churches across New England, New York, and Ohio

Edward Beecher (1803–1895)
- President of Illinois College (1830–44)
- Made a famous defense of abolitionism
- Pastored churches in New Eng., Ill., and eventually Brooklyn, NY

Mary Beecher Perkins (1805–1900)
- Partnered with sister Catharine in founding Hartford Female Seminary
- Married to lawyer-politician Thomas Perkins
- Grandmother of Charlotte Gilman Perkins

Harriet (February–March 1808)
- Died in infancy

George Beecher (1809–1843)
- Abolitionist and agent of American Anti-Slavery Society
- Pastored churches in Ohio and New York

Harriet Beecher Stowe (1811–1896)
- Famous novelist and antislavery writer
- Advocate for women's rights, postwar Reconstruction, Black education, Native American rights

Henry Ward Beecher (1813–1887)
- Most famous pastor in America during his lifetime
- Antislavery and women's rights leader
- Pastor of Plymouth Church in Brooklyn

Charles Beecher (1815–1900)
- Musician, pastor in New England, Middle Atlantic, the West
- Abolitionist
- Public educator in Reconstruction South (Florida)

continued

m. Harriet Porter 1817
Daughter of Dr. Aaron Porter of Maine;
her uncle, William King, was the first governor of Maine

CHILDREN:

Frederick (1818–1820)
• Died at age two

Isabella Beecher Hooker (1822–1907)
• Suffragist
• Leader in spiritualism
• Married to lawyer, judge, and
  politician John Hooker in Hartford,
  CT

Thomas K. Beecher (1824–1900)
• Well-known pastor in Elmira, NY
• Educator in Philadelphia and
  Hartford

James Chaplin Beecher (1828–1886)
• Led Black regiment during Civil War
• Missionary to the South China Sea
• Pastored churches in New York

m. Lydia Beals Jackson 1836
Lyman Beecher and Lydia Jackson had no children

The
BEECHERS

INTRODUCTION
Fire, Impulse, and Beecherism

ON A WARM SUNDAY afternoon in May of 1830, Lyman Beecher stood up to preach. Gripping a King James Bible with his large, muscular hands, Beecher was as comfortable behind a pulpit as his blacksmith father had been with an anvil. His unrelenting blue eyes scanned the sanctuary of the church, filled to capacity. In Philadelphia for the Presbyterian General Assembly, the man known as "Brimstone Beecher" was something of a celebrity for his ability to kindle spiritual revival. One local well-to-do church had invited him to be their pastor because his "reviving influence" abounded "to a degree which very few men in our country have ever had."[1] Born in New Haven, Connecticut, in 1775, raised by his aunt and uncle on a farm in Guilford, educated at Yale under the grandson of Puritan revivalist Jonathan Edwards, and later becoming pastor of Hanover Street Church in Boston, Beecher was a Yankee of Yankees. He even preached like the Puritans of old. After expositing a text, Beecher moved onto doctrine. After doctrine, he moved to application, what his daughter Harriet called "the heart of his discourse."[2] The only thing Lyman Beecher loved more than reading the Bible was doing something about it.

In Philadelphia, a city of lapsed Puritans and Quakers, there was plenty of work to be done. According to Beecher, sinners needed to be converted from an array of evils, including Catholicism, Unitarianism, Universalism, Deism, French infidelity, German infidelity, Episcopalianism, hyper-Calvinism, and Arminianism. After he reformed their souls, Beecher believed it was his duty to reform the way they lived, beginning with their consumption of alcohol. New England's preeminent revivalist was also America's leading crusader against drunkenness, the enemy of physical effort and "moral energy."[3] Beecher's reputation as the national spokesman for temperance transcended geographical, theological, and even racial lines. On this particular Sunday afternoon, Beecher was not preaching to Scotch-Irish Presbyterians. As shouts of "Amen!" and "True! True!" began to rise in the sanctuary, Beecher ignited a crowd of two thousand Black Methodists with his anti-drink gospel. A bishop in the African Methodist Episcopal Church had invited Beecher personally, hoping that the famous preacher might exhort his parishioners to pursue holiness and abstain from alcohol.[4] Beecher didn't disappoint.

By the end of the service, Beecher had persuaded a tenth of his listeners to stop drinking alcohol completely. He couldn't keep the news to himself. "Two hundred came forward and subscribed a pledge of entire abstinence which I wrote for them—the largest Temperance Society, I believe, ever organized at once, and promising to carry it through all the colored families of the land," Beecher bragged to his eldest son, William, who was preparing to attend Yale in the fall. As America's most famous motivational speaker, Lyman also knew how to motivate his children. After lamenting Andrew Jackson's infamous "Indian Bill" in Georgia which expelled the Cherokee from their reservations and out of the state, the teetotaling father set out a strict daily schedule for his son and urged him to "pursue my plan rigidly." If indeed William was to follow in his father's footsteps as a minister of God, he would need to "follow [his] example for the first ten years of [his] life."[5] Beecher had high standards for his sons. On his wife's deathbed in 1816, Lyman had promised Roxana that *all* of his sons would become ministers. In the house of Lyman Beecher, reform was more than an ideal. It was the family business.

However, the art of persuasion was not enough to revive America. People also needed to be *enlisted*. The next month, he wrote to his eldest daughter, Catharine, in Hartford and called her attention to the same issues, including the one closest to her heart: Native American reform. In the previous year, Catharine had formed a women's auxiliary, circulated petitions, and wrote a pamphlet entitled "To the Benevolent Women of the United States" to advance the cause of the Cherokee. It was the first cause to be taken up by one of Lyman's children.[6] But Lyman was recruiting Catharine for a new kind of mission. In the letter to Catharine, Lyman implored his daughter to join him on a journey to "the majestic West," namely Cincinnati, "the London of the West." In his quixotic mind, the fate of the entire country rested on this sacred mission to the frontier. As he explained to Catharine, "If we gain the West, all is safe; if we lose it, all is lost." Lyman Beecher, New England's most famous (and most villainized) preacher, was known for speaking in such black-and-white terms. Although it often drew the scorn of his foes, it was a useful tool for attracting his listeners to his various causes, like the Domestic Missionary Society, which he helped establish in 1820, or the American Temperance Society, which he cofounded in 1826. Lyman Beecher believed he *would* revive America. The future was certain. The Bible had revealed (at least as he interpreted it) that his reforms would culminate in a golden age for the church, a millennium under the rule of Jesus Christ. But he could not accomplish this work on his own. He needed help.

For his skills as an organizer, Beecher has earned a host of nicknames from scholars through the years, some more fitting than others. In the words of one historian, he was the "commander in chief of the 'Second Great Awakening,'" marshalling people and resources for the ultimate aim of revival.[7] Another has called him "a self-appointed cheerleader and coach of a generation," a peacemaker and bridge-builder, but always for the sake of a larger fight.[8] In his biography of Beecher, Vincent Harding has dubbed him "the apostle of unity among the orthodox," a rather appropriate title for a man who provided the mold for American evangelical cooperation for generations.[9] In his daughter Catharine he found a similar mind. Like her father, Catharine was a tenacious reformer and organizer, having founded Hartford Female Seminary, one of the first educational institutions for women in the United States, with her sister Mary in 1823. Of Lyman's eleven adult children (two died in infancy), Catharine shared perhaps the most intimate connection with her Puritan father. According to many, she was the most determined, even domineering, of Beechers. Lyman once called her "the best boy [I] had."[10] Therefore, when Lyman pleaded with his daughter to join him on such an epic quest, he found a listening ear.

But Lyman was not simply asking Catharine to come along. He wanted *all* the Beechers to join him on his journey to Ohio, where a "great battle" was being waged between the forces of good and evil, and where "Catholics and infidels have got the start on us." Time was of the essence. Like an Old Testament patriarch preparing for the land of Canaan, he persisted, "if I go, it will be part of my plan that *you* go, and another that Edward, and probably all my sons and all my daughters who are willing to go." Lyman's epistle was a word of prophecy for the entire Beecher family. By the end of the summer, his next oldest son, Edward, would accept a new position as the inaugural president of Illinois College in Jacksonville. Except for Mary, who remained in Hartford, and Henry, who would join his family after graduating from Amherst, the Beechers were going west *together.* "We shall succeed," he declared, "the Indians will be saved!"[11] In an era of history that has been called "the transformation of America," no figure seemed to embrace the optimism and progress of the infant nation more than the most famous preacher in New England.[12] And no one imbibed his optimistic and progressive spirit more than his own children.

"A GREAT REFORMER"

In 1830, the entire nation seemed drawn to the magnetic personality of Lyman Beecher. In March, a friend in New York City informed him of a call from Bleecker Street Church. But he also confessed, "You are wanted in Boston, I know, and where are you not wanted?" He continued, "The Bible Society, the Tract Society, the Education Society, and, above all, the Home Missionary Society, all want you. You may do a great good in Boston, but could you do as much good the next four years of your life any where on earth as in New York??"[13] Indeed, a pulpit in the nation's largest city would have increased the scope of Beecher's influence (and salary) considerably. But he was not interested in moving up, but *out.* As the Northeast embroiled itself in intramural debates over the nature of the human will and the role of the Holy Spirit, there was real work to be done. Like so many of his era, Lyman Beecher was convinced that his own efforts could hasten the return of the Savior and introduce Christ's millennial reign upon the earth. The writings of the great Puritan theologian Jonathan Edwards had convinced him that the "millennium would commence in America."[14] Beecher had been called by God to save souls *and* society, and he possessed the unique ability to mobilize others on this divine enterprise, including his family.

In 1830, Lyman Beecher firmly believed that the most pressing issue facing America lay not on the Eastern Seaboard, but on the frontier. Not even an invitation by his dear friend Nathaniel W. Taylor, professor at Yale Divinity School, to serve at his alma mater could divert him from his course. The need was of global proportions. "The moral destiny of our nation, and all our institutions and hopes, and the world's hopes, turns on the character of the West," he pressed Catharine. With his daughter, Lyman was rehearsing the very same arguments for the evangelization of the West that he would make to the American public five years later in *A Plea for the West* (1835). One minister believed the work "ought to be in every family, and read by every adult in the great valley, who feels any interest in the preservation of our free and happy institutions."[15] Indeed, if Lyman Beecher was a catalyst for moral and social change in the early United States, his children likewise became a catalyst for their father. In the wake of the infamous "Trail of Tears," Catharine's sympathy for the Cherokee in the West had now ignited a similar burden in Lyman. America had a moral, not just a manifest, destiny. This was more than simply Lyman Beecher's vision of America. This was "Beecherism."

However, the previous year had demonstrated just how difficult it would be to reform a nation. Just as Lyman Beecher had a skill for making new friends, he also had a talent for making enemies. In May 1829, professor of sacred rhetoric at Andover, Ebenezer Porter, wrote a letter to excoriate Beecher for his tendency to "exalt . . . human agency" and his emphasis on human responsibility. To many New England elites, it appeared that Beecher, along with Nathaniel Taylor, was diminishing the doctrine of original sin. This so-called "New Haven Theology," or "Taylorism," was the *cause célèbre* in the land of the Pilgrims, and it would follow him all the way to Cincinnati, where Old School Presbyterians charged him with heresy.[16] Porter warned, "Brace up now, Brother Beecher, and bear a while with my plainness like a man as you are. Once in a century or two the Church needs a Great Reformer to arise. Some of your remarks have seemed to mean . . . that you were born for that end, and that the theology of New England is the theatre of operation."[17] Beecher wasn't just a moral or social reformer. He was also a theological innovator in the tradition of Jonathan Edwards who stressed the value of human ability and the importance of spiritual and civic responsibility. Edwards's grandson, Timothy Dwight, had cemented these ideas into Beecher at Yale. Lyman Beecher believed in human potential. In certain orthodox circles of New England, this was a dangerous idea.

To many, it appeared that Lyman Beecher was a self-appointed reformer of the church, in the mold of a Martin Luther or a John Calvin.

Like the Reformation itself, Beecher's reforms were not welcomed by the ecclesiastical authorities, at least those at Andover, the nation's first graduate school where Edward, his son, had attended seminary and where his future son-in-law Calvin Stowe would serve as professor. Even Unitarians, his avowed enemies, had accused him of abandoning Calvinism, even suggesting that he was a kind of crypto-Unitarian. Somewhere between the ultraorthodox and the heterodox stood Lyman Beecher. Within a month of receiving Porter's letter, he wrote back with his signature combination of fire and friendliness: "if I was not born to be a reformer (of which I never dreamed), it has always been my opinion that I was not born to be a coward."[18] Lyman Beecher never backed down from a fight.

Unfortunately, 1830 had not begun under the most auspicious of circumstances. On a chilly January evening, a fire in the chimney of Hanover Street Church had engulfed the entire building. When the volunteer fire companies arrived at the scene of the blaze, the firemen (who were part of working-class drinking clubs) had allegedly refused to work their engines, singing with jeering voices, "While Beecher's church holds out to burn, / The vilest sinner may return." This version of events may be as apocryphal as Charley Stowe's account of President Lincoln telling Harriet Beecher Stowe that she caused the Civil War. Still, there was little doubt that Lyman Beecher, the "Great Reformer" of New England who incessantly reminded his community of the evils of drinking and theater and Sabbath-breaking and Catholicism, was not beloved by every corner of Boston society. Nevertheless, as he often did, Beecher saw the hand of providence behind the tragedy, telling his son William that the "prospect of usefulness is, my apprehension, greatly increased by the event."[19] By his estimation, sixty "inquirers" had come forward the previous Sunday in their temporary meeting place to pursue church membership.

As his children knew well, Lyman Beecher saw the world in very cosmic, black-and-white terms. With the specter of "infidelity" lurking behind every rock and tree, God was always accomplishing a greater good and guiding history to a more glorious end. After Edward departed with a degree of controversy from Park Street Church in Boston in order to move to Illinois, the congregation awkwardly asked Lyman to supply his son's pulpit for the next three months.[20] Everywhere he turned, it seemed, Lyman Beecher had an audience for his gospel of progress and reform. And just a couple months later, he was approached about becoming the first president

of Lane Seminary in Cincinnati. When he announced his decision to leave
for the West to his church on July 5, 1832, he declared that Lane would
become a "revival seminary" designed to "convince gainsayers, allay fears,
soothe prejudice, inspire confidence, and co-operation in revivals and public charities, and all good things on the part of all, of every name, who sub-
stantially hold fast the truth, and love our Lord Jesus Christ in sincerity."[21]
Whether from the classroom or from the pulpit, Lyman Beecher's goal was
the same: the spiritual and moral reform of America.

A FAMILY OF INFLUENCERS

For the Beecher family, the trip to Cincinnati became, in the words of one
historian, "part pilgrimage, part crusade."[22] After young George watched
his father preach the good news of salvation to a crowd in Wheeling, Virginia, he wrote that Lyman "gave them the Taylorite heresy on sin and decrees to the highest notch; and what amused me most was to hear him
establish it from the Confession of Faith. It went high and dry, however,
above all objections, and they were delighted with it, even the strong Old
School men, since it had not been christened heresy in their hearing."[23]
Lyman Beecher was reforming Calvinism *and* the country right before his
children's eyes. And they were taking notes. But the young Beechers were
more than spectators. They were also *participants* in their father's quest
to change the world. The Beechers were, as Stuart C. Henry has described
them, "gospel gypsies, singing hymns, scattering tracts and, between private prayer meetings, engaging strangers in conversations about the soul."[24]
At Wheeling, George preached five times and Lyman four. Along the way,
George distributed religious tracts to various passersby, "peppering the
land," his sister Harriet recounted, "with moral influence."[25] As Harriet described years later, "Dr. Beecher and his sons, it was soon found could race
and chase and ride like born Kentuckians, and that 'free agency' on horse-
back, would go through mud and fire, and water, as gallantly as ever 'natural inability' could."[26] Religious and moral reform went hand in hand in the
Beecher mind, which is why the children, no less than their father, were so
theologically and socially minded.

Lyman's sons and daughters endured much at the hands of their exacting, overbearing father, to be sure. However, if the impulse to construct
America into a theocratic republican society was the driving force behind

Lyman Beecher's entire ministry, this same desire to compel others toward a moral and theological vision manifested itself early on in almost *all* of his children. At Yale, where he was valedictorian in 1822, Edward delivered a graduation oration on "Moral Influence."[27] At eighteen years old, even young Harriet gave a speech to students at her sister's school on "modes of exerting moral influence."[28] This innate tendency to overlap the spiritual and the material was, according to one historian, "Stowe's gift" as a writer.[29] For the Beechers, the sacred and the secular were interwoven, and they defined sin and redemption in largely social and even national terms. For this reason, Lyman Beecher expressed to Catharine in 1830 that he wished to "consecrat[e] all my children to God in that region [Cincinnati] who are willing to go."[30] God had given the Beechers a holy assignment. If Lyman believed he could change the world, he believed that his children would play a critical part in that transformation. Indeed they did, but not always as he expected.

Beginning nine months before American Independence and ending nine days after the Emancipation Proclamation, the life of Lyman Beecher is, quite arguably, the story of American evangelicalism in the early republic. However, due to their common cause in reforming America, it is difficult to tell one Beecher's story without telling them all. Just as Lyman helped write his children's stories, so they helped write his—literally. The "so-called autobiography" of Lyman Beecher was in fact a project carried out by several of the Beecher children, principally by Charles.[31] And the children did the same for one another. Charles wrote his brother Edward's autobiography, and Catharine did similarly for her brother George. As the once-widowed father of eight small children at the age of forty, and the twice-widowed father of eleven children at the age of fifty-nine, Lyman, who did not know his own mother and had no relationship with his father, forged an especially affectionate bond with his sons and daughters and became a connection point between the Beecher siblings long after they had left the Cincinnati residence at Walnut Hills. In fact, by the 1850s, when distance and personalities divided them, many of the Beechers longed for "the early unity of the family."[32] Therefore, that Lyman's children continued his legacy of reform and that several surpassed their father in notoriety was perhaps to be expected.

Discussing Lyman Beecher's politics, for example, historian Daniel

Walker Howe could not avoid mentioning his children. Calling Beecher "the Henry Clay of the ecclesiastical realm," Howe then notes:

> The son of a blacksmith, Beecher fathered one of the truly great families in American history. Among his five daughters and eight sons were Harriet the novelist, Edward the abolitionist, Henry Ward the preacher, Isabella the suffragist, and Catharine, the founder of home economics. His own father had been stern and unloving, but Lyman involved himself wholeheartedly with his children. He encouraged them in both intellectual and religious seeking and succeeded in imbuing them with his strong sense of mission. In an age when education for women was a novelty, Beecher devoted as much concern to his daughters' minds as to his sons'. His drive for himself, his family, and the cause of Christ knew no bounds.[33]

In such an enlightened and well-known family, the father was somewhat overshadowed by his children. Transcendentalist Theodore Parker once called Lyman Beecher "the father of more brains than any other man in America."[34] So notable was the entire Beecher family by the late nineteenth century that a reference to one Beecher often begged mentioning another. When the *New York Evening Express* praised the ministry of Henry Ward Beecher at Plymouth Church in Brooklyn, the editor called America's most famous pastor "a worthy scion of the name," as if celebrity was simply to be expected of Lyman Beecher's son.[35] Like his father, Henry had become the most famous preacher of his generation and "the Billy Graham of his era."[36]

However, Beechers weren't just compared with their father. Sometimes they were confused with one another. In 1863, when Henry visited Britain, where his sister's *Uncle Tom's Cabin* (1852) was an overwhelming sensation, he was once accidentally introduced as the Reverend Henry Ward Beecher Stowe.[37] Nevertheless, Henry would become almost as well-known in England as his sister. At his residence in London, the famous Baptist preacher Charles Spurgeon was once nearly swindled by a con man claiming to be "Captain Beecher, the son of Henry Ward Beecher." Thankfully, Spurgeon did not fall for the ruse. He replied warily, "If you are really Mr. Beecher's son, you must be able, through the American consul, or some friend, to get your cheque cashed, without coming to a complete stranger."[38]

Whether in pretense or in truth, the name of Beecher was known through-out the Anglo-American world. At the funeral of Lyman Beecher in 1863, Rev. Dr. Leonard Bacon famously commented that the nation was inhab-ited by three types of people: saints, sinners, and Beechers.[39]

In a golden age of oratory and print, the Beechers were, one could ar-gue, the most recognizable family in nineteenth-century America. Not-ing their signature style of communication, Unitarian Thomas Starr King described "the rhetorical and emotional friskiness of the Beechers." Even Samuel Clemens, or Mark Twain, known for his own "rhetorical and emotional friskiness," described the lesser-known Thomas as "a famous Beecher." Thomas officiated Clemens's wedding to Olivia Langdon in 1870. Clemens was also known to drop by the Stowe residence in Hartford quite regularly, pretending to ask advice from his fellow celebrity novelist. So re-nowned was the entire family that Isabella complained of being overshad-owed by her other siblings: "Everywhere I go, I have to run on the credit of my relations. Nowhere but at home can I claim to a particle of individual-ity, to any distinction of goodness, smartness, or anything else whatever."[40] In 1868, Isabella even published a couple of articles on women's suffrage anonymously because she desired the essay to "make its own way, [rather] than be helped by my Beecher name."[41]

A NEW HISTORY OF THE BEECHERS

With such fame and influence, it is somewhat surprising that only one book has ever been written on the Beechers as a whole. As it stands, Mil-ton Rugoff's six-hundred-page *The Beechers: An American Family in the Nineteenth-Century* (1981) is still the only comprehensive account of one of the most influential families in American history. Then again, consid-ering how extensive is Rugoff's work and how daunting is the task of ex-amining such a large family, perhaps it is not completely shocking that another Beecher biography has not been attempted in the last forty years. Nevertheless, while incisive, Rugoff's tome is riddled with inaccuracies and stereotypes about New England Puritanism that often obscure how much the Beecher children resembled their father.[42] Rugoff has not been alone in such generalizations, which began as soon as histories were being writ-ten of the Beechers. In an 1887 tribute following Henry's death, Colonel

Robert G. Ingersoll wrote, "Henry Ward Beecher was born in a Puritan penitentiary, of which his father was one of the wardens—a prison with very narrow and closely-grated windows. Under its walls were the rayless, hopeless and measureless dungeons of the damned, and on its roof fell the shadow of God's eternal frown. In this prison the creed and catechism were primers for children, and from a pure sense of duty their loving hearts were stained and scarred with the religion of John Calvin."[43] While acknowledging Ingersoll's vitriol toward orthodox religion, Rugoff sympathizes with his views of Lyman Beecher's parenting, concluding that Beecher subjected his children to "certain of the most oppressive Puritan dogmas" and plunged them into "the Puritan labyrinth of obsessive concern with the self and the next world as against society and this world." According to Rugoff, it was Beecher's "vanity and pride" that compelled him to spend "his life telling everyone else how to live."[44]

At the very least, Rugoff's depiction of Lyman Beecher is incomplete. At worst, it perpetuates a distorted and rather simplistic religious narrative of the entire Beecher family.[45] Contrary to Rugoff, the Beechers were extremely concerned with the world in which they lived. Throughout his book, for example, Rugoff devotes much more time to dissecting the weaknesses of Calvinism than to exploring the optimistic view of history and humanity that pulsated through Lyman Beecher's entire family. Although it is true that Beecher venerated the famous Puritan theologian, Jonathan Edwards, almost to the point of worship, it is equally true that Beecher promoted a republican brand of Calvinism known as "New Haven Theology" that represented a significant departure from Edwards and which animated his view of, well, everything. Theologically and socially speaking, Beecher had as much in common with Charles Finney as he did with Jonathan Edwards (although he did not think so himself). For his time and place, Lyman Beecher was just as innovative as the younger Beechers were in theirs. And his children understood this well. After all, many of them were present at his heresy trial. When his New School congregation withdrew from the local presbytery in Lawrenceburg, Indiana, Henry relished being "the son of the Arch-Heretic."[46]

Although Lyman Beecher has become something of a cliché in history books for his revivalism, his belief in a "benevolent empire" of social causes, and his anti-Catholicism, he was not always stereotypical for his era.[47] Beecher was a rather complex, dynamic figure in his own right. He reflected the America he sought to reform. In the words of Harriet Beecher Stowe in *Oldtown Folks,* "every individual is part and parcel of a great picture of a society in which he lives and acts, and his life cannot be painted without reproducing the picture of the world he lived in."[48] The same was true of Lyman Beecher. Over the latter half of his career, Beecher shifted his views on slavery, Finneyism, and the disestablishment of religion, just to name a few. Once we understand Lyman Beecher as an evolving figure subject to culture and politics, we can make better sense of the dynamic relationships and changing thought endemic to the entire Beecher clan and that many understood as "Beecherism." As a result of Rugoff's emphasis on Romanticism rather than republicanism, his work tends to highlight the differences between Lyman and his famous children while overlooking the striking similarities between them. Instead, what is needed is a book that can explore the "family business" of moral influence and explain how Lyman was able to pass on this American enterprise to his children even with so many theological and social divisions among them. This is such a book.

Beecher historiography has always tended to focus on the individual members of the family because there was plenty of individuality to go around. The first biography of the family, *Saints, Sinners, and Beechers* (1934), written by Lyman Beecher's great grandson Lyman Beecher Stowe, provides portraits of each Beecher rather than telling one story chronologically.[49] Marie Caskey's religious biography in 1978 is structured in much the same way, providing vignettes of each member of the family rather than chronicling their lives together as one narrative.[50] To an extent, even Rugoff's tome is divided up in this fashion. Of course, there has been no lack of individual biographies. Harriet, the most famous Beecher and one of the most celebrated novelists in American history, has never lacked for biographers.[51] However, a true chronological biography of the *entire* Beecher family has never been attempted.

Beginning in the 1970s, substantive portraits of Lyman Beecher began to surface.[52] Still, when historians reintroduced us to the so-called "great gun of Calvinism," they foregrounded his role as minister and neglected his role as father.[53] Three works by Raymond L. Wood, Stuart C. Henry, and James W. Fraser are primarily biographical studies which focus on Beecher's contributions to American religion during the Second Great

Awakening.[54] While these do not discount the role of Lyman's children in his life and career, they are somewhat peripheral to the story, sometimes relegated to the index. In 1991, Vincent Harding's impressive *A Certain Magnificence: Lyman Beecher and the Transformation of American Protestantism, 1775–1863* continued many of these same religious themes while laying a greater emphasis on moral and social reform.[55] In the past twenty to thirty years, however, the focus has shifted to Lyman's children. In these works, scholars have tended to accentuate the differences between father and children, particularly on matters of religion, since there was a good bit of difference between many of them. Joan Hedrick's *Harriet Beecher Stowe: A Life* (1995), Barbara Anne White's *The Beecher Sisters* (2003), Debby Applegate's *The Most Famous Man in America: The Biography of Henry Ward Beecher* (2006), and Nancy Koester's *Harriet Beecher Stowe: A Spiritual Life* (2014) are just four of the most recent works that explore how far the apples fell from the Puritan tree.[56] As a result, the prevailing narrative of Lyman Beecher's religious parenting has included at least two assumptions: (1) Lyman inadvertently pushed his children *away* from much of Puritan religion, thereby sparking their rebellion from Calvinism and sometimes evangelicalism, (2) but he successfully indoctrinated his children into a kind of New England conservatism. Admittedly, there are shades of both in the Beecher story. Catharine, who followed her father on his quest to Cincinnati, provides the most vivid example. In fact, Catharine's experience laid the foundation for the rest of her siblings.

In 1822, Catharine's fiancé, Alexander Metcalfe Fisher, a professor at Yale in natural philosophy, was lost in a tragic shipwreck off the Irish coast. Instead of comforting her in a moment of unspeakable pain, Lyman traumatized his daughter by turning the unknown fate of Fisher's soul into a desperate, insensitive, yearlong attempt to ensure Catharine was converted. Ever the revivalist, Lyman chose evangelism over empathy, one might say. This harrowing experience was the turning point of Catharine's life personally, professionally, and religiously. In the summer of 1831, when a young Angelina Grimké visited Hartford Female Seminary before Catharine resigned as principal to leave for Cincinnati, Beecher related to her the story of Fisher's death and "how completely the whole course of her life had been changed by it."[57] Yet even still, Catharine did not cultivate an anti-evangelical spirit to the degree of a James Fenimore Cooper or a Nathaniel Hawthorne or other educated nineteenth-century New Englanders. Instead, she modeled her own ambitious initiatives after her father's evangelical networks, like when she founded the Central Committee for Promoting National Education, an organization which deployed "missionary teachers" to "save" the American West.[58] In *A Treatise on Domestic Economy* (1841), a book that established her as a nationally recognized authority on the health and well-being of the home, Catharine painted a picture of a healthy family remarkably similar to the one of her upbringing. In her chapter "On Domestic Amusements and Social Duties," for example, Catharine made oblique references to Lyman on several occasions, from gardening to music to games to circular letters. Defining a good father, she wrote, "It is far more needful, for children, that a father should attend to the formation of their character and habits, and aid in developing their social, intellectual, and moral nature, than it is, that he should earn money to furnish them with handsome clothes, and a variety of tempting food."[59] (Always strapped for cash, Lyman somehow managed to afford a premier education for most of his children.) If the Beecher children were indeed raised in a "Puritan penitentiary," it is curious that Catharine would offer Lyman Beecher as a model for proper parenting and "intellectual companionship."[60]

While Catharine rejected the predestination of a Calvinist God (and eventually wrote her own essay on the freedom of the will in 1839), she wrestled with doctrines like divine providence and goodness rather openly with her father. In her biography of the oldest Beecher child, Kathryn Kish Sklar observes, "This confrontation between Catharine and her religious heritage was the most formative experience of her life. It so profoundly engaged her mind and emotions that, even while she resisted certain doctrines of her father's religion, she became irrevocably committed to the larger issues of that heritage."[61] Her independent spirit never led her to question, for instance, the authority of men in the home. Criticizing the women's rights movement decades later, Catharine, who never married, demonstrated a rather traditional view of gender roles. She once opposed women's suffrage due to the threat of "foreign and domestic priesthood," leading one scholar to hear "echoes of Lyman Beecher's going to Cincinnati to save the West from the Catholics."[62] Like their father, the Beecher children were strangely conservative and progressive at the very same time, albeit in varying degrees. And like Lyman, they progressed with the nation itself. The antebellum generation was both a reflection of *and* a reaction to the revolutionary generation, and one can gain no better view of that continuity and complexity than the relationship of the Beechers to their progressively Puritan father.

With his deep moorings in Puritan custom and thought, Lyman Beecher actively *encouraged* his children to embrace a life of moral, social, and even religious reform. From circular letters to personal correspondence to spiritual testimonies, the Beechers attested to how deeply the seeds of reform were sown by their father, even when those seeds bore fruit in ways that Lyman never predicted or, at times, approved. While their theological leanings could sometimes be explained by the Episcopal influence of their maternal side, the Beechers' sharp consciences were inherited unmistakably from their father.[63] As historian Marie Caskey has noted, "New England's God and New England ways were the only ones the Beechers knew. To be sure, when the children visited their Anglican relatives, they were awakened to the fact that some segments of New England did not worship as they did, but their loyalty was still to the Puritan tradition of their father."[64] Amazingly, Isabella traced her views on women's rights back to family discussions around the dinner table in Cincinnati: "I date my interest in public affairs from those years between eleven and sixteen, when our family circle was ever in discussion on the vital problems of human existence, [where] the United States Constitution, fugitive slave laws, Henry Clay and the Missouri Compromise alternated with free will, regeneration, heaven, hell, and 'The Destiny of Man.'"[65] If Lyman Beecher was ever guilty of indoctrinating his children, he did so in a way that invited both open discussion and free inquiry, the very style of debate he had witnessed so boldly modeled for him at Yale by his own "father" Timothy Dwight, the man who had converted him to the faith.[66] The political and the moral and the theological almost always bound together in the Beecher home.

If one will permit the anachronism, the Beechers were, in some sense, the nation's first family of social justice warriors, united less by doctrine than by common ideals they imbibed from their father in "long discussions lasting past midnight and resumed at every meal."[67] In fact, Beecherism was one of the first identifiable (although often ill-defined) movements for social or public justice in the history of the United States, directly shaping other young reformers like abolitionist William Lloyd Garrison. While Lyman did not succeed in making good Calvinists of his children, they *were* thoroughly catechized in the Yankee school of moralism and social reform, beginning with the oldest. According to Catharine, "our house became in reality a school of the highest kind, in which [Lyman] was all the while exerting a powerful influence upon the mind and character of his children."[68] Edward, for instance, recalled long conversations with his father around the family table on the nature of justice. Although he eventually disagreed with Lyman on the subject of "social sins" and the issue of abolition, he maintained a commitment to justice throughout his lifetime. Whereas Lyman had been a leading critic of dueling after the death of Alexander Hamilton and chided those who "pervert justice" and "aid in the prostration of justice" by taking the law into their own hands, Edward also wielded his pen against the injustice of street violence, but in a different way.[69] After the murder of the abolitionist and journalist Elijah Lovejoy in 1837 at the hands of a pro-slavery mob in his state of Illinois, Edward wrote *A Narrative of Riots at Alton: In Connection with the Death of Rev. Elijah P. Lovejoy* (1838) to defend freedom of the press and freedom from slavery. It was the first abolitionist stand taken by a Beecher.[70] Lamenting that "in a Christian land even the show of justice is laid aside," Beecher pleaded that his friend had "died in defense of justice, and of the law, and of right: and with the instrument of justice in his hands."[71] Edward was much more outspoken than his father on the issue of slavery, but concepts like justice, moral influence, and the power of the press could all be traced to the family table.[72]

Although his presidency at Lane was rocked by the abolitionist controversy and Lyman himself never supported immediate emancipation, somehow Harriet credited her antislavery views to her father, once telling Frederick Douglass that Lyman's prayers for "poor, oppressed, bleeding Africa" turned her into an "enemy of all slavery."[73] Whether or not this was completely true, Harriet became, like her father, only a moderate reformer. Even as the celebrated author of *Uncle Tom's Cabin*, her views on slavery were never as extreme as that of Douglass (whom she invited to her home) just as Isabella's or Harry's views on women's rights were never as radical as those of Susan B. Anthony or Elizabeth C. Stanton. The Beechers were innovators, not iconoclasts. (Historian Molly Oshatz has identified Edward as a forerunner to Protestant liberalism due to his moderate arguments against enslavement.)[74] As Sklar notes, "Much of the effectiveness of the Beecher family lay in its ability to seize the power of social definition during a time of widespread change."[75] Their story was so much more than a struggle between a fundamentalist patriarch and his freethinking children because Lyman was not an ordinary Puritan and the children could be surprisingly conservative in their beliefs. As one historian has noted, the "evangelical united front" that coalesced between 1790 and 1837 largely by Lyman Beecher's efforts also brought about "the rise of American Victorianism," which several of his children embodied thoroughly.[76] In such a diverse family, the Beechers were tethered not by theology, geography, or even sometimes morality, but rather by their Beecherism. And this reformist gene developed rather strongly in the family even after Lyman's death, becoming the basis for some of their greatest divisions as well as their greatest achievements.

"BEECHERISM"

Historians have consistently identified a theological break between Lyman and his children because the Beechers did so themselves. In 1867, Henry Ward Beecher remarked to Ralph Waldo Emerson that "he did not hold one of the five points of Calvinism in a way to satisfy his father."[77] In 1927, Sinclair Lewis went so far as to call Henry "the archbishop of American liberal Protestantism."[78] Although Lewis was guilty of a bit of hyperbole, a liberal spirit certainly indwelled Beecher from a young age. "What is orthodoxy?" Henry once asked his readers at the *Independent*. "I will tell you. Orthodoxy is *my* doxy, and Heterodoxy is *your* doxy, that is if your doxy is not like *my* doxy."[79] In terms of style, Henry's ministry appeared to have more in common with the Methodists and Baptists than the Congregationalists or Presbyterians. Catharine and Harriet both joined the Episcopal Church of their deceased mother Roxana, curiously, after Lyman's death.[80] Harriet later urged her brother Charles to convert to Episcopalianism and become a minister. During one of their late dinner-table discussions, Lyman and Charles once engaged in a shouting match over the theology of Jonathan Edwards.[81] Even Edward, who adhered to many of his father's beliefs, also held to a mystifying view of the preexistence of the soul which he articulated in his poorly received *The Conflict of the Ages* (1855). Lyman once half-joked to his son, "Edward, you've destroyed the Calvinistic barns, but I hope you don't delude yourself that the animals are going into your little theological hencoop."[82] Needless to say, the Beechers were a diverse bunch. Lyman Beecher was, as George Marsden has called him, "the man who unquestionably best embodied [the] broad New School spirit" in American Presbyterianism, integrating modern ideas and moral reform into a confessional faith.[83] On one hand, Lyman failed to pass on this Edwardsean theology to most of his eleven children. On the other hand, almost all of them would adopt his "New School spirit" in some way, particularly in his pursuit of reform.

In both the North and the South, contemporaries of the Beechers often had a word for their sense of moral superiority and characteristically bold approach to reform: Beecherism. It was generally *not* a compliment. Before the Beechers had even arrived in the West, a local pastor was warning Cincinnatians about "Beecherism."[84] In the slaveholding South, where Harriet Beecher Stowe's *Uncle Tom's Cabin* was anathematized as a work of the devil, Beecherism was a monster under the bed. Richmond's *Southern Literary Messenger* struggled to define the creature:

> The old proverb, which divided the English into three classes—"Saints, sinners and Herveys," has of late received a cis-atlantic application, and the citizens of the new world have been designated as "Good, Bad and Beechers," the latter being supposed to be an intermediate class between the others. Proprietors of too much genius and goodness to be summarily condemned, and of too much ultraism and singularity to be commended, the Beechers defy both natural and artificial methods of classification, and can be ranked only in the catalogue of American curiosities. As we direct travellers to a hot spring or a mammoth cave, as the peculiarity of American nature, so we point out to him the Beecher family as the freak of American humanity.[85]

The name Beecher could even serve as an adjective. After the publication of Harriet Beecher Stowe's second antislavery novel, *Dred,* the *Southern Literary Messenger* denounced Stowe's "Beecherly boldness," calling her Beecherism a form of "total depravity."[86] Like their father, the Beecher children also had the gift of making enemies.

In an age full of various "isms" such as Finneyism, Taylorism, perfectionism, mesmerism, and spiritualism (all of which at least a few Beechers subscribed to in some degree), Beecherism was less of an idea and more of a bravado. In an 1857 editorial entitled "Beecherroyalty" in the *Brooklyn Times,* Walt Whitman accused Henry Ward Beecher of the worst kind of pastoral hubris. "We cannot help regarding hero worship as a great evil, whatever the characteristics and position of the hero himself," Whitman scoffed. "Mr. Beecher is doubtless a very able and sincere teacher of the people, but if the general effect of his teaching may be judged by the influence which his ministrations produced on the mind of the author of 'notes from a Plymouth Pulpit,' we may well doubt whether he is not making people Beecherites instead of making them Christians, and teaching them to worship him instead of that Creator whom he so eccentrically defines as a 'dim and shadowy effluence.'"[87] Whitman's concern was not completely unfounded. The Sunday ferries which transported hundreds from Manhattan to Brooklyn to listen to Henry were dubbed "Beecher Boats," and Plymouth Church where he preached was even nicknamed "Beecher's Theater."[88] When Plymouth Church sent loads of rifles to antislavery combatants in "Bleeding Kansas" one year earlier, they were known as "Beecher's Bibles," inflating the Beecher reputation for antislavery reform, and, in the opinion of many, the Beecher ego. In the *Autobiography of Mark Twain,* Samuel Clemens opined, "Mr. Beecher may be charged with a *crime,* and his whole following will rise as one man, and stand by him to the bitter end."[89] Henry was also a leader in the women's rights movement with his sister Isabella Beecher Hooker, who, not surprisingly, was also accused of shamelessly promoting the family brand. When Elizabeth Cady Stanton discovered in 1870 that Isabella had preferred not to include her at the lobbying convention for the National Woman Suffrage Association in Washington, DC, she scoffed, "The Beecher conceit surpasses understanding."[90]

Although Beecher fame never rose so high as it did with Harriet or Henry, and despite the fact that the Beechers were not as extreme in their views as many of their contemporaries, the braggadocio of Beecherism had in fact begun with Lyman himself. At a Mission Board Conference in New York in 1845, when a speaker was introduced in his place and announced that, "owing to the infirmities of age or the fatigue of travel, the celebrated Dr. Beecher" would not be able to deliver an address, the old reformer leapt out of his seat and gave a speech on missions, in his words, "full of fire, impulse, and Beecherism."[91] The Beecher children harkened back to their father's stage presence on numerous occasions, including Harriet on her public reading tour in 1872, when "the spirit of the old preacher was revived in her veins."[92] As Robert Merideth has noted in his biography of Edward, "ironically, the difficulties (which so consistently led them toward heresy that in the forties and fifties their eccentricity was called 'Beecherism') may be traced partly to the father."[93] However, Beecherism was more than mere theological eccentricity; it was the public swagger and social consciousness that came with it. And it lasted well after the 1840s and 1850s. In some sense, Beecherism was the moralistic *spirit* with which the family stumped for their various causes, not the causes themselves. According to some, this was precisely the problem with the Beechers' "eccentricity." Their subjectivity was fueled by their sense of superiority.

According to activist and public intellectual Orestes Augustus Brownson, a slippery tendency to avoid points of doctrine was shared by most of the group. In a scathing article in the *Catholic World* magazine in 1871, "Beecherism and Its Tendencies," Brownson exposed what he believed to be the dangers of their family philosophy: "Beecherism, as we understand it, errs chiefly not in asserting what is absolutely false, but in mistiming or misapplying the truth, and in presenting a particular aspect of truth for the whole truth." With a not-so-small Catholic bias (Brownson converted from Transcendentalism in 1843), he warned, "Beecherism is even more unintellectual than the Protestantism of the reformers themselves."[94] But Brownson did more than make generalizations. He named names. For instance, Brownson distinguished Thomas from Henry, "who is more frank and outspoken than his cunninger, more cautious, and more timid brother." Still, Brownson did not even consider Thomas to be a Christian, "regarding the Beechers as deepening into the darkness of unbelief, not as opening into the light of faith." Criticizing Thomas's alleged claims that all religions were essentially the same, the author mocked, "This Beecher can swallow any number of contradictions without making a wry face." Comparing Henry to "an india-rubber band," Brownson raged in disgust, "You see clearly enough what he is driving at, but you cannot catch and hold him. His statements are so supple or so elastic that he can give them any meaning that may suit the exigencies of the moment." Ironically, similar accusations had been hurled at Lyman's father in Cincinnati, the warden of the alleged "Puritan penitentiary."

Condemning Beecherism for its lack of rationality and its emphasis on subjective feelings, Brownson compared Thomas's beliefs to a new "edition of Bushnell-ism" (after Horace Bushnell, the Congregationalist minister of Hartford and the so-called father of American religious liberalism), claiming that Beecherism was guilty of immortalizing man and humanizing God. "Beecherism undeniably anthropomorphizes God," he scorned, "and regards him, as does Swedenborg, as the great or perfect Man, or as man carried up to infinity." So venomous was Brownson's critique of the Beechers that he even accused them of denying the doctrine of the Trinity, the Incarnation, and the new birth. Therefore, he reasoned, "Beecherism loses Jesus Christ himself," and "the Beechers have no Christian standing, even in simple human faith." A more serious indictment could not have been laid against another American in the middle of the nineteenth century.

However, Brownson did not save his invectives just for the brothers. Calling attention to the four Beechers who questioned the concept of eternal Hell, he insisted, "Beecherism, without explicitly affirming universal salvation, decidedly doubts that the sufferings of the damned, if any damned there are, will be everlasting, as we may see in *The Minister's Wooing*, and in the *Defence of Lady Byron*, by Mrs. Beecher Stowe," also noting her leanings toward mesmerism and spiritualism.[95] In the Beechers, Brownson saw the very worst of American society and the inevitable conclusion of Protestantism:

> Beecherism jumps astride every popular movement, or what appears to it likely to be a popular movement, of the day. It went in for abolition, negro suffrage, and negro eligibility, and now goes in for negro equality, in all the relations of society, female suffrage and eligibility, and reversing the laws of God, so as to make the woman the head of the man, not man the head of the woman. Henry Ward Beecher is at the head of the woman's rights movement, so earnestly defended by his lackey of the *Independent*. Beecherism goes in also for liberty of divorce, and virtually for polygamy and concubinage of free love, and free religion, while it retains enough of its original Calvinistic spirit to require the state to take charge of our private morals, and determine by statute

what we may or may not eat, drink, or wear, when we may go to bed or get up.[96]

Brownson obviously indulged in a bit of exaggeration in his screed against the Beechers. Nevertheless, it is revealing that even someone as vitriolic as Brownson could not help but notice how much of the old religion they still carried with them. As a former Unitarian and ardent Catholic, Brownson begrudged the Beechers for neither repudiating Transcendentalism nor completely shedding their Calvinism. (In this sense, Debby Applegate has rather aptly described Henry as a "Christian Transcendentalist.")[97] Anticipating criticism for lumping an entire family into the same heresy, Brownson clarified, "the Beecher family are singularly united, and all seem to regard brother Henry as their chief. No one of the family, unless it be Edward, the eldest brother, is very likely to put forth any views decidedly different from his, or which he decidedly disapproves. They all move in the same direction, though some of them may lag behind him while others may be in advance of him."[98] In terms of shifting views and theological camps, some might have concluded that Orestes Brownson was, like the Beechers, unique. However, for all of its flint-hearted animosity, Brownson's article is notable for at least one reason: it identified a common family trait in one of America's most eclectic families. Whereas modern scholars have often noted the differences between the Beechers, their opponents saw a family "singularly united."

THE POWER OF THE INDIVIDUAL

With twenty-six years between the oldest and youngest Beecher children, two different mothers, and so many different social and political and religious views among them, one might reasonably wonder if something like "Beecherism" was even possible. In 1835, when all eleven of Lyman's children gathered at the home in Cincinnati after his trial and second wife's death, the publicized family reunion was the first time that some of his children had ever met. James Beecher, the youngest of Harriet Porter's children, called Charles, the youngest of Roxana's children, "Uncle Charles."[99] Furthermore, how could a family known for its moral subjectivity and doctrinal ambiguity share anything in common? And if something as simple as justice linked the family together, how were the Beechers any different from the host of other reformers in the nineteenth century? In truth, the Beechers were not relativists, and they were far more than social justice warriors. They held firmly to at least three fundamental beliefs that tied them to one another. Although not every sibling adhered to these beliefs to the same degree, and while a couple of Beechers served as outliers in the group, these three basic tenets—along with the powerful legacy of Lyman Beecher—were enough to unite their family through conflicts and controversies, producing a distinctly progressive *and* conservative set of values that many recognized as Beecherism.

The first and most important Beecher ideal concerned the power of the individual. As Stuart C. Henry has stated, Lyman Beecher himself was "a living illustration of an evolving optimistic anthropology in American religion."[100] The same could be said of the entire Beecher family. Almost every Beecher possessed a generally optimistic outlook on world events that included a belief in the indomitable potential for human beings to change themselves and their fellow humans. Although this was not necessarily unusual in the earliest decades of the nineteenth century, it was especially acute in the Beecher mind and particularly noticeable during and after the Civil War when national optimism weakened. Not surprisingly, the Beecher children adopted this ideal honestly from their father. When Lyman Beecher was put on trial for heresy in Cincinnati, he was accused by Old School Presbyterians of denying the doctrine of total depravity and the power of the Holy Spirit in the rebirth. In the ultraconservative view, the New Haven Theology left far too much room for human ability and seemed to diminish human sinfulness and the work of God in the sinner. Instead of simply waiting for the return of Jesus Christ, Lyman believed with most New School Presbyterians that Christians were given the responsibility of ushering in the kingdom of God themselves through evangelism and good works. God would introduce a thousand-year reign of Christ, a golden age of religion, science, medicine, and prosperity across the globe. Later dubbed "postmillennialism," this was a rather sanguine view of the end of days, and it served as the engine for Lyman Beecher's revivalism and reform and the impetus behind his move to Cincinnati.[101] Lowell Mason, the choir leader at Beecher's Boston churches, recollected how Lyman's "full belief that the millennium was coming" had undoubtedly "imparted to music, as it had to theology, an entirely new spirit." Beecher not only introduced new songs to the church liturgy, but under his leadership, "music assumed a bolder, livelier, more triumphant character."[102] Beecher added a bit of flavor to traditional Puritan worship, not unlike Henry Ward would do years later when he integrated Methodist elements to the singing at Plymouth Church in Brooklyn. From music to voluntary societies to anti-slavery, it is difficult to overstate the extent to which Beecher's confidence in his ability to change the world imbued every facet of his life, family, and ministry. After all, part of his vision for Lane Seminary was to "inspire confidence" to the West and to the watching world.

While his children did not all subscribe to a postmillennial end-times theology, the sense of optimism and confidence in human ability became nothing short of a family trait. For example, Henry's belief in the power of progress led him to support Darwinian evolution. As scholars have suggested, Henry even seemed to believe in a kind of moral evolution and "higher love" that landed him in the middle of a highly publicized sex scandal that ultimately stained his legacy.[103] Quite naturally, the sense of progress and personal transformation that animated the family even made its way into the realm of the spiritual. In the 1830s, Henry's older brother George began to subscribe to the doctrine of perfectionism, the idea that a Christian could choose to live without sin. When the topic was discussed in a family circular letter that was passed around in 1836, Henry gave a rather revealing response: "As to perfectionism, I am not greatly troubled with the fact of it myself, or the doctrine of it in you (George); for I feel sure that if you give yourself time and prayer you will settle down right, whatever the right may be." While fond of the idea of human sinlessness, Henry still abided by his signature policy of attempting to hold multiple positions. Brother Charles and Calvin Stowe, on the other hand, were more skeptical of the idea that sinful human beings could achieve any sense of perfection. At the end of the circular, George replied, "I am quite amused with the sympathy of all my brothers, and their fatherly advice touching perfectionism, as if I were on the verge of a great precipice, but I trust in Him that is able to keep me from falling."[104] But indeed he was not far from the precipice. Just a few years later, in 1843, George was found dead in his garden with a self-inflicted gunshot wound. Although his brothers and sisters struggled to come to grips with his apparent suicide, it seemed that the expectation to change oneself could sometimes be a burden instead of a blessing.

Although not every Beecher entertained the doctrine of perfectionism, almost every Beecher had an uneasy relationship with the doctrine of original sin, beginning with Catharine Beecher's crisis of faith after her fiancé's death at sea. In a July 1822 letter to her brother Edward (who would soon formulate the doctrine of the preexistence of souls as an attempt to explain Adam's Fall), she wrestled with the idea of human depravity: "The difficulty in my mind originates in my views of the doctrine of original sin, such views as seem to me sanctioned not only by my own experience, but by the language of the Bible." Catharine could not reconcile this Puritan doctrine with her own feelings. In some ways, her head did not agree with her heart. "When I look at little Isabella," she wrote, "it seems a pity that she ever was born, and that it would be a mercy if she was taken away. I feel as Job did, that I could curse the day in which I was born. I wonder that Christians who realize the worth of an immortal soul should be willing to give life to immortal minds, to be placed in such a dreadful world. I see that my feelings are at open war with the doctrines of grace."[105] That a young woman would contemplate issues of morality, human dignity, and divine justice so earnestly in her soul, even challenging her father and brother, is itself remarkable. She was, after all, Lyman Beecher's daughter. But she was also her mother's daughter. Roxana, who hailed from an affluent and well-traveled Episcopalian family, had wrestled similarly with Lyman during their engagement to the extent that Lyman had nearly called off the wedding due to their theological impasse.[106] As Catharine would write to Lyman months later, she rejected the idea that God had "made us mere machines, and all our wickedness was *put into us*."[107] Catharine's quest to educate and raise the status of women became the defining theme of her life, convinced that women were shaped more by their own domestic virtues than by Adam's sin.

Even though Catharine opposed women's rights, her sister Isabella was one of the chief organizers of the movement and remained hopeful of women's suffrage to the very end of her life. Isabella was known as somewhat of a peacemaker between the more conservative, New England–based American Woman Suffrage Association (AWSA) and the more radical, New York-based National Woman Suffrage Association (NWSA). As Barbara White has shown, even Spiritualism (a religion that involved communing with the dead), which Isabella and other Beechers sometimes practiced, was itself very "woman-centered and optimistic."[108] The Beecher siblings thought often about death, as their own mothers had died relatively early and Roxana in particular was canonized as the patron saint of the family. In turn, their view of the afterlife was even more optimistic than their view of the present. As Orestes Brownson was quick to point out, at least four Beecher children rejected the idea of eternal punishment.[109] By 1878, Edward rejected the idea of divine retribution in Hell in favor of a kind of Protestant purgatory wherein all souls are eventually restored to eternal life. Charles once speculated to Henry that Lyman's "whole career" would have been completely different and "his whole influence upon us modified" had the idea of Hell simply been struck "out of his mind."[110] Indeed, the disagreements between Beecher siblings on religion and politics did not so much concern the general direction of humanity as they centered on the best way to go about improving it. For Catharine and Harriet, who published dozens of books between them, the path was through moral influence. For Isabella, who published only one book, it also involved lobbying and legislation. Not all Beechers were as optimistic as their father (Thomas had a rather dim view of humanity and the world), but most of Lyman Beecher's children believed that their efforts in moral and social and political reform were directly shaping the nation for a better tomorrow.

THE IMPORTANCE OF THE FAMILY

The second Beecher belief concerned the household. All of Lyman Beecher's children were certain that the family unit was the building block of American society, and they absorbed this ideal from their own upbringing. If we envision the Beecher residence as simply a classroom or laboratory for ideas about God and the world, we are mistaken. Harriet once joked, "My father was famous for his power of exciting family enthusiasm." From fishing and hunting excursions with the boys to climbing apparatuses in the backyard (all of which Catharine mentioned in her book on home economics), Lyman found a multitude of ways to activate his sons and daughters. Perhaps the most cherished family possession was the gift of music. While in Litchfield, Lyman once brought home an upright piano, and as only Harriet could describe it, "The ark of the covenant was not brought into the tabernacle with more gladness than this magical instrument into our abode."[111] Soon Lyman learned to play the violin as Catharine and Mary played the keys, filling the house with concerts and singing. This was a Beecher pastime that the children often continued in their own families. Years later, Edward brought the first piano to Jacksonville, Illinois. Charles eventually became a music minister and composed hymns. In the early days, Sunday evenings after church were particularly electric, when tunes such as "Auld Lang Syne," "Bonnie Donn," and "Mary's Dream" would permeate the air. On rare occasions, the Puritan preacher would forget his sense of decorum and begin to indulge the "double shuffle," a dance that was frowned upon by women at the church. (Interestingly, Catharine also mentioned this.) Even Lyman's bedtime prayers were sometimes characterized with a "hilarious cheerfulness" that inspired and amused his children.[112]

One does not have to strain to imagine the colorful personality of such a figure, the son of a blacksmith who enlivened the home with physical *and* mental activity. Lyman was fond of "working off nervous excitement through the muscles" with loads of sand in the cellar (also symptomatic of his "dyspepsia"). On the other hand, Lyman and his children were also voracious readers, consuming both religious and secular novels (although far more of the former than the latter). In this sense, the Beechers' inclination to embrace moral and social and spiritual causes was but an extension of the kinetic energy and religious fervor that already animated their home.[113] Lyman's knack for "exciting family enthusiasm" took various forms, from singing around the piano to combating infidelity on the frontier.

Due to their experiences in this kind of domestic environment, the cathected Beechers each developed a very high view of the family, and according to many, their *own* family. One of the critiques of Beecherism was the perceived self-importance of its members as they fulfilled their quest to change the world, a sense of pride no doubt born in a home where the fate of the world rested on their shoulders. As a result, the value and significance of families was a hallmark of the various Beecher causes, beginning with the founder of home economics herself, Catharine Beecher. In fact, when Catharine wrote about the responsibilities of women in the home, she seemed to channel her inner Lyman Beecher, claiming that the "great moral enterprise" of mothers is a subject "involving the destiny of the whole earth."[114] For this woman with no children, motherhood was next to godliness. According to Sklar, Catharine believed that the family "was the chief agency for shaping the conscience" as well as "the means of elevating the status of women rather than confirming traditional patriarchy."[115]

In addition to Mary, who settled in Hartford with her husband, Thomas Perkins, and became the most conservative of the Beecher sisters, Harriet and Isabella were also distinguished by their traditional family values. While *Uncle Tom's Cabin* has been called a "feminist book" for its attention to the plight of women, so much of the novel's gripping power was found in Stowe's ability to graphically illustrate the wrenching apart of enslaved families.[116] When Mrs. Shelby experiences a crisis of conscience at her husband's selling of Eliza's child "down river," she exclaims, "I have talked with Eliza about her boy—her duty to him as a Christian mother, to watch over him, pray for him, and bring him up in a Christian way; and now what can I say, if you tear him away, and sell him, soul and body, to a profane, unprincipled man, just to save a little money?"[117] Slavery was not just inhumane; it made liars of slaveholders and orphans of slaves. One of the most sinister evils of human bondage was its desecration of the holiest of institutions: the family. Drawing from the thought of her older sister Catharine, Harriet extolled the family unit as the basis for Christian society to the extent that she compared the state to a large family.[118] For Isabella the suffragist, women had the right and duty to vote. However, in her view, they did not have the right to impugn the sanctity of marriage. Isabella "deplored" the idea, held among certain women's rights reformers, that divorce should be made easier for women and that "free love" was an acceptable practice.[119] In modern parlance, one could say Harriet and Isabella were both pro-women and pro-family. Indeed, they eventually embraced the women's movement (Isabella before Harriet) only because they were so devoted to the concept of the family. For Catharine and Mary, on the other hand, their commitment to traditional Puritanical and Victorian family values precluded involvement with the women's movement. In Catharine's case, it sparked hostility and outright opposition. And no Beecher sibling would more publicly—and perhaps more hypocritically—defend the sanctity of the family than Henry Ward, who declared that the "family is *the* most important *institution on earth*." So holy was the family in Henry's mind that he believed any question about God could be tested "on the analogy of a truly Christian family."[120]

A key to understanding the Beecher ideal of family is the concept of change. In an epoch of American history that one scholar has called a "a generation of change," few families seemed to adapt to change quite like the Beechers.[121] In fact, change was one of the most consistent themes in their lives, beginning with their parents. After the death of Roxana in 1816 and Lyman's marriage to Harriet the following year, the oldest children soon took to calling his new wife "mother." After Harriet passed in 1835, the sixty-one-year-old traveled back east to Boston the following summer and returned with a third wife, Lydia. Lyman's pastorates were also somewhat of a revolving door. From East Hampton Church in New York (1799–1810) to Litchfield Church in Connecticut (1810–26) to Hanover Street Church in Boston (1826–30) to Bowdoin Street Church across town (1830–32) to Second Presbyterian Church in Cincinnati (1832–51), Beecher's ministry was constantly in flux, as he entertained numerous invitations to other churches and institutions, from Philadelphia to New Haven to New York. Lyman also changed denominations, providing no small amount of controversy. In the midst of these transitions, the family unit became for the Beecher children a spiritual constant in an ever-changing material universe. When Catharine, Mary, Edward, and George were boarding together in 1824 across the state in Hartford, Lyman still rejoiced in "the idea that we are all one establishment."[122] Over the next few decades, the family-centeredness of the Beechers could bring them together across great distances, from Ohio to New York and from Connecticut to Florida. They collaborated on books, arrived at others' houses unannounced, vacationed together (most often at the water cure in Elmira, New York), and even accompanied one another on tours to Europe. Their circular letters are evidence of just how close they became and of the breadth of topics they discussed despite great distances between them. And Lyman Beecher, as one might expect, was a unifying force. In one such circular letter, he wrote to his eldest son:

> William, why do you not write to your father? Are you not my first-born son? Did I not carry you over bogs a-fishing, a-straddle of my neck, on my shoulders, and, besides clothing and feeding, whip you often to

make a man of you as you are, and would not have been without? And
have I now always loved you, and born you on my heart, as the claims
and trials of a first-born demand? Don't you remember studying theology with your father while sawing and splitting wood in that wood-
house in Green Street, Boston, near by where you found your wife?[123]

The starting point for understanding one of the most influential families
in the nineteenth century lies in small notes such as these. Just as Lyman
Beecher's children needed their father, so the man who grew up largely un-
important to his own father seemed to need his children.

CHRISTIAN REPUBLICANISM

The third principle of Beecherism was the belief that republican virtues
such as freedom, disinterestedness, self-sacrifice, temperance, and justice
were perfected in the teachings of Christianity and indeed that the fate of
the young nation rested upon these values. In a group of people that included megachurch pastors, celebrity novelists, sailors, education reformers, and various species of abolitionists and women's rights advocates, the
ideal of Christian republicanism was in fact the family religion.[124] Whether
or not the entire Beecher clan qualified as "evangelical" in any theological
sense, they were certainly united in the conviction that evangelical values
were in the best interest of the nation. So thoroughly did Lyman Beecher
embrace Christian republicanism that he once delivered a sermon entitled
"The Bible a Code of Laws" and a lecture years later entitled "The Republican Elements of the Old Testament." In the lecture, Beecher praised the
"administration of justice" of the Israelite government, "especially in respect of the poor, the stranger, the widow, and the fatherless."[125] When Lyman preached against drunkenness (which he often associated with Roman
Catholicism), he stressed that Christianity was "indispensable" to a healthy
republic. "It is admitted," he declared in a sermon on the evils of intemperance, "that intelligence and virtue are the pillars of republican institutions,
and that the illumination of schools, and the moral power of religious institutions, are indispensable to produce this intelligence and virtue. But who
are found so uniformly in the ranks of irreligion as the intemperate?"[126]
In other words, without intelligence and virtue, the American experiment

would fail. And without Christianity, intelligence and virtue would disappear. Although the Beechers belonged to various denominations and sometimes disagreed on points of doctrine, this seminal idea lasted generations in their family. Indeed, it endured the events leading to and following the Civil War.

For example, in 1853, one year after her wildly successful *Uncle Tom's Cabin* awakened the American conscience to the evils of slavery, Harriet Beecher Stowe met the man southern evangelicals referred to as "the father of New England abolition": William Lloyd Garrison.[127] Although Garrison's belief in the power of moral influence over legislation was shared by most Beechers, and although Garrison himself had once preached in Edward's church in Boston, the Quaker Garrison and the daughter of famed Presbyterian minister Lyman Beecher had significant theological differences that worried Stowe, whose antislavery views were not as extreme as Garrison's. Although Stowe eventually became an Episcopalian, she retained many of her evangelical beliefs and remained convinced that these beliefs were essential for a healthy republic.[128] Consequently, upon meeting Garrison, Stowe immediately addressed her concerns with the fiery editor of the weekly newspaper the *Liberator*. "Mr. Garrison, are you a Christian?" she asked abruptly. He then replied that her question was too vague. "Well," she persisted, "are you such a Christian as I am?" But Garrison replied that this question was even more vague. Finally, Stowe struck at the heart of what she perceived to be the essence of her Christian faith: "Well, Mr. Garrison, do you believe in the atonement?"[129] While Garrison hardly expounded upon the penal substitutionary nature of Christ's death, his answer nevertheless satisfied Stowe, demonstrating the importance of faith to the Beechers in their civic duties, regardless of their religious affiliations.[130] If abolitionists could not acknowledge the demands of divine justice, Harriet reasoned, how could they be expected to enforce human justice for the rest of the nation?[131]

Younger brother Henry was likewise convinced that only Christianity would save the republic. One week after the assassination of Abraham Lincoln, Henry offered a word of encouragement to his congregants at Plymouth Church that would have made his father proud: "Republican institutions have been vindicated in this experience as they never were before; and the whole history of the last four years, rounded up by this cruel stroke,

seems now in the providence of God, to have been clothed with an illustration, with a sympathy, with an aptness, and with a significance, such as we
never could have expected or imagined. God, I think, has said, by the voice
of this event, to all nations of the earth, 'Republican liberty, based upon
true Christianity, is firm as the foundation of the globe.'"[132]

Although theologically worlds apart, Henry Ward Beecher was indeed
his father's son. The Beecher children were not always committed evangelicals, but they were avowed republicans who believed that America's
"moral destiny" would be fulfilled through Christian values. Like their father, they were quite willing to impress those values upon their own generation. Indeed, it would be no exaggeration to suggest that the infant
republic appeared, at times, like the Beecher family writ large. As the nation was changing, so were the Beechers, and vice versa.[133] For example,
Lyman's heresy trial in Cincinnati presaged the New School–Old School
schism in the Presbyterian denomination just two years later. The family's
disagreements over slavery, abolitionism, and colonization were a small
picture of the large debates taking place at the national level at the very
same time. Catharine's impasse with her father over original sin was, in
effect, a picture of the larger conversation between the Puritan generation
and the republican one springing from it. Harriet's literary success typified
the rise of women novelists and fiction writing in the antebellum age. Lyman defended state religion and then later celebrated disestablishment,
as so many clergymen would in the earliest decades of the nineteenth century. His embrace of Finneyism after originally repudiating Finney's "New
Measures" characterized American evangelical culture from the 1820s
to 1850s. And Catharine's mission to educate women generated the rise
of women educators between the 1840s and 1880s. Beecherism was remarkably ahead of its time *and* typical for its time. Can we tell the story of
nineteenth-century America without the Beechers? Perhaps. But it would
be very difficult—and much less interesting.

Chapter 1

A NEW ENGLAND "ESTABLISHMENT" (1823-1832)

LYMAN BEECHER CHANGED pastorates according to two things: finances and foes. In 1810, when the Congregationalist church of Litchfield, Connecticut, invited him to preach a trial sermon, Lyman was in the middle of a salary dispute with his congregation in East Hampton, New York, who refused to increase his annual sum of $400 to $500. The timing was providential. Litchfield offered double. However, fifteen years later, he was still making $800 a year. In debt and with mounting education expenses for his sons, Lyman resigned his post at Litchfield and one day later was invited by Hanover Street Church in Boston to be their minister—at an annual salary of $2,000. But his career move to Cincinnati was not guided by the same kind of opportunism. Lyman Beecher was motivated by far more than income or standard of living. He also relished the challenge of a formidable opponent. Every one of Lyman Beecher's pulpits was marked by a new enemy that posed a supposedly cataclysmic threat to Christian civilization.

After witnessing Timothy Dwight brazenly confront deism at Yale College, Lyman Beecher's life was defined by a similar quest to combat the hydra of irreligion wherever it poked its skulking head. At East Hampton, the local "infidel club" quieted the fervor of revivalism in the area, prompting Lyman to write to his fiancée, Roxana, in 1799 that "Everything is at stake."[1] In 1806, he delivered a "Sermon on Dueling" in the wake of the infamous Alexander Hamilton duel with Aaron Burr, thrusting the name of Lyman Beecher into the national spotlight for the very first time. Dueling was, in his words, "a great national sin."[2] Although as early as 1803 Beecher had called for the establishment of a Society for the Suppression of Vice and the Promotion of Good Morals, it was not until he witnessed clerical drunkenness in the state of Connecticut that he launched his war on intemperance. By 1826, after preaching to his Litchfield congregation about the evils of social drinking, he published his *Six Sermons on the Nature, Occasions, Signs, Evils, and Remedy of Intemperance*, which was eventually translated into several languages.[3] In Boston, the new adversary was the menace of Unitarianism. In 1832, Lyman set his sights upon the West to counter Roman Catholicism, where "the great battle is to be fought in the Valley of the Mississippi."[4] In the Beecher family, each cause was larger than life. And every city presented a new challenge. Therefore, long before the family crusade to Cincinnati, the instinct to reform and the expectation to succeed had become almost second nature among Lyman's oldest children. In fact, without Catharine and Edward, the majority of their siblings may never have embraced their father's quest to change the world.

"WE ARE ALL ONE ESTABLISHMENT"

Although Alexander Fisher's tragic death at sea exposed some of the deepest divisions between Lyman and Catharine over the character of God and the nature of sin, it also provided an opportunity for Lyman to give Catharine a friendly push in the direction that would eventually define her life. When Lyman took Catharine to visit Hartford to talk to the Rev. Joel Hawes, pastor of the First Congregationalist Church, to discuss the theological arguments that Lyman apparently could not win with his daughter, Hawes "lamented the want of a good female school." Catharine initially dismissed the remark, but Lyman did not. His son Edward, who had been "consecrated to the ministry" from his "mother's womb," was already operating a grammar school in Hartford to help pay for his theological studies.[5] His other son, George, would soon attend the school under Edward's tutelage.[6] With Thomas Gallaudet, Lyman had supported the first school for the hearing impaired, the Connecticut Asylum for the Education and Instruction of Deaf and Dumb Persons, in Hartford.[7] He later suggested that Catharine rethink Hawes's proposal. While Lyman knew very little about girls' schools, his belief in the value of education to improve the morals of his children *and* society was unwavering. Whatever Catharine chose to do, she ought to do it with excellence: "I should be ashamed to have you open, and keep only a commonplace, middling sort of school," he cautioned her.

"It is expected to be of a higher order; and, unless you are willing to put your talents and strength into it, it would be best not to begin." In other words, do it well or don't do it at all. This would become a Beecher maxim.

As Barbara A. White explains, "Lyman Beecher's daughters were disadvantaged in being girls, who could not be ministers—but this was no excuse for becoming commonplace and middling. The Beecher sisters had to show that they were 'of a higher order.'"[8] While Catharine never adopted Lyman's view of original sin, she did take her father's professional advice. "This and your advice have led me to wish to commence [a school] there," she wrote back to him. Within a month, Lyman had scouted the community, obtained commitments from students, and arranged the school to open in just six weeks.[9] Catharine soon brought Mary and Harriet with her. When the Hartford Female Academy opened in May 1823, Catharine served as administrator, Mary performed most of the teaching, and Harriet, only twelve, became a student. Until her marriage to Calvin Stowe in 1836, Harriet would look to her sister Catharine as a maternal authority. Between Litchfield and Hartford, Beecherism as an engine of moral and social reform was now a dual threat. The four oldest in Hartford—Catharine, Edward, George, and Mary—boarded in the same home.

Catharine still needed a bit of motivation from her father. After just one term, she wanted to relinquish her administrative duties to her sister, Mary, and return to Litchfield. Catharine's roots in the idyllic, somewhat old-fashioned town of her youth still ran deep. But Lyman was adamantly against her decision, insisting that her commitment to found the academy was a long-term endeavor. "It will not answer for you to leave that school," he urged. "You must not think of it."[10] Lyman, the son of a blacksmith, was determined to instill his New England work ethic in his children. Even across the state, Lyman envisioned the family as a single unit with a common goal. As a result, to alleviate the financial burden upon himself and his children, Lyman wished to pay off his property in Litchfield "to make the old establishment free from debt." Despite the distance apart, he reminded his children of "the idea that we are all one establishment."[11]

Several years after the death of Timothy Dwight (1817) and the disestablishment of the Congregationalist Church in Connecticut (1818), that Lyman Beecher chose to describe his house in Litchfield as the "old establishment" and his family in terms of "one establishment" reveals how he conceived of the Beecher alliance. With the collapse of the so-called "Standing Order," the union between Congregationalist clergymen and the magistrate, the family was to him the last bulwark of religion, morality, and support in the new religious landscape. The separation of church and state, which he later celebrated as the "best thing that ever happened to the State of Connecticut," placed the future of Christianity solely on the churches, which, in the Congregationalist and Presbyterian denominations, were composed of family units.[12] In a rapidly changing America, Lyman relied upon his own children as he once did the traditions of the church. In an 1823 letter to his children in Hartford, he confessed, "I find myself continually more attached to my children, and beginning, in feeling, to look back and lean on them as once I looked for support to those of the generation which is gone; and it is my hope and prayer that you may all be continued and prospered to give support and consolation in the afternoon and evening of my day."[13] At times, Lyman the overbearing father could be as insecure as he was absolute.

Lyman Beecher had replaced Timothy Dwight as New England's leading proponent of revivalism and reform as social control, but his vision for society had evolved from his days at Yale.[14] He explained to his hearers in 1826 that "our charitable institutions . . . are the providential substitutes for the legal provisions of our fathers, now inapplicable by change of circumstances. . . . Now, unless the salt of the earth contained in Christian institutions, can be diffused through the land, the mass will putrify [*sic*]." To fulfill God's special blessing upon the American people, the Christian magistrate was being "substituted" with voluntary societies as the primary means of generating revival and reform. The assistant to the church was now the reform agency, not the civil sword. "In other words," explains Jonathan D. Sassi, Beecher "concurred with the vision of the American church sanctifying society. He played an important part in conceiving both strategies that evangelical Congregationalists used to connect Christianity and society in the 1820s."[15]

But Beecher was more than a social strategist. He also viewed societal transformation on a personal level. The strength of the church no longer rested in the state, but upon the family. In fact, his earliest opposition to both drinking and slavery seemed to begin with the notion that these vices separated "whole families" and left them "robbed of fathers, brothers, husbands, friends."[16] While preaching on the importance of family, Lyman was ever mindful of his own. He employed several methods to unite the family "establishment," including the power of guilt. In another letter to Hartford in 1823, he upbraided Edward, Catharine, Mary, and George for not writing him. "Not a line do I get from any of you," he scolded. "I unrolled the surtout, and out dropped a letter for your mother and for William, but none for me. I felt disappointed, as I had long been hungry for a letter; so I searched my pockets and found none, and felt sad."[17] Indeed, Lyman Beecher was determined to keep his family together because he *needed* his family. Likewise, Catharine relied heavily upon her father. She decided to stay in Hartford at Lyman's instruction, and although she was distanced from her father by theology, gender, and now geography, her vision for America was no less religious, family-centered, or national in scope. After visiting Litchfield one summer, Catharine was reminded of just how much she admired her father. She bragged to Edward, "Yesterday I heard two of father's best sermons. The afternoon sermon perfectly electrified me. I wish it could be heard by all young men in the country." She then added, "The fact is, I never heard any body preach that makes me feel as father does; perhaps it may be because he is father. But I can not hear him without its making my face burn and my heart beat."[18] Transfixed at Lyman's power and magnetism behind the pulpit, Catharine viewed her own work "as a complement to her father's."[19] In turn, Lyman wrote often and affectionately to his eldest daughter. He considered her, after his sister Esther, "my nearest contemporary."[20]

By 1826, the Beecher "establishment" had shifted east, but the aim of reform and Lyman's tendency to direct (or control) his children's steps remained the same. After Lyman left the "Land of Steady Habits" in Connecticut and moved into the pulpit at Hanover Street Church in Boston, Edward was invited to pastor the reputable Park Street Church on the corner of Boston Common. Not surprisingly, Lyman had a hand in his son's call to Boston. Park Street, the "Gibraltar of orthodoxy," was the site of Lyman's ordination sermon for Sereno Edwards Dwight in 1817, later published as *The Bible a Code of Laws*.[21] In September of 1826, he wrote a letter to Edward attempting to disabuse him of the notion that he was simply moving his son closer to himself.[22] As was often the case, the Lord's will happened to be Lyman's will. (There was a fine line between Lyman motivating his children and *maneuvering* his children.) Lyman charged his son to accept the invitation from Park Street: "Do it without fail."[23] However, as Stuart C. Henry explains, "Lyman Beecher thought it no injustice (to say nothing of impropriety) to plan his children's lives. Rather it was a duty." After all, Roxana's last request to Lyman on her deathbed was that all her children enter the ministry.[24] There was a standard to uphold. Henry adds, "The children of Lyman Beecher did not necessarily resent this autocratic trait in their father and, indeed, though they did not always accede to it, were sometimes quite pleased by the developments it occasioned."[25]

Nevertheless, when Catharine visited Boston in the spring, she was thrilled at the opportunity to witness her father and brother transform the city for good. "The Lord I think is raising a standard there and calling his children to gather round it," she later wrote Edward, quoting the prophet Isaiah. "With the moral influence which He may enable such men as Papa and you to exert, we may hope for great things in Boston."[26] In the Beecher mind, "moral influence" lay at the intersection of the human and divine wills, the space which recognized both creaturely freedom and the sovereignty of the Creator. In a nation that had erected a "wall" between church and state, and in a state that would soon disestablish the Congregationalist Church altogether (the last state church would fall in Massachusetts in 1833), "moral influence" and the power of the human will to exercise public virtue was the new American civil religion.[27] Was there a more important field to harvest than the Land of the Pilgrims? Lyman started almost immediately reforming the city, cofounding the Hanover Association of Young Men in January 1827, a prototype for the Young Men's Christian Association, or YMCA.

Edward also wasted little time seeking to improve Boston society. On February 10, just a few months after he had taken the pastorate at Park Street, Edward delivered a lecture at the request of the Auxiliary Education Society of the Young Men of Boston on "the importance of the christian ministry, and the duty of men to extend its influence and to increase its numbers." The *address*, later published in revised and expanded form, was Edwards's very first exhibition of the theme of cosmic warfare that he would later illustrate so clearly in *Conflict of the Ages* (1853). If Boston was the heartbeat of American religion, the world was the "waterloo of the Universe," and Christians were engaged in a "great moral conflict" with the forces of the devil. While Edward never adopted the histrionics of his father or his more famous brother, he certainly had a penchant for the dramatic. But he was also being shaped by his Boston context. Edward had already developed his unique doctrine of the preexistence of souls as a response to the Unitarian belief in human free will, but he yielded "to his father's request to postpone utterance of his new views."[28] Lyman Beecher could not stomach an outright rejection of original sin like that of his daughter just five years earlier, but when Edward engineered an "adjustment" to orthodoxy in order to explain Adam's Fall, he managed to accept his son's theological innovation, albeit reluctantly. This was, after all, similar to what Lyman was doing himself.

MOBILIZING WOMEN IN HARTFORD

By the fall of 1827, Mary was wedded to a local Hartford lawyer named Thomas Perkins and largely retired from public life. According to Lyman Beecher Stowe, Harriet's grandson, Mary was "an anomaly, she was the only purely private Beecher."[29] But her sister Catharine was not a private woman. Next to the men of the family, she was an influencer in her own right. The Hartford school had completed a new building, boasted eight teachers, and was steadily becoming one of the elite academies in New England. Catharine's vision had also expanded. The school was now a seminary, designed not just to refine women but to educate them in social, moral, and religious principles so that they could be sent out as teachers. In the spring, just before she taught her first class on moral philosophy, she published an article in the new *American Journal of Education* proposing her reforms.[30] Although the wealthy families around Hartford were slow to embrace her vision of women's education, she was as stubborn and hard-driving as her father.

Catharine was already training young Harriet in the family business of reform. Although she was the administrator of the school, Catharine did not particularly enjoy teaching, so she passed on many of her classroom duties to her precocious teenage sister. Once when Catharine was in Boston, eighteen-year-old Harriet penned her a letter to assess the "moral character" of her students. "This morning I delivered a long speech on 'modes of exerting moral influence,' showing the ways in which an evil influence is unknowingly exerted and the ways in which each and all can exert a good one," she dutifully reported. Even at the age of eighteen, Harriet seemed to view the world as her father and brother did: as a kind of Manichean battle between good and evil. Moral influence was about spiritual warfare. Later in the same letter, Harriet boasted, "The other teachers also say they never saw the classes form in more perfect order and go and return with so little noise." She then confided to her sister, "I feel as if we are holding the helm, and can turn the vessel the right way. The force of *moral influence* seems equal to that of *authority,* and even stronger. When the girls wish what is against my opinion they say, 'Do, Miss Beecher, allow just this.' '*Allow* you?' I say. 'I have not the power; you can do so if you think best.' Now, they cannot ask me to give up my opinion and belief of right and wrong, and they are unwilling to act against it."[31] In Harriet's incipient teaching philosophy one can hear the faint echoes of Jonathan Edwards in *Freedom of the Will* (1754), contending that "the will always is as the great apparent good is."[32] This near-holy respect for the freedom of human decision-making was, in effect, the most controversial point of Lyman Beecher's New School Calvinism and the way that *every* Beecher envisaged individual and societal change. Contrary to the old Puritan magisterial way of thinking, people could not be coerced into modifying their behavior. Christians "have not the power" to make decisions for other people. However, they *did* have the power to "influence" their decisions so that they might turn away from their sin "if they think best."

Harriet was applying the same idea in the classroom that Lyman exercised from the pulpit: human beings were driven by their own motives. As William once pleaded to an unconverted George in 1825, "know that God never forces men contrary to their own wills to love him."[33] The greatest gift that one person could give to another was to motivate them to do good, similar to the way that God encouraged obedience from "free agents" in his "moral government."[34] Even the Holy Spirit Himself was an influencer. In his 1817 sermon "The Bible a Code of Laws" at Park Street, Lyman asked, "What is family government; what is civil government; what is temptation, exhortation or persuasion; and what are the influences of the Holy Spirit; but the means, and the effectual means, of influencing the exercises of the human heart, and the conduct of human life?"[35] For Lyman, all of human existence was defined by influences. On another occasion, he preached to his hearers, "even [God] can govern them, as such, *only by moral influence*, in accordance with their accountability and the laws of mind."[36] Moral influence was not about manipulation, but about honoring both the free agency *and* responsibility of human beings. According to Joan D. Hedrick, "the principle that Harriet drew from this became the guiding star of her prophetic career."[37] At eighteen years old, by observing the effect of moral influence rather than brute authority to motivate the will of her students, Harriet Beecher had already learned a valuable lesson from her sister and father and grasped the source of her true power as a public figure. In time, she would wield that power as few Americans ever had.

As Beth Barton Schweiger notes, education itself was also changing during this time. "Memorization began to slip from favor in the nineteenth century when a Romantic pedagogy emerged that redefined learning as creativity. Students began to be perceived not only as vessels but as agents who could produce as well as receive ideas."[38] The Beechers fully employed this new pedagogy, both at home and in the classroom. Learning meant responding. As pioneers in women's education, the Beecher sisters viewed education in terms of service to the public good. This was, at least in their minds, a *Christian* virtue. Establishing valuable social connections with the local Congregationalist church and even igniting a small revival at the school (in which Lyman warned her of "the very high state of excited feeling"), Catharine understood the role of religion in shaping the mission *and* the reputation of the academy.[39] For instance, with Catharine in Boston, Harriet conducted prayer meetings and celebrated four students who "wish to make a public profession of religion."[40] Aspiring to improve the plight of *all* women in America and elevating her own public voice, Catharine had developed a presumptuous habit of delegating tasks she did not wish to do herself. Harriet had wanted to open her own school in Groton, Massachusetts, where her brother George was "directly engaged in building up his cause in the world."[41] But she was persuaded by Lyman and Catharine to continue under her sister's supervision. She acquiesced. At such a young age, Harriet, whose voice would eventually surpass all other Beechers, did not mind "acting as an extension of Catharine."[42]

The spirit of public duty that propelled the Hartford Female Seminary was also evident to outsiders. Angelina Grimké, who eventually came to blows with Catharine years later over the issue of slavery and the role of women, visited the academy in 1831. Grimké was rather impressed that many of Catharine's students "had become teachers simply from the wish of being useful."[43] On one hand, to a woman who had been raised in gentility on a South Carolina plantation, the inveterate Yankee sense of moralism and productivity must have appeared quite admirable. On the other hand, for the young woman who had lost her mother at the age of sixteen and had been thrust into maturity for the sake of her younger brothers and sisters, life had always been devoted to "being useful." In many ways, Catharine knew of no other way.

Catharine's sense of duty extended well beyond the classroom. Meanwhile, Lyman's influence was never far away. In 1828, while spending time with Lyman and Edward in Boston, Catharine met Rev. Jeremiah Evarts, a friend of Lyman's, who was the secretary of the Congregationalists' American Board of Commissioners for Foreign Missions. Evarts, who also played a role in calling Edward to Park Street, captivated Catharine with accounts of the Cherokee people in Georgia being forced from their homes by the American military at the direction of President Andrew Jackson. As a missionary-activist, Evarts had lobbied Congress and organized rallies on behalf of the Cherokee. As Catharine later recounted, he urged that "American women might save these poor, oppressed natives, and asked me to devise some method of securing such intervention."[44] Another powerful idea had been planted in Catharine's mind. On her return to Hartford, Catharine mustered her powers of moral influence and composed a pamphlet, *To Benevolent Women of the United States*, to plead for the help of Hartford's elite. The ensuing petition drive, as Daniel Walker Howe has noted, "set a pattern that would be followed by the antislavery movement in years to come."[45] The circular was passed from household to household. Soon the students and teachers of Hartford Female Seminary got involved and sent Catharine's letter to friends, family, and throughout New England, soliciting signatures.[46]

Forming women's auxiliaries to aid Lyman and his minister friends in Boston in their own anti-Jacksonian protests, and arranging public meetings on behalf of the Cherokee, Catharine's organized protest from 1828 to 1830 was "the first Beecher campaign for a social cause," at least among Lyman's children.[47] Although Edward would take the first public step on behalf of abolition nearly a decade later, paving the way for his siblings while

Catharine remained only moderately antislavery, it was in fact Catharine who pioneered racial reform among the Beechers when she so publicly condemned the tyranny of the Jackson administration against the Cherokee.[48] As Catharine's biographer has noted, "All the Beecher children were influenced by the power of Lyman's example, but Catharine did much to create the mold that her younger siblings followed."[49] Among the Beechers, moral influence was always a family affair. While Lyman Beecher's children were often bolder and more outspoken on the issue of race than their father, their crusades against racism and injustice were never completely independent of Lyman himself, who often encouraged and even assisted in their various endeavors. In fact, one Beecher crusade seemed to lead to another. In July 1830, when Lyman unveiled his plan to travel west to Catharine, the Cherokee were on his mind:

> In respect to the Indians the prospect brightens. The tide of the West is turning, and running strong against the Jackson administration. A great meeting has been held in Cincinnati, and one in another place, disapproving the measures of the present administration, and among the rest of the Indian Bill, a Mr. Evarts says, exactly right, and proposing that their members of the Senate be requested not to ratify any treaty made in pursuance of it, and that their members in the House be instructed to make no appropriations. It is in contemplation to get up similar meetings in Philadelphia and New York, and Hartford, Northampton, and Boston, and through New England and the land. We shall succeed; the Indians will be saved![50]

Native American reform was no longer just Catharine's pet cause. It was now a Beecher family crusade. This was the collective power of Beecherism. Motivating one another and drawing upon common resources, they were "one establishment."

A "GREAT MORAL AND SOCIAL INFLUENCE" IN BOSTON

Aside from paying the bills for his growing family, moral influence was the very reason Lyman Beecher had arrived in Boston in the first place. As a pragmatist at heart, Beecher measured success in the kingdom of God in terms of converts and causes. Therefore, he relished the chance to speak to *more* people and lead *more* campaigns in the name of Christ. In a letter to Edward months before he would join his father in Boston, Lyman rejoiced, "The more I become acquainted with my work and opportunity, the more I am satisfied that my opportunity to do good is increased tenfold. For example: at these united prayer meetings I can instruct and influence all the orthodox churches in Boston on the subject of revivals with more ease and as much effect as my own single church in Litchfield."[51] Lyman had a much larger audience in his new urban context. In September, a month after dissuading Edward from accepting a professorship at Dartmouth, he wrote to his son to inform him that the prestigious Park Street Church intended to extend him a call to be their pastor.

On one hand, Boston was the land of freedom and opportunity. "I know not how a minister can desire any thing better than to preach the Gospel in Boston," his wife, Harriet, wrote shortly after arriving in the city. On the other hand, Harriet also felt somewhat unworthy of this new mission field. "This soil was pressed by the feet of the Pilgrims, and watered by their tears, and consecrated by their prayers. Here are their tombs, and here are their children who are to be brought back to the fold of Christ."[52] Tradition was never far from the Beechers' minds. Like the prophets of old, they had come to deliver a message from God to a stiff-necked people. Lyman Beecher desired this same prophetic work for his son Edward. Convinced that "it is here that New England is to be regenerated," Lyman wanted his son to play a critical role in shaping America. Lyman expected nothing less than a second birth of civilization, indeed a "resurrection of New England."[53]

In Lyman Beecher's mind, the spiritual battle for Boston was truly a war of good versus evil. To a friend he rejoiced "that orthodoxy in Massachusetts is becoming a phalanx terrible as an army with banners."[54] He also envisioned his Hanover Street Church Young Men's Association as an army of sorts, calling it "a disciplined moral militia."[55] Years later, the Hon. Amasa Walker, who served on the association with Lyman, recalled "the vast influence which Dr. Beecher exerted while in Boston, through the various agencies he set in motion." According to Walker, Lyman's true legacy in the city was not theological per se, "but of that great moral and social influence which he exerted."[56] In many ways, the next six years would be the zenith of Lyman's pastoral career. For good reason, Harriet Beecher Stowe looked back upon Lyman's ministry in Boston and called it "the most active, glowing, and successful period of his life. It was the high noon of his manhood, the flood-tide of his powers; and a combination of circumstances in the history of Massachusetts brought him in to labor there just as a whole generation were on the return-wave of a great moral reaction."[57] As state-sponsored Christianity was nearing its end in Massachusetts, Lyman Beecher offered an evangelical alternative with an equally comprehensive vision for American society: a voluntary religion of the heart aimed at spiritual revival and moral reform. At Hanover Street, he gained a platform that he never could have achieved in Connecticut. And he was bringing his son along for the ride.

However, if Lyman gained more followers in his new city, he also made new enemies. In the more refined and aristocratic Boston, the homespun preacher known as "Brimstone Beecher" appeared a bit provincial and unsophisticated next to the Unitarian elites who dominated the city.[58] Increasing in private endowments and growing more secular in its emphasis, Unitarian-led Harvard cozied up to wealthy merchants and financiers in the Boston area, a fact that provoked the disgust of Transcendentalists (themselves Unitarians).[59] According to Fanny Holmes, the wife of Oliver Wendell Holmes Jr., "In Boston you had to be something, and Unitarian was the least you could be."[60] With eighty churches in Boston and many of the wealthiest patrons in the city, Unitarians—rationalistic Christians who denied the tri-unity of God and emphasized virtue as essential for Christian living—established themselves as the intellectual and social gatekeepers of Boston.[61] But Lyman Beecher had not come to the hub of New England because he loved the theater. The hardy son of a blacksmith had come for a fight. In a sermon in October of 1827 before the American Board of Missions, Beecher put the conflict in the most black-and-white terms: "If Unitarians are right, we are idolaters; and if we are right, Unitarians are not Christians."[62] There was no room for debate. Over fifty years later, Henry Ward Beecher contended that his father and the Unitarian leader William Ellery Channing were "standing together, and travelling in precisely the same lines, and toward precisely the same results."[63] But this was revisionist history on the part of Henry, whose theology had more in common with Channing than his father by the end of his life. In the early nineteenth century, Lyman Beecher was persona non grata in the Unitarian community.

In 1827, Lyman Beecher founded the *Christian Spectator,* a monthly magazine which promoted evangelical doctrines and values to challenge the intellectual and high-minded periodicals of the Unitarians like the *North American Review* and the *Christian Examiner.*[64] Lyman was vying for the hearts *and* minds of Boston. In this bustling cosmopolitan city, the entrepôt of New England, the "establishment" went to the Unitarians, and Lyman's children were fully aware of the new power dynamics. As Harriet Beecher Stowe recalled bitterly, "All the literary men of Massachusetts were Unitarian. All the trustees and professors of Harvard College were Unitarians. All the elite of wealth and fashion crowded Unitarian churches. The judges on the bench were Unitarian, giving decisions by which the peculiar features of church organization, so carefully ordained by the Pilgrim fathers, had been nullified."[65] In Litchfield, Lyman enjoyed close ties with local officials and the administrators at the law school and local girls' academy. However, in Boston, the Beechers first embraced their role as cultural and political outsiders.

In Litchfield, a town that Harriet described as "half Hebrew theocracy, half ultra-democratic republic," Lyman had embraced state-supported Christianity.[66] He was, as George Marsden has called him, "one of Connecticut's champions of antidisestablishmentarianism."[67] Until he arrived in Cincinnati, he did not fully realize how much the religious establishment shaped his assumptions about religion. However, in Massachusetts, the state church presented a unique challenge. Not every Congregationalist was an orthodox Calvinist. Like President John Adams decades earlier, who attended Harvard and became a Unitarian, many Congregationalists in eastern Massachusetts were raised in churches that slowly pushed aside orthodox beliefs.[68] Harvard itself had been censured for its progressive theology as far back as the 1740s, when arch-evangelist George Whitefield publicly criticized the school for the "bad books" in its classrooms.[69] By the 1820s, the result was a church united in ecclesiastical polity but very divided in theology and politics. Two hundred years after the Pilgrims landed at Massachusetts Bay, Boston was already a decidedly *un*-evangelical city in many ways, and the balance of political power favored the Unitarians. According to Daniel Walker Howe, "The ecclesiastical arrangements that the Beechers found so objectionable gave control of meetinghouses and the hiring of ministers to the legally constituted 'parishes' of the Standing Order in Massachusetts, rather than to the converted members of the 'church.'"[70] Theological conflict was tearing the established church apart.

This division within the official state church between orthodox Calvinists and Unitarians was perhaps the last nail in the coffin for the state church in Massachusetts, and Lyman Beecher was holding the hammer.[71] Arguing for the abolition of the Standing Order and the creation of two distinct denominations, he appealed to the holy cause of liberty:

> Have not Unitarians the privilege of forming churches of their own; and have not all denominations the right of judging for themselves what are the qualifications for membership? It is the *essence* of liberty of conscience, that Christians of similar views in doctrine and experience should be allowed to associate for mutual usefulness and edification. It is the exercise of this right which constitutes different denominations of Christians; and if, according to the doctrinal views of the Orthodox, Unitarians cannot be received into fellowship, have they any claim upon us? Let them go to their own company, and be at peace. We do not ask to be admitted to their churches;—why, should they demand fellowship in ours?[72]

As a Calvinist, a revivalist, and a defender of voluntarism, Lyman could no longer see the benefit of an established church that accommodated opposite faiths.[73] Amanda Porterfield simplified Lyman's project a bit when she wrote that Beecher "hitched the wagon of New England covenant theology to the freedom-loving horses of Methodist and Baptist supernaturalism."[74] Still, against the "infidelity" of Enlightenment liberals and the unorthodox, Beecher had more in common theologically and socially with his other evangelical brethren than with his liberal Congregationalist counterparts. In some ways, this problem had long existed in New England. Historically, revival and state-funded Christianity did not mix well in Massachusetts. Nearly a century earlier, many "New Light" evangelicals during the First Great Awakening had contended for "Separate" congregations due to their dissatisfaction with the moribund spirituality of the state church. By the 1820s, during the *Second* Great Awakening, a similar movement was taking place, as evangelicals like Lyman Beecher objected to the heresy of the religious establishment and desired to leave it altogether. As Richard J. Carwardine has noted in his work on evangelical politics in antebellum America, Beecher's "conversion to the merits of disestablishment"—begun in Unitarian Boston—was "legendary" in American history, as it had a considerable impact upon the nation and indeed his own children.[75]

HENRY'S "REAL BEECHER BLOOD"

In addition to the steep cost of Yale College, the fact that Lyman convinced young Henry in 1830 to attend Amherst, a school recently founded by anti-Unitarians, was no mere coincidence.[76] (Andover, where his son Edward had studied, was likewise established as a response to the Unitarianism of Harvard.)[77] Lyman accomplished this strategic maneuver by arguing that Henry, who then desired to be a sailor, would improve his chances at becoming a commodore with a college education. It was an enticing idea for the adventurous and ambitious Beecher. Lyman always seemed one step ahead of his children. Showing a common northern prejudice against the South during the Nullification Crisis, Lyman was also worried that his son might be "susceptible to Southern influence assailing him on the side of honour & spirit" if he attended Yale. Amherst was a good Yankee school. He wrote to his friend, President Heman Humphrey, "I understand that teaching by professors and having smaller classes & more particular attention can be & is paid to each student than might be practical at Yale."[78]

Henry experienced a conversion of some sort at Mount Pleasant Academy and expressed his desire to enter the ministry. But he was also known for his sense of humor and general lack of seriousness. Lyman's concerns were both spiritual and professional. Nevertheless, he prophesied, "I shall have the boy in the ministry yet."[79] At Mount Pleasant Academy, the initial seeds of reform had begun to grow quietly in the young Beecher, but they were probably only observable to Harriet, the sibling with whom he shared the most intimate connection. In a letter to Harriet in March of 1830, Henry considered the morality of card playing. Although he claimed not to have made up his mind about the forbidden activity, he carried a small amount of guilt for not confronting his classmates who "don't think there is any harm in it any more than there is in playing chess."[80] As a sixteen-year-old, Henry already displayed a contempt for gaming and gambling that would only increase throughout his life, an aversion that was still evident in his eulogy of General Ulysses S. Grant over half a century later.[81]

However, at Amherst, where he matriculated in the fall, Henry finally found the courage to speak up, at least on a few issues. As John Raymond Howard observes, in college, "he was interested in matters of reform, having decided anti-slavery views and being a total abstainer from ardent spirits; made himself a power in the class prayer-meetings; and always attracted the attention of his fellows by the ability and originality of his essay-writing and his fluency and eloquence in debate and extempore speaking."[82] In a debate for the Athenian Society on the issue of colonization, he was assigned to defend the negative side of the question, "and in preparing to speak I prepared my whole life," he later reflected. "I contended against colonization as a condition of emancipation—enforced colonization was but little better than enforced slavery—and advocated immediate emancipation on the broad ground of human rights."[83] Henry was hardly an abolitionist, having accepted the task of arguing a particular point. However, his argument that "all men are designed by God to be free" would germinate in his teenage mind. With the help of his siblings—and northern political culture—it continued to grow.

Still tormented by his father's doom-and-gloom theology, Henry took refuge in poetry and literature, including Byron, Coleridge, and Wordsworth. He also digested German Romanticists like Goethe and Lessing.[84] Eager to be liked, Henry was also anxious to make his mark in the world. In the years at Amherst, he and a friend visited nearby towns and lectured on phrenology, an emerging pseudoscience which taught that a person's intelligence and character were determined by the shape of their head. While Beecher lectured, his friend measured the heads of his listeners. Although the lectures brought in very little money, Beecher got his first taste of public speaking, foreshadowing his brilliance on the lyceum circuit.[85] Noting Henry's penchant for humor, one classmate later described his reputation as "a reformer and an earnest man." A future businessman and philanthropist, Lewis Tappan, also in the class at Amherst, recalled, "In logic and class debates no one could approach him. I listened to his flow of impassioned eloquence in those my youthful days with wonder and admiration."[86] For all of his distinctions, Henry resembled his father in oratory and conviction.

Reluctant to divulge his thoughts to his father but eager to throw himself into the family business of moral influence, Henry found a convenient sounding board for his ideas and aspirations in Harriet. In a letter in the spring of 1831, he revealed to his older sister:

> I want to consult you on a *plan* that I have formed—for I possess real Beecher blood in the matter of *planning*. It is this: In my six weeks' vacation, and in the four weeks' one, I mean to attach myself as some kind of agent to the Bible, or Tract, or Education, or some other society, wherever I can, and travel round to the small towns at a distance, and collect funds and distribute Bibles and tracts, or something like that, or do something or other—of course I can't tell what they may want me to do.
>
> I shall in a month or two be eighteen years old, and I think that that is old enough to begin to do something. I can get letters of the president and professors here and of gentlemen of Boston to establish my mission, so that folks will not think that I am collecting my own purposes under the name of some society. Will you write to me about it? Tell C. that I have engaged one to hear me recite botany. I am going to establish a daily prayer-meeting here, and pray for a revival. Pray for us, too. Mount Pleasant is in a very bad state. Lotteries are here without number—five dollars is the highest prize—and books and everything else, morals and all, are going, I believe, and the masters (blind fellows) know nothing of it, although one of the monitors handed in to Mr. Fellowes a *lottery scheme* instead of his report in the division.
>
> Give my love to Mary and husband, Catharine, Cos. Elizabeth, and all who care for me, taking a goodly portion to yourself.

Your Brother,
H.C.B.[87]

In western Massachusetts, Henry was still planted firmly in the Beecher family "establishment." Although he would "not dare go to [his] father" about his spiritual trials, he was able to confide in and solicit advice from his sister in Hartford.[88] Henry's relationship with Harriet was not unlike young Thomas's relationship with Isabella, who was urged by her mother,

Harriet, to lead her eight-year-old brother to Christ. The older Beecher sisters often served as confidantes, counselors, and cheerleaders for their younger brothers as they experienced the conflict of seeking to imitate their father while simultaneously distancing themselves from his control.[89] In Thomas's case, this internal angst became the "central tension" of his life.[90] In Henry's case, his relationship to Lyman was even more paradoxical. With a mixture of fear and affection, he longed to imitate his father *and* to escape him. Plotting his first major endeavor into moral and social reform, Henry was determined to be a moral influencer, relying upon Lyman's connections in New England and his contacts in Boston to get him started. Quite naturally, he drew from his father's playbook. While Lyman, "New England revivalism's greatest engineer," was awakening Boston, his son was engineering prayer meetings and praying for revival at Amherst.[91] Henry even took aim at the lotteries, which Lyman had attacked with his Hanover Street Church Young Men's Association. Desiring to be "some kind of agent" for a benevolent society, young Henry Ward Beecher was starting to show his Beecher colors. Indeed, he had "real Beecher blood" in his veins. However, these plans proved a bit too ambitious. Henry was unable to convince the trustees and the societies that he could be useful. He settled for a teaching position at a school for the summer.

Henry overestimated a few things during his college years. His belief in phrenology was motivated by the idea that human mental capacity could be increased. According to Clifford E. Clark Jr., "phrenology encouraged Beecher to believe in progress and the possibility of the perfection of the individual. Phrenology not only offered an alternative to metaphysical explanations of human behavior, it also seemed to point the way to a new understanding of the laws of nature." As president of the Natural History Society, Henry presented a lecture on phrenology to "exhibit and defend its *fundamental principles*."[92] Just a few months later, he graduated from Amherst and joined the rest of the family in Cincinnati.

Like Catharine, Henry resisted his father's spiritual authority even while simultaneously aligning himself with Lyman's various causes. In Boston, for example, when Lyman made such a public foray against the Unitarians, Henry perceived for the first time that the name of Lyman Beecher "was in everybody's mouth, I had the vague impression that my father was a man of a great deal of public renown." Henry never adopted much of his father's Calvinist theology, but their shared sense of mission and Lyman's seeming courage in the face of opposition endeared the impressionable son to his father. As Debby Applegate notes, "He didn't understand all the details of these battles, but the attacks only made him more loyal to his father. What choice did he have? 'Remember that neutrality is treason,' as Lyman liked to say, 'and if persisted in, is fatal.' Had he given the critics a fair hearing, Henry would have been surprised at how closely they reflected his own troubled feelings toward his father's demanding doctrines."[93] Also like Catharine, whose school he attended in Hartford when he was ten (where he was the only boy among forty girls), perhaps the strongest doctrine that Henry imbibed from Lyman was the doctrine of *doing*.[94] Even though he did not yet have a clear direction for his "mission," he wanted to "do something" for the cause of Christ. Lyman believed in practicing what he preached, and of all the critiques laid against him by his children, the charge of hypocrisy was never among them.

THE DARK SIDE OF "MORAL INFLUENCE"

In truth, Lyman Beecher's enemies in Boston included more than the Unitarians. As Lyman's wife, Harriet, wrote in February 1827, "Almost every minister of every denomination has set up evening meetings, and preach against us without mercy."[95] Whether or not *every* minister in *every* denomination was actually preaching against Lyman Beecher, this belief fostered a not-so-subtle complex among the Beechers that they were evangelical Davids facing down the heretical Goliaths of their age. In their minds, it was the Beechers against Boston. Among those groups whom Lyman Beecher opposed were Universalists, Finneyite revivalists, high Episcopalians, and most hated of all, Roman Catholics.[96] However, unlike his view of the more democratic Charles Finney, with whom he eventually reconciled after the New Lebanon Convention of 1827, Beecher's disdain for "Papal Superstition" never relented.[97] In fact, it became so strong that young Harriet believed it was her father's "great motive in going to Cincinnati."[98] In 1831, Lyman delivered a series of lectures in Boston on the looming threat of Roman Catholicism, including warnings of plots by the Vatican to seize control of the United States. Moral influence had a dark side.

Like countless Americans before him, Beecher entertained conspiracies about a Roman Catholic takeover of the American republic. However,

Beecher was also generating a new brand of nationalist ideology. In what John C. Pinheiro has called the "Beecherite synthesis," Lyman fused traditional Protestant beliefs about the papacy with nativist fears to produce, or at least contribute to, a new anti-Catholic prejudice in America which helped stoke anti-Catholic riots in Boston a few years later.[99] While denying any connection to the violence and also asserting his support for the civil liberties of Catholics, Lyman alluded to these riots in *A Plea for the West* (1835), scoffing at "the idea that the Catholic religion should be advocated on the ground that of its power of protecting Protestant republicans, against the violence of its people." The real dangers, he argued, were the "threats of a Catholic mob," not the unbridled chaos of republicanism. For Beecher, the city of Boston represented the potential risks for the rest of the nation if the tyranny of Roman Catholicism was not held in check. Boston also had the power to "illustrate the peril and commotion which a small body of Catholic population may produce in spite of clerical power."[100] Frenchman Alexis de Tocqueville, whose *Democracy in America* was likewise published in 1835, and who was himself a Catholic, resented that, in America, "the Catholic religion has erroneously been looked upon as the natural enemy of democracy."[101] Perhaps no clergyman in Boston—and in the West—had done more to promote that idea than Lyman Beecher.

Like most of his other beliefs, Lyman Beecher's virulently anti-Catholic bigotry made its way into the pulpit, into his reform efforts, and even into his own children. Although Edward Beecher would not compose *Papal Conspiracy Exposed* until 1855 (at the end of his second pastorate in Boston), his view of Protestantism and Catholicism fit nicely into the dual framework he had constructed in the 1820s of cosmic warfare. His biographer Robert Merideth has even suggested that "Beecher's anti-Catholicism" was a "metaphoric illustration of his vision of the good and bad societies."[102] Edward's primary objection to Roman Catholicism, aside from his interpretation of Scripture, was the priestly abstinence from marriage. As one historian has noted, "Edward Beecher, like his contemporaries, saw a diabolical cleverness in the combination of clerical celibacy with the confessional. It placed unrequited desires in the breasts of the clergy at the same time that it gave the priest extraordinary power over his female penitents."[103] In Edward's mind, this stood *against* the exclusive and intimate marital union designed by God and diminished the importance of families. "Whoever would become eminently holy," he later argued of Roman Catholicism, "whether man or woman, must first of all abjure marriage and take the vow of perpetual celibacy and chastity."[104] As Robert Merideth has also shown, by the late 1820s, Edward followed a powerful trend among New England Protestants to frame the Pope as the grand nemesis of religious and civil liberty. In fact, the ideal of combating Catholics in the West was one of the factors that propelled the young Beecher westward even before his father.

Anti-Catholicism was a prejudice that imbued the thinking of almost every Beecher from an early age. Only after multiple visits to Rome in the 1850s, for example, could Harriet begin to unmoor herself from this Puritan aspect of the family worldview. Scholars have noticed that Henry did not halt his attacks on Roman Catholicism until he moved out of the West and had ministered for years in New York City.[105] This prejudice was difficult to shake because "moral influence" included both social and ethnic components. When Lyman Beecher led his campaigns against Sunday recreations and alcohol consumption in the city of Boston, it was resisted most vehemently by working-class Catholic immigrants. It certainly did not help matters that Beecher compared the "insatiable desire of drinking" during saints' days to the evil of "papal indulgences," or money given to the medieval Church to reduce time spent in purgatory.[106] Both of these activities, Lyman argued in 1828, "dissolved . . . the bonds of order" by eroding the morals of the community.[107] Catholicism was not the same as, for example, Masonry, a subject on which Lyman counseled his children to remain tight-lipped.[108] It was an enemy to be openly and publicly renounced. Grounded in a millennial expectation that God would achieve ultimate victory over the anti-Christian forces of the Roman Catholic Church, Lyman's anti-Catholicism also helped him to justify a world without state religion.

In an 1827 sermon delivered at Plymouth, "The Faith of Our Fathers," Beecher boasted, "It has been contended, that christianity cannot exist in this world without the aid of religious establishments. But, with more truth it might be said, that, from the beginning to this day, it has existed in spite of them. It took possession of the Roman Empire in the face of a formidable establishment of false religion, and has survived the deadly embrace of establishments nominally Christian, and now, bursting from their alliance, finds in them the most bitter opposition to evangelical doctrine and vital godliness."[109] In other words, the history of the Roman Catholic Church embodied the very worst of religious establishment. Therefore, in his mind, the Church should be disestablished completely. Of all of Beecher's arguments against Catholicism, no doubt his appeal to the "republican form" of Christianity resonated most powerfully with his children, who were not as quick to stereotype Catholics as drunks and gamblers but who were nonetheless prone to resist almost anything (including Lyman) which might significantly limit their religious freedoms.

However, it was not Lyman Beecher who had the last laugh in Boston. On a frosty December night in 1830, when the fire bell rang in the North End, it was discovered that Hanover Street Church was engulfed in flames. Upon realizing that it was Lyman Beecher's church, the firemen, many of whom were Catholics, refused to put out the fire. In an instance of unbelievable irony, the church basement, rented out by a local merchant who had been secretly storing jugs of rum, began to explode. Boston's "temple of temperance" was now overflowing with liquor.[110] Unable to resist themselves, the firemen jeered at the "hell-fire" of the catastrophe. "Only smell the brimstone!" the bystanders mocked. "I wonder what 'Old Hell-fire' will do now that his shop is burned?" In the eyes of his enemies, Lyman Beecher, Boston's moral crusader, had received the very judgment he had called down upon others. In a moment of delicious justice, many Catholics relished the opportunity to speak back to the Protestant voice of New England. And the name-calling did not stop with the blaze. Shortly after arriving in Cincinnati, Lyman had offended so many German and Irish Catholics that a local newspaper dubbed him "The Right Reverend and Awful Lyman Beecher, D.D.—the wily political priest."[111] In a free nation, Lyman was vilified by many Catholics for imposing his Protestant and evangelical will upon outsiders.

THE NEW ENGLAND WAY

By the time the Beechers departed for Cincinnati in 1832, Lyman Beecher had established himself as the most popular—and most villainized—preacher in New England and perhaps the United States. Before the family took on truly "national" status in Ohio, the personal and public lives of the Beechers in Massachusetts and Connecticut had ripple effects for their careers and indeed for the nation itself. The Hanover Association of Young

Men, which Lyman founded in 1827, introduced the city of Boston to the Lyceum movement, which later hosted abolitionists such as William Lloyd Garrison and Frederick Douglass.[112] Like Lyman Beecher, Garrison himself had come to Boston for the moral improvement of America. He entered the temperance ranks under the influence of Lyman's preaching in Boston in the late 1820s.[113] On Independence Day in 1829, Garrison delivered his first antislavery address in Boston at Edward's Park Street Church at the invitation of the local Congregational societies. Although Edward did not personally invite Garrison, he sat on the platform, and it was perhaps on July 4 that young Edward first heard slavery referred to as a "national sin."[114] In the months following the sermon, as a member of Lyman Beecher's congregation, Garrison became more radical in his views of immediate emancipation. He famously recanted his colonizationist views two years later. However, on July 4, over a year before Edward left for Illinois, Garrison certainly struck a chord with the young Beecher when he declared, "We have seen how readily, and with what ease, that horrid gorgon, Intemperance, has been checked in his ravages. Let us take courage. Moral influence, when in vigorous exercise, is irresistible. It has an immortal essence. It can no more be trod out of existence by the iron foot of time, or by the ponderous march of iniquity, than matter can be annihilated. It may disappear for a time; but it lives in some shape or other, in some place or other, and will rise with renovated strength. Let us, then, be up and doing."[115]

Although more radical in tone, Garrison was still speaking a language that Edward Beecher understood well. If anyone believed in the inevitability of progress and the power of moral influence, it was the family of Lyman Beecher, the man largely responsible for checking the "horrid gorgon" of Intemperance. Garrison also foreshadowed Edward's path to reform when he beseeched, "I call upon the great body of newspaper editors to keep this subject constantly before their readers; to sound the trumpet of alarm, and to plead eloquently for the rights of man. They must give the tone to public sentiment. One press may ignite twenty; a city may warm a State; a State may impart a generous heat to a whole country."[116] Less than two years later in Boston, Garrison founded the *Liberator,* the premiere antislavery newspaper in the United States. In less than a decade, Edward published *Narrative of Riots at Alton,* an account of the death of the abolitionist editor Elijah Lovejoy in Illinois.

In the months after Garrison's address at Park Street, a group of former Yale Divinity School students who served in the Illinois Association invited Edward to become president of Illinois College. As a tutor at Yale, Edward had left an impression upon these men, known as the "Yale Band." However, as Merideth observes, "As always . . . the Beecher name and influence helped him."[117] While Edward may have beaten his father and siblings to the West, it was his family who paved his road to Illinois. These former students of Nathaniel Taylor, Lyman's best friend, were united in their mutual admiration for Lyman. Asa Turner, who corresponded with Edward in 1829, came to Boston in the spring of 1830 at the request of George Beecher to study with Lyman. Jonathan Baldwin Turner, professor of rhetoric and belles lettres at the college, described himself as an "old and well-tried friend" of George. Truman Marcellus Post, professor of languages, applauded Lyman's "wise treatment" of his "religious difficulties" and for providing a "great service" to him. William Collins, who made the "largest single subscription" to the school and served as a trustee, was a former deacon at Lyman's church in Litchfield. Nathaniel Coffin, who became the treasurer of the college, was a relative of the Beechers.[118] In some ways, Lyman followed his son to the West. In other ways, Edward followed his father. Nevertheless, both Edward and Lyman were following a growing trend among New Englanders to migrate westward for the sake of educating—and evangelizing—the frontier.[119] As would become their habit throughout the nineteenth century, the Beechers were influencing and being influenced by their New England context at the very same time.

Quite naturally, New England was also the lens through which the Beechers viewed their journey westward. When Catharine, who resigned from Hartford Female Seminary in 1831, accompanied Lyman to Cincinnati in the spring of 1832 to survey Lane Seminary and the city, she wrote back to her sister Harriet that "this is a New England city in all its habits, and its inhabitants are more than half from New England." Since the end of the eighteenth century (Cincinnati was founded in 1788), New Englanders had transported their customs, institutions, and religion into the Midwest, from western New York to Ohio to Illinois. By leading new colleges and erecting new academies, the Beechers were part of this great Yankee migration. (The first *Plea for the West* was actually published in 1826 by the Episcopal bishop of Ohio, Philander Chase, a New Englander.) With a combination of magnificent hills, verdant forests, and rich soil, Cincinnati must have appeared somewhat like New England. More than any of her siblings and more than any other woman of her age, Catharine would embrace this project to Hellenize the West with New England ideals. Concluding her letter to Harriet with a spirit of optimism, Catharine wrote, "As to father, I never saw such a field of usefulness and influence as is offered to him here. I see no difficulties or objections; every thing is ready, and every body gives a welcome except Dr. Wilson's folks, and they are finding that it is wisest and best to be still, and we hope that before a great while they will be *friendly*." She added, "Father is determined to get acquainted with Dr. Wilson, and to be *friendly* with him, and I think he will succeed."[120] Originally from Kentucky, Rev. Joshua Wilson was not from New England. He did not share Lyman Beecher's brand of theology or his view of slavery. Two elders at Second Presbyterian, most likely through Wilson's influence, wrote to Lyman warning him that, if he came to Cincinnati, there would be "a considerable secession from the Church."[121] Eventually taking to the New York press to campaign against Lyman, Wilson was not as friendly as the Beechers would have hoped.

Chapter 2

THE WILD, WELD WEST
(1832-1837)

IN THE 1830s, Cincinnati was a burgeoning metropolis of seeming contradictions. The so-called Queen City was a small town with big aspirations, a western frontier with New England sensibilities, and a northern entrepôt with southern sympathies. Upon arrival in 1828, Englishwoman Frances Trollope was impressed with the size and energy of the "infant Hercules," despite its poor drainage system, unrefined citizens, austere architecture, and roaming pigs. "Though I do not quite sympathize with those who consider Cincinnati as one of the wonders of the earth," she demurred with a bit of British condescension, "I certainly think it is a city of extraordinary size and importance, when it is remembered that thirty years ago the aboriginal forest occupied the ground where it stands; and every month appears to extend its limits and its wealth." With twenty-eight thousand people laboring in farming, wool, milling, brewing, and pork production (the city was nicknamed "Porkopolis"), Cincinnati was a rising industrial center in the Ohio River Valley.[1] New Englanders had also brought their Federalist and Whig politics to the city, from land offices to banks to pro-business policies.[2] Cincinnati was a city on the move. Frances Trollope was not alone in her opinion that the "population is greater than the appearance of the town would lead one to expect."[3]

With waves of eastern migrants pouring into the city, Cincinnatians adapted rather well to change—but not always. In the middle of a transportation revolution and in the most intense period of land speculation in American history, the clash of eastern and western cultures was the background for Lyman Beecher's call to Lane Seminary.[4] When the first professor at Lane, George Beckwith of Massachusetts, resigned in the fall of 1830 due to a shortage of funds, the chairman of the Board of Trustees, Old

Schooler Joshua L. Wilson, expressed his lack of confidence in "obtaining aid from eastern men and eastern funds."[5] But to Wilson's dismay, the East delivered men and money. After Lyman Beecher was elected president and professor of theology a year later, Wilson's letter of resignation to the board left little doubt that his objections were as regional as they were theological: "You may call this Beecherism or Taylorism, or Bostonism, or what ISM you please, except Bibleism and Presbyterianism."[6] Whether in Boston or Ohio or Indiana or New York, the nature of Beecherism was to appropriate certain prevailing movements and ideologies of the age as its own. This is why it was somewhat difficult for Wilson and others to define. This was also its power. In its official invitation letter in January 1832, the seminary board noted the rising tension in the city that foreshadowed the crisis Lyman would face in the years to come: "The minds of many Western Christians are becoming alienated from their brethren at the East by the fierce and bitter controversies which now agitate the public mind. Missionaries who come out from New England are held up as heretics, and every obstacle is thrown in the way of their efficiency and success." In short, frontier religion did not seem to coalesce well with the scholasticized, New School theology of Yale and Andover.

On the other hand, the Ohio Valley was the ideal place for a preacher-president who could cut through the web of complex doctrines and deliver a simple gospel. As Methodist circuit rider Peter Cartwright once observed, "The great mass of our Western people wanted a preacher that could mount a stump, a block, or old log, or stand in the bed of a wagon, and, without note or manuscript, quote, expound, and apply the word of God to the hearts and consciences of the people."[7] Cincinnati was no place for a patrician Timothy Dwight or an erudite Nathaniel Taylor, but perhaps for the revivalist Lyman Beecher it was tailor-made. In their letter to Beecher, the board members at Lane entreated, "Will you not, under these circumstances, come over and help us? Will you not come immediately? The case is pressing and urgent. The armies of Israel need a leader."[8] For a man who framed his entire ministry in biblical proportions, such an invitation was irresistible. Lyman Beecher did not leave Boston with a victory over the Unitarians or the Catholics. However, the real battle for the soul of America, and indeed the world, was no longer in New England. One teacher in Kentucky called the Ohio Valley "the great battlefield between the powers of light and darkness."[9] Reverend John Jay Shipherd, founder of Oberlin College in upstate Ohio, called it the "valley of moral death," alluding to Psalm 23.[10] To some, including many in his own church, the fifty-seven-year-old Beecher was too old to start a new life in the West. But as he had boasted to Catharine in his fateful letter in 1830, "When I stop I expect to stop in heaven, and not linger long on earth after my active usefulness is ended."[11] Lyman Beecher had not yet begun to slow down. As usual, the family followed in his optimistic footsteps. On the way to Cincinnati, Harriet wrote to a friend, "Father says we are in hands of Providence; but mother and Aunt Esther seem to demur, and think they should rather trust Providence by the way."[12]

A CITY AT THE CROSSROADS

In an 1851 essay entitled "Cincinnati—Its Destiny," a resident named S. H. Goodin predicted that his city would become America's great metropolis. According to simple laws of centralization, he reasoned that Cincinnati was primed to become *the* crossroads of the United States.[13] Although citizens in St. Louis and Chicago disputed this prediction, one can certainly see Goodin's point. Along one of the two great arteries of trade in the United States and centered at the nexus of North and South, East and West, Cincinnati was positioned for progress. When the Beechers disembarked after their steamboat adventure down the Ohio River in 1832, they truly believed that Cincinnati was America's next great city. Quoting from Joel 3:14, Lyman called the Ohio Valley the "valley of decision."[14] A year after arriving, Harriet wrote her first book, *Primary Geography*, generously sharing credit with her sister Catharine. (The first advertisement listed Catharine as the sole author!)[15] In the book, which she wrote to "exert an influence" over the minds and morals of children, the twenty-one-year-old Harriet concluded, "This city of Cincinnati has for these few years, been constantly growing larger, and in a few years more, it may become one of the greatest in the world." After noting the unsettled regions of Ohio, she added confidently, "But people are constantly coming from New England, and from the eastern and southern states, to settle in this country."[16] For the Beechers, the best was yet to come in Cincinnati.

In truth, the city was a melting pot or a tinderbox, depending on which person you asked. Although slavery had been outlawed in Ohio since the Northwest Ordinance of 1787, race relations in Cincinnati were hardly calm. Due to its proximity to slavery-friendly Kentucky and its own trade practices with slaveowners, Cincinnati was divided along racial lines and its elites were highly suspicious of abolitionism. The substantial free Black population was relegated to a portion of the community known as "little Africa."[17] Most free Blacks were former slaves who lived in shacks, spoke poor English, and worked as laborers in the city. Some actually *were* slaves, having escaped across the Ohio River from Kentucky, a fact bemoaned by Kentucky Senator Henry Clay in his famous speech to the Senate in 1850.[18] Whether slave or free, *all* Blacks in Cincinnati lived in constant fear of being kidnapped and claimed as fugitives by agents of southern masters, the very kind described in Harriet's monumental book. When Alexis de Tocqueville visited Cincinnati in late 1831, just before the Beechers' arrival, he wrote to his mother in France that "everything that is good and bad about American society stands out here with such relief that it is like reading a book with large letters intended to teach children how to read."[19] Hopes and fears, freedom and slavery, prosperity and poverty, grew together in Cincinnati.

As Kathryn Kish Sklar has described it, the Beechers "entered an already established society where New Englanders, Middle-Atlantic state emigrants, and Southerners were dedicated to suppressing the issues that could potentially divide them."[20] Those issues had rocked the city in 1830 in the form of race riots and would eventually explode the city again during the riots of 1836. Cincinnati was volatile because the nation itself was turbulent. Recent events had exposed the deep political, racial, and religious fissures that already existed in the country, pushing Americans closer to civil war. In August 1831, in Southampton, Virginia, preacher and slave Nat Turner led the largest slave revolt in American history, killing nearly sixty white people. In *Confessions of Nat Turner*, conducted while Turner was awaiting execution, Mr. Thomas Gray asked the self-proclaimed prophet, "Do you not find yourself mistaken now?" Turner allegedly replied, "Was not Christ crucified?"[21] The very same year William Lloyd Garrison founded the Boston-based abolitionist newspaper the *Liberator*, launching his attacks against slaveowners, colonizationists, and anyone who stood against the immediate emancipation of slaves. In 1833, the American Anti-

Slavery Society was founded in Philadelphia by abolitionists Garrison and Arthur and Lewis Tappan, benefactors of Lane Seminary. Cincinnati felt the shocks from this kind of seismic activity in the East.

In such an environment, the "conservative abolitionist" Lyman Beecher initially seemed well-suited because he knew how to play to every side.[22] Shortly after becoming president of Lane, he joined the Cincinnati Colonization Society. However, in his first semipublic comment on slavery in 1833, he wrote to Arthur Tappan and confessed that he saw no "inconsistency" between abolitionists and colonizationists. If it "were in my power to put an end to slavery immediately, I would do it," he assured the abolitionist New York businessman.[23] Although Lyman seemed willing and able to hold the middle during these early years in Cincinnati, the seeds of abolitionism were already being sown in the hearts of some of his children. By 1833, twenty-three-year-old George had become awakened to the antislavery cause, becoming the second Beecher to take a sincere interest in the movement. George was a man of conviction and conscience, much like his father, and his abolitionism would have ripple effects for several of his siblings. Against his father's wishes, he soon began trying to convert William to the cause.[24] Evangelical by nature, Beechers never kept their beliefs to themselves. (Years later, his activism had a significant impact upon the New School Presbyterian churches of Indiana where he and Henry and Charles would later minister.) Unlike New England, Cincinnati thrust the Beechers into a world where slaves and slaveowners lay just outside their door, demanding a personal, if not public, response. That summer, a former student invited Harriet to visit her home in Washington, Kentucky. It was Harriet's first and only known visit to the South and to a plantation with slaves, providing valuable material for a young mind that would later produce *Uncle Tom's Cabin*.

WALNUT HILLS

Nevertheless, as social and political forces swirled around them, the Beechers remained relatively undivided by the issues that divided the world outside their home at Walnut Hills. Reflecting upon her first years in Cincinnati with no small degree of nostalgia, Harriet described their brick, L-shaped home as a place surrounded by furry creatures, birds, and towering trees, but most importantly, filled with energy and love: "It was an exuberant and glorious life while it lasted. The atmosphere of his household was replete with moral oxygen—full charged with intellectual electricity. Nowhere else have we felt any thing resembling or equaling it. It was a kind of moral heaven, the purity, vivacity, inspiration, and enthusiasm of which those only can appreciate who have lost it, and feel that in this world there is, there can be 'no place like home.'"[25] As evidenced by works like *Oldtown Folks,* Harriet developed a somewhat rose-colored lens of her upbringing through the years. Still, her description of Walnut Hills as a "moral heaven" filled with "moral oxygen" suggests that it was not quite the oppressive "Puritan penitentiary" later historians have framed it to be. Most revealing is the apparent "intellectual electricity" that charged the home. The residence at Walnut Hills was a house of ideas, and the Beecher children were not isolated from relevant concepts like public justice, free speech, and human rights.[26] They were introduced to these ideas in conversation with Lyman, who also hosted students and faculty in the house.[27] Conversations took place at the table, by the large fireplace in the winter, and on the veranda in the spring. With thirteen members of the household, including four servants, the house was full of people and intellectual exchange. Friends like Ormsby Mitchel, professor of mathematics and astronomy at Cincinnati College, and his wife, Louisa, were also known to drop by the Beecher homestead. Even Thomas "did not escape the family debates."[28] As Barbara White has noted, the Beecher children received their "most influential learning not from the Institute or Semi-Colon Club, but from the family dinner table."[29] Lyman Beecher was so convinced of the power of moral influence that he practiced it in his own home. After all, if he could not influence his own children, what hope was there of changing the world? Unfortunately for his career, Lyman would not be as open to honest discussion when it came to the issue of slavery.

If Lyman indeed played the role of the Puritan preacher to his children, then he appeared less as the cartoon of Jonathan Edwards delivering "Sinners in the Hands of an Angry God," which has become so popular among some historians today, and more as the leader of a voluntary society in which the participants could only be made to share his social, political, and theological commitments through their own free will. In an era of Lyceum lectures and revival prayer meetings, such a conversational style of teaching was not as unconventional as it might sound. Cincinnati had also softened Lyman a bit. He was no longer the stalwart leader of the conservative cause, but the alleged liberal trying to pull sides together. As the Beecher siblings would attest years later, they engaged rather extensively with their father in these family discussions, and the disagreements that occasionally arose about religion and politics did not stem from being isolated from ideas, but in the interpretation of the ideas themselves. Things like "purity, vivacity, inspiration, and enthusiasm" were the very same qualities that Lyman sought to generate in his Bible and Tract and Temperance societies, his revivals, and at Lane Seminary. Therefore, a more fitting comparison of the Beecher home, at least in the Cincinnati years, is one of a New School classroom and not of a prison.

Thanks to the Plan of Union (1801), which united Congregationalist and Presbyterian churches for the sake of western expansion and helped to proliferate New School ideas along the frontier, Lyman Beecher left the Congregationalist Church in Boston to join the Presbyterian Church in Cincinnati, all without leaving his New England Theology behind—much to the chagrin of provincial Old School Presbyterians like Joshua Wilson. The Beechers changed states, denominations, and cultures, but they did not have to change the core values of human responsibility and potential, the hope and certainty of the millennium, and the relative compatibility of American and divine governments. Not surprisingly, these were the chief values that the Beecher children imbibed from their father. Brokered in Timothy Dwight's parlor at Yale, the Plan of Union itself was a joint venture by two formalist denominations to evangelize and bring moral order to the West.[30] Although the Presbyterian Schism of 1837 would spell the official end of "Presbygational" churches, the moral reform and the innovative New England Theology that long troubled the confessionalist Presbyterians in the South and West would in fact live on in the Beechers, who were less concerned with points of doctrine and more concerned with the moral fabric of America.[31]

The Beecher catechesis was so effective that Old Schoolers saw Lyman's New School spirit in his children. In 1833, when George faced the local presbytery for his ordination, what followed was a roast. Lyman turned to his conservative opponents defiantly and declared, "we shall still live; we shall stand on God's earth, and breathe his air, and preach his Gospel as we believe it." In response, the waspish Joshua Wilson launched a thirty-minute attack against New Haven Theology and professed his view that "the candidate was not a Christian, and knew nothing experimentally about Christianity, and that . . . he, and all who held the same sentiments with him, 'would never see the gates of eternal bliss.'"[32] In essence, young George was condemned to hell by his father's enemies. From the Old School point of view, such theological hair-splitting between natural and moral ability and between freedom and bondage of the will was the difference between salvation and damnation. For the Beecher children, it was the worst kind of religious hypocrisy. Setting the scene, Charles mocked years later, "The candidate is Mr. George Beecher, a *New School man;* but that is not the worst—a *Taylorite!!*"[33]

George had imbibed a heavy dose of New Haven Theology at Yale, graduating from the college in 1828 and the seminary in 1832 before following his father to Cincinnati. Due to poor health, including a two-year loss of vision, George's studies at Yale had been interrupted, so his father had recommended a year of study at Lane.[34] Such an accusation that George was outside the Christian faith only pushed the young Beecher further down the New School path, leaving a bitter taste in his mouth for rancorous theological debate and for Old School dogma. Despite the verbal assault, George passed his ordination. But it dealt a psychological blow to an already weathered mind. In college, George had felt "as if no one cared for me, or could feel respect or affection for me."[35] Those feelings would plague him the rest of his life. With the insistence of his father and the encouragement of his siblings, George soon left to pastor a church in Batavia, Ohio, with the American Home Missionary Society.[36]

In 1832 and 1833, events like the reelection of Andrew Jackson and the Nullification Crisis in South Carolina were signs to the Beechers that the nation was possessed by the spirit of populism and individualism, but not always for the good. Although Lyman hoped that Jackson might become "a great blessing to the civil & religious interests of the nation," the Beechers generally were spiritual, not political, democrats.[37] Headlines from Washington were not the primary topics of conversation in the Beecher household. They had more pressing matters on their minds. Almost as soon as they arrived in Cincinnati, so did cholera. The epidemic was no respecter of color or class, sweeping through all parts of Cincinnati and lingering for several years. At one point, the disease was killing twenty to thirty people per day, sometimes within just a few hours of their first symptoms.[38] The disease wreaked havoc at Lane Seminary, where it took the lives of several students. It also endeared the students to a new classmate who arrived in the spring of 1833 named Theodore Dwight Weld, who ministered to the sick and dying. Harriet Porter herself was also slowly passing away, having exchanged the safe confines of her native New England for a frontier ridden with disease and disorder. The young woman originally admired by the Beecher children for her beauty and elegance had become bitter, then distraught, then depressed, and then broken. Harriet was paying an emotional and psychological toll for being the wife of a somewhat absent-minded crusader such as Lyman Beecher and for being the mother of so many children in an unfamiliar place. And Lyman was quietly suffering as well, watching his wife slowly retreat from the world. To make matters worse, Harriet's best friend, Eliza Stowe, died from cholera in 1834, leaving behind her husband, Calvin Stowe, professor of biblical literature at Lane.

In a season of death and deterioration, the Beecher children relied less upon their mother and more upon one another. When Harriet Porter fell ill, as she often did, the younger Harriet cared for her stepmother alongside Aunt Esther, who was basically in charge of the household. When William visited the house from Putnam, Ohio, he confided in his sister about the harsh criticisms that he had received from his church about his frank remarks. He also asked her about the best way to broach the subject to Lyman. As Noel B. Gerson has put It, "No relationships under the roof of the seething Beechers were simple."[39] Harriet welcomed her role as counselor for her brothers in their complicated relationship with their father. In fact, as the most dynamic Beecher, Harriet played different roles for different siblings. For George, who struggled with his calling, she was a cheerleader. Along with Edward, who came in from Illinois, she encouraged George not to leave the ministry altogether and to continue his studies at Lane. For Henry, she was a companion. When Henry visited from Massachusetts, he and his sister picked up where they had left off in their fondness for one another.[40] At the time of Eliza's death in 1834, when her stepmother's health was plummeting, young Harriet was attending Henry's graduation at Amherst in Massachusetts. She was the only sibling to attend.

The Beechers were a complex of relationships, some closer than others. For example, young Thomas admired his half-brother Edward, over nineteen years his senior, as an almost untouchable example of intellect and virtue. Yet, because they were a bit closer in age, he revered his other half-brothers, Henry and Charles, as his "heroes."[41] Still yet, he considered his older sister Isabella "his lifelong confidante, sharing with her his joys, sorrows, and doubts."[42] Before the 1840s, nothing in the way of sibling "rivalry" or division had developed inside or outside the home. Roxana's children and Harriet's children got along relatively well in these years, even with age and distance and DNA between them.

BUILDING A NETWORK

Outside the sylvan confines of Walnut Hills, the first few years in Cincinnati were a time of building relationships, institutions, and influence. Almost as soon as they moved to the city, Harriet began to publish stories and essays in the *Western Monthly Magazine,* a literary journal modeled after regional magazines in the East. Her sister Catharine's first and only publication in the magazine was a temperance song for the Youth's Temperance Society of Cincinnati.[43] Like their father, the Beecher sisters used seemingly every medium available to advocate for reform. In Cincinnati, "the literary capital of the Mississippi Valley," newspapers and magazines were especially important for the dissemination of ideas.[44] A prevailing "ideology of literacy," as historian James McPherson has phrased it, extended well beyond periodicals.[45] Around this time, both sisters were invited to join a literary society known as the Semi-Colon Club, Cincinnati's premiere social and intellectual group, comprised of doctors, lawyers, professors, clergy, and businessmen. Lyman was also in the club, and his daughters benefited from their Beecher name.

Lyman also enjoyed the perks of such ambitious company. Among the members of the Semi-Colon Club, for instance, was a local lawyer originally from New England named Salmon P. Chase, the future leader of Ohio's Liberty Party, a founder of the Free Soil Party, future governor and senator, and eventual chief justice of the U.S. Supreme Court. As the nephew of the venerable Philander Chase, Ohio's first Episcopal bishop, Salmon was already connected to an impressive network of prominent figures in the state. Within a few weeks of the Beechers' arrival in Cincinnati, Chase had already begun attending Beecher's church and praised Lyman's sermons in the pages of his diary.[46] Beecher even married Chase and his first wife Catherine Jane Garniss in 1834. One of the most notable members of the Semi-Colon Club was Uncle Samuel Foote, a well-traveled former sea captain and the brother of Lyman's first wife, Roxana. Foote had founded the club along with other New Englanders who valued reading and the life of the mind. The Beechers were in their element.

For Catharine, the Semi-Colon Club was a networking tool to meet various important figures in Cincinnati who could support her education initiatives. For Harriet, it was a launching pad into a life of writing. When one of Harriet's pieces was read aloud in the group, editor James Hall "chased down the identity of the author." Hall urged Harriet to enter her piece in his magazine *Western Monthly* in a contest for a fifty-dollar prize. She won the prize, and her story, "A New England Sketch," was published in April 1834. It was her "first signed fictional piece."[47]

The gritty and sometimes nettlesome Catharine was leveraging her father's relationships in other places as well. The Western Literary Institute and College of Professional Teachers was an organization that grew out of a conference on education in Cincinnati in 1831. While the group was limited to men, Catharine participated as an observer since Lyman became one of the group's most important members. The group also met frequently in Second Presbyterian Church, where Lyman was ordained as pastor in 1833. (The church had once formed as the result of a split from Wilson's congregation at First Presbyterian.) From this organization, Catharine drew resources and support for her next major endeavor in female education. In the spring of 1833, after raising five hundred dollars from local philanthropists, Catharine opened the Western Female Institute on the corner of Sycamore and Fourth Street. Consistent with her father's overarching project for the West, the aim of the school was for "mental and moral development." As in Hartford, the school was truly a team effort by the Beechers. In addition to Mary Dutton and Anne Tappan, who were teachers, Harriet was an associate principal with her sister.[48] By the fall of 1834, due to her father's circle of friends and her own Beecher tenacity and ambition, Catharine had established herself in the elite social circles of Cincinnati. And as in New England, church and state were sometimes hard to distinguish. On Sunday mornings, she often rode to Second Presbyterian with the wife of an Ohio Supreme Court judge.[49]

THEODORE DWIGHT WELD

Lyman Beecher's belief in human progress was the engine that powered his revivalism, his moral reform, and indeed his own home. But the issue of slavery turned his optimism into a weakness. In the eyes of abolitionists, merely expecting slavery to someday be abolished, unless coupled with action, was no better than defending the institution itself. In the spring of 1833, Lyman Beecher encountered a young, revivalistic, education-promoting, temperance-advocating, antislavery influencer who also saw the world in black-and-white terms. He was, in many ways, a younger version of Lyman Beecher. Both men had been born into the world just inches away from death. Both also had very complicated relationships with their fathers that shaped them profoundly. But Theodore Dwight Weld did not possess one of the key attributes of Beecherism: moderation. When faced with Weld's call for immediate emancipation, Beecher's caution began to look like cowardice, and his optimism naivete. What transpired on the campus of Lane Seminary in the middle of the 1830s would change Beecher himself, his children, and according to some, the course of American history.

Theodore Dwight Weld was converted by the revivalist Charles Finney in Oneida County, New York, in 1825. In the years that followed, Weld, filled with angst at the austere Puritan ways of his upbringing, became Finney's "most talented protégé and trusted aide," embracing Finney's bold, anti-authoritarian style.[50] Ironically, while Lyman Beecher was leading the opposition to Finney in Boston, Weld was a Finneyite to the hilt. The two met in Boston just months before the failed New Lebanon Conference in 1827, and one can only speculate how this meeting might have influenced Weld's estimation of Beecher when he stepped on campus. In a letter to Finney in 1828, Weld confessed he had "indulged in a wicked asperity of feeling against Mr. Nettleton, Beecher, etc. I know I have often advocated brother Finney's cause, and those called 'new measures,' with much of the unhallowed feeling of a political partisan."[51] More than anxious benches or women-led prayer meetings or any of his "new measures," the most lasting idea that Finney implanted into the New Englander's soul was the belief that "faith without works is dead" (James 2:26). If a Christian really believed in loving his neighbor, he or she would do so. "As was true of most of the 'isms' of the day," historian George Marsden has noted, "abolitionism drew much of its strength from Western New York; and as was true of most New School supported 'isms,' abolitionism grew out of the revivals associated with Charles G. Finney."[52] From the soil of Finney's democratic revivals in this "burned-over district" grew a works-oriented, perfectionist, activist religion that produced reform movements such as manual labor and temperance and abolitionism.[53] Baptized in the frenzied waters of Finneyite revivalism, Weld was fully imbued with this reformist spirit.

Therefore, in 1827, at the age of twenty-fix, Weld entered the manual training school at the Oneida Institute in New York. Shortly after, he began traveling throughout the Midwest and South as an agent of the National Manual Labor Society, lecturing on manual labor, temperance, and even female education.[54] According to Nancy Hardesty, Weld became "the archetypical example" of a reform lecturer in the early nineteenth century in his ability to convert others to an urgent cause.[55] His commission, in which he was tasked with seeking out a location for "a great manual training institution," was significant for at least two reasons. First, his experiences in the South afforded him a firsthand look at the evils of plantation slavery, leaving him with memories he would never forget. Weld had witnessed something of slavery during his early days as an itinerant lecturer in mnemonics (the study of improving memory), but his second tour through the South left a bitter taste in his mouth and also introduced him to men like James A. Birney, a slaveholder with an uneasy conscience.[56] Secondly, these journeys also brought him to Lane Seminary, where he believed a manual training school might find great success.[57] While in New York, Weld befriended the influential Tappan brothers, Arthur and Lewis, relaying to them what he saw and conveying his surprise that students from the South attended Lane. He was not unlike William Lloyd Garrison in that he was initially drawn into Lyman Beecher's orbit through his advocacy of social causes that did *not* relate to slavery. But like Garrison, slavery soon became Weld's all-consuming ambition. In 1833, Beecher and Weld had both come to Cincinnati because of their mutual belief in the power of moral influence. But they were each facing a different direction. Whereas Lyman envisioned a training center for revivalists to convert the West, Weld saw an abolitionist headquarters in the North to convert the South.

Although only a student at Lane, Weld had earned a reputation in New York as an evangelical orator. Franklin Vail, the agent of Lane who had gone east to find "men and money" for the school, had actually offered him the professorship of sacred rhetoric.[58] Weld also came to Cincinnati with his own entourage, bringing with him a cadre of young, like-minded zealots from western New York of the Finneyite flavor. To make matters even more interesting, during his travels Weld had made disciples of a group of white southerners, including former Alabama slaveholder William Allan, who had renounced slavery and had followed their leader to Lane. Years later, Lyman reflected upon Weld's magnetism and described the young reformer as a "genius" and a "god of a man" to his peers. He was "as eloquent as an angel and as powerful as thunder," Beecher recalled.[59] Weld was clearly more than a student, one hundred of whom were on campus in the spring of 1833. Beecher's quixotic attempt to drive a middle way between abolitionists, colonizationists, and the proslavery camp was under threat from within his own institution.

However, the movement that took place at Lane Seminary was not due simply to Weld's personality or his oratorical power. Had Weld been convinced that political antislavery was more expedient to abolition than moral influence—like a number of young Whigs in the Cincinnati area—he would never have sparked the kind of student revolt that ensued in 1834. Devoted to a singular message of saving a people, Weld was an evangelist at heart. And his evangelism took on the characteristics of a revival. Almost as soon as Weld and his lieutenants arrived on campus, they began converting their fellow students to the abolitionist fold. In the winter of 1834, when the fifty theological students at Lane decided to debate the issue of slavery at the direction of Weld, the forum was made possible by Lyman himself, who had assured Arthur Tappan that he would not stand in the way of honest discussion. Over the objection of most of the seminary faculty, Weld staged eighteen days of student debates. But to call these gatherings "debates" is a bit misleading. They were rallies for abolitionism, converting even James A. Thome, a Kentuckian from a slaveholding family. In fact, by the end of these revival-like meetings, three-quarters of the students had been converted to abolitionism.[60] The moral awakening at Lane Seminary had begun.

Similar to a typical revival, these meetings generated reform efforts. In the spring, with the financial assistance of Tappan, the students began teaching literacy and religion to Black children on the other end of town. After the anti-Black riots in 1829, Black-sponsored schools in Cincinnati had been in steep decline. In 1831, the Ohio state legislature had prohibited "black or mulatto persons" from attending Cincinnati public schools.[61] However, Weld was undeterred. Refusing to bow to public pressure, Weld ate, socialized, and worshipped amid the Black community. To those who doubted his motives, Weld fired back, "If any one wishes to know what my *principles* and *practice* have been and are as to Intercourse with the Colored people, I say let him ask the three thousand colored people in Cincinnati."[62] In addition to starting a school, Weld and his band of reformers hosted lyceum debates and opened a library. Two students even left the seminary to work exclusively in the Black community, also known as "Bucktown."[63] Once again, Beecher did not stand in their way. After all, this was a familiar playbook during the Second Great Awakening. Revival bred reform. Had not Lyman Beecher championed the moral improvement of America? Had not the Beechers come to educate the West?

From this revival movement at Lane also sprang voluntary groups, like the almost schoolwide Anti-Slavery Society.[64] Among the rebels was a young Henry Stanton, future agent for the American Anti-Slavery Society and husband of feminist Elizabeth Cady Stanton.[65] Weld and his "Weldites" were, in some sense, out-Beechering Beecher.[66] Although Lyman was quick to point out that Lane had been the first seminary in the United States to admit a Black student, James Bradley, this was not nearly enough for the Lane rebels.[67] If, as historian Marie Caskey has noted, "religion was at the heart of the Beecher family's identity," religion played an equally significant role in the millennial abolitionism of Theodore Dwight Weld, who adopted the revivalist spirit he had witnessed in western New York.[68] "We believe that faith without *works* is dead," Weld wrote.[69] If Lyman Beecher envisioned himself as the Apostle Paul following the Macedonian Call to the West, Weld explicitly compared himself to John the Baptist, demanding repentance from America's Pharisees.[70]

Abolitionists like Weld saw a clear parallel between the biblical idea of immediate repentance and the political idea of immediate emancipation. After all, if God had commanded his people to follow his precepts, they should not delay their obedience. When William Lloyd Garrison confronted Lyman Beecher with this logic in the fall of 1830, Beecher reportedly responded, "Oh, Garrison, you can't reason that way. . . . Great economic and political questions can't be solved so simply. You must take into account what is expedient as well as what is right."[71] In February of 1834, when the students at Lane petitioned Beecher, Calvin Stowe, and church history professor Thomas Biggs to an open discussion, they posed two questions to their teachers: (1) Is it the duty of the people of the slaveholding states to abolish slavery immediately? (2) Are the doctrines, tendencies, measures of the American Colonization Society such as to render it worthy of support by the Christian public?"[72] While most of the students answered with a resounding "yes" or "no," the faculty postponed the meeting. Such a debate was, in their estimation, "inexpedient."[73] Beecher's reluctance to convert immediately to the abolitionist faith was not unlike Catharine's refusal to submit to the terms of her father's evangelical faith a decade earlier. After postponing their decision, they eventually made no decision at all. And by making no decision, they each made their decision.

As historians like Vincent Harding have shown, Lyman Beecher's optimism also blinded him to the volatility at Lane. "In a sense, his failure to see the depth of the Lane situation was tied up in his inability—or refusal—to plumb the depths of the complexity of the human spirit and its capacity for choosing self-defeating pathways."[74] When Lyman defended the benevolence of shipping Blacks to Africa at the Colonization Society in June, one New Yorker dismissed his ideas to Weld as mere "hallucinations."[75] Student James Bradley, who had been kidnapped into slavery directly from Africa, found the idea outrageous.[76] The teaching ministry of the Lane students to the Black community and their willingness to enter the houses of Black people was inflammatory in a city that had worked hard to sever Blacks from whites. Their open discussion of such a taboo issue was seen as dangerous to the trustees of the school, who wanted to live on peaceful terms with southerners and northerners alike. Therefore, when Lyman Beecher left Cincinnati in the summer to travel east, advising the trustees to wait until he returned in October, the trustees did the opposite. Agreeing with the findings of a special committee, the trustee board abolished the Anti-

Slavery and Colonization societies on campus and added "that the Executive committee has the power to dismiss any student from the seminary when they shall think it necessary so to do."[77] The executive committee also decided to prohibit further discussion of slavery in the school, even dismissing one faculty member who had openly sided with the students.[78] This was *not* a picture of moral influence. Garrison's *Liberator* called the school "a Bastille of oppression" for its silencing of free speech and dissent.[79]

Asa Mahan, the New School pastor of Sixth Presbyterian Church (another congregation formed after a split from Wilson's church), was the only trustee to vote against restricting the students' rights. Appalled by the "Draconian code" passed by the board, Mahan immediately wrote to Beecher, convinced that Lane's president would reject such measures.[80] But Beecher was more ambivalent than Mahan imagined. He was angered by the committee's decision but even more so by the students. His view of Weld was a mix of respect and utter frustration. Weld's methods, at least as Beecher saw them, were self-defeating. As Robert H. Abzug has framed it, "At Lane, Beecher's task was not quite so simple as telling off an adamant abolitionist. He wanted both public support and the loyalty of his students. He walked a tightrope."[81] Still, Weld would not relent. He would not cease his interaction with the Black community, having previously insisted that "any reference to color, in social intercourse, was an odious and sinful prejudice."[82]

The sight of white students "walking to and from the seminary with colored women" only incensed the trustees further.[83] In an age of mob violence, it was also brazen. The bloody race riots of New York and Philadelphia in July and August had rocked the Eastern Seaboard. Finally, in an effort to quell the movement, the trustees closed the seminary. Forced to find lodging off campus, Weld wrote to Beecher and implored him to return to Cincinnati. However, on the East Coast, the president was somewhat insulated from the fracas and had probably decided that it was best not to rush back into a lose-lose situation. As one historian has remarked, Lyman seemed "more like Jonah fleeing to Tarshish than St. Paul pressing toward Macedonia."[84] When Beecher finally *did* return in October and approved of the trustees' actions in a "Declaration of the Faculty of Lane Seminary," the exodus began. It took only a week for thirty-eight of the fifty theological students, and fifty of the sixty literary students, to request an "honorable dismission" from Lane.[85] With power in numbers, Weld and most of the student body quit the seminary in protest. Almost overnight, Lane was "gutted."[86]

The Lane rebels eventually moved to the pro-abolitionist Oberlin College, where Weld was offered a professorship, where Asa Mahan became its first president, and where, fittingly, Charles Finney was soon appointed professor of theology. Declining the position, Weld instead became an agent for the American Anti-Slavery Society, accelerating what Marilynne Robinson has called the "cultural colonization of the Middle West by abolitionists."[87] Upon hearing of Weld's decision, the abolitionist James Birney wrote in his diary, "I give him one year to abolitionize Ohio."[88] On one hand, Lyman Beecher broke his promise to Arthur Tappan *not* to repress Weld. On the other hand, Beecher had simply allowed "free discussion" to take place without him, leaving the hardest decisions to be made by others. This was, in some sense, the conflict within Beecherism and the early American republic itself: optimistic, but not completely disinterested. Either way, by Christmas 1834, Lane had lost nearly all its students.[89]

FATHER AND SONS

American history sometimes begs the counterfactual. Instead of telling historical *facts*, historians occasionally conjecture about what might have occurred in the past if something else had happened differently. For example, what if the immortal Jonathan Edwards had condemned slavery as did his disciple Samuel Hopkins or his own son Jonathan Edwards Jr.?[90] Would Lyman Beecher have been so reluctant to oppose slaveholding? Or what if William Lloyd Garrison had been an orthodox Calvinist instead of a Quaker? Would abolitionists still have been stigmatized as religious and social fanatics? One cannot help but wonder how these simple facts might have altered the course of American history. Indeed, a biographer of Garrison even speculated about the life of Lyman Beecher not long after his death. Oliver Johnson, a former member of Lyman Beecher's church in Boston, proposed his own hypothetical: what if Lyman Beecher had stood *with* the Lane rebels instead of against them? His conclusion is a rather severe arraignment upon the reformer's legacy:

> I verily believe that, if Lyman Beecher had been true to Christ and to liberty in that trying hour, the whole course of American history in

regard to slavery would have been changed, and that the slaves might have been emancipated without the shedding of blood. The churches at that hour were halting between the good and the evil side, and it only needed the example of one strong man like Dr. Beecher to rally them to their legitimate place as the foremost champions of justice and liberty. He sacrificed a great opportunity . . . and linked his name forever with those of the trimmers and compromisers of that day. He inflicted a wound upon his own reputation from which he never recovered. He lost the confidence of the friends of freedom; while the champions and apologists of slavery respected him far less than they would if he had shown himself worthy of the New England blood.[91]

While Johnson's prediction is a bit idealistic, it bespeaks the enormous weight that the name of Lyman Beecher carried in antebellum America. For those who believed in the power of moral influence (including Garrison and Johnson), no figure wielded more potential for nation-shaping than America's most famous organizer and moral crusader. Beecher was, in Johnson's words, one of "the foremost champions of justice and liberty." He did not live up to those principles in 1834. However, in Beecher's defense, if indeed there were others in the antebellum period capable of rallying America's churches together, then Beecher was not the only "strong man" who failed this Herculean test.

Still, another historical counterfactual has never been posed: How would Lyman Beecher's children have evolved on the issue of slavery if they had *not* seen their father's debacle at Lane? Would they have come to oppose slavery differently if they had not witnessed the abolitionist revival in Cincinnati? What did they learn from Theodore Weld? Of course, we can only speculate but what is undeniable is that, in the immediate months and years after Weld's exodus from Lane Seminary, most of the Beechers stepped beyond their father into the realm of abolitionist thought. Before 1835, according to Charles, "most of the Dr's children including Edward, agreed with him."[92] But this soon changed. While the Beechers were almost always characterized by moderation, and in fact one Beecher would become an avowed anti-abolitionist due in part to the events at Lane, *every* one of Lyman's children eventually took a side in the debate.[93]

Surprisingly, the events at Lane in 1834 only made Lyman Beecher more "expedient" and cautious on the issue of slavery. He'd suffered the reproach of the press, the loss of friends, and a devastating blow to his school, but somehow remained convinced that the noncommittal option was the safest. On Christmas Day 1834, partly by Beecher's design, Boston Congregationalists launched a new benevolent society, the American Union for the Relief and Improvement of the Colored Race, which opposed slavery but rejected neither immediate emancipation nor colonization outright. With its first convention, in January 1835, the entire project epitomized Beecher's *via media* approach. Not surprisingly, William Lloyd Garrison was repulsed by it.[94] With a foot in both the abolitionist and the colonizationist camps, the American Union really stood in neither. As a result, it was a failure from the start. The American Union was Lane all over again. And Lyman Beecher's pragmatism on the issue involved more than voluntary societies. As a father, he counseled his children *not* to take sides. In a letter to his son William in July, he prodded:

> As to abolition, I am still of opinion that you ought not, and need not, and will not commit yourself as a partisan on either side. The cause is moving on in Providence, and by the American Union, and by colonization, and by Lyndy in Texas, which is a grand thing, and will succeed, as I believe; and I hope and believe that the Abolitionists as a body will become more calm and less denunciatory, with the exception of the few he-goat men, who think they do God service by butting every thing in the line of their march which does not fall in or get out of the way. They are the offspring of the Oneida denunciatory revivals, and are made up of vinegar, aqua fortis, and oil of vitriol, with brimstone, saltpetre, and charcoal, to explode and scatter the corrosive matter.[95]

Blinded by optimism and wounded by the "vinegar" of the abolitionists, Beecher's reference to "he-goat men" was certainly a reference to Theodore Weld, whom he still viewed as a product of western New York. Beecher scorned the "Oneida denunciatory revivals" for their lack of moderation and deference toward ministerial authority. Their willingness to publicly "denounce" their opponents was thus confirmed at Lane. As one like-minded colonizationist complained in 1835, "I find that where New Measures flourish there Abolition (and kindred fanaticisms), flourishes."[96] Lyman was trying to pull his older children in his centrist direction but already losing grip on their thinking. They were Beechers, after all.

At least one of Lyman Beecher's sons began to drift in the abolitionist direction *during* the student rebellion at Lane. While George was being anathematized at his ordination by the proslavery Presbyterians, Lane students were looking on with as much disgust as the rest of the Beecher siblings. Among these students was Theodore Dwight Weld, who sat fully "awake, nodding from side to side, and scarce keeping still a minute together."[97] Against the cruel imprecations of the conservatives, George and Weld stood *together*. For a somewhat fragile young man who craved friendship and acceptance, the support of his fellow students could not have been overlooked. They were united in their opposition to the Old School. If Theodore Weld represented the social extreme to Lyman's left, he appeared a bit more palatable when standing on the side of Lyman's son against the proslavery extreme to his right. George's quiet introduction to abolitionism coincided with his disillusionment with conservative religion and his attraction to the student revival meetings at Lane, neither of which escaped the attention of his father.[98]

Another one of Lyman's sons was also changing his mind on the so-called "negro question." According to Charles Beecher in his unpublished "Life of Edward Beecher," 1835 was the year that his older brother finally concluded that "gradual emancipation was fallacious."[99] In 1830, Edward left for Illinois, fully believing in the wisdom of gradual emancipation, but no longer. He now found himself somewhere between the Oneida school of abolitionism and that of his father. Edwards's limbo was not altogether surprising, considering that Jacksonville, the so-called "Athens of the Middle West," was much like Cincinnati, with northern *and* southern interests.[100] Also in 1835, Edward published his *Six Sermons on the Nature, Importance, and Means of Eminent Holiness throughout the Church*. With an emphasis on practical Christian living and good works, he contended, "No sin should be deemed trivial or venial. All should be abhorred. There should be the feelings of heaven on this subject. The evils of moral pollution should be felt, and mourned over as they would be in heaven, before the throne of God, where every robe is pure and spotless. And if the church will commune with God as she ought, she can gain this also."[101] With the goal of killing sin and increasing holiness, Edward now took aim at "moral pollution." According to Merideth, "the sermons revealed a state of mind congenial to immediate abolition."[102]

Lyman's children had a tendency of slowly breaking away from their father while imitating him at the same time. Edward's own work sounded like Lyman's in 1827: *Six Sermons on the Nature, Occasions, Signs, Evils, and Remedy of Intemperance.* Edward even mentioned temperance in his publication, but not in the most favorable light: "Thus to one the cause of Sabbath-schools may easily become the most important of all; to another, foreign and domestic missions; to another, the discussion and defense of doctrinal truth, and the exposure of error; to another, the cause of temperance; and to another, the circulation of tracts, or of the word of God. These and similar enterprises are, without doubt, great and glorious beyond conception. But neither one of them is or can become the leading and most important enterprise of the present age."[103] Interestingly, the cause of abolitionism was not mentioned. However, Beecher did urge his fellow Christians to avoid the "unchristian feeling exhibited in some of the great movements and discussion of the day," which is "alike humiliating and surprising."[104] Whether this was a subtle reference to William Lloyd Garrison or Theodore Dwight Weld or both, Beecher was still wary of aligning himself with abolitionists despite gravitating toward their ideas.[105]

After all, it was still a dangerous time to be an abolitionist, from the East Coast to the Mississippi River. In October, William Lloyd Garrison was dragged through the streets of Boston. The same month, the editor of the *St. Louis Observer,* Elijah Lovejoy, published the statement of principles of the American Antislavery Society and declared that he agreed with most of them. Under pressure to resign, Lovejoy, a Presbyterian minister, wrote to Beecher to see what he should do. Edward replied, "I think the time for silence has gone by. . . . even the religious party at the South are more erroneous than I had supposed." Bristling at various resolutions in the church which defended the institution of slavery, he added, "If religious men do not understand this subject any better than that, it is time that some one teach them. . . . I say go on."[106] Edward's private support for an abolitionist was significant for the entire Beecher family because it would not stay private long. As his father, Edward saw the slavery issue through a religious, even gradual, lens. However, unlike Lyman, he believed that the time for patience was coming to an end.

TRIALS OF VARIOUS KINDS

In several ways, 1835 was a turning point for the *entire* Beecher family. Prior to 1835, the Beechers had never collectively experienced as much grief and anguish and suspense as they did in that year. Conversely, *after* 1835, they would never again be as united. Despite his optimistic spirit, Lyman was understandably shaken in the aftermath of the Lane rebellion. His integrity and his leadership had been questioned. His relationship with Arthur Tappan, who now backed Oberlin College, had grown icy. After the trustees squelched the students' freedom of speech, the *Evangelist*, a New York newspaper, had asked in outrage, "In what age do we live? And in what country? And who are the persons thus restrained? And with whose endowments was the seminary founded? And who is its president?"[107] Ironically, ten years later, the *Evangelist* would print Harriet Beecher Stowe's first piece on slavery, "Immediate Emancipation."[108]

In the fallout from Weld's exodus, Lyman's children, big and small, rallied around their father. Isabella, then only eleven years old, remembered her father's compassion. "I can see him now, joining them in the little log house just opposite ours—pleading, remonstrating, with tears and almost with groans," she recalled of Lyman with the students. "I was but a child, but was in such sympathy with his distress that I never could forgive the young men for departing from such a loving guide and friend."[109] Harriet, no stranger to the woes of Beecher men, surely felt Lyman's anxiety.[110] In fact, she would spend the rest of her life defending her father's legacy. In *Men of Our Times* (1868), Harriet described Weld's admittance to Lane as political subterfuge. While posing as students, the Lane rebels, "headed by that brilliant, eccentric genius, Theodore D. Weld," had actually come "that they might make of the Seminary an anti-slavery fort."[111]

Catharine, now thirty-four, showed no signs of diverging from her father's grand vision for the frontier. In 1835, at the request of the American Lyceum, she published her first detailed plan for educating the West: *An Essay on Education of Female Teachers*. To address the growing threat of lower-class ignorance and dissolution on the frontier, America needed to raise up *women* teachers who could inculcate moral and religious principles into the minds and hearts of those who had lost touch with the church. With their potential for self-sacrifice and their ability to do the most important work in the least desirable places, women were the key to saving the American conscience. Like her father, who had enlisted her to the West, Catharine was skilled at the art of mobilization, calling upon the wealthy to finance this vast educational program. According to Sklar, Catharine "fell back in 1835 upon her father's formula of asserting the need for evangelical leadership to meet the threat of national wickedness and corruption."[112] In an era of railroads, canals, and other "internal improvements," Catharine was convinced that the nation needed *moral* improvement. As another scholar has noted, with her inveterate fear of Roman Catholicism and foreign, anti-republican ideas, "Beecher echoed her father's antagonism to the Irish Catholic immigrants of Boston." Even so, Catharine herself stepped beyond Lyman's Puritan worldview, acknowledging Catholics' support for women's education, sometimes more so than Protestants.[113] In his *Plea for the West* (1835), published the very same year, Lyman made no such concession, declaring unequivocally that Roman Catholics have always "been hostile to civil and religious liberty."[114] Despite setbacks at Lane, and despite these subtle differences in their thinking, Lyman and his children had not abandoned their quest to save the West *together.*

However, Lyman was on trial—literally. In June, the truculent Joshua Wilson finally succeeded in putting his New School foe on trial for heresy. Although Lyman was acquitted ten-to-one, an appeal by Wilson to the Synod meant that he would make a second defense upstate in Dayton in October.[115] Years later, an aged Lyman remembered the atmosphere before the Synod. "The Old School had raked and scraped all the old dead churches where they could get an elder, and thought they might carry the day. It looked squally."[116] These interrogations not only foreshadowed the Presbyterian Schism of 1837, but they demonstrated just how inextricably linked religion was to the politics of the age. Social order and theological order overlapped. Marsden explains, "Southerners who previously had not much direct contact with New School theology were, with the addition of the antislavery threat, becoming champions of strict orthodoxy."[117] As Beecher was being vilified by the abolitionist press for his opposition to Finneyites like Theodore Weld, he was suspected of heresy by proslavery Presbyterians due to his perceived sympathy for Finney himself.[118] If, as historian C. C. Goen has famously contended, the denominational schisms of 1837 and 1844 and 1845 presaged the Civil War, cementing a national divide, then some of the initial fissures appeared in Ohio in 1835.[119] On the surface, conservative Presbyterians were grilling Lyman Beecher on the nature of original sin and the human will. But underneath the issue of the freedom of the will lay the freedom of the slave. The reason that moral influence was such a dangerous idea to the Slave Power was its potential for personal and societal change. Theodore Dwight Weld had once written to William Lloyd Garrison that upon every human being God "has stamped his own image, by making him a *free moral agent.*"[120] Free choice was now an explosive topic. Thanks to Beecher's theological acumen and pulpit bravura, and to Wilson's dismay, Lyman was acquitted at both the presbytery and synod levels. With his characteristic optimism, Beecher later claimed, "my trial was the greatest blessing."[121] However, the experience also came with a cost. As one might imagine, Lyman's children never forget what they saw.

Watching their father, the living embodiment of Calvinist doctrine, treated like an enemy of the faith did at least two things to the Beecher children: (1) it evoked a natural desire to defend their father, and (2) it cemented a lifelong distrust for dogmatic, confessionalist (and for some, orthodox) Christianity. Isabella Beecher, only thirteen years old, could not understand how men of faith could attack her father, "such a good man."[122] Harriet felt similarly, using her pen to defend Lyman for years to come.[123] Henry, who had recently begun his theological education at Lane after graduating from Amherst, recalled, "I never saw so many faces of clergymen and so few of them intellectual faces."[124] In this theological and political gauntlet, the Beecher children were rushing *to* their father but running *away* from his religion. If this was the fruit of Calvinism, the Beecher children wanted nothing of it. Along with Henry, the experience was especially traumatic for Charles, recently graduated from Bowdoin College, who was so disillusioned by the "sectarian bickering" that he would eventually follow in his father's footsteps as a tried (and actually convicted) heretic.[125] The events in 1835 changed the way Lyman's children viewed not only theology, but the authority of the church itself.

The following year, in *Letters on the Difficulties of Religion* (1836), Catharine showed her allegiance to Lyman when she attempted to explain the theological controversies in the Presbyterian Church. In her view, it was not the "new school men" but their opponents who should "go out from the Presbyterian church and form another denomination." She then derided the Old School men: "I do not see any just ground for the two parties to feel enmity or ill will; if they only can exercise the charity and patience and meekness of the gospel they profess, all can be terminated amicably and quietly. They only need to allow that their brethren *honestly* differ in opinion, and to feel willing that each partly should act according to their views of right; and if they find their principles so opposite that they cannot dwell in one family, to separate kindly, as did Lot and Abraham, and dwell in two different enclosures."[126] This was a rather prescient word to the Presbyterian Church just a year before the denomination decided it could no longer "dwell in one family." In turn, Old School men made little distinction between Lyman and his children. Joshua Wilson scoffed that Catharine was just as much a heretic as her father.[127] The Beechers had left Boston as the guardians of orthodoxy; now they were a family of heretics! As one historian has put it, the preparation for Lyman's defense before the Synod in October 1835 became a "family affair," as Henry helped him find his books, Thomas packed his trunk into the cart, Charles drove the horse to the boat, and George accompanied him in Dayton.[128] This experience had a centripetal effect upon the Beechers, drawing them closer together and allowing the children to support their patriarch emotionally in ways they never had. Indeed, Lyman needed his children like never before.

HARRIET PORTER'S DEATH

But Lyman needed help with more than his luggage or his theological arguments. He was hurting tremendously. In fact, when he left the house for his first defense in June, doctrine was the furthest thing from his mind. "My wife was lying at home on her dying bed," he recalled. "She did not live a fortnight after that."[129] On July 7, Harriet Porter passed away of consumption (tuberculosis) at the age of forty-five, almost twenty years after Roxana Beecher, forty-one, died of the same disease. She was buried in the cemetery at Walnut Hills. Her death, like Roxana's, had been a slow demise. While Milton Rugoff was a bit too morbid when he characterized Harriet's existence as a "shadow life," there is some substance to his assertion that she "had remained a visitor—a troubled, pensive transient. Increasingly, she had been unable or unwilling to cope with that swarm of individualistic children and their father . . . nor did it help matters that most of the children were not her own and were ever ready to compare her with the increasingly idealized image of their first mother."[130] Indeed, for the older children, who had always acknowledged a distance between themselves and their stepmother, Harriet's death was a sad reminder of their own up-bringing.[131] However, for Harriet's biological children, the loss was especially difficult. In their view, she was no mere "visitor." To Isabella, Thomas recalled the "beauty & brilliancy of mothers look" before she died. "Can you ever forget that morning," he asked, "I never can—memory & imagination paint it anew with fresh colors—every time I reflect at all." Thomas and Isabella would never forget their mother praying incessantly for their salvation and that of their siblings. Like Harriet and Henry, who were only five and three respectively when Roxana died, Thomas (thirteen) and Isabella (eleven) and James (seven) would elevate their deceased mother to Protestant sainthood. Thomas recollected, "During all her sickness she exhibited no fear of death and has shown to all the power of the Christian's hope in overcoming death."[132]

Nevertheless, while the Beechers did not share the same relationship to Harriet Porter, they still faced her loss *together* in the fall of 1835. Upon returning from Dayton and stepping into the parlor at Walnut Hills, Lyman was thrilled to discover that *every* one of his children had convened at the house to be with their father. It was probably the fondest memory of his life. Charles recounted the occasion with no small degree of nostalgia:

> When Edward returned, he brought on Mary from Hartford; William came down from Putnam, Ohio; George from Batavia; Ohio; Catharine and Harriet were here already; Henry and Charles at home too; besides Isabella, Thomas, and James. These eleven! The first time they all ever met together! Mary had never seen James, and she had seen Thomas but once. Such a time as they had! The old doctor was almost transported with joy. . . . There were more tears than words. The doctor could not speak. His full heart poured itself out in a flood of weeping. He could not go on.[133]

The man paid to make speeches was speechless. The glowing patriarch walked around the room and gave each of his children a kiss. After a year of controversy, political turmoil, financial uncertainty, and the loss of his wife,

Lyman's heart was full. And in typical Beecher fashion, Lyman consecrated the event with prayer, the singing of hymns, and of course, preaching. The next morning, Edward preached from his father's pulpit at Second Presbyterian, followed by William in the afternoon and George in the evening. If the exodus of the Lane rebels and the heresy trials had ever caused Lyman to question victory in the West, the sight of his three oldest sons preaching in his pulpit was a reminder that his promise to Roxana had been kept. The Beecher gathering was publicized in the local press. In the West, where "the newspaper was king," the article in the *Cincinnati Journal* was the first indication that the Beechers were becoming a somewhat famous family.[134] This was the first time—and the last time—that the entire Beecher clan would be together.

RIOTS IN CINCINNATI

The issue of slavery was certainly a topic of conversation during the Beecher family reunion. After being defeated in the Synod, Joshua Wilson had appealed to the General Assembly, which was meeting the following year in Pittsburgh. Lyman was not out of the woods yet.[135] In Pittsburgh, Lyman intended to ask the assembly to support the American Union. (Not surprisingly, it was rejected.) Lyman's children were also involved in their own antislavery endeavors. George's presbytery, centered in nearby Chillicothe, was one of the most abolitionist in the state of Ohio. In November, Chillicothe enacted and sent out a series of nine resolutions on slavery to be considered by other presbyteries. The first resolution was "That the buying, selling, or holding of a slave for the sake of gain, is a heinous sin and scandal, requiring cognizance of the judicatories of the church." One resolution sought to prohibit slaveowners from participating in communion, and another asked that those who aided in the capture of fugitive slaves would be likewise barred from the Lord's Table.[136] When the resolutions made their way to the floor of the Cincinnati presbytery in April 1836, Lyman objected to a motion to bypass discussion on the resolutions. He had prevented, or at least avoided, free discussion on the issue of slavery at Lane just a year earlier. He would not make the same mistake again. Although Lyman did not agree with all of the measures, the Cincinnati presbytery finally adopted seven out of the nine resolutions.[137]

Since the late eighteenth century, the Ohio River had increasingly become a kind of loose boundary between two forms of Christianity. These faiths were by no means exclusive to the North or South, but their points of emphasis diverged over time and eventually boiled over in Cincinnati. Below the Ohio River, Kentuckians identified resistance to federal authority as a mark of true republicanism and adherence to points of doctrine as the ground of salvation. In 1798, Kentucky State Assemblyman John Breckinridge, whose son Robert became an Old School Presbyterian minister, introduced the so-called Kentucky Resolutions, which declared that John Adams's Alien and Sedition Acts were "altogether void, and of no force." The resolutions were strongly in favor of states' rights and free speech, drafted by Thomas Jefferson himself.[138] In the 1810s and 1820s, evangelicals in the Midwest also noted certain theological differences with Kentucky. Baptist missionary John Mason Peck, a former Congregationalist from New England, noted in his diary around 1820 that a group in Southern Illinois was hostile to certain voluntarist ideas. "A set of crude and erroneous notions had been stereotyped in their minds, in Kentucky, about gospel doctrine and moral obligation, and they were fixedly resolved to learn nothing else." Peck then noted a degree of fatalism in their ranks: "They maintained that missions, Sunday-schools, Bible societies, and such-like facilities, were all men's contrivances, to take God's work out of his own hands."[139] Remarkably, Peck traced this aversion to "moral obligation" in the lower North to Kentucky.

In contrast with transplanted Virginians in Kentucky (like Breckinridge), the Midwest was full of transplanted Yankees (like Peck) who believed in a more missional, educational, socially responsible faith. The Northwest Ordinance of 1787, which outlawed slavery, was strong evidence that Ohioans were a bit more amenable to federal authority than their counterparts to the South. The heresy trial of Lyman Beecher, a Yankee, at the hands of Joshua Wilson, a Kentuckian, illustrated that purveyors of the New England Theology were not always as fixated on theological precision as those in the Bluegrass State. Indeed, if Kentuckians were accused of resisting initiatives for "moral obligation," Ohioans were often accused of "ultraism," or holding extreme positions on social issues.[140] George Beecher, for example, had witnessed the effects of ultraism at Lane with Theodore Weld's crusade, and he was steadily gravitating in that direction himself.

In 1836 (just years after being anathematized by Joshua Wilson), he wrote in his diary that he reorganized the Temperance Society in Batavia "on the principle of *entire* abstinence."[141] The antebellum period was truly an age of extremes. Cincinnati itself was on the verge of civil unrest between catalysts of social change who believed there could be no compromise between darkness and light and those who resisted change for the sake of political and social and even theological order. The race riots of 1836 thrust the younger Beechers into the middle of this war, evoking, in a new way, their basic convictions about the nature of freedom.

In early 1836, an abolitionist named James G. Birney arrived in Cincinnati to establish his antislavery newspaper, the *Philanthropist*. Birney was a unique kind of moral influencer because of his past. Having once owned slaves in Kentucky and Alabama, he freed them and converted to the abolitionist cause. Therefore his hatred for slavery was particularly hot. Although the *Philanthropist* was not as radical as Garrison's *Liberator*, it still threatened the city's connections with the South, and his presence was a liability to the trade which benefited the city's most influential families. By the summer, when southern buyers came to the city for their semiannual business, Birney's "abolition rag" triggered the anger of the Cincinnati elites and their "mobocrats."[142] On July 12, a mob broke into Birney's printshop and damaged his press and type, threatening worse if Birney did not stop printing. But he continued, fixing the press and putting out a new edition. The vandalism kindled something in Henry, who responded to the lawlessness with an editorial condemning mob violence. Drawing upon the principles of moral influence, his rationale was that mobs were an assault upon the right of private property and "the first, the highest, the most sacred, the last deserved right of freedmen, the right of free discussion."[143] The banner of free speech was once again being raised by a Beecher on the hallowed ground of free discussion. And Henry was not the only Beecher sibling waving the banner. At Henry's urging, his sister Harriet wrote an anonymous letter for the local paper defending freedom of the press and private property. Writing under the pseudonym "Franklin," after the patriot printer from Philadelphia, Harriet knew that Cincinnatians were less prone to read something penned by a woman.[144] But "Franklin" did not take a stand on slavery.

After another week in the sweltering Cincinnati heat, the tension in the city matched the temperature outside. When a citizens' meeting was called on July 21, the same day that Harriet's "Franklin" letter appeared in the paper, over a thousand men showed up at Lower Market Street to exercise their own "free discussion." Led by Judge Burnet, a committee of thirteen, "including many good Presbyterians," essentially voted to threaten Birney with yet another mob.[145] They issued an ultimatum to the meddling outsider: cease publication or face five thousand angry Cincinnatians. Birney had until noon the next day to fold up shop. However, with no small amount of courage, he refused. Birney delivered on his word to remain. And so did the mob. The riots that ensued on July 31 were not the first in Cincinnati's history nor the last, but they were in fact the worst. In a tumultuous cloud of hate-filled shouting and obscenities, an angry mob smashed the printing press and threw the wreckage in the Ohio River.[146] Watching helplessly, the feckless mayor merely told the crowd to go home after they were done. Nevertheless, the unsatisfied crowd began marching in the direction of Birney's boardinghouse. But they were greeted by the young lawyer Salmon P. Chase, in a moment of genuine bravery, who barred them from entering. Instead, the rioters meted out their wrath upon all manner of Black-owned houses in Bucktown.

Continuing the next day, the race riots which convulsed the city of Cincinnati had an enormous impact upon the Beecher family and on the infant nation. "It was the mob attack on Birney's press," historian Eric Foner has stated, "which brought Chase into the abolitionist camp."[147] Chase's work in the Liberty Party and then the Free Soil Party would help lay the foundation for the antislavery ideology of the Republicans in 1860. As for James Birney, he was succeeded as editor by Gamaliel Bailey after moving to New York to become the secretary of the American Anti-Slavery Society. However, Birney continued to publish the *Philanthropist* until 1843, using the publication as a literary weapon against Kentucky slaveholders. In an 1838 issue, a commentator beseeched Ohio legislators, "Kentucky, they are told, 'will not idly menace.' We say again, that the anger of Kentucky is waxing warm."[148] As history would have it, Gamaliel Bailey eventually moved to Washington, DC, and started the *National Era,* the antislavery paper that would be the first to publish *Uncle Tom's Cabin.*[149]

The riots also had significant consequence for Henry, who was emboldened not to become an abolitionist, but to take a very public stand against anti-abolitionist mobs. With the threat of further vandalism and violence, Henry volunteered to join the street patrols around town. As Debby Applegate has described him, "Henry was no Salmon Chase, but by now his heroic impulses were thoroughly aroused, and he volunteered for the patrol."[150] Although he never fired a shot, Henry left home each day with two loaded pistols.[151] One night at Walnut Hills, Harriet found an excited Henry over the kitchen stove, pouring melted lead into a mold: "What on earth are you doing, Henry?" she asked. "Making bullets, to kill men with, Hattie!" he replied. "I never saw Henry look so terrible!" she later recalled. "I did not like it, for I feared he was growing blood-thirsty."[152] Indeed, of all the Beechers, Henry struggled the most with the non-compulsive nature of moral influence, particularly on the slavery issue. In the 1850s, when he famously sent Sharps rifles to abolitionist fighters in "Bleeding Kansas," he remarked that rifles had "greater moral agency than the Bible."[153] Nevertheless, still reluctant to yoke himself with abolitionism, Henry had taken his first public stand on behalf of free speech, free discussion, and free sidewalks. It was only a matter of time until he and his sister followed Salmon Chase to his belief in "free soil, free labor, and free men."

ON THE NATIONAL STAGE

Across the West, another Beecher was emboldened by mob violence, but on the Mississippi River instead of the Ohio. In May, Elijah Lovejoy's printing press in St. Louis, Missouri, was destroyed by an anti-abolitionist mob. Lovejoy soon moved to Alton, Illinois, where Edward Beecher became his "closest associate."[154] Although Edward would not completely embrace the moniker of "abolitionist" until Lovejoy's second *Observer* was demolished by yet another mob, he began to garner a reputation for antislavery in the Jacksonville area. As months passed, Edward also attracted attention at the national level. "Respected even by Garrison, who thought of him as the staunch friend of Lovejoy, Beecher became something of a national figure in the abolition movement," Merideth has explained.[155] In Ohio, brother George joined a local antislavery society, making him the "first Beecher to take a radical stand" on the issue.[156] If 1835 was a crucible for the Beecher family, 1836 was in fact a gestation period for the Beechers' public persona, pushing them ever further into the national spotlight. 1836 was also a critical time for Catharine's career. In the spring and summer, she toured the East Coast to promote her ideas of training women as teachers. During this time, she "was received as a spokeswoman for the West."[157] The mantle for "saving the west" was slowly being passed from father to daughter. And during Lyman's visit east in 1836, he was also well received—by his new wife. Wasting very little time as a widower, Lyman found love once again, marrying Mrs. Lydia Jackson of Boston, a widow with several children.

In some ways, 1836 was a season of new beginnings after a season of trials. In fact, it began with yet another marriage in the Beecher family. In January, Harriet was married to Calvin Stowe in a relatively private wedding. In addition to friend and colleague Mary Dutton, it was a family ceremony. Harriet jokingly quipped, "and as there is a sufficiency of the ministry in our family we have not even to call in the foreign aid of a minister."[158] Already at thirty-five, Stowe was the second leading Hebrew scholar in America of his time, next to Moses Stuart at Andover. As Lyman's colleague at Lane, he had also experienced a great deal with the family, and they with him, during the loss of his first wife, Eliza. Harriet matched her husband in intellect, and the two paired rather well in their unusual interest in both the literary and the preternatural. With Calvin's droll sense of humor and Harriet's quick wit, they also seemed to complement personalities. In September, Harriet gave birth to twins, Eliza and Isabella (later changed to Harriet or "Hattie").

Lyman Beecher's experience at the General Assembly in May characterized much of the Beecher family in that year: expectation, suspense, relief, and joy. Lyman's rival, Joshua Wilson, relentlessly prosecuted him all the way to Pittsburgh, demonstrating that the Old School menace would not soon go away. When Wilson saw that he would not win his case, he consented to withdraw the charges of heresy and hypocrisy. Beecher escaped his third and final test from the highest Presbyterian court. After the Synod in Dayton had cleared him of any charges, they had also concluded that Beecher had not been crystal clear in his explanation of certain doctrines. They ordered him to publish his views, and Lyman's *Views in Theology* (1836) was the result. In his section on "Natural Ability," Beecher submitted, "a free agency, that has no power of a right action, is in that respect no free agency. There must be an agent qualified to act as he is required to act—something in his constitution which qualifies him to be governed by

law—and rewards and punishments—as matter and animals are not qualified."[159] Human beings were not animals. They were capable of free choices
under a moral government. Whether Lyman realized it or not, his children
believed that the logical conclusion to this kind of "free agency" and "natural ability" was the emancipation of the slave. So did his opponents. And
they were not finished making war on the New School.

Portrait of Lyman Beecher, 1842, by James Henry Beard.
National Portrait Gallery, Smithsonian Institution.

Edward Beecher, the inaugural president of Illinois College (1830–1844).
Harriet Beecher Stowe Center, Hartford, Connecticut.

View of Cincinnati, Newport, and Covington, by Adrien Mayers. This painting captures a view of Cincinnati and northern Kentucky in 1832, the year that the Beechers arrived in the West. Amon Carter Museum of American Art, Fort Worth, Texas.

Timothy Dwight Weld, follower of revivalist Charles G. Finney and leader of the Lane "rebellion" in 1834. Library of Congress.

Catharine Beecher, the oldest of the Beecher siblings, in 1848.
Schlesinger Library, Harvard Radcliffe Institute.

Harriet Beecher Stowe, 1852, the year *Uncle Tom's Cabin* was published.
Schlesinger Library, Harvard Radcliffe Institute.

Henry Ward Beecher (ca. 1855–1865), pastor of Plymouth Church in Brooklyn and widely considered the most famous man in America. Library of Congress.

Henry Ward Beecher at a "reverse slave auction" in New York,
raising money to emancipate enslaved persons.

The final reunion of the Beecher family in New York, photographed by Matthew Brady
in 1859. Standing (*left to right*): Thomas, William, Edward, Charles, Henry Ward.
Seated (*left to right*): Isabella, Catharine, Lyman, Mary, and Harriet.
Schlesinger Library, Harvard Radcliffe Institute.

James Beecher, the youngest of the Beecher siblings, in his Union military uniform.
Schlesinger Library, Harvard Radcliffe Institute.

Henry Ward Beecher and Harriet Beecher Stowe.
J. Gurney & Son, 1868.

Charles Beecher, a hymn composer, pastor, and the only Beecher to be found guilty of heresy by an ecclesiastical authority. Harriet Beecher Stowe Center, Hartford, Connecticut.

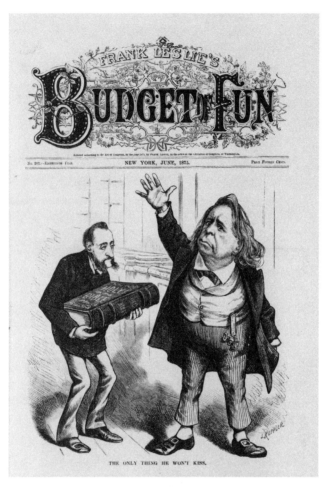

"The Only Thing He Won't Kiss." Satirical cartoon of Henry Ward Beecher during his highly publicized sex scandal with Elizabeth Tilton. Cover of *Frank Leslie's Budget of Fun*, June 1875, Joseph Keppler, Library of Congress.

Suffragist Isabella Beecher Hooker and her husband John Hooker in 1891.
Library of Congress.

Thomas K. Beecher, the ecumenical pastor of Park Church in Elmira, New York,
in 1893. Center for Mark Twain Studies, Elmira College.

Chapter 3

NEW SCHOOL KIDS
(1837-1847)

IN JACKSONIAN AMERICA, to be *for* something was to be *against* something else. To promote temperance was to condemn drunkenness, Roman Catholicism, and sometimes immigration. To endorse manual labor was to reject elitist education. As one might expect, the spirit of opposition also animated the politics of the age. To be a Whig was, at the very least, to oppose Andrew Jackson. Princeton theologian Charles Hodge was a so-called "Cotton Whig" who sympathized with southerners and Democrats alike, but nothing roused his Whiggery quite like Jackson (ironically, a fellow Presbyterian).[1] Opposition was very often the strongest tie that bound certain members of a particular group. For example, with the rise of women's rights, abolitionists were sometimes united around little more than their mutual hatred for slavery. The American Anti-Slavery Society split over the role of women.[2] Angelina Grimké exemplified the emerging tension within the abolitionist movement when she wrote to Theodore Weld in 1837 that she endorsed female ministers. She then asked playfully, "Is brother Weld frightened at *my ultra-ism*?"[3] (Grimké and Weld had much more in common than antislavery. They were married in May 1838.) Religion was likewise oppositional. Presbyterians were divided into Old School and New School camps. Unitarianism, one of the most intellectually fashionable churches in the new republic, was, according to Daniel Walker Howe, "the most antidenominational denomination in the country."[4] Even moral influencers began to define themselves against one another. William Lloyd Garrison was horrified to learn that fellow abolitionist Elijah Lovejoy used weapons against anti-abolitionists when he was attacked and murdered by a mob in 1838. Moral influence could be employed in all manner of ways, he argued, but it was always *non*violent. After all, could there be *moral* influence without morals? Wrestling with the meaning of freedom, equality, and the unfulfilled promises of the American Revolution, the spirit of the age in the 1830s was the spirit of opposition.

UNITED IN OPPOSITION

The responsibility to publicly oppose the forces of evil was a mantle that Lyman Beecher passed down to his children from an early age and an instinct that united the Beecher family in a period when their individual beliefs and convictions were in fact diverging. In 1837, the Beechers were already a mixture of general antislavery, outspoken colonizationism, sympathy for abolitionism, and abolitionism. They were a small picture of the northern United States, and in a city which "continued to be a microcosm of the larger conflict that was gripping the nation."[5] Although their views on the slavery issue were not identical, their combined opposition to Garrisonian abolitionism *and* Wilsonian proslavery remained firm. When Henry became the temporary editor of a local publication, the *Journal and Western Luminary,* he attacked both radical abolitionists *and* mobs. Although his stand against extremism was not quite as "courageous" as Clifford E. Clark Jr. has described it, Clark is most certainly correct that Henry drew his positions on free speech from "the New School theology on God's moral government, a concept that had played a central role in the father's theology."[6] His sister Catharine was also opposing extremes at the national level. In her *Essay on Slavery and Abolitionism with Reference to the Duty of American Females* (1837), in which she challenged Angelina Grimké's connection between abolitionism and women's rights, Catharine spent more time critiquing abolitionism than defending colonization. Arguing for women's *improvement* inside a natural hierarchy of American society, Catharine's essay was a polemic against ultraism, calling William Lloyd Garrison an "avowed opponent" of Christian institutions.[7]

Indeed, a common religious enemy ensured that the Beechers still had more in common theologically than they had differences. And they had many differences. By the late 1830s, some of the older Beechers' religious leanings were beginning to shift away from the Puritanism of their father. Continuing Lyman's Edwardsean project to modify Calvinism, Edward sought to attain the "highest power" of personal holiness, pursuing a degree of sanctification which resembled Methodism more than Presbyterianism.[8]

Having already lost three of six children, he had witnessed the fleeting nature of human existence and was determined to live with purpose.[9] Like
Catharine, Edward resisted the doctrine of total depravity, and with time
he would also question the traditional idea of original sin.

In the western New York town of Batavia, George was also obsessed
with holiness. He consumed William Wilberforce's *A Practical View of
Christianity* (1797), expressing his admiration for the British abolitionist.[10]
Pastoring a well-established church in the so-called "Burned-Over District,"
George inevitably sampled the local theological flavor. After reading the
sermons of his father's rival, Charles Finney, Lyman's third son was so determined to achieve holiness that he now believed Christian perfection (a
state of sinless moral purity) to be possible and even required for salvation. In the family circular in 1836–37, George's new views were a topic of
discussion. Brother Charles was wary of the idea, reminding his brother
that the human heart was deceitful, while Henry was "not greatly troubled"
by the matter.[11] In a letter to George in 1837, a concerned family member
(most likely Lyman) warned, "Reading Mr. Finney's sermons is just the
thing I would not recommend to one of your temperament, who are dis-
posed to look on the dark side of your own character and prospects." The
author later urged, "But I beseech you, remember, that the gospel system
is one which, while it requires perfect holiness as the thing to be aimed
at, where faith and love to Christ exist, accepts the least degree of it."[12] In
other words, nobody's perfect. By faith in Christ, there was forgiveness of
sins. Did religion play a role in George Beecher's spiraling depression? If
so, it was Finneyite moralism—and not just Puritan introspection—which
appeared to lead him down a path of self-doubt. Nevertheless, it is not a
coincidence that, as George was drinking deeply from the well of abolitionism and joining the Antislavery Society, he was also exploring the theological ideas of Charles Finney. He joined the ranks of "non-Antinomian"
groups who were beginning to sprout up and form conventions in western
New York.[13]

However, even as Lyman's older children did not align with his views
on sin, sanctification, or necessarily slavery, they were singularly united
against the Old School. Edward was now himself a leader in the New
School party and the "chief supporting player" of the abolitionist drama
unfolding in Alton, Illinois.[14] Between 1836 and 1840, classes at Lane aver-
aged a mere five students.[15] Therefore, Henry was quite literally one of his

father's *only* pupils during his time in Cincinnati, sitting under the tutelage of Lyman's New School faculty (or what was left of it). At Amherst, Henry had been fond of Charles Finney and had begun to silently reject the fossilized, angular Calvinism of his father. In Cincinnati, his aversion to conservative Presbyterianism turned into antagonism when theology became bound with politics.[16]

After witnessing the onslaught against his father and the ferocity of the anti-abolitionist mobs, Henry finally confided to a friend that he identified himself as an abolitionist, just not the kind "full of brimstone and *damnation* for all of other opinions, proud as Lucifer and inflexible as a mountain."[17] As Debby Applegate explains, "publicly he was in a bind. Besides his loyalty to Lyman, there was the fact that nearly every girl he knew had a father who was staunchly anti-abolition. One thing Henry refused to be was a social pariah. But as the summer wore on he found it increasingly difficult to balance conscience and popularity." Impressionable and a bit impetuous, Henry was not, however, without a brain or a conscience. He was beginning to completely rethink the strict, predestinarian theology that would compel some people to hold other people in chains. "For the first time since he began keeping a diary," Applegate notes, "the pages began to fill with long, technical, theological proofs, practical notes on potential sermons, and professional tips. Any hints of doubt are less about religion per se and more about the all-or-nothing nature of Calvinism."[18] Henry, like his older siblings, was firmly entrenched with his father in New School Presbyterian thought. But whereas the Old School forced Lyman to more carefully articulate Edwardsean Calvinism, they caused his children to completely reevaluate the entire Calvinistic system. More than any other single event in their lives, the General Assembly of 1837 cemented the Beechers' break with the Puritanism of their upbringing, setting in motion a course of events that pushed them further away from their father's eighteenth-century faith and impelling almost all of them to join the abolitionist side.

"THEY WILL FIGHT LIKE DEVILS"

In 1837, most Americans were not optimistic about America's immediate future. Due in large part to the risky lending practices of banks during the western land bubble of the 1830s, the United States experienced an economic depression that severely depreciated the value of paper money, sending the nation into a financial crisis that had devastating consequences for western communities. In the so-called "Panic of 1837," many of the benefactors of Catharine's Western Female Institute were unable to continue their support. With a sense of Yankee superiority and a somewhat abrasive personality, Catharine had developed a knack for rubbing Cincinnati's most prominent families the wrong way. When their patience dried up, so did the funding for the school.[19] The panic was the last nail in the coffin for the Western Female Institute. Kathryn Sklar adds, "Catharine quite ruthlessly appropriated all the money for herself and left Mary Dutton and Harriet to bear the financial losses of the school."[20] Lyman also found himself in a financial pinch. In 1837, Arthur Tappan suspended his support payments to Lane Seminary, a consequence of the economic crisis and Lyman's unwillingness to turn Lane into an Oberlin.[21] But Lyman once again relied upon his children, eventually asking George for $200, a request that demanded no small amount of swallowed pride.[22] He and his wife, Sarah, obliged. The father who had taken his children to the West to "save the nation" himself needed saving.[23] The late 1830s was not the most auspicious time to be in education.[24] Farther west in the hinterlands of Jacksonville, Edwards's presidential salary at Illinois College was still only a modest $1,100.[25]

However, Americans were concerned with more than just an economic collapse. The nation itself was in danger, it seemed. The ominous clouds of civil war were already looming over the infant republic, leading some to predict unprecedented bloodshed. In 1836, on the floor of the House of Representatives, South Carolina congressman James H. Hammond proposed the option of murdering abolitionists, "ignorant, infatuated, barbarians as they are."[26] Hammond was not alone in this sentiment. After the debates in the general assemblies of 1835 and 1836, Presbyterian pastor Robert F. Witherspoon of South Carolina wrote to Lyman Beecher to express his indignation at abolitionists and his drab view of the national destiny. Beecher had survived the arrows of Joshua Wilson, he demurred, but the Union might not survive the coming storm. In Witherspoon's view, the fault lines forming in the denomination represented the United States as a whole: "Division I do most sincerely and deeply deplore; and *if* it must, as a dernier resort, come to this, I am strongly inclined to the opinion that Mason and Dixon's line must be the *ridge*." Witherspoon's words were prophetic. Less than a year later, at the next General Assembly, southerners overwhelmingly opposed the New School side, fifty to nine. But Witherspoon went a few steps further. By his estimation, the United States was on the brink of war.

As a South Carolinian and a slaveholder, Witherspoon stood opposite of Beecher on the slavery issue. While he was willing to dialogue with moderate antislavery men and even conceded the evil of slavery, he was angered by the ultra-abolitionists. He warned:

> Yet so *it will be* if the Abolitionists rule. Our land must be deluged in blood by a contest fiercer and more bloody and unrelenting than even *Tory* warfare during the revolutionary struggle. When men contend for *liberty*—an *opinion*—they will *fight like devils. This cause* will arm son against father, daughter against mother, and prostrate the strongest and most tender ties of life. I have been a slaveholder from my youth, and yet I detest it as the *political and domestic curse* of our Southern country; and *yet I would contend to the death* against Northern interference with *Southern rights,* and would follow *Dr. Beman to the scaffold on Charleston Neck* if he continued to hold the sentiments he expressed at Pittsburg in 1835. I give you, Brother Beecher, my honest, undisguised sentiments. They may be *wrong,* but I think them *right.*[27]

A more prescient depiction of the United States in the late 1830s could hardly be found. Affirming the doctrine of total depravity, Old School Calvinists like Witherspoon were right about one thing: sinners would "fight like devils." The infant nation was heading inexorably toward civil war, when the soil would be "deluged in blood" and brother armed against brother. Offering no solution to the problem of human bondage, Witherspoon only knew that southerners like himself would never be told when and how to emancipate their slaves. Abolitionists would not stop in realizing their vision of liberty for the United States, and neither would slaveholders. Letters like these only further convinced Lyman Beecher that extremism was *not* the answer to the country's problems.

THE "SCHISM" OF 1837

But the denomination had already reached a boiling point. Although Southern Presbyterians like Witherspoon and Virginia pastor Benjamin Rice maintained amicable and even light-hearted relations with Beecher, friendships were never the same after the turn of affairs in Philadelphia in 1837. With the heresy trial of Albert Barnes in 1836 over a controversial New Divinity doctrine known as the moral governmental theory of atonement, Old Schoolers finally decided that it was time to sever ties with churches influenced by the New England Theology.[28] Before the assembly, they adopted a "Testimony and Memorial," listing New School errors and calling for the dissolution of non-Presbyterian churches. They took aim at four western synods, in Ohio and western New York. These synods were made possible by the Plan of Union (1801), which had become strongholds of New School Presbyterianism and antislavery sentiment. Because the *cause célèbre* in Philadelphia was along doctrinal lines, historian George Marsden has argued that, while "slavery played a major role in shaping the course of the division," it was not in fact the "primary cause." At the root of the division, he contends, was the New England Theology. Indeed, Lyman Beecher had been a kind of test case for the entire controversy. Men such as Joshua Wilson, for example, had laid their charges against Beecher on theological, not political, grounds. However, as the entire Beecher clan knew quite well, the two were inextricable.

What changed after 1836 was not the correlation between proslavery politics and Old School theology, but Southern Presbyterians like Robert Witherspoon. As Marsden notes, "By the opening of the General Assembly of 1837, the South had been won solidly into the Old School camp."[29] Ignited by the antislavery controversy, the South became an Old School voting bloc. While they kept relatively silent on the topic of slavery *at* the assembly, this was a calculated (and apparently successful) attempt to gain the support of their northern counterparts. With the help of some questionable parliamentary maneuvering, the Old School amassed enough southern votes to abrogate the Plan of Union and eliminate sixty thousand church members from the denomination. At the same moment that Angelina Grimké was giving an impassioned speech against slavery across town in Abolition Hall, the General Assembly was descending into an uproar. The result was a split between New School and Old School Presbyterians, between those who adhered to the ideas of Jonathan Edwards and opposed slavery (Lane, Oberlin), and those who promoted a stricter adherence to the *Westminster Confession* and defended slavery (Princeton, Union). In one of the great ironies of American history, Jonathan Edwards, a slaveowner, spawned an entire tradition of antislavery theologians.[30]

On the face of things, the terms of the Presbyterian schism were theological in nature. However, if slavery was "not central to the division," as George Marsden has contended, it was not so obvious to many Presbyterians, including the Beechers. After attending the General Assembly with his friend Elijah Lovejoy, Edward believed that abolitionism was at the heart of the matter. When he was asked months later to call a convention to form an Anti-Slavery Society in Illinois, he attributed part of the reason "to the impression produced on many by the violent proceedings of the General Assembly of the Presbyterian Church in 1837, and the belief that such unjust measures had been introduced into the church to defend slavery." Clearly, many westerners saw the invisible hand of the Slave Power orchestrating the proceedings in Philadelphia. According to Edward, these same Illinoisans were also provoked by the so-called "Texas question" and the western expansion of slavery.[31] At the very least, as historian and Presbyterian pastor Sean Michael Lucas has observed, "the debates over slavery provided the larger context in which the division of 1837 occurred."[32] Philadelphia was a bellwether for the nation. In the end, for Lyman Beecher, the Old School–New School schism was a theological problem that inevitably took political form. Reflecting on the events in Philadelphia years later, he charged, "John C. Calhoun was at the bottom of it. I know of his doing things—writing to ministers, and telling them to do this and do that. The South finally took the Old School side. It was a cruel thing—it was a cursed thing, and 'twas slavery that did it."[33]

Whether or not Calhoun actively whipped votes for the Old School side, his "positive good" speech, delivered just months earlier on the U.S. Senate floor, had ripple effects for the entire slavery debate. In the most famous defense of slavery in American history, Calhoun declared, "I take the higher ground. I hold that in the present state of civilization, where two races of different origin, and distinguished by color, and other physical differences, as well as intellectual, are brought together, the relation now existing in the slaveholding States between the two, is, instead of an evil, a good—a positive good."[34] Calhoun unashamedly advanced an argument that went well beyond the usual paternalistic models promulgated by most slaveholders. South Carolina Presbyterian James Henley Thornwell, who saw himself as a father figure to his slaves, had conceded that slavery was "not absolutely a good—a blessing."[35] But Calhoun's speech went even further in its justification for slavery, and it only emboldened the slavocracy and its hierophants. Robert Elder explains, "In its force, clarity, and content, Calhoun's argument marked a significant departure in the political debate over slavery. Although fragments of his argument could be found scattered throughout the preceding four decades . . . Calhoun consciously molded these defensive elements into an aggressive political ideology designed to counter the abolitionist campaign. Racial slavery, Calhoun argued, was not a moral abomination, a hidebound anachronism, or even a necessary evil; it was an institution uniquely suited—morally, economically, politically—to the conditions of the modern world."[36]

Lyman Beecher's knowledge of the Deep South was never firsthand. There is no evidence to suggest that Calhoun intervened in ecclesiastical affairs or that he embraced separationism before the late 1840s.[37] Lyman might as well have identified Eli Whitney, the inventor of the cotton gin in 1794 (and a Yale graduate with himself and Calhoun) as the real culprit behind the schism. However, Calhoun was in fact a Presbyterian, and he wielded considerable influence in the South in 1837. Regardless, for Beecher, there was no question that the real culprit behind the denominational split was slavery. In the late 1830s, with names like Calhoun, Jackson, Lovejoy, Finney, Weld, Beecher, and Thornwell, it seemed that the fate of the abolitionist movement and of the nation itself was tied to the Presbyterian denomination.

Behind the political intrigue, Charles Beecher saw something even more basic than the slavery issue. As a moral influencer, he understood where all agents of change drew their true power. After quoting his father in the *Autobiography*, he added: "And it was ideas that did it. It was ideas concerning God and man—ideas concerning the divine administration, the government of the universe, the origin of evil—that convulsed the Church and convulsed the nation: and why should they not? Theology and politics are next of kin. Their study is but the study, in different relations and connections, of the fundamental principles, and historical facts, and moving powers of the universal government of God."[38] In many ways, this was the Beecher mind on the issue of slavery. The concept of "moral government" applied to both the human sphere and the divine. If one did not believe human beings were free, responsible, moral agents *before God,* he or she would likely not embrace the idea that human beings were responsible to their fellow man. Theology was not *a*-political; it was the politics of the cosmos. In 1896, Charles expressed a similar idea: "It may not be clear at first to the ordinary mind why slavery and theology should go hand in hand, in national affairs. But if we reflect that theology is but another name for the politics of the universe, or the kingdom of God, the problem becomes simple."[39] In this sense, the schism of 1837 was waged over the very nature of government. Since 1801, Presbyterians and Congregationalists had forged a precarious union for the sake of evangelism. However, their concepts of polity—church and state—could never be truly reconciled. Finally, by 1838, Lyman lamented, "The Rubicon is passed, never to be passed again."[40]

THE MARTYRDOM OF ELIJAH LOVEJOY

Between 1800 and 1850, the Beechers evolved on the slavery issue like the majority of northerners, from toleration to troubled acceptance to condemnation. They also followed a conventional path during the Second Great Awakening, from prayer circles to reform groups. In 1837, at roughly the same time that his half-brother Thomas was having a spiritual conversion, William, the oldest, was having a political conversion, becoming the third Beecher to publicly support immediate emancipation when he joined the local Anti-Slavery Society.[41] When Harriet traveled to Putnam, Ohio, in the summer to escape the mosquito-ridden humidity of Cincinnati, William's new opinions were no doubt a topic of conversation.[42] Harriet and William probably also discussed the plight of their brother George, who had likewise joined the Anti-Slavery Society. However, Edward's road to abolitionism was a bit more dramatic. When he first arrived in Jacksonville, Edward's position on slavery was not much different from his father's. He too believed in a "big tent" approach to reform, including different groups. Edward was careful, like Lyman, to exercise prudence with proslavery men in the lower North.[43] However, also like Lyman, he became a mouthpiece for reform once he encountered violence in the streets. For Lyman, it was dueling that launched his writing career and national reputation. For Edward, it was anti-abolitionist mobs.

When Edward first met Elijah Lovejoy at the commencement ceremony at Illinois College in September 1834, the two became friends. Originally from New England, Lovejoy was also an orthodox Presbyterian minister. Whereas Beecher was "decidedly hostile to the doctrines of immediate emancipation," Lovejoy was the editor of the abolitionist newspaper in St. Louis, called the *Observer*. However, just a few months later, Edward changed his mind on emancipation. Eventually, he "became satisfied, from a careful examination of the history of experiments on this subject, that the doctrine of gradual emancipation was fallacious, and that of immediate emancipation was philosophical and safe."[44] Whether this change occurred as a result of Lovejoy or the Lane rebels is difficult to tell. Edward gave a fair hearing to all points of view. In Boston, he had been so "touched" by the sermons and writings of Unitarians that he had modified his own theological system accordingly.[45] Nevertheless, as abolitionists often preached, there was a significant gap between believing and *doing*. Edward was not yet ready to act upon his beliefs. When Lovejoy asked him to call a convention for the Illinois Anti-Slavery Society, Beecher replied that it was not a conciliatory organization and therefore not accepting of *all* antislavery positions. "On the whole I decidedly preferred to stand on my own ground," he recalled, "to join no society—and to speak as an individual, if I spoke at all."[46] Indeed, he did not speak much.

In 1836, Lovejoy's *Observer* press was burned to the ground by an anti-abolitionist mob. To distance himself from rioters, he moved the press across the river to Alton in Illinois, a free state. When he came to nearby Jacksonville, he spent time with Beecher's family and again asked Beecher to convene the Anti-Slavery Society. But this time Edward had a counterproposal. If the meeting could be opened to "friends of free inquiry," uncommitted to abolitionism but convinced that slavery is a sin and must be ended, he would allow Lovejoy to use his name to call the meeting.[47] Lovejoy accepted these terms. In the months that followed, Edward Beecher slowly became an abolitionist and Lovejoy's "closest associate." Robert Merideth's description of Edward's stance during this period as a "reticent radicalism" is oxymoronic, but apt. After all, to be publicly branded as a radical abolitionist was a dangerous gamble. Just a month after returning from the General Assembly, a mob destroyed the second *Observer* press in August 1837. According to Merideth, this event "changed the complexion of things for Beecher."[48] While he was still cautious in public, there was no turning back in his mind. At the commencement at Illinois College in September, Edward proposed to alter the "character of the convention" so that "friends of free discussion" could attend the Anti-Slavery Society in good conscience. Wielding the hammer of free discussion to drive in the nail of emancipation, Edward was employing a familiar Beecher tool.

The Jacksonville area was filled with pro-southern sympathizers. This was typical of the so-called "Butternut region," or the southern portions of Ohio, Indiana, and Illinois.[49] Understandably, Edward was hesitant to stand unabashed with radical extremists. But he had already gone too far to claim neutrality. When the Anti-Slavery Society was convened, anti-abolitionists and colonizationists like Rev. Joel Parker disrupted the proceedings. To make matters worse, the third *Observer* press was destroyed prior to the convention. In his first public act of defiance against the pro-slavery agenda, Edward managed to draw up a "Declaration of Sentiments," asserting that slavery is in all cases sinful and denouncing any instance when an individual was regarded as property.[50] Edward was also on a three-person committee to prepare an address to the citizens of Illinois, and he comprised a committee of one to propose topics for discussion at the next annual convention.

By November, the next *Observer* press was on its way to Alton, inspired by the success of the *Philanthropist* in Cincinnati after the riot of 1836.[51] However, a town hall meeting was called to reach a "compromise" between Lovejoy and his opponents. Local politicians and businessmen called for Lovejoy to resign, but the editor refused to accept any terms which silenced his right to free speech. In *Narrative of Riots at Alton: In Connection with the Death of Rev. Elijah Lovejoy* (1838), Edward records Lovejoy's response with a bit of theatrical flourish. Redolent of Martin Luther at the Diet of Worms, Lovejoy declared, "by the help of God, I will stand. I know I am but one and you are many. My strength would avail but little against you all. You can crush me if you will; but I shall die at my post, for I cannot and will not forsake it." Clearly, Edward remembered his dear friend as a Luther-type figure, a man of conscience standing up to the tyrannical popes of the frontier. He then records Lovejoy's next words:

Why should I flee from Alton? Is not this a free state? When assailed by a mob at St. Louis, I came hither, as to the home of freedom and of the laws. The mob has pursued me here, and why should I retreat again? Where can I be safe if not here? Have not I a right to claim the protec-

tion of the laws? What more can I have in any other place? Sir, the very
act of retreating will embolden the mob to follow me wherever I go. No,
sir; there is no way to escape the mob, but to abandon the path of duty:
and that, God helping me, I will never do.[52]

If these were *not* the exact words of Elijah Lovejoy to the officials at Alton,
they were certainly Edward Beecher's to America. Lovejoy's harrowing experience was the final confirmation for Beecher that there could be no middle ground with anti-abolitionists. Retreat was not an option. In Beecher's
view, the brute force of mobs was the very opposite of moral influence.
Physical coercion did not rely upon the power of argumentation and example, but upon fear. As a result, mobs were "a virtual surrender of the
foundations of our civil government and of all religious toleration."[53] They
were un-Christian and un-American. Conversely, Lovejoy's selfless sense of
duty was the model of true republicanism.

The next Monday, on November 6, the fourth and final *Observer* press
arrived in Alton. Edward left for Jacksonville, believing that the situation
had calmed. However, it would be the last time he saw his friend alive. In
the late hours of the night, a rancorous mob of over thirty people stormed
down to the warehouse in Alton where the new press was stored. Anticipating the worst, Lovejoy and others armed themselves in defense of the
press. When the attackers fired on the building, Lovejoy fired back, killing
one of the rioters. Further enraging the crowd, Lovejoy was gunned down
by a sniper.

The tumultuous episode in Alton invited multiple interpretations. After all, a man had defended his freedom of speech by killing another man.
Local colonizationists like Baptist John Mason Peck framed Lovejoy as an
extremist "who was represented as having fought like a hero."[54] A couple
of months later in Springfield, a young lawyer named Abraham Lincoln
took a more ambivalent approach in his Lyceum Speech, calling for "so-
ber judgment" against "wild and furious passions."[55] However, beyond Illinois, Lovejoy's death touched off a wave of abolitionist paeans in his honor,
extolling Lovejoy as an example of courage and hope. Clergyman David
Root, an agent for the Anti-Slavery Society in Ohio, even compared Lovejoy to Jesus Christ: "Yes, Lovejoy is no more. That beloved brother, that
champion of liberty, that Christian hero, that uncompromising friend of

the defenceless, down-trodden slave, whose movements in the cause of the oppressed for the last six months we have contemplated with admiration, has been sacrificed, by wicked hands, upon the altar of his country's liberty, in bearing testimony to the truth, and his name is henceforth to be enrolled upon the calendar of Christian martyrs."[56] Indeed, the fallen editor had become a Christlike martyr for the abolitionist movement. However, it was Edward Beecher who would immortalize the name of Elijah Lovejoy into the American consciousness. *Narrative of Riots at Alton* chronicled the events leading to the chaos, dramatized the days and hours before the murder, and established Lovejoy—warranted or not—as "the first martyr in America to the great principles of the freedom of speech and of the press."[57] Merton L. Dillon, in his 1961 biography of Lovejoy, called Beecher's work "probably the most eloquent defense of freedom of inquiry ever written in this country."[58] Edward Beecher thus became a critical figure in the burgeoning American abolitionist movement, gaining the respect of figures like William Lloyd Garrison and demonstrating that the power of the press could not be stopped with a bullet. Just as importantly, Edward became the first Beecher to stand with the radical abolitionist camp.

As Lovejoy's "interpreter," Beecher was branded almost immediately as a maverick by local anti-abolitionists.[59] Although the faculty at Illinois College supported his views, Beecher was blamed by others for Lovejoy's death. One Wisconsin newspaper falsely reported with "unalloyed pleasure" that the trustees had dismissed him.[60] But Beecher's resolve to end slavery did not abate. Lovejoy's death was a turning point in his life and in the life of the nation. As a matter of fact, Harriet Beecher Stowe was *not* the first Beecher to harness the power of narrative to awaken the American conscience to the wickedness of slavery. *Narrative of Riots at Alton* was half history and half hagiography, designed to offer the American public an example of bravery, sacrifice, and sincere conviction in the face of evil. In the early 1850s, Harriet would draw upon the life of runaway slave Josiah Henson in a similar way to write *Uncle Tom's Cabin,* but in the genre of fiction. For Edward Beecher, the cause of abolition was the cause of Christianity itself. "Until this question [of slavery] is decided no man can tell what the gospel is," he declared.[61] The political was bound up with the ethical and the spiritual. This was the Beecher way.

A BEECHER NETWORK

As Edward was blazing his own trail in Illinois, Henry was also stepping out on his own. In a matter of months in 1837, Henry graduated from Lane, married Eunice Bullard White, and moved to Lawrenceburg, Indiana, to take his first pastorate. He was eager to leave the confines of Walnut Hills. No longer under his father's authority, Henry was free to be his own preacher. Like his brothers, he yearned for independence, but he was still a Beecher. No less committed to evangelistic preaching than Lyman, Henry adapted various elements of Methodism into his western ministry. He also inherited his father's belief that gospel ministers were "watchmen set upon the walls of Zion to descry and announce the approach of danger."[62] His crusade against intemperance was instinctive. Upon discovering several bars and brothels that littered the town, Henry called Lawrenceburg a city "with two distilleries and twenty devils in it."[63] Years later, in the *Indiana Farmer and Gardener,* a new bimonthly newspaper which he edited, Henry attacked a Christian distillery in Lawrenceburg, proving that he was willing to risk his own reputation among local businessmen for the sake of the sacred Beecher cause.[64] He was a moral influencer at heart.

Only a short steamboat commute from Cincinnati, Henry could not outrun his father or his father's enemies. While his new church was excited to receive Lyman Beecher's son as their pastor, his new presbytery was staunchly Old School and not thrilled with the idea of a rabble-rousing Beecher in their midst. Although Henry passed his ordination exam, his opponents found another way to silence him, passing a motion declaring that the Presbytery of Oxford was officially with the Old School National Assembly. Henry's church had a choice to make: Old School or New School. They sided with Beecher. Withdrawing from Oxford Presbytery, they become Independent Presbyterian Church. Henry had left Cincinnati only to join the same assembly as Lyman. The forces that had torn the Presbyterian denomination apart were simultaneously pulling father and son together. Swelling with pride, Henry confessed, "My case may stand for many. A graduate of Lane (that propaganda of heresy)—the son of the Arch-Heretic—has received the imprimatur of Orthodox Oxford!"[65] Lyman gave his official approval, ordaining Henry along with Calvin Stowe on November 9, 1838. If Lyman's trial had ensured that there would be *two* Presbyterian sects, Henry's experience made certain that no Presbyterian church in the state could remain neutral. When the Beechers split presbyteries, they split the entire denomination.

Indeed, it is difficult to imagine a time and context in American history more subject to change and division than the antebellum West. From city to city, and from church to church, political coalitions and theological affiliations were as unpredictable as the New Madrid fault (which produced giant earthquakes in 1811). When Presbyterian missionary Timothy Flint floated down the Mississippi River, he noted divisions in the Presbyterian churches: "Even among our own brethren, it is well known, that there is some feeling of a questionable nature, some rivalry between the pupils, the doctors, and schools, of Andover and Princeton." He added regretfully, "The Cumberland Presbyterians, with all the freshness of a new sect, are not found lacking in this order of things."[66] The frontier in the 1830s witnessed a level of atomization never before seen in American society, producing a movement that Nathan O. Hatch has called "the democratization of American Christianity."[67] Since arriving in the West, the Beechers had adapted to every imaginable variable, from deadly pathogens to college protests to race riots to economic depressions to church splits. In some ways, change was the only constant—that is, besides family.

For the Beechers, as for many western settlers, the family unit was their *only* pillar of stability and support. As the Beecher siblings scattered across the Midwest, they remained connected to one another through their two primary modes of moral influence: ministry and education. For example, after the Panic of 1837 finished off the Western Female Institute where she was attending, Isabella, only fifteen, was sent by Lyman to Batavia, New York, to teach and study at a school near her brother George. Sarah Buckingham, the daughter of an affluent Batavia family whom George had just recently married, offered to board Isabella. However, when it was later found that the school had no openings, Harriet, her former teacher and mentor, convinced Lyman that it was best for Isabella to move to Hartford to stay with her sister Mary Perkins and Mary's husband, Thomas. After only being allowed one year at Hartford Female Seminary—founded by Catharine and run by Mary—Isabella met her future husband, John Hooker, a clerk in Thomas Perkins's law office.[68] With years and even decades between them, the Beechers found support in one another. And when Beechers finally started their own families, they were *still* tied to their brothers and sisters. In 1838, Henry and Eunice welcomed their first child, Harriet Eliza, named after his sister. In the same year, Harriet and Calvin named their first boy, Henry, after her brother.

The center of gravity in the Beecher universe was, of course, Lyman. With more geographical distance between family members, the aging patriarch employed various ways to mobilize his children, with or without a college education. For the oldest, William, the only Beecher son of seven not to graduate from seminary, Lyman had to pull strings just to get him licensed to preach.[69] However, as William began to fulfill his own predestined ministry in Putnam, father partnered with son in the family business of revival. In February 1839, from Columbus, Lyman wrote to William, updating him on a local awakening. With the urgency of an itinerant evangelist, he exhorted, "dear son, make haste, and come on as fast as your horse can bring you, to help your father and do good, besides all the comfort it will give me to see you. I know you so well that I have confidence that you will come if possible—a true chip of the old block—to do the Lord's work, at all events."[70] Lyman had not abandoned his vision of redeeming the West with his children. Revival brought the Beechers to the West, and it kept them together.

For Lyman's daughters, however, his vision for the West was implemented much differently. Years later, Isabella criticized her father for pressuring her to begin a teaching career shortly after Western Female Institute closed, when she was still a child. When the Panic of 1837 laid a financial stress on the family, Isabella's school days were cut short. "At fifteen my dear good father (instigated of course by his new wife) came to me and suggested that I should begin to teach school now and support myself. I, who had never been to school in earnest, for two years together in my whole life." Just as her brothers were beginning their education, she bemoaned, "mine was finished. . . . Till twenty three, their father, poor minister as he was could send them to College and Seminary all *six*—cost what it might, but never a daughter cost him a hundred dollars a year, after she was sixteen."[71] This proved to be one of the most biting criticisms ever leveled against Lyman by one of his children. Lyman clearly favored his sons, producing a feeling of bitterness from the woman who would later become a voice in the women's rights movement. Harriet had begun her teaching career at almost the exact same age at Hartford Female Academy in 1827, but Isabella was promised only one more year of schooling in Hartford with her sister Mary. Nevertheless, despite her quiet resentment for a male-dominated family and the coldness between her and Lyman's third wife, Isabella continued to admire her father, who she envisioned as "filling the place of my own mother."[72]

"I AM LONESOME"

The family dynamics at Walnut Hills were changing by the late 1830s. Worn down from eleven children and recent bouts of controversy in the church, Lyman's Calvinistic edges were a bit smoother now. The atmosphere around the dinner table was full of personalities that rivaled his own, as the children challenged his ideas with more frequency and boldness. Charles, for example, had a shouting match with his father over the theology of Jonathan Edwards. While Edwards's *Freedom of the Will* convinced many, including Lyman, that human free will was compatible with divine sovereignty, it turned Charles into "a confirmed fatalist."[73] His sister Catharine was also not afraid to express her opinions or to criticize the views of her more "educated" brothers. In 1839, Catharine became so heated in a debate with Charles and Edward over "slavery, predestination or free will and preexistence," that Lyman believed she had badly wounded her brothers with her words.[74] In an increasingly divided church and country, the Beechers were wrestling with the providence of God, the direction of history, the role of decision-making in the course of human events, and sometimes, with one another. Ironically, as Catharine was formulating her ideas about the American home and becoming an expert in household living, she was also becoming an expert in domestic argumentation and testing the patience of her family. Although Catharine chose *not* to adopt the spinster role that her Aunt Esther had assumed during her childhood, she remained convinced that "the nation's moral center [was] in the home."[75]

These sorts of household arguments contributed to Charles's decision in 1838 to move to New Orleans, far away from his father's professional and spiritual control. Forced to take a job as a clerk at a wholesale house while serving as a local church organist, Charles was working out his relationship to organized religion *and* to his deeply religious family. He was also experiencing the world. In his letters to Harriet, he recounted his experiences on the slave plantations while collecting debts from planters, providing valuable material that his sister would use in *Uncle Tom's Cabin.*[76] However, when Charles published a poem in New Orleans that questioned the eternal state of his deceased mother and lamented that he had no more close friends, Henry showed Lyman the newspaper clipping. The poem read:

> "Oh, must I live a lonely one,
>> Unloved upon the thronged earth,
> Without a home beneath the sun,
>> Far from the land that gave me birth?

> "Alone—alone I wander on,
>> An exile in a dreary land;
> The friends that knew me once are gone;
>> Not one is left of all their band.

> "I look upon the boiling tide
>> Of traffic fierce, that ebbs and flows,
> With chill disgust and shrinking pride,
>> That heartfelt misery only knows.

> "Where is the buoyancy of youth,
>> The high, indomitable will,
> The vision keen, the thirst for truth,
>> The passions wild, unearthly thrill?

> "Oh, where are all the bounding hopes
>> And visions bright, that were my own
> When Fancy at her will could ope
>> The golden doors to Beauty's throne?

> "My mother! whither art thou fled?
>> Seest thou these tears that for thee flow?

Or, in the realms of shadowy dead,
Knowest thou no more of mortal woe?

"In that still realm of twilight gloom
Hast thou reserved no place for me?
Haste—haste, oh mother, give me room;
I come—I come at length to thee!"[77]

All of Roxana's children idealized their mother to cope with their father's lack of parental warmth. As years passed, maternal love became the
center of their religion. "For many people," explains historian Timothy
Larsen, "an early expression of their devotional sense is the cult of motherhood."[78] This was true for all of the Beecher children. But Charles's poetic
plea reverberated with an unusual amount of pain. Pleading for his mother,
Charles Beecher felt trapped. He could find no comfort in life or in death.
He had no help from "friends" on earth and no certainty of a life beyond the
grave. (He resisted the doctrine of hell for the rest of his life.) Charles had
run away from his family *and* their faith, and, unwittingly, from the hope
of ever seeing his mother again. The poem was thus a judgment upon his
controlling father and a cry for help. But on this occasion, perhaps due to
his past experiences with Roxana and Catharine, Lyman did not respond
with his characteristic burst of theological argumentation. He resisted the
urge to preach a sermon to his son about the doctrines of heaven and hell
and the immortality of the soul. Instead, the college president chose a less
professorial approach to parenting. In one of the most compassionate letters he ever penned, Lyman Beecher wrote to his son to remind him of "the
trembling solicitude of a father's love."

Indeed, Lyman insisted that Charles would always be loved—no matter
what he believed. Although "our opinions may differ," he wrote, their time
apart had only produced "a more intense interest, solicitude, and sympathy" for him. His father missed him. Lyman had softened a bit since his
days arguing over disinterested benevolence with his fiancée in the 1790s.
He assured Charles that he would not interfere in his personal affairs. Expressing a deep sadness for Charles's agony, Lyman only wanted him to
know that he dreamed of his "returning home." Nevertheless, for Lyman
Beecher, no conversation was devoid of some biblical allusion, comparing

Charles to the lost sheep of Luke 15. Although this was a bit on the nose for a son grappling with spiritual doubt and resentment, given the circumstances, the analogy was not entirely inaccurate. Of all the Beecher children, Charles was the first to *literally* run away from his father.

Still, a more appropriate metaphor for Lyman's relationship to Charles would have been the story of the prodigal son in the very same chapter of Luke. In fact, this parable was almost certainly on Lyman's mind when he pleaded with Charles not to abandon his faith and his family. Charles had fled from his father's house, but the father was still waiting expectantly for his return. "Oh, my dear Charles—the last child of my angel wife, your blessed mother—you can never know the place you fill in your father's heart, and the daily solicitude and prayers of his soul for your protection and restoration to equanimity, satisfaction, and joy of heart in communion with God." Ultimately, Lyman saw Charles's departure as a crisis of faith, and he wanted him to know that the *entire* Beecher clan was in his corner. "Whenever the temptation comes over you to feel that you are friendless," he charged, "remember . . . that your father lives, that Aunt Esther lives almost only to suffer and pray for you, and that every one of your brothers and sisters are united in a weekly concert of prayer for your preservation and restoration to joy and peace in believing." If Roxana could speak, Lyman wrote to Charles, she "might speak to your troubled soul" and remind him to trade despondency for joy.[79] Even in death, Roxana Beecher still managed to speak into the lives of her children, who always possessed a "fierce and worshipful loyalty to their mother's ghost."[80] Indeed, few correspondences in the Beecher family illustrate more clearly the power of her name to inject hope and healing into a broken family. Months later, Charles returned to Cincinnati.

The late 1830s saw a Beecher diaspora across the United States, from New Orleans to New England to the Indiana backwater. In every case, regardless of how they felt about Lyman, his children eventually found themselves within his grasp, if not control. Henry, Charles, and Isabella all exhibited a bit of rebellion against their father, but the power of Beecherism was strong. Lyman's influence over his children's lives was the power of *moral* influence, the call to shape the destiny of a nation. They no longer shared the same house, but they shared a similar vision for America. Nevertheless, as his children began to leave the nest, Lyman felt more isolated in his Cincinnati residence. Not even an eternal optimist like Lyman Beecher was immune to the feeling of loneliness. Beecher was especially prone to bouts of depression. He missed his children, particularly his sons. Thomas had departed for Illinois College in 1839, under the watchful eye of his big brother.[81] In a letter to George (who also knew the feeling of loneliness), Lyman wrote, "I am at length so entirely and distantly separated from my sons as I have never before been since the birth of my first-born, having always had one or more with me, and others so near as to secure frequent intercourse, and aid in public action, but having now not one within two, four, and eight hundred miles." With so much distance now between himself and his sons, Lyman confessed, "I am lonesome, and am stirred in spirit to bring my dear sons around me by correspondence, by which our sympathy and co-operation may be sustained, otherwise my quiver full of them may not avail me to speak with the enemy in the gate."[82] More than likely, the "enemy" that Lyman referenced was the Old School sectarians. In the letter to George, he reported that the lines were finally "drawn between Old School and New," and that if he ever left the seminary, "it would go into the hands of the Old School infallibly and immediately."[83] In Lyman's mind, Lane was a New School institution, and he needed the "co-operation" of his sons to combat the "enemy" of the Old School. The Beecher men were pastoring different churches, but on the same team—a New School team.

Lyman also felt a bit of pressure in the city of Cincinnati, as he did not possess the same level of cachet in the community as he once had. By the late 1830s, with the Presbyterian Schism, the Panic of 1837, and Catharine's habit of rubbing certain patrons the wrong way, Cincinnati's polite society had begun to grow somewhat tired of the Beechers. Kathryn Sklar notes, "The Beechers were middle-class Yankee evangelicals, and their moral edges were often too sharp to move smoothly in genteel Cincinnati society."[84] Although Lyman bragged to George that Lane was on better financial footing, the state of things in Cincinnati forced the father to ask his son for two hundred dollars, a request to which George acquiesced.

"CONSERVATIVE ABOLITIONISTS"

In his letter to George, Lyman described most of the students at Lane Seminary as he now described himself: "conservative Abolitionists."[85] Just a few years earlier, he would have balked at any self-designation with the word "abolitionist," regardless of the adjective before it. Lyman refused to be associated with "men such as Garrison" because they would not practice "peaceful reform."[86] But much had changed in just a few years. With the increasingly proslavery agenda of the Old School and the recent antislavery work of Edward and George, it became less radical for Lyman to qualify his abolitionism. In fact, George was slowly and indirectly shaping Lyman's official position on slavery. In 1840, the New School General Assembly passed a resolution requiring every minister to preach at least one antislavery sermon a year. The measure had been originally proposed by George, who was now an up-and-coming leader in the abolitionist movement.[87]

As Owen W. Muelder has speculated, George Beecher may have even been part of Theodore Dwight Weld's famous "Seventy," a band of lecturers and agents of the American Anti-Slavery Society recruited by Weld to evangelize the United States with the abolitionist gospel.[88] The reference to "Seventy" had a twofold meaning. It was a rough number of enlisted agents *and* an allusion to the tenth chapter of the Gospel of Luke, when Jesus Christ sends out seventy-two disciples to heal the sick and declare the kingdom of God. Whether George was personally selected by Weld or just appointed as a local agent by the national society, his contributions to the Anti-Slavery Society were enough to earn him a reputation as an abolitionist. Perhaps Lyman saw George in some of his students. John G. Fee, for example, would soon come to Cincinnati to attend Lane, where he adopted abolitionist views. Shortly after his time at Lane, Fee began working for the American Missionary Association (AMA), an organization headquartered in New York. Fee pastored a church in Bracken County, Kentucky, where he served as an organizer for local AMA activity, handing out antislavery tracts throughout the upper South.[89]

In truth, by 1840, the majority of Beechers could have been reasonably classified as "conservative abolitionists" in one form or another. While Henry was not yet willing to align himself with the likes of Weld or to preach an antislavery sermon, he now repudiated colonization.[90] He was pushed in that direction by the local distiller and church member C. G. W. Comegys, who had pointed out that Beecher was righteous enough to harangue the evils of drinking but oddly silent on slavery. Leaving the tiny crossroads of Lawrenceburg, Henry accepted a call in 1839 to pastor the newly formed Second Presbyterian Church in Indianapolis.[91] It was a few steps up the professional ladder for Henry, aside from the pesky issue of mosquitoes. Henry had convinced Eunice that Indy was free of malaria, only to discover that virtually everyone in town had the illness. After their second child was born dead, Eunice moved in with her parents in West Sutton, Massachusetts, for almost a year. In addition to mosquitoes, marital problems, and financial troubles, Henry could not escape the slavery issue. The motion by the General Assembly now put pressure upon Henry to condemn slavery from the pulpit. Although Henry would not actually preach his first antislavery sermon until 1843, George's resolution helped lessen the stigma of "conservative abolitionism" for his brother.[92] Indeed, George's abolitionism had a radicalizing effect upon the entire family far greater than perhaps historians have ever recognized. In Putnam, Ohio, William lost his pastorate when his congregation became uneasy with his views against slavery and intemperance.[93] After George left his church in Batavia over salary issues, he relocated briefly to Rochester and then to Chillicothe, Ohio. In turn, William replaced George at Batavia, perpetuating the Beecher preaching carousel and providing William a pulpit to voice his views.

In New England, Henry's sisters followed the lead of their husbands on the matter of slavery. Thomas Perkins, Mary's husband, was already heading in the abolitionist direction. By 1840, John Hooker had converted to the abolitionist gospel. Incredibly enough, he then converted Isabella to the cause by appealing to Lyman! When Isabella objected to the insulting language of abolitionists, John responded with a clever rebuttal: abolitionist rhetoric sounded very similar to the kind employed by her father against dueling decades earlier. Were abolitionists as abusive against slaveholders as Lyman Beecher had been against his enemies? John's argument was not lost upon his wife, who admired her father deeply. Lyman Beecher was still the highest moral standard in her eyes. The question before her was simple: either her father had been in grievous error or abolitionism was acceptable. In time she affirmed the latter. As evidenced by Isabella's internal struggle, once Lyman bequeathed a legacy of moral influence to his children, he could not always determine the shape that legacy would take. After only a year and a half of marriage, and inspired partly by the example of her father, Isabella became a "whole-souled abolitionist" like her husband.[94] As her older, more reserved sister Mary watched this transformation, she feared that young Isabella might become a "public woman" like Catharine and Harriet. The latter had recently published her first piece commenting directly on a social issue, entitled "Drunkard Reclaimed."[95] Although bound by the instinct to exert moral influence, some Beechers were more "conservative" than others.

"YOUR SON GEORGE IS DEAD"

In 1840, William Henry Harrison was elected to the U.S. presidency in a campaign that billed Harrison as a war hero and something of a common man. One of these two caricatures was grounded in fact, and the other was not. "Ole Tippecanoe" did boast an impressive service record after fighting the British and their Native American allies in the War of 1812. However, during the campaign, he was also depicted as having lived in a log cabin, a detail that was not exactly true. Nevertheless, on the frontier, it was a rather effective symbol of grassroots, working-class values.[96] For the Beechers, Harrison's victory was auspicious for two reasons. First, Harrison was a Whig, defeating the incumbent Martin Van Buren, Jackson's Democratic successor. He represented industry, entrepreneurship, temperance, economic progress, and other things the Beecher family prized. Just as importantly, Harrison was emblematic of the rising importance of the American West in national affairs. Not only had Harrison earned his military achievements in the Old Northwest, but he was a well-known figure in Cincinnati and southern Ohio. Harrison owned a farm in North Bend, about ten miles outside of Cincinnati. He had served as clerk on one of the city courts. He'd also attended and addressed a meeting of the Young Men's Bible Society, of which Lyman was a leading figure.[97] Harrison's wife, Anna, even gifted Henry and Eunice with some home furnishings for their wedding.[98] In William Henry Harrison, moral influence and politics were not so far apart as they might have been under another president. Nevertheless, after delivering a lengthy inauguration speech on a blustery, wet winter day, he caught a cold. Thirty-one days later Harrison died of pneumonia, concluding the shortest presidency in American history. Harrison was the second-to-last Whig to ever be elected to the nation's highest office. In many ways, this was a fitting picture of the triumph and tragedy of the Beecher family in the 1840s.

Like America itself, Lyman Beecher had great expectations for his children. When he asked his oldest daughter, Catharine, to come along with him to the West, he already knew her potential as a moral influencer. She had founded one of America's first educational institutions for women in Hartford. Indeed, she continued that work in Cincinnati with the Western Female Institute. But Catharine exceeded even her father's expectations when she became America's leading expert in home economics.[99] Her *Treatise on Domestic Economy* (1841), written to the women of America, became the standard how-to manual for household living in the United States, explaining everything from sewing to cutting to mending to crossstitching.[100] Catharine had learned many of these crafts as a young woman under the tutelage of her Aunt Esther, who "made war upon dirt and disorder with the same indignant zeal that Lyman turned on the unconverted."[101] Drawing from her own experience in a frenetic home of Yankee practicality, Catharine's reasons for writing the treatise were both personal and philosophical. On one hand, she had witnessed too many wives and mothers— including her *own* mother—decimated by the physical burden and "mental taxation" of raising a family.[102] From her years in the West, Catharine knew all too well that even young women—including her stepmother—were "unusually subject to disease."[103] Her *Treatise on Domestic Economy* was thus a resource to help alleviate the toil of nineteenth-century housework.

But it was much more than an instruction booklet for women. In the words of historian Linda Kerber, it was a picture of the "republican mother."[104] More specifically, Catharine's *Treatise* was an exhortation toward Christian republicanism. Repackaging her father's ideas for a new audience, she stated unequivocally at the beginning of the work, "The principles of democracy . . . are identical with the principles of Christianity."[105] Catharine was showing her fellow women how to sustain and improve the most basic element of the American republic: the home. By exerting moral influence upon the family, Catharine aimed at nothing less than the "intellectual and moral elevation of her Country."[106]

For this reason, to classify the *Treatise* as a feminist work misses Catharine's very Beecher-esque project. As Milton Rugoff has explained, "Her concern was not women's rights but women's self-improvement."[107] In Catharine's mind, male and female roles in American society were not interchangeable. Rather, women were to exercise the liberty they had been afforded by government to excel in the sphere they had been allotted by God. It was "in America alone," she argued, "that women are raised to an equality with the other sex." Therefore, women should take advantage of their opportunities to lift themselves up, physically, intellectually, and spiritually. The founders of the nation "have secured to American women a lofty and fortunate position." However, this position was not relegated to a nuclear family. No doubt describing herself, Catharine declared, "No woman is forced to obey any husband but the one she chooses for herself; nor is she obliged to take a husband, if she prefers to remain single."[108] Although she was bound to a traditionally female role in American society, Catharine did not feel bound to a traditional home. Quoting extensively from Tocqueville, Catharine's treatise also featured some interesting interpretations of the Bible. In chapter 14, "On Habits of System and Order," Catharine argued that women directly violated the command "Thou Shalt Not Kill" when they risked or shortened their own lives by neglect or misuse. In her estimation, the wife who did not take care of her own body was guilty "as if [she] should intentionally run a dagger into a neighbor."[109] In other words, to neglect personal discipline and order in the home was tantamount to murder! Beecher moralism could sometimes adopt its own form of "ultra" extremism. With a combination of common sense, moral absolutism, and Yankee ingenuity, the *Treatise on Domestic Economy* enjoyed immediate success and catapulted Catharine into national fame.[110]

Her brother Henry was also exceeding expectations. As the middle brother, Henry ranked behind William, Edward, and George in the Beecher dynasty of ministers. He did not possess William's status as firstborn, Edward's intellect, or George's heart, but he certainly had his father's charm and personal appeal. After traveling to Indianapolis from college to visit his brother, Thomas wrote to Isabella, "I think I like Henry the best. He is the most like father of all his sons—and as a speaker and writer far surpasses any divine I have ever heard, in my opinion."[111] In 1841, the comparisons between Lyman and Henry only increased when Henry's new church experienced a lengthy revival, eventually making it the largest Presbyterian church in the state.[112] Despite accusations that he was disconnected from his congregants, Henry's warm, informal preaching style was a sensation with his frontier audience. It appealed especially to Thomas, who sometimes bristled at the doctrinal preaching of his father. Thomas had "once almost worshipped Edward," but no longer. At Illinois College, he grew to despise his older brother's byzantine theological formulations and now believed that Edward was perhaps "not a Christian." Instead, it was Henry, not Edward, who occupied the hallowed space next to Lyman. "[I]f I could be a second *Father* or Henry, untold wealth would not swerve my choice!"[113] A mixture of adoration and contempt for these two men would define Thomas's entire ministry for decades to come. Still, that Thomas would question the piety of Edward, who had established himself as a courageous figure in the abolitionist movement, while praising the "warmth of affection" and "domestic usefulness" of Henry, who had yet to preach an antislavery sermon, reveals Thomas's direction on the slavery issue and his aspirations at an early age. Meanwhile, Lyman took note of Henry's rising stardom in evangelicalism and his esteemed place in the eyes of his younger brothers.

Signaling a turning point for his mission to the West, Lyman began sending Henry's younger brothers to Indianapolis, investing Henry with a newfound authority in the Beecher tribe. In 1842, with his new wife, Sarah Coffin, Charles moved to Indianapolis to become Henry's assistant.[114] Thomas joined him a year later. Even the young troublemaker James was sent to Indianapolis for a time, but with little success. Henry had his hands full. In addition to gardening, Henry explored phrenology and mesmerism at the advice of Harriet, seeking to relieve a nervous disorder he likely inherited from his father.[115] For nearly a decade, Cincinnati had been the Beecher base of operations, launching various members of the family into new churches and schools and moral causes. However, as the sun was setting on the Beechers' time in Cincinnati, Lyman unofficially designated Indianapolis as a kind of second headquarters for the family. In 1842, he even assisted Henry in a revival in Terre Haute.[116] Conversely, in the spring of 1843, Lyman resigned from his pastorate at Cincinnati's Second Presbyterian Church, acknowledging the limitations of old age.[117] The spirit of revival was moving westward from Ohio to Indiana, and *within* the family itself. Lyman was brought to tears when he received word from Henry that Charles had surrendered to the Lord and returned to the fold of God, the last of Lyman's children to experience conversion.[118]

After employing his brother as an organist and choir director, Henry became for Charles what Lyman had been for most of his children. He arranged for the twenty-nine-year-old to be examined before the local presbytery in August 1843 and then found him a pastorate the following May in Fort Wayne, Indiana, at the newly organized Second Presbyterian Church.[119] Even in northeast Indiana, the Old School–New School stalemate was inescapable. As Charles's church was an offshoot from First Presbyterian, where many Old School leaders attended and had blocked Henry's calling there, his new congregants expected their new preacher to "put in [his] best licks" and "knock the socks off those Old Schools folks!" Exhausted by the same theological fighting he'd witnessed in Cincinnati, Charles replied that he "had nothing particular to say for New School" because he "always supposed his father knew all about that."[120] In other words, Charles was not interested in fighting his father's battles.

In the Beechers' quest to save souls, they could not save one of their own. Shortly after resigning his pastorate, Lyman made an East Coast fundraising trip with Edward and William, the latter of whom was now serving in George's former pulpit in New York. Stopping in Philadelphia, New Haven, Hartford, and Boston, Lyman once again played the role of cheerleader on behalf of the evangelization and reformation of the frontier. The Beechers were still making their collective "Plea for the West."[121] At the end of July, after considerable success during the campaign, Lyman was approached on the street by a friend with a newspaper in his hand, who asked, "Have you heard the dreadful news which has come into the city this morning?" Startled by the question, he said he had not. The man then replied, "Your son George is dead." On July 4, George Beecher was found dead of a self-inflicted shotgun blast to the mouth. Stepping outside to presumably drive away birds from his beloved cherry trees, he was later discovered by a female servant in an apparent suicide. Grabbing an issue of the newspaper, Lyman read the article with so much devastation and shock and horror that he immediately fled to his hotel room, sobbing.

Understandably, the news was a bombshell upon the entire family. Henry learned of George's death in a similar manner while returning from Jacksonville, where he delivered the commencement address at Illinois College while Edward was on his fundraising trip. "I suppose you have heard the news?" one of his elders asked. When Henry replied in the negative, the elder exclaimed, "Why, your brother George has killed himself!" In one of the few speechless moments of his life, Henry was in such disbelief that Eunice later recalled, "Henry did not speak, but drove rapidly on. I just glanced at his face. It was like marble, and I can never forget the agony I saw there."[122] More than any other brother, Henry was most shaken by George's death. The following year Henry named his son George Lyman Beecher after his fallen older brother, the one who shared his love of gardening.[123] Henry was no longer a middle child.

As Harriet confessed just a couple years later, George's apparent suicide was an explosion, sucking the "moral oxygen" out from a family known for its ebullience and buoyant optimism. An incredible feeling of sadness and confusion blanketed the group. "The sudden death of George shook my whole soul like an earthquake; and as in an earthquake we know not where the ground may open next, so I felt an indistinct terror as if father, brothers, husband, any or all, might be just about to sink."[124] For their own sanity and sense of purpose, the Beechers struggled to come to grips with the idea that George had killed himself. In a family of moralists, suicide was a clear violation of the Sixth Commandment. The tragedy also left the Beechers with a sense of guilt, as Catharine had visited her brother just a day before his death. In his very last letter, George had voiced his loneliness, crying out, "Dear Brothers and Sisters, all hail!—I only wish I had you all here, and every room in my house stowed full. When, think you, Henry and Charles, shall I see your faces here? Can you not come, one or both, this summer?"[125] With unbearable sorrow, regret, and a challenge to their belief in self-improvement, the Beechers tried to lean upon the providence of God and their own optimistic understanding of history.

Rather than admit the fairly obvious, Lyman chose to emphasize George's character. In his letter to George's widow, Sarah, he proudly recalled that his consecrated son had been "ripening fast in holiness." God's plan for George was not for this earth. "God was preparing him for more esteemed usefulness in a higher, nobler sphere; and, though we see not exactly what it is, we may confide in him who reigns above that there is no mistake," he boasted.[126] Catharine also tried to see the silver lining of tragedy. With more guilt than most, she composed her brother's journals and papers in an autobiography "to aid those, who, while compassed with infirmities, are still aiming at *high attainments* in Christian character."[127] God never wasted adversity. Even in calamity, the Beechers found moral influence. However, as historian Marie Caskey observes, with George's death, "the family had lost its most militant abolitionist."[128] Although Henry finally mustered the courage to deliver his first anti-slavery sermon in May, "The New Testament View of Slavery," a vacuum was left in terms of moral leadership in the family.[129] George's voice was not as thunderous nor his pen as sharp as his siblings', but he spoke prophetically into the family conscience. Despite his tragic end, he left a powerful example for his more moderate brothers and sisters.

LOOKING FURTHER WEST, HEADING BACK EAST

By the end of August, Lyman made a nostalgic and somewhat symbolic trip with his two eldest sons to East Hampton, New York. For the first time in over twenty years, Lyman returned to the small fishing village where his ministry began and where he made his name as a moral influencer. It was also the first time that either William or Edward had been back to the place of their birth. In the wake of George's ignominious death, Lyman enjoyed valuable time with his sons by doing the one thing he enjoyed most: preaching. All three Beechers sermonized at the Presbyterian Church, in the morning, afternoon, and evening. Like the family reunion after his wife Harriet's passing, preaching once again proved to be a cathartic exercise. Although Lyman had to defend himself from the recent charges of heresy that had made their way East, he counted the trip a success in more ways than one. He wrote from Massachusetts, "If Edward and myself could spend a year together in the field we could do up the business."[130] God had provided for another year of redeeming the West. The Lord giveth and taketh away.

But Edward was no longer looking westward. During his fundraising adventures, he strengthened some of his New School connections. Just as he had been the first Beecher to travel west, so he was the first to return to the East Coast. The following summer, after fourteen years as president of Illinois College in Jacksonville, Edward returned to Boston, as pastor of Salem Street Church. Edward once again served as a kind of compass for the family. His move was the beginning of a slow, reverse migration of the Beecher family back to their stomping grounds in the older part of the American republic. However, Edward was not leading from the front. The emerging *de facto* leader of the Beecher clan was still influencing in Indianapolis. Henry's seven lectures "to young men" in 1843–44 were published by the Indiana Synod and circulated to every church in the state. A dozen other publishers printed the lectures throughout the United States and in Europe, giving the young preacher his first taste of national recognition.[131] Like his father, Henry was introduced to the American public as a moral crusader, as he condemned everything from theaters to intemperance to gambling to youthful "vulgarity." No series of sermons ever revealed Henry to be the son of Lyman Beecher more than these orations, when he warned "corrupters of youth" of the "iron rod of vengeance" and the "appointed time of judgment."[132] Just as Edward was formulating his theory of "organic sin" in response to slavery, Henry likewise attacked the "economy of vice" overtaking the nation's youth.[133]

Back in Cincinnati, Catharine established herself as one of the most "public" women in the United States. Beginning in 1843, she published three subsequent works which codified the views of religion and womanhood that had slowly been incubating in her mind for two decades. In *Evils Suffered by American Women and American Children* (1843), Catharine railed against the fleets of male-led missionary groups and voluntary societies who ignored the needs of women and small children "growing up in heathenish darkness, enchained in ignorance" in their own backyard. She charged, "Where is there a single man sustained by Christian benevolence to operate on their behalf?"[134] The cause of women had been neglected. Catharine was *not* abandoning the voluntary model of her father. Rather, she argued that the "benevolent empire" did not go far enough. Her diatribe against the hypocrisies of men was a call to exert moral influence upon their fellow women, who would in turn shape the country with "the great power and influence they thus command." The destiny of America was tied to the destiny of women. Once the plight of women was improved and their potential unlocked, "a whole nation will have received its character and destiny from her hands."[135]

If *Evils Suffered by American Women* was an admonition for men to educate women, Catharine's next work, *The Duty of American Women to their Country* (1845), was a call for women to improve themselves. Women, especially affluent women, could not simply wait to be empowered; they were to empower others. Drawing from her father's doctrine of natural ability and his relentless evangelical preaching, Catharine reminded her female readers that they were the nation's only hope: "This is the way, and the *only way*, in which our nation can be saved from impending perils. Though we are now in such a condition that many have given over our case in despair, as too far gone for remedy—though the peril is immense, and the work to be done enormous, yet *it is in the power of American women to save their country.*" Catharine was preaching from a paper pulpit. Margaret Fuller, an editor at the *New York Tribune,* published her wildly successful *Woman in the Nineteenth Century* (1845) in the same year, arguing for complete equality with men. But Catharine's message was more evangelical and less egalitarian in purpose. Like her father, she believed that she could save America and indeed the world. To save America, Catharine had to convince others to change *themselves,* not just the laws of society. "All that is needed is a knowledge of the danger, and a faithful use of the means within their reach," she contended.[136] According to Catharine's moral gospel for America, salvation lay within. The following January, her sister Harriet made her own *cri de coeur* for the soul of America in a series in the *New-York Evangelist* entitled "What Will the American People Do?" According to Joan Hedrick, the articles, which pushed for Protestant education against the rising tide of Jesuits and Roman Catholic nuns in the West, were a "reminder of just how strong the family culture was."[137] Catharine was a chief developer of this culture.

The final treatise in Catharine's trilogy was *An Address to the Protestant Clergy of the United States* (1846), a republican rebuke of Protestant ministers who sought power over the public good. Not surprisingly, the solution to this problem was women's education. For Catharine, the most "distinctive peculiarity" of Christianity is "self-denying benevolence." This ethic alone could save the republic. To become self-sacrificial, women needed Protestantism. And to be good Protestants, they needed education. Historians Eleanor Flexner and Ellen Fitzpatrick, in their work on the woman's rights movement, *Century of Struggle,* judge that Catharine Beecher "was obsessed with the need for good teachers."[138] By 1846, education was for Catharine all-consuming because it was bound with her religion. In her view of the American destiny, education was salvation. Her clarion call for teachers was her evangelism to the nation. To establish proper institutions of education, America needed the Protestant clergy to stop acting like Catholics, so Catharine's logic went:

The indispensable condition of eternal life is *character,* and this character is secured only by *faith in Jesus Christ;* a faith that "works by love,"
and not by fear. "Now faith cometh by hearing, and hearing by the *word
of God.*" Hence the Bible is the gift of the Protestant church to *all the
people,* and with it, the education and intelligence needful to read and
understand. From this comes INDEPENDENCE OF MIND, and with it civil
and religious freedom, and ten thousand blessings in their train. From
this comes the fact, that the Protestant clergy hold their authority and
influence, only so long as they can maintain a reputation with *their people* for unblemished morals, intelligence, and piety. The Catholic priest
depends on the sanctity of his *office,* and on the blind submission of his
flock to the authority he administers.[139]

In Catharine's view, biblical education was a win-win for all Americans.
When Protestant ministers cultivated the minds of the people, they promoted the common good *and* their own job security. When they did not,
she argued, they undermined the republic. By tying Protestantism to the
ideal of freedom and Catholicism to "blind submission" to authority, Catharine was retooling her father's ideas for a more egalitarian purpose. Indeed, *An Address to the Protestant Clergy of the United States* illustrates
why historian Marie Caskey identified Catharine and Isabella, reformers of
very different stripes, as the so-called "moralists" of the family. "Both sisters
came to view religion in almost exclusively moral terms, as the stimulus to
right actions undertaken for disinterested (socially useful) reasons."[140] Although Catharine did not contend for woman's rights in its most extreme
form, her purpose for religion was no less political and utilitarian in nature.

Traditionally, historians have argued that the woman's rights movement
sprang from abolitionism, citing leaders like Angelina Grimké, Elizabeth
Cady Stanton, Susan B. Anthony, and other figures from the Seneca Falls
Conference in 1848.[141] However, Catharine Beecher provides a bit more
complexity to this narrative. Before Catharine advocated for the emancipation of slaves by abolitionists, she trumpeted the salvation of America by
women. She was pro-women and antislavery yet opposed to both woman's
rights and abolitionism, believing that, if women could be given the chance
to educate the masses, they could "preserve this nation" from the "fierce
contest on the subject of slavery, that internal cancer which inflames the

whole body politic!"[142] Catharine's path represented much of the progressive wing of American evangelicalism in the 1840s, willing to improve the plight of women's education but less willing to do so for Blacks, at least at first. For example, Oberlin was the very first college in the country to provide higher learning for *both* sexes at the same institution. However, of the thirty-eight women enrolled at the school in the summer of 1834, twenty-three had left by the time its first two Black students, Charles and Gideon Langston, arrived in the fall of 1835. Oberlinites were originally more accommodating of women than they were of Blacks. By the beginning of the Civil War, Oberlin educated more Black students than all other institutions of higher learning combined. But this was only after cofounders and trustees initially cried "Mad!" to the idea of interracial education. Change did not come all at once. The movement for women's education, pioneered by women like Catharine Beecher, laid a foundation for Black equality. "A key difference between Lane and Oberlin," historian John Frederick Bell has noted, "was the presence of women, a factor that amplified fears of race mixing."[143] Due to his own beliefs and his more conservative context, Lyman Beecher was willing to integrate races at Lane (that is, James Bradley) before he was willing to integrate Catharine's students with his own, a decision that Catharine never protested due to their similar hierarchical view of society.

As the nation barreled toward Civil War, the Beechers literally found themselves at the crossroads of controversy. In 1842, while traveling north from Cincinnati in his wagon before dawn, a farmer named John Van Zandt met nine Black people walking along the road. He offered them a ride and they accepted. A couple of hours later, two white men stopped Van Zandt and claimed that the Blacks were fugitive slaves from Kentucky. As they were being taken back, one from their group, a man named Andrew, fled into the woods. Their owner, Wharton Jones, sued Van Zandt for five hundred dollars in federal circuit court under the 1793 Fugitive Slave Act for loss of Andrew's services. Tried by local antislavery lawyer and family friend Salmon P. Chase, the case went to the Supreme Court, which eventually ruled that the Fugitive Slave Act was constitutional.[144] Chase was known in the Cincinnati area for defending fugitive slaves, as the city had become a major stop along the "Reverse Underground Railroad" and a testing ground for the Fugitive Slave Act.[145] It was also a proving ground for Harriet Beecher Stowe, who witnessed these injustices in the city and was now absolutely convinced of the evil of slavery, even assisting with her husband in the Underground Railroad.[146] In 1845, the same year that Salmon P. Chase was awarded a silver pitcher by local Black leaders in Cincinnati for defending a runaway slave named Samuel Watson, Harriet finally doffed the conservativism of her father and published her first antislavery story in the *New York Evangelist,* "Immediate Emancipation— A Sketch." It was an inflection point for her blossoming career as a writer and reformer.

In a scenario very familiar to anyone living in Cincinnati, Harriet's "Sketch" featured a slave named Sam who is sent by his southern master on an errand. When Sam does not return, his owner discovers he has run away with the help of a Quaker. Once the master tracks down Sam and his friendly accomplice, he is then persuaded by the Quaker that any man in Sam's condition would naturally desire to be free. Even if Sam lived well as his slave, through debt and resale Sam "may come to be a field hand, under hard masters, starved, beaten, overworked—such things do happen sometimes, do they not?"[147] As historian Joan D. Hedrick astutely observes, "This is, in a nutshell, the story of Uncle Tom."[148] The primary difference was that, unlike Mr. Shelby, this master acquiesced and freed his slave. Stowe claimed that she held an actual letter in which a master had wished his slave well. Nevertheless, the story was unmistakably birthed from Cincinnati's unique context, as Stowe recounted "literal matters of fact occurring in the city of Cincinnati, which have come within the scope of the writer's personal knowledge [and] have merely been clothed in a dramatic form, to present them more vividly for the reader."[149] If indeed the Fugitive Slave Act of 1850 was the impetus for *Uncle Tom's Cabin,* it was in fact the wrenching of families in Cincinnati under the Fugitive Slave Act of 1797 that set Harriet along the abolitionist path. Joan Hedrick summarizes: "In ways subtle and pervasive, the bordertown of Cincinnati, with its race riots, commercial trading, runaway slaves, disease, and death, and Walnut Hills, with its gardens, nurseries, and parlors, its poverty and its hopes for a better world, formed the tide-mud of 'the Real' out of which emerged Stowe's most powerful work of fiction."[150] She was the first Beecher woman to publicly defend immediate emancipation. Like her sister Catharine, she'd also found her pulpit. Noticing that her letters were "turning into sermons," she once boasted to her brother George, "I was made for a preacher."[151]

In 1846, the issue of slavery on the frontier finally ignited an actual war. After President James K. Polk annexed Mexican territory, Mexican forces killed eleven American soldiers during a skirmish on April 25, 1846. Polk asked Congress to declare war. A freshman congressman from Illinois, Abraham Lincoln, questioned Polk's claim that the war "shed American blood upon American soil."[152] He introduced so-called "spot resolutions," demanding to know the exact spot where blood was spilled, but to no avail.[153] Congress granted Polk his declaration. To most New Englanders, and to the Beechers, the Mexican War was a war of aggression, a shameless maneuver by the Slave Power to extend slavery territory west. A young Transcendentalist author named Henry David Thoreau was so disgusted by the naked self-interest that he refused to pay taxes in protest of the war and was taken to jail. Although opposed to Polk's agenda, the Beechers were not concerned with resolutions or civil disobedience, but with moral influence. (Lyman bemoaned "the shameless infidel fanaticism of the transcendental party.")[154] In that year, Lyman traveled to England to deliver lectures on temperance, forty years after his "Sermon on Dueling" in East Hampton launched his national platform as a moral crusader.[155] In early 1847, with the help of Vermont governor William Slade, Catharine organized her first group of "missionary teachers" for the West, most from New England, dispatching half to Indiana and half to Illinois.[156] Although less convinced of evangelical religion than she had ever been, Catharine was determined to implement her father's evangelical strategy for redeeming the nation. Her "plan to educate the children of the West with missionary teachers was directly modeled upon her father's efforts to train ministers for the West."[157]

As Beechers looked west, they were also heading east. In 1847, with soaring popularity and flocks of new listeners, Henry left Indianapolis to become the pastor of the prosperous Plymouth Church in Brooklyn, New York. His departure signaled a transition from the frontier that would soon pull almost all the Beechers east with him. In these days, with nearly all of Lyman's children out of the house, the old patriarch grew lonely in his empty estate at Walnut Hills. Lyman Beecher had been largely ignored by his own father. He had also buried two wives. Therefore, that his identity was partially wrapped up in his children is more than understandable. In the mid-1840s, without the strength of his children, the so-called "Great Gun of Calvinism" had become a bit more delicate and even helpless. Thomas recalled:

I remember that father's income had ceased. He was living by gifts literally. Every morning at prayer he would pray for the needed supplies, and in phrases of varied simplicity speak forth our Lord's suggestion, "Give us this day our daily bread." One morning, after I had brought him the mail, I came back to the study and found him tear-blind, and trying to explain a letter in his hand. "Tom, you can get some boots now—here's some money; and your mother can get you a vest from —— (whose slightly-worn wardrobe had kept me clothed at second-hand for years); and *now* you'll stay with me."[158]

In old age, Lyman was still a man of faith, believing that God would provide for his every need. Yet even his love for his son was not completely disinterested. Lyman could give away his money, but he could not seem to let go of his sons. As Thomas was preparing to leave for Illinois College, Lyman implored him with a cracking voice, "Tom, I love you; you mustn't go 'way and leave me. They're all gone—Jim's at college. I want one chicken under my wing." This was perhaps Lyman Beecher at his neediest. Thomas nevertheless remained under the power of guilt, adding, "Of course I staid by until I left with a blessing."[159]

When Thomas finally left for college, Lyman got a dog named Trip to keep him company in the house. He kept a comb in his pocket to groom his new best friend. Thomas recalled, years later, "Visiting home during one of my school vacations (1847), I found father at last without a child to love or govern, and it seemed to me that his long-trained faculty was keeping itself fresh in training a very stubborn and active terrier named Trip. Trip had taken my place in the study and by the table. At every interval of rest from writing, father would talk a word or two to Trip."[160] Walnut Hills still had a bit of energy left. Although he learned how to say goodbye to his sons, Lyman would always long for companionship. In 1847, when he learned that Thomas had begun attending an Episcopal Church during his time in Philadelphia, he charged his son, "Tom . . . your mother loved the Episcopal Church. . . . She was a good woman. The Episcopal Church is as good as any. Go there, if you can do any good by going; I have no objection at all; only, whatever Church you go to, be a Christian and work."[161] This was, in essence, the heart of Beecherism: a broad evangelical identity defined by orthopraxy, not orthodoxy. Ultimately, with the help of his wife's ghost, Lyman Beecher held his children closer than his doctrine. The man who once tried to read "Sinners in the Hands of an Angry God" to his wife Roxana had mellowed with age.[162] Lyman did not remember that Roxana, the former Episcopalian, was not actually Thomas's mother. That was his second wife, Harriet. Nevertheless, with the memory he still had, he remembered to pass on the only immutable Beecher creed: to "be a Christian and work."

Chapter 4

SHALL WE COMPROMISE? (1847–1857)

BY THE LATE 1840s, the Beechers were no longer facing westward. But they were still looking into the future. When Henry departed in 1847 for Brooklyn, arguably the fastest-growing city in America, he left on the very first train to ever leave Indianapolis, on the Madison and Indianapolis Railroad. He had arrived on the frontier in the age of the steamboat, and he was leaving at the beginning of the railroad era.[1] Two years later, when Plymouth Church burned down in the dead of winter (oddly enough, just like Lyman's in 1830), Henry oversaw the construction of a new kind of church building. "I want the audience to surround me," he told the architect, "so that I shall be in the centre of the crowd, and have the people surge all about me." Shedding his pulpit for a platform, Henry was helping to usher in the dawn of the attraction-style megachurch.[2] Catharine was also a trailblazer in her field. In 1847, with the encouragement of education reformer Horace Mann, she founded the Central Committee for Promoting National Education, an organization designed to "save" the nation by sending out hundreds of female missionary teachers into the American West. The ambitious project signaled a shift in the teaching profession for the next forty years in American life, as women slowly replaced men in the classroom.[3] In the vanguard of nineteenth-century social movements, the Beechers had the unique distinction of being *behind* the most progressive leaders in American reform yet still *ahead* of the times. Even Harriet, not yet of international fame, was part of a new cadre of mostly educated women beginning to publish short stories and other works of fiction, promoted by groups like the Semi-Colon Club. While not the first woman to write tales and parables for the American public, she would soon become the face of the movement.

As a relatively young nation, the United States was still a land bursting with energy and idealism. In his celebrated essay "Self-Culture" (1838), Unitarian William Ellery Channing typified the confidence of the age when he adjured his readers, "You cannot, without guilt and disgrace, stop where you are. The past and the present call on you to advance. Let what you have gained be an impulse toward something higher."[4] Americans in the 1840s were generally a forward-looking people, but the future seemed less certain than it had only two or three decades before. Sparking an Adventist movement known as "Millerism," Baptist minister William Miller famously predicted that the Lord would return in 1843.[5] Unfortunately for the Millerites, he did not. Nevertheless, after the "Great Disappointment," a millennial expectation in America steadily grew. In 1848, the Mexican War officially ended with the Treaty of Guadalupe Hidalgo, ceasing an unpopular conflict that had claimed the lives of thousands of America's sons, including Henry Clay Jr. Meanwhile, slavery, the issue largely believed to have started the war, was still unsettled. Texas remained a slave state. In August, the Free-Soil Party was born, cofounded by Beecher family friend Salmon P. Chase. As Edward Beecher lamented, "Good men are at this day as really and as thoroughly divided against good men as they ever were."[6]

Charles Beecher saw war on the horizon. After witnessing the atrocities of the slave plantations in New Orleans, he returned with a new abolitionist spirit. In a May letter to his sister Harriet, who was editing a series of lectures he was about to publish, Charles prophesied, "Tell father that the great tribulation is begun. This guilty land will not escape." Drawing from the Book of Revelation, he painted a grim, apocalyptic picture of the end of days: "The Woman will first ride the Democratic beast & become drunk with blood. Then she herself will be destroyed. Democracy become Anarchy, & universal confederacy against God. Antichrist will rise to the surface, & ride on the foam-wave, & then will come the End.—Father may not live to see it. But I for one expect either to die by violence or to live in the fastnesses & retreats of the forest.—The plot is laid. The explosion will come soon."[7] The postmillennialism of the older generation—the Edwardsean belief that American advancements in science, education, politics, and technology would introduce a golden age under the reign of Jesus Christ—was gradually being exchanged for a less sanguine view of history. Even Lyman Beecher, the man who epitomized the optimism of the infant nation, had lost some of his former excitement about the future. In a letter on April 30 to his sister Esther, who was visiting Charles at his new church in Fort Wayne, Lyman confided, "This winter, for the first time since I had children, I have been without one at home, or near me, and really good as my wife is, it will seem lonely, and makes time often hang heavy on my spirits."[8] In the twilight of his career, with his fame and prestige eroding and his strength diminishing, Lyman Beecher was unable to summon his ebullient spirit as quickly as he once had. But he continued to hope for the best. "Come and let us pray together," he insisted to Esther, "and give thanks together for what the Lord has done for us, and, if the Lord will, come to be no more separated from me till he shall call us home to be reunited to those happy spirits, Roxana, Mary Hubbard, Harriet Porter, George Beecher, and the multitude with whom we have taken sweet counsel in joy and sorrow, and Sabbath worship, and missions, and revivals, which have filled up so many of our days."[9]

When gold was discovered in California in 1848, it seemed to vindicate the notion of "manifest destiny," a phrase coined by newspaper editor John O'Sullivan to describe the sense of divine progress and western expansion that seized Americans during this epoch of history.[10] However, for a people of destiny, the future had become increasingly difficult to square with the American past. For proslavery politicians like U.S. senator Stephen Douglas of Illinois, the Missouri Compromise of 1820 was a roadblock to progress, as it did not allow for slavery in western territories north of the 36° 30' line (and prevented him from securing a railroad through his state). As a result, the "little Giant" introduced the Kansas-Nebraska Bill of 1854, which would overturn the compromise and allow for the Kansas and Nebraska territories to decide for themselves on the slavery issue. Conversely, for antislavery moral influencers like William Lloyd Garrison, the U.S. Constitution itself was a barrier to abolition, as it neither promoted nor proscribed the institution of slavery. Consequently, in a radical act of defiance in 1854, Garrison publicly burned a copy of the Constitution. Drawing from Isaiah 28, he called the founding document a "covenant with death" and an "agreement with hell."[11]

Indeed, Americans in the 1850s were a Janus-faced people, looking backward *and* forward in the same moment, attempting to reconcile the present with the past. Nothing would evoke this national schizophrenia more than the Fugitive Slave Law of 1850, a draconian measure which permitted slaveholders to capture suspected runaway slaves and return them to the South without due process of law. Invoking the Fugitive Slave Law of 1793, the new law gave the federal government the power and the responsibility to oversee the retrieval of the enslaved, forcing free states to be complicit in the great southern evil. Chained to a barbaric past, the future of the infant nation had never seemed so precarious. In one of the most tumultuous chapters of American history, the Beechers were progressive enough to become some of the loudest voices in the growing choir of abolitionism yet conservative enough to entice the listening ears of an evangelical audience. Lyman Beecher's children still believed that America had a "moral destiny." However, if the United States was to be born again, it would need to be a New School rebirth: being made new without completely destroying the old.

"CITY OF CHURCHES"

When Henry Ward Beecher arrived in Brooklyn in the fall of 1847, it had already become the fourth largest city in America, doubling in size to eighty thousand in less than a decade. Removed from the hustle and bustle of Manhattan, Brooklyn was a sprawling bedroom community for those who wished to escape the commercial world of Wall Street. The market revolution had produced the age of the suburb. In contrast with the secularized society across the East River, Brooklyn boasted a distinct religious culture.[12] Nicknamed the "City of Churches," by 1855 the city was home to over 130 congregations from virtually all denominations.[13] The relationship between Manhattan and Brooklyn was thus mutually beneficial. Whereas curious Brooklynites could ferry across to Manhattan to enjoy the forbidden fruits of theater and music, work-weary Manhattanites could visit Brooklyn to hear some of the best preaching in the United States. In the frenetic metropolis of New York City, one did not need a map to locate Henry's Plymouth Church. To find it, Manhattanites joked, "just follow the crowd."[14] In just a couple of years at Plymouth, the silver-tongued Henry Ward Beecher, with his unorthodox style and his father's crisp delivery, became a phenomenon. Thousands of curious New Yorkers flocked to see the New England preacher with the flair of a western revivalist. The bravado of the frontier had come to the financial district.

Beecher's *extempore* style, dispensing with his notes during sermons, appealed to a wide array of churchgoers, from the businessman to the politician to the chimney sweep. One observer called him a combination of Saint Paul and P. T. Barnum.[15] To some New Englanders, Beecher's fresh, and at times feverish, approach was distasteful. Theodore Parker, who had once attended Lyman Beecher's church in Boston and mocked his homespun style, likewise balked at his son: "he is eternally young, and positively wears me out with his redundant, super-abundant, ever-recovering and ever-renewing energy."[16] However, to thousands more, Henry Ward Beecher was captivating. Among those Brooklynites who deeply admired Beecher was a young journalist and aspiring poet named Walt Whitman. The moralistic reformer wrote, "The Plymouth Church, the new place of worship where Mr. Beecher officiates, is one of the amplest in the United States, and is always filled with a congregation when the pastor preaches."[17] Whitman was among those who ferried across to Manhattan to watch the theater, a particular activity of which Henry did not approve. Nevertheless, what appealed to Whitman the most about Beecher was that he seemed so unclerical. "It was only fair to say of Beecher that he was not a minister," Whitman deduced. "There was so much of him man there was little left of him to be minister."[18] In Brooklyn's religious marketplace, Henry offered something more than the typical Sunday morning experience. After attending Plymouth Church one Sunday, Catharine reported to her father that Henry had delivered one of the most inspired sermons she had ever heard.[19]

On one hand, Beecher was not the only New York preacher with an unconventional style. Across the river in Manhattan, the arch-revivalist Charles Grandison Finney attracted thousands at Broadway Tabernacle, a church financed by Arthur and Lewis Tappan and other wealthy New York businessmen like William Green and Isaac Dimond. Built according to Finney's own specifications, the circular auditorium allowed him to look virtually every listener in the eye.[20] However, in the wake of the Old School–New School conflict, accusations of heresy plagued Finney, prompting him to leave the Presbyterian Church. Eventually resigning his pastorate in 1837 to move to abolitionist Oberlin College, Finney was as divisive as he was magnetic.[21] Henry Ward Beecher, however, possessed his father's ability to reform certain aspects of evangelical religion while avoiding the stigma of fanaticism. "Henry was no wild-eyed radical," notes Debby Applegate. "He was too much of a Beecher for that."[22] At Plymouth, Beecher innovated *within* the bounds of orthodoxy. At Andover Theological Seminary, Professor E. A. Park wrote to the president of Harvard that Beecher "is, 'for substance of doctrine,' orthodox. He has an immense power over the *people* and he is *read* by the learned."[23] Beecherism transcended classes and creeds. For Walt Whitman, an anticlerical, Quaker-influenced, anti-abolitionist, progressive Democrat, Beecher was a spectacle to behold. After listening to one of Beecher's sermons in 1849, Whitman wrote, "He hit me so hard, fascinated me to such a degree that I was afterwards willing to go far out of my way to hear him talk."[24] In an era of urbanization and increasing mobilization in American life, Henry Ward Beecher maximized the scope of his influence by building an "auditorium" that seated over two thousand people and injecting a bit of Broadway into the pulpit. In 1852, Ralph Waldo Emerson listed Beecher among the four most powerful and virtuous men in the country, alongside Horace Greeley, Theodore Parker, and Horace Mann.[25]

Henry Ward Beecher was not overly concerned about theological precision. "To the extent that he had a theology," summarizes Gary Dorrien, "Beecher preached a watered-down New School revivalism rooted in his belief in the love and righteousness of God, the regenerative influence of Christ, and the moral capacity of human beings to turn from sin."[26] But Henry still believed in being careful. Although Plymouth Church was slowly swinging in the antislavery direction by the time Beecher arrived, it was still opposed to abolitionism. Slavery was still a volatile issue in the North. Consequently, William G. McLoughlin explains, "Beecher quickly developed a marvelous facility for threading his way among diverse views and yet seeming to be uncompromisingly dedicated to liberty and equality." In short, Henry knew how to speak out of both sides of his mouth. As McLoughlin notes, Beecher's primary approach to ministry can best be described as "moral suasion."[27] In a nation fractured over theology and politics, and in a city with several different social classes, basic moralism was Henry Ward Beecher's Nicene Creed. "In so far as individual men are concerned," he preached, "religion aims first and mainly at the production of character."[28] In fact, by the late 1840s, almost *all* the Beechers were adapting their ideas about religion to the orthodoxy of human freedom and character formation.

THE BIBLE AND SLAVERY

Henry had once coached Charles through his ordination exam, teaching his younger brother how to be sufficiently vague enough to navigate the maze of questions about the freedom of the will and other points of Presbyterian dogma.[29] However, by 1847, in his new post in Fort Wayne, Charles had developed a penchant for heterodoxy that Lyman and Henry were trying to keep under wraps. For Charles's ordination exam in the New School Assembly, Henry encouraged him to keep things "practical" and "popular." But Charles had already earned a reputation around Fort Wayne as a quasi, if not full-blown, heretic. Local Old Schoolers labeled Second Presbyterian as a group of Unitarians, and Charles was branded as "unsound" in his beliefs.[30] In 1846, Charles published *The Bible a Sufficient Creed,* a philippic against dogmatic, creedal religion. Demonstrating an inveterate Beecher hostility to the Roman Catholic Church, "mother of harlots," Charles also took aim at the *Westminster Confession:* "Three hundred and twenty-five years were necessary to produce the Nicene creed; but it took one Protestant denomination only forty years to turn what their own Assembly scouted as an unwarrantable imposition, into an iron rule. This shows the rapid movement of Protestant apostacy."[31] Not surprisingly, the work did not go over well with Presbyterians. Charles no longer subscribed to any interpretation of the Bible other than his own. His commitment to human freedom was sacrosanct.

Likewise, one year earlier, Charles stood with other New School ministers in urging the General Assembly to denounce slavery as a sin. He now saw the Old School–New School in more black-and-white terms. "Old School theology enthrones a great slave-holder over the universe; New School enthrones a great Emancipator."[32] In May 1847, he stepped out even further. In a letter to the *Fort Wayne Sentinel,* Charles expressed concern over the condition of African Americans in Indiana. While commending his fellow ministers in the local presbytery who had recently passed two antislavery resolutions, Charles wished they would have passed a third: "Resolved, that the disenfranchisement of free people of color as practiced in the state of Indiana is a crime analogous to that of slavery." Charles's letter was a sharp rebuke to his fellow midwesterners and northerners who prided themselves on their antislavery politics. The letter helped gain Charles a nationwide reputation for abolitionism, attracting the attention of a prominent antislavery Congregationalist church in Washington, DC, funded by Lewis Tappan.[33] But Charles did not accept the position, more than likely because he feared that they would not tolerate his radical ideas about the Bible and creeds. For Charles, almost any external religious structure was tantamount to Roman Catholicism: "The creed system is now exerting upon the clergy of the Protestant churches, a secret, unsuspected, but tremendous power against the Bible—a power of *fear*."[34] Although Catharine and Harriet have traditionally been highlighted as the first in the family to officially depart from evangelicalism, joining the Episcopal Church, Charles was in fact the first Beecher to make such a public leap from Presbyterian doctrine. Although he did not leave the denomination of his father, his distaste for Old School hypocrisy had now become a repudiation of traditional Protestantism. He insisted that "liberty of opinion in our Theological Seminaries, is a mere form."[35]

Within the Beecher family, Charles's ideas were still eccentric. Even Edward was concerned. In a twenty-five-page letter, he argued with Charles about the sentiments espoused in the book.[36] In many ways, Edward understood Charles's internal conflict more than most. Edward was formulating his own attenuation of Presbyterianism, seeking to reconcile the justice of God with original sin. Like Charles, he did not find his answer in the *Westminster Confession*. Instead, he engineered a brand-new doctrine on the preexistence of the soul. On the outside, the Beechers were seeking to rectify human bondage inside a free society. On the inside, they were seeking to reconcile the Calvinist faith of their father with the republican notion of freedom. Lyman himself had found the answer to this problem in Nathaniel Taylor's New Haven Theology. However, by the 1840s, *all* of Lyman's children had abandoned their father's Calvinism for the sake of continuing his project of moral influence.

Technically speaking, neither Catharine nor Harriet was the first to join the Episcopal Church. Jaded by the Old School–New School controversy, twenty-two-year-old Thomas had become so disillusioned with formal religion that he rejected nearly all forms of spiritual authority. As principal of Northeast Boys' Grammar School in Philadelphia, he began attending the local Episcopal church, preferring its style of worship and even joining the choir. He was allergic to the rigid liturgy of the Presbyterians. Writing somewhat fearfully to his father, he confessed that he had *not* joined a church because he did not believe *any* creed or confession to be true. Furthermore, he regarded the Bible as a "sealed book" and no longer bothered to read it. For Thomas, the essence of Christianity was love, not law. "I shall always love Christ—love my parents & friends—& shall always wish to love—& make a friend of every man I meet & associate with."[37] With Lyman's reluctant approval, Thomas eventually joined the Episcopal Church, but not for long. Although he escaped the guilt-inducing tendrils of his father, Thomas had not gone far enough to evade Lyman's vigilance entirely. Nearby Third Presbyterian was pastored by Rev. Thomas Brainerd, who had served as co-pastor with Lyman Beecher at Cincinnati's Second Church from 1833 to 1837. Brainerd had supported Thomas's father through his heresy trial, and he now supported Thomas in Philadelphia.[38] While away from the city, Brainerd opened his home to the young Beecher. Thomas stayed with Brainerd's wife, Mary, and befriended Brainerd's family. Quite naturally, Thomas Beecher then joined Third Presbyterian Church, also known as Old Pine Street Church. But his religious skepticism remained.

Finally, in 1848, Thomas discovered a brand of religion that satisfied his emotional hunger and suited his beliefs about education and the importance of the family. Leaving Philadelphia, he moved to Hartford, Connecticut, to serve as principal of a public high school. Staying with the Hookers and Perkinses, he was still ensconced in the Beecher network. While in Hartford, Thomas was introduced to Horace Bushnell, pastor of North Congregational Church and the man widely regarded as the father of American religious liberalism. For the next two years, Bushnell became Thomas's mentor and close friend. According to Myra C. Glenn, "The Hartford years, then, were a watershed in Beecher's life."[39] Influenced by English Romanticist Samuel Coleridge, Bushnell believed the essence of religion lay not in cold, lifeless doctrines but in knowledge based on intuition. Rather than adhering to a strict, literal theological system, Bushnell believed that all religious language was metaphorical. With an emphasis on religious emotion and practical Christian living, Bushnell was not unlike most of the Beecher children by mid-century. "He was both a Yankee and a Puritan," describes historian Robert Bruce Mullin, "a Yankee in his love of innovation, a Puritan in his abiding trust in the values he first learned as a child in Connecticut."[40] No wonder he attracted the attention of the Beechers. In particular, what impressed Tom and his sister Mary in 1848 was Bushnell's concept of Christian nurture.[41]

A year before Thomas arrived in Hartford, Bushnell's *Discourses on Christian Nurture* appeared, offering a rebuttal to American revivalism with the central idea that Christian formation was a formative process, not a dramatic decision. Acknowledging the "social power" of the church and seeking to recover a Puritan vision of the Christian home, Bushnell contended that revivalism was too fleeting and too impotent to effect lasting moral change. "Never is it too early for good to be communicated," Bushnell insisted. "Infancy and childhood are the ages most pliant to good. And who can think it necessary that the plastic nature of childhood must first be hardened into stone, and stiffened into enmity towards God and all duty, before it can become a candidate for Christian character!"[42] For Thomas, who nursed a quiet resentment against the authority of his father, one of the most famous revivalists in America, Bushnell's gospel was a welcome alterative to the pressure-packed, decisionistic culture in which he had been raised. After reading *Christian Nurture*, he remarked, "Mr. Bushnell has got hold of the life of religion."[43] Christianity was something which should be fostered gradually and lovingly, not by manipulation or force, he reasoned. As one of the major ideas to spawn the Christian education movement in the United States, Christian nurture breathed life into Thomas's vision of the home and school as the primary loci for developing a child's faith and instilling Christian values.[44]

Bushnell's concept of "organic unity" in the family only bolstered Thomas Beecher's commitment to moral influence, as it established that a parent could "teach, encourage, persuade, and govern" a child "prior to the age of reason and deliberative choice."[45] In other words, Christian nurture *increased* the potential for moral influence. To a degree, in a house filled with "moral energy" and family discussions, the Beecher children had been raised in a home that Bushnell was describing. Bushnell was also a defender of their political values, once describing Andrew Jackson's ultrademocratic ideas as "Gospel Jacobinism."[46] Regardless, Bushnell's attack upon revivalism left Lyman Beecher suspicious of his fellow Puritan. In 1849, when Bushnell published his controversial *God in Christ,* his local association selected five clergymen to examine the soundness of his views. Two of these ministers, Noah Porter and Joel Hawes, were good friends with Lyman Beecher. Although the report vindicated Bushnell, it still left doubt as to the actual orthodoxy of *God in Christ.* Consequently, Lyman requested that Bushnell make a summary statement of his beliefs about the Trinity, the atonement, justification, and the doctrine of Christ.[47] Upon this summary, the association would make its final judgment of Bushnell. Coming from a man who had been asked to summarize his *own* views in writing, Lyman's request was motivated at least in part by his alertness to Bushnell's sway over his own children. With his pulpit gone and his ministry fading, Lyman still knew an influencer when he saw one. He was also a keen judge of his children's thoughts. Although the Hartford clergy ruled that the book contained "dangerous errors," Bushnell was acquitted of heresy. Nevertheless, if Lyman was worried that his children were drifting in a more liberal direction under the guidance of Bushnell, he was right. On March 5, 1849, Thomas joined Bushnell's North Congregational Church. Bushnell also preached at Thomas's ordination in June of 1851, later exchanging pulpits with him.[48] In 1849, Bushnell was even present at Henry's examination in Brooklyn, although Henry was not quite as taken with the Hartford minister as his younger brother. Freeing the church from the shackles of monkish dogma, Bushnell also helped free some of the younger Beechers from the burden of orthodoxy.

THE YOUNGEST BEECHER

With striking blue eyes and a pugilistic personality, James Chaplin Beecher (1828–1886) had every bit of the youngest-child syndrome. He was generally regarded as the handsomest of the Beecher children and was often pampered for that very reason.[49] As a result, he was also the unhappiest. When he was suspended from Dartmouth in 1845 for assaulting another student, the president of the school arraigned Beecher as "rude, ungoverned . . . [and] impatient of discipline."[50] Lyman himself compared James to a volcano.[51] In many ways, James Beecher was more western than eastern.

Born twenty-seven years after his oldest sibling and twelve years after Roxana's youngest child, James was raised in a home with less Yankee strictness than the older Beecher children. His own mother, Harriet Porter, had passed away when he was only seven years old. By the time he graduated from Dartmouth in 1848 (due largely to his Beecher name), his half-sister Harriet had just given birth to her sixth child, Samuel Charles, "in remembrance of the beauty story of Samuel in the Old Testament—'Long as he liveth he shall be lent to the Lord.'"[52] However, in the late 1840s, James appeared less like a prophet and more like a Philistine.

By the time his last son went to college, Lyman Beecher had mastered the art of using guilt to motivate his younger children. For example, Thomas had been induced to stay longer at Walnut Hills by his father's pitiful pleas for companionship. And Lyman could employ this method from hundreds of miles away. Writing to his sister Esther in Indiana, he sulked, "Love to all at Fort Wayne. Ask Charles why he don't write to me in my lonely, childless state—that old gentleman that rode seventy miles in twenty hours to see him safely launched in ministry."[53] Lyman's technique of laying guilt upon his children was also a kind of moral influence. As James continued his spree of unholy behavior in New Hampshire, Lyman resorted to an extreme form of emotional manipulation, writing to his youngest son that, if he could not begin "mending his ways," his father's health would precipitously decline.[54] In other words, if James did not straighten up at school, he would inadvertently kill his father. This proved to be an effective, albeit shameless, tactic because James's performance at Dartmouth improved. But James also had help from his siblings. Taking it upon himself to mentor his younger brother, Thomas invited James to Philadelphia one summer so that he could "build up a Christian character in him—at least as much, as good as my own." After James returned to college, Thomas was conflicted. He wrote to his father that James owed him $110 and that his brother was "a singularly deceived & disproportionately noble man."[55] In short, James had admirable qualities about him, but he was hard to love. In this sense, the youngest Beecher, James, was not unlike the oldest Beecher, Catharine, who was founding a national organization for teachers at the same time that James was testing the patience of his. (After establishing the "Central Committee" with former Vermont governor William Slade as its secretary and general agent, Catharine eventually became dissatisfied with the organization and cut ties with Slade, who renamed the organization "The National Board of Popular Education.") Like Catharine, James was gritty but not always agreeable.[56]

After graduating from Dartmouth, James decided he would no longer be subject to his father's—or anyone else's—control. Like the prophet Jonah fleeing on a boat to Tarshish, the impulsive, twenty-one-year-old Beecher declared that he was shipping out to the Orient, the farthest place he could imagine from the life he knew. Not surprisingly, Lyman did not approve. But James didn't care. He wanted to be a sailor. During his days in Boston, Henry Ward had once dreamed of becoming a sailor, too, only to be cunningly convinced by his father that commodores must be college-educated. But James already had his degree. College had not extinguished his gypsy spirit. Thomas described his younger brother as someone who excelled in wickedness and who possessed a "sad proclivity toward vulgarity—bestiality." In effect, he already had a sailor's mouth. Probably for this reason, Thomas supported James's decision to leave for the Pacific. After all, where else could such a tempestuous soul be calmed but on the raging seas? Thomas urged his father and his brother Henry—the two patriarchs of the family—to approve of James's plan. A voyage of this sort could be "good medicine" for a restless youth, he interceded. The time away at sea could also allow James to "cut loose from the family restraints, only to find more inexorable ones in the dealings of Providence with him." James was in God's hands. According to historian Myra C. Glenn, this was an unexpected move on Thomas's part:

> It is surprising that Thomas supported James's request to become a sailor. The life of a seaman in the nineteenth century was a very difficult one, characterized by poor living conditions, harsh punishments, and rigorous labor. Seamen also had an unsavory reputation in mid-nineteenth-century America. . . . Henry and especially Lyman were understandably reluctant to let James become a sailor. Thomas's support of James's desire to ship off to sea seems all the more surprising in light of the family's misgivings about James's plan. No doubt Thomas's resentment of James's continued dependence on him played a role in his support of the latter's desire to go to sea. Perhaps Thomas viewed James's sea voyage as a way to get rid of him and the emotional

and financial burden that he represented. Yet Thomas's advocacy of James's plan to go to sea was also motivated by a genuine concern for his brother. . . . Having struggled so hard to achieve his own independence from the family nest, Thomas well understood how painful and difficult the process of achieving autonomy from Lyman could be.[57]

Thomas did not care for James's profane language or his sordid way of life. In fact, after Isabella saw her brother in the summer of 1852, she confessed to her husband that James was "an odd fish & troubles me continually."[58] Nevertheless, in 1849, Thomas was an advocate for James to his father. Lyman Beecher had a way of pushing his children away from himself and *toward* one another. Although Thomas and James did not agree on much, Lyman's two youngest sons both believed in the right to choose one's "moral destiny." As thousands of Americans flooded California to strike gold, James headed to San Francisco to seek his own independence. For the next five years, Lyman Beecher's *second* prodigal son worked on clipper ships in the East India trade, first as a seaman and then as an officer.[59] Lyman had taken his entire family west only to watch his youngest son go further west, and farther away from his family, than he ever imagined.

With the anxiety of an older sister, Isabella wrote of James, "I wish I could forget him or he could annihilate himself for five years or more—if he would then come out strait & good. I can't tell where the fault is—but somehow I don't love him much—or any body else, who is always ridiculing every body & every thing." She finally concluded, "If it were not for my Mother, I could shirk him entirely—& find perfect rest & comfort in my own husband & children. But I am haunted with the . . . responsibility that she laid on me in regard to my brothers—I am so thankful Tom is moored at last."[60] Indeed, it would take more than five years for James to come out "strait & good." Before he could find his moorings in the family establishment, he wandered the turbulent seas of drunkenness and made a shipwreck of his faith, the two great Beecher apostasies.

THE COMPROMISE OF 1850

In a troupe of pastors, teachers, writers, and moral reformers (and sailors), there were virtually no politicians. Thomas ran for numerous political offices in the 1880s, primarily under the Greenback and then Prohibition parties, but he never won an election. He once joked that he was the most nominated but least elected candidate.[61] Only one member of the family was ever voted into public office, but it was suspiciously brief. In a bid to vindicate himself after being convicted of heresy in 1864, Charles ran for the Massachusetts General Assembly in the same year. As moral influencers, the Beechers believed the best way to bring about lasting change in American society was by persuasion, not by legislation. The human heart had to be convinced, not coerced. Although the Beechers never completely shed their New England Federalist way of thinking about the social order, before 1850 they often distrusted those who became too engrossed in politics. In May of 1847, as Presbyterians in Ohio became increasingly fractured along theological and political lines, Lyman wrote to his son William, urging him to attend the next Ohio Assembly. "South and West slaveholders in civil matters are mad," he scoffed, "and the clergy are bound hand and foot to their chariot-wheels, drive they never so furiously."[62] As soldiers in the army of God, ministers were not to become overly entangled in civilian affairs, especially in defense of slavery. Leading up to the 1848 election for the Indiana seat in the House of Representatives, Charles, now a strident abolitionist, reminded his congregants in Fort Wayne that Christians were not obligated to vote for either Whigs *or* Democrats. In the spring he reported to the American Home Missionary Society, "Moral influences came to a head in that year tendi[n]g to drive me away. Odd fellowship, Sons of Temperance, Infidelity, and Universalism, had all received rebuke, & grown restive. Politics also had felt a little sore."[63] Committed to the seminal idea of human potential, the Beechers believed that reform, not political bickering, was the spirit of their age. Henry declared, "The questions of our day are questions of . . . progress of reforms. The spirit of our people and, I think, God may say *the public spirit* of the world, is for amelioration and expansion and growth toward individual and social excellence."[64]

But as so many already knew by 1850, the Beechers were certainly not anti-political. They were, in fact, political creatures. In the mid-nineteenth century, religion and politics were alchemized together, and neither would ever be the same. As some historians have shown, America was arguably more "evangelical" on the eve of the Civil War than at any time in its history.[65] This meteoric rise in evangelical religion was due in large part to

Lyman Beecher and his children, who canvassed half of the infant nation during the Second Great Awakening attempting to proselytize town after town with their gospel of anti-drink, anti-theater, anti-gambling, anti-Catholic and eventually antislavery reform. Even Whig politicians sometimes felt the weight of the Beechers' outspoken moralism. When Henry Clay—the son of a Baptist preacher from Virginia—ran against Democrat James K. Polk for the presidency in 1844, Lyman Beecher strongly disapproved. Although a leading Whig, Clay had violated one of the most fundamental laws of Beecherism. In 1838, Clay helped his fellow Kentuckian, Rep. William Graves, compose a formal challenge to a duel with Rep. Jonathan Cilley of Maine. Graves killed Cilley on the third shot. On top of the cacophony of Democrats who branded Clay as "the murderer of the lamented Cilley," Beecher protested Clay's selection as the Whig candidate, claiming that Clay's hands were stained with blood. "The duellist is a murderer," he declared unequivocally, summoning the spirit of the young firebrand who had once denounced Aaron Burr for killing Alexander Hamilton in 1804.[66] From the wrath of Lyman Beecher, no politician was safe. In fact, in 1850, Clay managed to awaken the fiery judgment of the entire Beecher family.

After the Mexican War, the future of the American West was unclear. The slavery question appeared more volatile than ever, "tied as it was to the nature of . . . expansion," but America's recently inaugurated president, Zachary Taylor, did not push for the expansion of slavery.[67] Unlike Old Tippecanoe, "Old Rough and Ready" was an *actual* war hero, having won a series of battles against formidable Mexican forces. Born in Virginia and raised in Kentucky, Taylor was the owner of a Louisiana plantation with 145 enslaved persons, yet he was also a Whig. Before he could act on the issue, Taylor died of acute gastroenteritis on July 9, 1850, four months after his inauguration. He was succeeded by Millard Fillmore, the *last* Whig president in American history. To a degree, the Whig Party was a microcosm of the Union itself, splintering over the issue of slavery yet unable to overcome sectional interests. In the eyes of many, the illustrious Henry Clay was poised to once again stave off catastrophe. Whig Horace Greeley's *New York Tribune* had asked in 1848, "Who . . . is better prepared to . . . safely guide the Ship of State beyond the reach of the impending storm than Henry Clay?"[68] Indeed, Clay genuinely desired to save the Union, as he ostensibly had in 1820 with the so-called Missouri Compromise and again in 1833 with the compromise tariff that ended South Carolina's nullification crisis. Yet, as much as these achievements redounded to his legacy as the "Great Pacificator," Clay was also a Kentuckian at heart.

Although Clay had lambasted the Mexican War as a "war of aggression" and prioritized unionism over states' rights, he was still a slaveholder who opposed immediate emancipation.[69] Despite the political diversity in the Bluegrass state, the Ohio River between Clay's Kentucky and Harriet Beecher Stowe's Ohio (the same river crossed so precariously by Eliza in *Uncle Tom's Cabin*) had become a liminal space between North and South, antislavery and proslavery. When Ohio senator Charles Anderson, originally from Kentucky, proposed eliminating a provision of a law prohibiting Blacks from testifying in civil and criminal court cases, he was accused of "niggerology" and excoriated by his fellow Kentuckians for betraying his heritage.[70] The state of Kentucky gifted the Union with both Abraham Lincoln *and* Jefferson Davis, but in 1850, it was overwhelmingly anti-abolitionist. For this reason, historian Sean Wilentz has called Clay's third compromise "more of a balancing act, a truce that delayed, but could not prevent, even greater crises over slavery."[71] On January 29, Clay presented a series of resolutions that eventually became known as the Compromise of 1850. On February 5 and 6, in a speech that lasted four hours and forty-five minutes, he implored Congress to save the Union.[72] After months of debate, and despite a torrent of northern criticism, the result was that California would be admitted to the Union as a free state; Washington, DC, would retain slavery without a slave trade; and the Fugitive Slave Law would force the North to return runaway slaves who were denied the right to a jury trial. Crafted by Clay, the compromise spelled the beginning of the end for his party and the Union itself.

In the spring of 1850, as the nation debated its future, Harriet Beecher Stowe was preparing to leave Cincinnati. Her husband, Calvin Stowe, had accepted the position of the Collins Professor of Natural and Revealed Religion at his alma mater, Bowdoin College, in New Brunswick, Maine. Harriet was ready to leave. At the end of 1849, her newborn son, Samuel Charles, or "Charley," had passed away of cholera during the epidemic that swept through the West. "It was at *his* dying bed, and at *his* grave," she later wrote, "that I learnt what a poor slave mother may feel when her child is torn away from her."[73] Aching with grief, Harriet wanted a new beginning. Historian Nancy Koester notes, "The move to Maine would not improve the Stowes' standard of living, but it would give them what they needed most: a fresh start in New England. It was time to go home."[74] In April, the Stowes left on a steamboat bound for Pittsburgh. For Calvin, he was returning to his first teaching post. For Harriet, she was returning to the New England of her upbringing. Similar to Lyman's tenure in Litchfield, the years at Bowdoin were the happiest, healthiest, and most productive years of Harriet's life.[75]

As the Stowes journeyed to Maine, they witnessed firsthand the outrage and division caused by the Fugitive Slave Law. In Brooklyn, where they stayed a few days with Henry, locals were still discussing New York senator William Seward's "higher law" speech in March before Congress against the Fugitive Slave Bill. Seward, a rival of President Millard Fillmore, who eventually signed the Bill into law, famously contended there was a "higher law than the Constitution" that ought to dissuade Congress from introducing slavery into western territories: the moral law. Stirring the religious sympathies of the North, well over a hundred thousand copies of the speech were distributed.[76] Meanwhile, Henry was also contemplating a higher law and distributing his own thoughts on the matter. In an editorial in the *Independent*, "Shall We Compromise?" he declared, "If the compromises of the Constitution include requisitions which violate humanity, I will not be bound by them. I put Constitution against Constitution—God's against man's."[77] Galvanized by the controversial bill, Henry took his most Garrisonian step toward radical abolitionism. Protesting that the Fugitive Slave Act had brought the "abomination of slavery to our very door," his subsequent antislavery sermons were widely published.[78] For the next decade, Henry would be one of the leading abolitionist voices in the public square. David B. Chesebrough has concluded that "one can trace the development of Northern thought on slavery by observing the evolution of Beecher's sermons on the same subject."[79] 1850 was a turning point for that evolution. At an antislavery rally in New York, Henry captivated Walt Whitman once again with his "bold masculine discourses."[80]

After hearing one brother denounce slavery, Harriet heard yet another. In Massachusetts, where the Stowes lodged with Edward's family, the furor from the "terrible decree" was even more rancorous.[81] On March 7, Massachusetts senator Daniel Webster made his fateful address opposing a ban on slavery in the new territories and accepting a fugitive slave code. To New Englanders, Webster's support for the compromise was nothing short of treason. Poet John Greenleaf Whittier called the great Whig orator "a fallen angel."[82] The Beechers were aghast at Webster's betrayal, and Harriet would later describe him as the "lost archangel of New England."[83] By the time Harriet arrived at Bowdoin College, after witnessing town after town embroiled in conflict over the issue of fugitive slaves, she had been activated to the cause. Previously beset by division, the abolitionist movement was being united in collective indignation against the Fugitive Slave Act. The North now seemed bound to the great southern evil. With habeas corpus effectively suspended, "almost no colored man is safe in our streets," reported the *New York Independent*.[84]

THE MAKING OF *UNCLE TOM'S CABIN*

Harriet Beecher Stowe was apoplectic. With her Beecher blood boiling, the normally mild-mannered professor's wife simmered with a quiet rage over the injustice of the Fugitive Slave Act. In a letter to Catharine, who was equally incensed, Harriet scorned "this miserable wicked fugitive slave business—Why I have felt almost choked sometimes with pent up wrath that does no good."[85] Harriet was beginning to question the very idea of a "union" between slave and free states. To Henry, who was quickly becoming a media sensation, she fumed over the case of Henry Long, a waiter at the Pacific Hotel in New York City. Long, a runaway slave from Virginia, was violently seized while waiting tables and taken to the U.S. Clerk's office to be claimed by a slaveholder. "Must we forever keep calm and smile and smile," she agonized, longing to "do something even the humblest in this cause."[86] She did something, indeed. After five years of relative silence, Harriet began to write again. And she also began reading. Shortly after arriving in Maine, she encountered the *Autobiography of Josiah Henson*, the story of a runaway slave to the North.[87] Harriet now had the compelling testimony, the imagination, the skill, and the motivation to compose a fictional work that would speak into the "Great Debate" over slavery. She just needed a little help from her family.

Although Harriet Beecher Stowe attributed the authorship of *Uncle Tom's Cabin* to God, the best-selling book of the nineteenth century after the Bible was in fact a Beecher family effort. In January 1851, as Harriet was busy plotting a sketch on the "capabilities of liberated blacks to take care of themselves" (a very Beecher-esque theme in itself), Henry came to visit while in the area giving lectures. The two stayed up all night talking about "the horrid cruelties" of the Fugitive Slave Law. When Henry described the mock slave auctions in New York to raise money to buy slaves' freedom, Harriet was transfixed.[88] At Broadway Tabernacle, for example, Henry had raised $2,250 to redeem Emily and Mary Edmonson, sisters in Virginia who had failed at an escape from bondage and were awaiting transport to New Orleans. Imitating the cries of an auctioneer, Henry called for bids to emancipate male and female slaves, a provocative performance he continued in the years leading up to the war.[89] Electrifying crowds who put thousands of dollars into a hat in a matter of minutes, the auctions were Beecher moral influence at its most dramatic. Henry drew his sister into his cause, as Harriet assumed responsibility for the education of the Edmonson sisters and purchased the liberty of two more children in the Edmonson family.[90]

Around the time of Henry's visit, Isabella Beecher, Edward's wife, wrote Harriet to update her on the recent atrocities endured by Blacks in the Boston area. In one of the letters, Isabella exhorted her sister-in-law to wield her mighty pen on behalf of freedom. "Now, Hattie, if I could use a pen as you can," she insisted, "I would write something that would make this whole nation feel what an accursed thing slavery is."[91] These were the words Harriet had been waiting to hear. For several months, she had contemplated whether she was a "Great Reformer" like her father. Just a month earlier, she had written to Calvin—back in Cincinnati finishing his final semester at Lane—that she wished "Father would come to Boston and preach on the Fugitive Slave Law as he once preached on the slave trade," for she hoped that "a Martin Luther would arise to set this community right."[92] It was time for a reformation, and she could no longer hold silent. After reading her sister-in-law's words, Harriet rose up from her chair and pledged, "I shall write that thing if I live."[93] The Beechers always needed a crisis to spark their moral crusades. For Harriet, that catalyst was the Fugitive Slave Law. Her family and her pen did the rest.

In truth, Harriet was not the first or even the second Beecher to be ignited into action by the Fugitive Slave Law. Emboldened by Edward and Henry, Charles attacked the statute in *Duty of Disobedience to Wicked*

Laws: A Sermon on the Fugitive Slave Law (1851).[94] Charles's work was so
controversial that the ministers of Newark, New Jersey, where he ministered, eventually expelled him from the Presbyterian Synod. Predictably,
the reasons for his expulsion were social *and* theological.[95] Charles and his
wife, Sarah, had already struggled to make ends meet with four children in
Fort Wayne, despite his popularity as a music leader. (A local newspaper
had even run an invitation for a "Donation Visit" for local residents to bring
clothes and other goods to the Beechers' home.)[96] When he finally lost his
pastorate in New Jersey, Charles had to be supported monetarily by Harriet, Henry, and Isabella.[97] By 1851 and 1852, Harriet had already witnessed
the courage—and to some extent the cost—of abiding by a "higher law."

Harriet's siblings provided more than inspiration. Receiving payments from editor Gamaliel Bailey (who had taken over the *Philanthropist* in 1838 when James G. Birney gave it up), Harriet issued her stories
about Uncle Tom in weekly installments in the *National Era* from June 5,
1851, until April 1, 1852. Eventually published in two volumes, *Uncle Tom's
Cabin* catapulted her to national fame. While Harriet was composing her
magnum opus and with Calvin in the classroom, Catharine supervised the
home in Brunswick, giving her sister time away from the children to devote herself to her holy task. As Kathryn Sklar notes, with no children of
her own, "Catharine's fierce loyalty to Harriet was an important dimen-
sion in her life." In some sense, Catharine felt that she too was writing the
book. "I am trying to get Uncle Tom out of the way," she explained to her
sister Mary. "At 8 o clock we are thro' with breakfast & prayers & then we
send off Mr. Stowe & Harriet both to *his room at the college*."[98] Who better
to run a house filled with children than the founder of home economics
and one of America's leading educational reformers? Catharine ran a tight
ship. For the next six years, Catharine devoted herself to the establishing of
Milwaukee Female College, hoping to create a home for herself in the upper Midwest.[99] The college would replace the missionary teaching agency
as the primary artery by which she could exert moral influence. "Horace
Mann, Horace Greeley and all that modern reform party who all stand
waiting for the moment when Catharine will come on their side," Harriet
boasted.[100] However, in 1851, she was the surrogate mother for Harriet's
children while their mother penned one of the most monumental books in
American history.

During the production of *Uncle Tom's Cabin*, Harriet was also comforted by the presence of her father, who had resigned his theological professorship at Lane in 1850. In May of 1851, he left Cincinnati and returned to New England, following his children back east. At the ripe age of seventy-five, Lyman was not unlike Father Mapple in Herman Melville's *Moby-Dick*, published that same year: "in the hardy winter of a healthy old age; that sort of old age which seems merging into a second flowering youth, for among all the fissures of his wrinkles, there shone certain mild gleams of a newly developing bloom—the spring verdure peeping forth even beneath February's snow."[101] Lyman's mission to save the West was now complete, albeit unfulfilled in many ways. Lane Seminary had not blossomed into a Yale or an Andover of the West, but it would remain a training center for pastors in Cincinnati until 1932, when it became part of McCormick Theological Seminary in Chicago. Lane also produced its fair share of moral reformers after Lyman's tenure, including Jonathan Fisher Crossette, who in 1868 helped establish the Women's Christian Association—which came to be the YWCA in 1893—and became a missionary to China in 1870.[102]

Although his body was failing in 1851, Lyman's mind was still sharp enough to write on several social, political, and theological issues. In the Stowes' large house in Brunswick, he prepared various works, including his *Lectures on Political Atheism, Sermons on Intemperance, Occasional Sermons,* and his *Views of Theology.*[103] Before traveling to Boston and renting a house near Edward in the fall, Lyman was completing his final theological treatises in the very same house that Harriet, his uncredentialed daughter, was composing a book that would shape the American nation far more than anything he had ever written. The sun was setting on the family patriarch as it was dawning for the most famous Beecher. Indeed, it cannot be missed that Harriet was somehow able to pen *Uncle Tom's Cabin* while arguably the two most boisterous, domineering Beechers were living under the same roof.

Further yet, Harriet also had help from her younger sister Isabella. Joan Hedrick explains, "While Catharine provided sisterly support by keeping Harriet away from the clatter and bang of domestic cares, Isabella acted as amanuensis, a laborious chore when documents had to be copied by hand to preserve a record. Aunt Esther's arrival soon after Isabella's completed the rallying of the Beecher women."[104] In some sense, from its origin to its aftermath, *Uncle Tom's Cabin* was a Beecher family accomplishment. Even after its publication, Stowe was assisted by her siblings to see the project through. When Rev. Joel Parker filed a libel suit against Harriet for quoting him in a very proslavery light, her brother Henry helped Calvin negotiate a settlement. As Harriet began to write *A Key to Uncle Tom's Cabin* in 1853 to defend the veracity of her novel against those who questioned its basis in reality, she sent her brothers on fact-finding missions to ascertain stories of cruelty against slaves.[105]

While Stowe was the only Beecher capable of writing a work with such overwhelming moral and emotional force, the book, which sold 300,000 copies in the United States in its first year alone, was filled with all the signature elements of Beecherism. For instance, Uncle Tom himself is a product of moral influence, having been converted at a revival, where he "got religion at a camp-meeting."[106] Not surprisingly, as a born-again evangelical, he was also known for his sobriety. As little Eva points out to Miss Ophelia upon their arrival in New Orleans, "he'll never get drunk."[107] Uncle Tom was a figure of which the temperance movement could approve. In fact, an entire litany of reforms can be found in the book, imbuing the novel with an unmistakable New School moralistic flavor. When Cassy explains how she was sold into slavery, she recounts how her lover was lured into a gambling addiction by a friend. "He got him to the gaming-houses; and he was one of the sort that, when he once got a going there, there was no holding back."[108]

Consistent with her Beecher belief in the natural ability of sinners, not only did Stowe effectively humanize slaves in a way that countless whites had never conceived, but she depicted "Tom's manly disinterestedness" in the mold of the Christian republican ideal.[109] Tom was not simply a Christ figure; he was also a paragon of American virtue. The harrowing drama of *Uncle Tom's Cabin* is thus an exhortation to the American, Protestant, evangelical, activist gospel upon which Stowe herself had been catechized in the Beecher home. "It seems to me, mamma," the dying Eva sermonizes, "the Bible is for every one to read themselves."[110] The character of Uncle Tom is the antithesis of the Old School, slaveholding Christ who neither related to sinners nor offered them hope in the midst of their sufferings. Instead, the meek yet mighty slave "manifested a tenderness of feeling, a commiseration for his fellow-sufferers, strange and new to them, which was watched with a jealous eye by Legree."[111] After watching her father, brothers, and sister convert thousands to their various causes, Stowe found her own literary pulpit to preach an antislavery gospel. It is a "great book," historian Ann Douglas stated, "not because it is a great novel, but because it is a great revival sermon, aimed directly at the conversion of its hearers."[112] As innumerable scholars have since recognized, Stowe's sermon landed powerfully upon the heart of the nation. Noting the evangelical nature of the book, Henry Louis Gates Jr. has called Stowe's protagonist "the most popular Black character in the history of American literature, the self-sacrificing Christ-like character whom people simply called Uncle Tom."[113]

The power of *Uncle Tom's Cabin* to awaken the American conscience to the evils of slavery is a story well told. A decade later, President Abraham Lincoln allegedly called Stowe "the little lady who wrote the book that started this great war."[114] In her recent work *Uncle Tom: From Martyr to Traitor*, historian Adena Spingarn concludes, "Although the Lincoln story is probably apocryphal, the sentiment was a common one. Many Americans— Black and white—across regions and the political spectrum—believed that Stowe's novel was a fundamental impetus for the Civil War."[115] As Spingarn demonstrates, the character of Uncle Tom was transformed through the decades by countless stage adaptations, "anti-Tom" shows, and "a kind of intraracial critique of an older generation by a younger one" during Jim Crow.[116] With a controversial legacy in which the book has been called everything from "romantic racialism" to "Everybody's Protest Novel," Stowe's fiction remained embedded in the American imagination almost from the second it was released into a ballooning national print culture in 1852.[117]

Nevertheless, when *Uncle Tom's Cabin* was first unleashed upon the American public, Stowe's contemporaries recognized the pulse-pounding book for what it was: moral influence. In an unsigned review of the novel for the *Liberator*, William Lloyd Garrison applauded that Uncle Tom "triumphantly exemplifies the nature, tendency and results of CHRISTIAN NON-RESISTANCE."[118] Poet Henry Wadsworth Longfellow wrote to Stowe soon after reading it: "I congratulate you most cordially upon the immense success and influence of *Uncle Tom's Cabin*. It is one of the greatest triumphs recorded in literary history, to say nothing of the higher triumph of its moral effect."[119] Whereas northerners celebrated the blockbuster novel as a

victory for humanity, in the South the work was anathema. In North Carolina, Methodist widow and small-town newspaper editor Frances Bumpass
received a request from a publisher in Buffalo, New York, who enclosed
two dollars to pay for an advertisement of Stowe's new book. Bumpass, an
ardent holiness advocate but a strong supporter of slavery, returned both
the letter and the money.[120] The *True Democrat* in Little Rock, Arkansas,
mocked "*Uncle Tom's Cabin-ism*" as nothing more than "blubbering sympathy" for the slave.[121] In Dixieland, the Beechers were gaining a reputation as
social agitators. Another newspaper in Little Rock estimated that the book
had been a "joint production of the entire family, manufactured for the
occasion, and as a means of raising the wind."[122] Years later, after Stowe's
second antislavery novel, the *Southern Literary Messenger* jeered, "Luckily,
she is only a Beecher."[123]

<h3 style="text-align:center">"CHRISTIAN ACTIVISM"</h3>

In a "free" nation filled with slaves and in a tenuous "union" between North
and South, the Beechers epitomized the inner conflict of a people who did
not always live up to their ideals. Catharine herself was a "bundle of contradictions."[124] She was a leading expert on home economics yet had no home
of her own. She taught others how to raise children but did not have any
children. While she wrote prolifically on evangelical religion (she would
publish five books in the 1850s), she had never experienced conversion. In
many ways, Catharine was the living embodiment of "do as I say, not as I
do." Although she rallied America's women to become teachers, she did not
enjoy the classroom. By the early 1850s, Catharine had created a reputable
brand as a "public woman" and thought leader, but she was also a troubled
reformer. Publicly, she did not follow the avant-garde in woman's rights. In
1851, she responded to the "Declaration of Sentiments" at the Seneca Falls
Convention point-by-point in her *True Remedy*. The following year, she
broke with the National Board of Popular Education, the organization she
had founded with William Slade, and eventually established the American
Woman's Educational Association in New York.[125] And Catharine would
soon experience conflict with her new institution in Milwaukee over a dispute about living quarters. Privately, Catharine continued to cause friction
within the Beecher tribe itself, as she quarreled with Lyman's third wife,

Lydia Jackson. For a woman who preached self-sacrifice and commitment to a generation of American women, Catharine struggled repeatedly to model these virtues in her own career and family. Catharine Beecher remained a reformer at heart, and she devoted herself to her father and sisters. Still, her relationships were often characterized by dysfunction.

Edward was yet another Beecher who exhibited a degree of angst and contradiction in his career as a reformer. As Catharine the pro-woman advocate was critiquing the woman's rights movement, her brother the Calvinist theologian was completely reenvisioning Calvinism. After years of concealing his unique views on the preexistence of souls, Edwards unveiled them to the world in his *Conflict of the Ages* (1852). With a cosmic metanarrative similar to Eastern religions, Edward argued that humans had in fact *not* been universally corrupted by Adam's original sin, but instead had been given a previous life cycle *before* their present stay on earth. In other words, sinners were not the result of one man's bad decision, but the reincarnated fruit of a past life. Attempting to navigate between the Charybdis of human freedom and the Scylla of human depravity, he contended that life on earth was a "moral hospital," and that "humiliation, confession of sin, and purification and pardon, are the final results of the truest and highest progress."[126] Edward engineered a brand-new account of human history to suit his rather optimistic appraisal of human potential.

Although Edwards's theology was somewhat bizarre and convoluted (and mocked by his father), his aims were no less ambitious than those of any other Beecher. He wanted to "revolutionize the world" with his ideas.[127] As Robert Merideth observes, Edward's work was "motivated in part by the slavery crisis" and his eccentric "theology was related to abolitionist politics."[128] On the heels of Henry's "Compromise" editorial, Charles's sermon on the Fugitive Slave Law, and finally Harriet's bestselling novel, Edward's less understood *Conflict of Ages* was an attempt to emphasize the importance of human accountability by taking aim at the central doctrine of Old School dogma: original sin. Edward believed himself to be revising both sides of the theological aisle, "that, after a careful examination of all the theories of the Old School and the New School divines for vindicating the fall in Adam, and its results, they are rejected as insufficient."[129] For Edward, the slavery issue could be boiled down to two competing views of the universe, and "instead of a God dishonorably ruining his creatures," Edward presented a God who was behind human moral improvement. Emancipation was thus a part of America's destiny.

Embracing a lengthier doctrine of human progress that spanned eons, Edward had evolved beyond the New School mind. His commitment to the Beecher creed of human freedom had now led him to reject the traditional notion of inherited sinfulness. Predictably, the book "startled the community" of orthodox and heterodox theologians.[130] New Schoolers and Old Schoolers alike submitted less than glowing reviews.[131] In Richmond, the *Southern Literary Messenger* joked, "Dr. Edward Beecher throws his parabola quite beyond the sphere of the earth, makes a novel excursion into the realm of the past, and comes back to publish on this planet his Rambles in Chaos."[132] Even Lyman himself had called Edward's idea of preexistence "your little theological hencoop." Lyman Beecher Stowe notes, "apparently the only theological animal of any standing who went into it was Edward's younger brother, Charles."[133] More than theology, the book also revealed Edward's personal turmoil. For over twenty-five years, since his last pastoral stint in Boston, the ostensibly conservative Beecher had quietly wrestled with the justice of God and how to reconcile orthodox Christianity with slavery. While attempting to straddle the line between Old School and New School, *The Conflict of Ages* placed Edward outside the pale of virtually every Calvinist camp.

Further south, Thomas Beecher was also a bundle of contradictions. In May 1851, after his tutelage under Horace Bushnell in Hartford, he was elected pastor of the New England Congregationalist Church in Williamsburg, New York, in Brooklyn. The people of Williamsburg, many of whom were rich businessmen, hired the younger Beecher in the hope that he could grow their congregation like his famous brother had multiplied Plymouth Church across town. But Thomas was not his brother, and he struggled with confidence in public speaking his entire life. It certainly did not help matters that he was perpetually in his brother's shadow. Thomas was also the first of his siblings to lose a spouse. Just two years after marrying Olivia Day, she died while pregnant in August of 1853. Thomas's refusal to weep over his lost wife and child troubled his sisters.

No stranger to sorrow or to adversity, Thomas carried a special burden for the poor and the downcast. While several Beechers have been identified by historians as forerunners of the so-called Social Gospel movement in the late nineteenth and early twentieth centuries, Thomas's ministry was perhaps the most comparable to that of Walter Rauschenbusch, which later arose in nearby Hell's Kitchen, or that of Washington Gladden, whose first pastorate was likewise in Brooklyn.[134] Armed with the liberal theology of Horace Bushnell, Thomas announced that the doors of the church were open to the poor and not just to the powerful. He desired an inclusive ministry that reached the "little people—all people." However, Thomas did not play well with the social prophets of his day. He was a Beecher, after all. By 1852, he became extremely critical of other reformers and abolitionists, calling them "crazy atheists & no government men" who undermined the public good.[135] As an alternative, Thomas put forward the idea of a "Christian activism" that marshaled energy and resources through the church, not through a plutocracy or the state legislature. In a public lecture, "Unity of Reforms," he lambasted abolitionists for singling out slavery as the only evil in society while ignoring others. At the same time that his sister Harriet was in Liverpool speaking at British Antislavery societies, Thomas curiously alluded to *Uncle Tom's Cabin* to make his point. Rich men, he excoriated, "willfully oppress[ed] a poor man, and torture[d] him as truly as ever Legree did a slave." Those who claimed the name of Christ but did not serve the poor were only "half-way Christian," in his judgment.[136] Thomas was, oddly enough, an anti-reformist reformer.

Like several of his siblings, Thomas often failed to live up to his ideals. In May 1853, John Hooker, Isabella's husband, took Thomas and Livy to a meeting of the American Anti-Slavery Society. They listened to speeches by William Lloyd Garrison, Wendell Phillips, Edmund Quincy, and his brother Henry Ward.[137] Even with members of Thomas's family and church present at the event, he was still hostile to abolitionism. Although he insisted upon caring for the poor, he did not see an urgent need to help the poorest. While insisting upon the importance of the church, he could not abide with his own people. Comparing his congregation to Pharisees and expressing disappointment at the lack of change in the church, he resigned from Williamsburg on May 16, 1854. Like Catharine and Edward and Charles and others, Thomas spoke *on behalf of* evangelicalism, yet his relationship *to* evangelicalism was rather uneasy and riddled with inconsistencies. As a so-called "Christian activist," he grew very impatient with other Christians and other activists.

Eventually, Thomas landed in the upstate New York town of Elmira, a city transformed by the canals and railroads of the transportation revolution. As a "busy station" in the Underground Railroad with an elite class of wealthy churchgoers, Elmira presented yet another challenge for the anti-abolitionist, ultrademocratic Beecher. According to Myra C. Glenn, Thomas "seemed almost obsessed" with the issue of wealth, denouncing a "separate caste in the village."[138] Nevertheless, Thomas remained a Beecher at heart. He preached against gambling, drinking, racing, and other Beecher themes. And in his aversion to creeds he rivaled his brothers Henry and Charles. Informing his church that he had "no ambition to found . . . or preserve a church" or to enforce orthodoxy, he declared that his "exclusive aim" was "to help men as individuals to be Christians." On one occasion, when a parishioner asked him about his views on the church creed, Beecher opened a desk drawer and remarked, "There is the creed." Closing the drawer, he declared, "And there it shall remain."[139] Protecting his freedom of religion at all costs, Thomas would not be bound even by his own congregation.

THE KANSAS-NEBRASKA CONTROVERSY

The Beechers did not believe in rigid doctrinal boundaries, but they did believe in the Bible. Therefore, anyone who questioned the preeminent authority of the Scriptures was suspect. In November 1853, Harriet Beecher Stowe wrote to William Lloyd Garrison that she would not endorse his newspaper or his party because of his biblical skepticism: "What I fear is that it will take from poor Uncle Tom his bible & give him nothing in its place—you understand me—do you not?"[140] The Stowes were quite literally a family of the Bible. After just two years in Maine, they had moved to Massachusetts, where Calvin had accepted the professorship of languages and biblical and sacred literature at Andover Theological Seminary. In December, when Garrison visited Andover and Harriet finally met the fiery editor of the *Liberator*, she did not beat around the bush. She pressed, "Mr. Garrison, are you a Christian?" He replied that her question was too vague. "Well," she persisted, "are you such a Christian as I am?" But Garrison replied that this question was even more vague. Finally, Stowe struck at the heart of what she perceived to be the essence of her Christian faith: "Well,

Mr. Garrison, do you believe in the atonement?" Interestingly, even while Harriet was departing from her father's beliefs about hell, revivalism, and the rebirth, she still fulfilled at least three out of historian David Bebbington's four criteria for an evangelical: biblicism, crucicentrism (emphasis upon the cross of Christ), conversionism, and activism.[141] Garrison's answer that Jesus Christ was the "redemptive spirit of love" satisfied Stowe. Even heretics were not beyond the pale of friendly cooperation. Nevertheless, curiously, when Garrison published some of their correspondence in his newspaper on December 23, he did not use Stowe's name. He simply referred to her as a "highly esteemed friend."[142]

By the 1850s, the business of reform was drifting from the church meetinghouse to the statehouse, causing serious divisions within the temperance and abolitionist ranks. In 1851, Maine was the first state to pass a law prohibiting the manufacture and sale of alcohol. Two years later, the same year that Edward delivered his *Address to the Citizens of Massachusetts* at the State Temperance Convention, the state of Vermont passed a similar law.[143] Foreshadowing the Eighteenth Amendment to the Constitution in 1919, the new laws turned moral influence into legal prohibition. Temperance, a traditionally voluntary movement, had become edict. Likewise, in abolitionist circles, the gap between moral influence and political antislavery was closing. By 1853, William Lloyd Garrison had severed ties with his former colleague Frederick Douglass over, among other things, politics. Once close friends on the abolitionist circuit, the two had become enemies as Douglass became more ambitious and politically active.[144] Merging his journal *Frederick Douglass' Paper* with the Liberty Party, Douglass no longer felt "glued to the non-voting theory."[145] He was also questioning the wisdom of nonviolence. During a speech in Salem, Ohio, on August 22, 1852, Douglass posited that "violence . . . in some circumstances [is] far more potent than Moral Suasion." "What is the use of Moral Suasion," he asked, "to a people thus trampled in the dust?" When Douglass waited a few moments for his words to land upon the hearts of his hearers, he was interrupted by fellow abolitionist Sojourner Truth. In a moment Douglass would never forget for the rest of his life, Truth, a Garrisonian, interjected, "Is God gone?" The so-called "Great Interruption," one that Harriet Beecher Stowe would invoke years later in her scathing rebuke to President Buchanan, implied that if God was on their side there was no need to resort to violence.[146] Douglass's departure from the Garrisonian camp had become a public dispute.

Stowe attempted to call a truce between the two feuding abolitionists. Although she remained above the fray, the movement could ill afford a fierce public squabble between its two most famous spokesmen. "You speak of him as an apostate," Harriet reproved Garrison. "Where is this work of excommunication to end—Is there but one true anti slavery church & all others infidel? & who shall declare which it is?"[147] Garrison was not the pope of abolitionism, Harriet chided. The Beechers were not sectarians of any stripe. Just as they would not submit to the rigid terms of the Old School Presbyterians, they refused to be pigeonholed into one faction of moral reform. On the lyceum circuit, Henry likewise took the stage with men with whom he did not fully agree. The Beechers' commitment was to the Bible, freedom of speech, and to freedom of Protestant religion (although even this last belief was bending, as Henry's *Plymouth Collection of Hymns* [1855], prepared by Charles, controversially included hymns by Unitarians and Catholics).[148] "I am increasingly anxious," Stowe later told Garrison, "that all who hate slavery be united if not in form at least in fact—unity in difference."[149] As reformers quarreled over the difference between voluntarism and voting, Stowe attempted to hold the line.

However, even the Beechers could not escape the political maelstrom of 1854. On January 4, U.S. senator Stephen Douglas of Illinois, the most dynamic Democrat in America, introduced a bill to Congress that would overturn the Missouri Compromise by permitting settlers of the Kansas and Nebraska territories to decide for themselves about slavery. Appealing to Americans' democratic sensibilities, Douglas's idea of "popular sovereignty" opened to slavery land that had previously been closed to it. On its face, the bill was a safety valve to release the flammable pressure of the slavery issue building in the East. But it only served to explode the West and enrage the North. Left to choose whether it would enter the Union as a free or a slave state, Kansas erupted in outright war as northerners moved into Kansas to vote against slavery and southerners moved into Kansas to vote for it.[150] Dubbed by Horace Greeley as "Bleeding Kansas," the battle in the West was the first war on American soil over slavery. Proslavery Missourians known as "Border Ruffians" crossed into neighboring Kansas to launch raids upon cities and intimidate antislavery settlers in the region.

Back in the East, the Kansas-Nebraska controversy was a call to action. In New Jersey, Charles Beecher was one of many clergymen in the northern states who published sermons condemning the Kansas-Nebraska Act.[151] He did not mince words. Richard J. Carwardine notes: "Critical evangelicals believed that the spread of slavery would not only blight the economic prospects of the new territory, but would transform it into a moral and religious wilderness. Charles Beecher and others spoke of Kansas and Nebraska becoming a vast 'dungeon-brothel,' where under slavery's moral code Bible-reading, education, marriage vows, and Christian family life would be obliterated, and where human beings would be bred and sold like cattle."[152] Harriet also raised her voice in "An Appeal to the Women of the Free States of America on the Present Crisis in Our Country." Leveraging her fame as a celebrity novelist, Harriet also drew up a petition against the bill with the help of Calvin, Lyman, and the support of Senator Charles Sumner, who routinely cited *Uncle Tom's Cabin* in his antislavery speeches. In all, Harriet collected the signatures of 3,050 New England pastors, professors, and presidents on a sheet of paper two hundred feet long.[153] The political landscape was shifting. In May 1854, the Republican Party was founded in Ripon, Wisconsin, by fifty-four citizens determined to defeat the Kansas-Nebraska Bill. That spring, a forty-five-year-old Abraham Lincoln, drawn out of his law practice and back into politics, began seriously formulating arguments against the institution of slavery. However, by the end of May, the bill was signed into law by President Pierce, who turned a blind eye to the chaos in the West.

The Kansas-Nebraska controversy was also a call to arms, enflaming an already volatile public discourse. New England was set ablaze in abolitionist sentiment when runaway slave Anthony Burns was arrested by a federal marshal in Boston, confined in a local courthouse, and taken back to Virginia after a weeklong trial. As mobs surrounded the courthouse, a thousand federal troops were called in to escort Burns to his ship. Abolitionist protesters like Wendell Phillips and Theodore Parker championed Burns as a martyr of the Fugitive Slave Act. Not long afterward, Henry David Thoreau delivered his searing address "Slavery in Massachusetts" and William Lloyd Garrison burned copies of the Declaration of Independence and the Constitution before a cheering crowd. On October 28, 1855, Thomas Beecher preached a sermon, "Declaration of Independence—A Lie," contending that not all men were equal in the United States.[154] Inevitably, the verbal became physical. In May of 1856, Charles Sumner, who had encouraged Harriet to write up her petition, delivered a thundering speech in the Senate, "The Crime Against Kansas," comparing slavery to rape and predicting a civil war. Two days later, Congressman Preston Brooks, a cousin of the South Carolina senator who had cowritten the Kansas-Nebraska Act with Stephen Douglas, savagely beat an unsuspecting Sumner with his cane on the floor of the Senate, heaving blow after merciless blow upon his bleeding head. The North was aghast. Although Brooks broke his cane and was levied a three-hundred-dollar fine for the assault, southerners mailed him replacement canes in support of the beating.

"Bleeding Kansas" was, in many ways, a civil war before *the* civil war. And like his night patrols in Cincinnati after the race riots of 1836, Henry Ward Beecher felt that he *must* do something to help defend freedom and public order in the West. He did a great deal, in fact. In the wake of the Kansas-Nebraska war, Henry armed, auctioned, and addressed the masses for the fight against slavery. In 1855, in his *Conflict of Northern and Southern Theories of Men and Society,* Henry described the manifold differences between northern and southern cultures, from morals to industry to education to religion. For Beecher, as for so many who lived above the Mason-Dixon Line, the North was not simply a free land; it was a superior society. As Eric Foner has explained, this belief was central to the "ideology" of the nascent Republican party: "It is impossible to understand the intensity of Republican opposition to the expansion of slavery in the West without bearing in mind their image of southern society, as well as their conviction that free land in the West provided an insurance of continuing social mobility in the North."[155] Few northerners embodied this social mobility more than Henry Ward Beecher, the small-town preacher from the frontier who became "the most famous man in America" in New York City.[156] According to Beecher, northerners were a more practical, even more authentic, people. Whereas Yankees were determined to *do,* southerners were only interested in *seeming.* In true Yankee spirit, Henry was committed to doing his part for the slave. Therefore, on June 1, 1856, just a couple of weeks after Senator Sumner was beaten on the Senate floor, Plymouth Church staged its first slave auction, raising over twenty-two hundred dollars to free enslaved Black girls from bondage. More than any sermon could achieve, the auction invited the people of Henry's church to participate firsthand in the antislavery cause. But Henry did not limit his influence to the church walls. On behalf of his congregants, he promised to do something more radical than perhaps any church in America had done to that point in the cause for freedom. Instead of prayers, they sent guns.

In New Haven, at a meeting to raise rifles for the Connecticut Kansas Colony, which was about to migrate west for the frontier, Henry pledged that, if twenty-five rifles could be raised on the spot, he would pledge an additional twenty-five from Plymouth Church. The fundraiser was a success. Plymouth delivered. Eventually, they raised enough for twenty-seven rifles at twenty-five dollars each. Loading Sharps rifles into boxes labeled "Bibles," Plymouth Church sent their pledged weapons with New Englanders on their way to join Free-Soil settlers in Kansas. The rifles earned the nickname "Beecher's Bibles," and the westward company of young men called themselves "Beecher Bible and Rifle Colony."[157] Henry had officially qualified himself and his congregation as radical abolitionists. In typical Beecher fashion, he was leading the charge against slavery *and* shrewdly gauging the winds of antislavery sentiment in the North. In the process, he was making abolitionism more acceptable for mainstream Americans. The public outrage from the guerrilla warfare in Kansas demonstrates Paxton Hibben's withering observation that Henry was "a barometer and record" of his times and that he was never "in advance of his day" but rather "precisely abreast" of it.[158] Henry earned a reputation in the South as a social fanatic precisely when it came with the least cultural risk in the North. Galvanized by the Fugitive Slave Law, the Kansas-Nebraska controversy, and then the beating of Charles Sumner, Henry finally decided that ultra-abolitionism was acceptable enough to most northerners that political activism would no longer harm his reputation in Brooklyn. "Despite his eccentricities Beecher was a bellwether," insists Debby Applegate. "If he was saying, plenty of plenty were thinking it."[159] He was a scientist *and* shaper of popular opinion. He was a Beecher.

By sending rifles into a conflict zone, Henry had blurred the line between militancy and moral influence. But his commitment to liberty remained unchanged. No longer was he a cheerleader on behalf of freedom of speech. He was now an armorer for Free-Soilers. According to William G. McLoughlin, the social and religious "revolution" that took place between

1840 and 1870 in American life needed a spokesman, and "Henry Ward Beecher was to this revolution what Thomas Jefferson was to the earlier one."[160] Although McLoughlin was probably guilty of a bit of hyperbole, Henry had undoubtedly become a bellwether for most of the Beecher family, who always seemed to follow his lead on the slavery issue. For instance, as Henry was answering the South, so was Charles. In 1855, in response to increasing southern appeals to the Bible to justify human bondage, the American Anti-Slavery Society published Charles's *The God of the Bible Against Slavery*. His argument was the same as any other Beecher's in the 1850s: "A *fair* Bible argument ought to show that slavery, as defined by the slave law, is agreeable to the character of God as revealed in the Bible."[161] Harriet also seemed to be growing bolder in her defiance of the South. In 1856, she published *Dred*, her last antislavery novel.[162] As the fictional son of the slave insurrectionist Denmark Vesey, Dred was a runaway slave and a somewhat darker and less Christlike character than Uncle Tom, demonstrating that Harriet's views on the subject were indeed evolving with the rest of the family.

Spread out across the Eastern Seaboard, the Beechers maintained the ability to remain together, an impressive feat that reinforced the similarities in their thinking. In 1856, Lyman moved permanently to Brooklyn to stay with Henry and Eunice, signaling that Henry had become, in many ways, the new head of the family. After a few months, using money that had long been owed to him by Lane Seminary and with help from friends in Boston, Lyman and his wife, Lydia, moved to their own residence on Willow Street.[163] He was a regular attendee at Plymouth Church and even made weekly prayer meetings. Yet Lyman Beecher, the once "conservative abolitionist," did not seem to frown upon his son's social extremism. "I thought I could preach till I heard Henry," he joked. No doubt he saw much of himself in his son. Lyman had pleaded with his generation to save the West, and Henry was doing the same in his own unique way. After Lyman's eightieth birthday, Catharine organized a family reunion at the Stowes' "Stone Cabin" in Andover. A few years later, they would gather again at Henry's for the now-famous photo of the family in Mathew Brady's studio.[164] As the nation barreled toward civil war, the Beechers stayed connected to one another.

LIFE AND DEATH

Just as Henry was assuming his official place as head of the tribe, Edward was moving back west. In 1855, the same year that he published *A Papal Conspiracy,* Edward became the pastor of First Congregational Church of Galesburg, Illinois, north of where he served as president of Illinois College. "I am a Western man once more," he boasted, again bucking the Beecher trend.[165] (When he moved again in 1871, he would retire next to Henry.) In Galesburg, "the chief city of the Abolitionists in Illinois," as described by one St. Louis newspaper, Edward resumed a familiar role as a leader in the Illinois antislavery movement. The Beecher house even became a station on the Underground Railroad. While juggling his pastoral duties, he also taught at Knox College, a hub of abolitionist activity in central Illinois. Notably, Knox was the first college in Illinois to award a college degree to a Black man.[166] Edward, the heady and at times obscure theologian, was still drawn to academia. He was, as Lyman Beecher Stowe has described him, "the scholar" of the family.[167] Occasionally, he was even invited to lecture at the new theological seminary in Chicago, although his theory of the preexistence of souls was deemed off-limits. When hard times fell upon his family, as they had during his first stint in the West, Edward was assisted by the affluent Stowes. Now reaching farther and wider than ever before, the Beecher network had lost none of its durability and dependability. Even James, the seafaring Beecher, had come to stay with Edward in Boston in 1854. After briefly trading his sailor hat for a business suit, James decided to return to the Pacific.[168] Likewise, for a short time, Charles, always admiring his older brother, moved to Galesburg and served as professor of rhetoric at Knox. Four of Charles's sons attended the school.[169]

The late 1850s were a time of deep reflection for many of the Beechers, a family already prone toward introspection. Death seemed not so far away. As Charles exhumed writings and correspondence for Lyman's *Autobiography,* he considered his father's legacy, his own destiny, and the weight of eternity. Editing Lyman's papers was "deeply affecting" him. He confessed to Henry in 1857 that it "is really one of the most solemn things I have attended to for a long time. It fills me with concern for my own children, and my own great Stupidity in regard to them, and above all my unbelief in regard to their danger." At the forefront of Charles's mind was the doctrine of hell. Charles did not believe in the idea of hell, but its impact upon his father was undeniable. "Is eternal punishment a reality? Father thought so. He never doubted. Strike that idea out of his mind, and his whole career would be changed, his whole influence on us modified," he wrote. "Yet Isabella and Mary, I fear reject father's belief on this point, and Hatty's mind is I fear shaken—do you believe in it? Do you really believe that the wicked will exist forever, and continue forever in sin?" Charles's task to compile his father's autobiography had turned into something much deeper and less sentimental. He inquired of his brother, "Do you believe this? How can we affect our children as Father did us, if we have not the same concern for them, the same sense of their awful danger?"[170] Now in his forties, Charles was having an existential and theological crisis. While he did not see the factual basis for hell, it was his father's sense of purpose and parental care that he coveted most. Lyman had lived his life with a singular aim to save and reform souls, including his children's. Charles questioned whether his own desire to do the Lord's work could ever compare with his father's. Could he ever see the world in such urgent, black-and-white, life-or-death terms? How could his parenting ever measure up to his father's? Even in his frailty, Lyman Beecher still set a high standard for his children.

Death was also knocking at the door. While Harriet was abroad in Europe, her teenage son Fred's drinking had become so excessive that they decided to send him to someone who could help. In June 1857, Fred was moved to Elmira, New York, with his Uncle Thomas, who had for "so many years . . . fought the same fight."[171] Fred stayed at the Elmira Water Cure, an oasis of rest and rehabilitation for several of the Beechers. Thomas, who was recently married to Julia Jones, the best friend of his deceased wife, watched over his nephew. He paid his board, assuring Harriet that God had granted him "victory over the same appetites which are ruining Fred."[172] Intemperance was the cardinal sin in the Beecher household, but in a family of evangelical convictions, there was always redemption.

However, it was not Fred but Henry, Harriet's oldest and favorite son, who needed saving. In July of 1857, during a swimming party on the Connecticut River by Dartmouth College where he was a freshman, Henry drowned.[173] He was nineteen. A dark cloud of sadness and grief loomed over the entire family. Harriet was despondent. It was the first time that she had buried one of her children since little Charlie had died of cholera in 1849. The way that Henry died also recalled memories of Alexander Metcalf Fisher, Catharine's fiancé, who had drowned at sea in 1822 without sign of conversion. The tragedy left a sharp pain in Harriet's soul and a deep questioning about her son's salvation. It also compelled her to write. The following year she began composing *The Minister's Wooing,* a comedy about New England Congregationalism in the early republic and the burdensome psychology of Edwardsean Calvinism. A young man named James Marvyn, an apparent unbeliever with whom the principal character, Mary Scudder, falls in love, is thought to be lost at sea. His soul is likewise thought to be lost. Even so, Stowe's thoughts about her deceased son are spoken by Mary's mother:

> "I have always had a trembling hope for James," said Mrs. Scudder,— "not on account of any of his good deeds or amiable traits, for election is without foresight of any good works,—but I felt he was a child of the covenant, at least by the father's side, and I hope the Lord has heard his prayer. These are dark providences; the world is full of them; and all we can do is have faith that the Lord will bring infinite good out of infinite evil."[174]

The most agonizing, unresolved question of Harriet's life could still be answered with the goodness of God. As Bruce Gordon observes, "Stowe, haunted by the question of whether God had willed her son, Henry, to die, desperately sought a deeper, more comforting mystery."[175] Mary Scudder's eventual choice for a husband, Rev. Samuel Hopkins, was an actual historical figure. As Jonathan Edwards's chief disciple and a staunch antislavery theologian, Hopkins supplied Stowe with the perfect character to illustrate—quite humorously at times—how the most rarefied theological formulas were still just attempts to explain the most basic commandments of God.

While lampooning the lofty doctrines of New England theologians, Harriet's overarching point was much more practical and human. "Why, Mary, you are a living gospel," James once praised the pious young woman. "I can't understand all the hang of predestination, and moral ability and natural ability, and God's efficiency, and man's agency, which Dr. Hopkins is so engaged about; but I can understand *you—you* can do me good!"[176] For Harriet, people made the difference, not theological arguments. Although she could see the virtue in doctrines such as "disinterested benevolence," she believed they were useless unless they were *practiced*. (Ultimately, Mary called off her marriage to Hopkins when her true love, James, returned miraculously from sea.) Tied to her own experience and upbringing, Harriet's characters were also grounded in history. For instance, Candace, one of Hopkins's faithful parishioners, was modeled after Sojourner Truth, the renowned abolitionist and women's rights advocate.[177] One scholar has speculated that the heroine, Mary Scudder, was probably inspired by Sarah Pierrepont Edwards, the wife of Jonathan Edwards, demonstrating that Harriet had not developed the negative view of Edwards that she would in a decade or so.[178] Her scorn was reserved for the character of Aaron Burr, the grandson of Jonathan Edwards and the man who killed Alexander Hamilton in a duel in 1804. Ultimately, *The Minister's Wooing* was a show-case of various Beecher reforms and a critique of Calvinism, vindicating Lawrence Buell's assertion that Stowe's New England fiction was "veiled autobiography."[179]

Whereas tragedy compelled Lyman to push for his children's conversion, it caused his children to relinquish the traditional idea of conversion altogether. (Several of Lyman's children would conveniently let go of his ideas after his death.) In what historian Mark Schantz has called a "culture of death," many Americans in the mid-nineteenth century, including the Beechers, sought to cope with the ever-present reality of death in various and sometimes unique ways.[180] After the loss of her unconverted son Henry, Harriet began to question the doctrine of hell and to alter her view of the hereafter. Seeking to communicate with her deceased son, Harriet dallied in the religion known as spiritualism. Begun by the Fox sisters in upstate New York, spiritualism was a popular movement in the nineteenth century, mostly led by women, that practiced communion with the dead.[181] Partly due to Harriet's "pastoral role" in the family and partly due to the loss of children experienced by her other siblings, several of the Beechers would come to accept this new faith. Spiritualism even interested Charles, who initially published a critique of the religion and then, in classic Beecher fashion, developed his own *sui generis* view.[182] William, the oldest, also dabbled in the art of clairvoyance and "animal magnetism."[183] In the midst of personal sorrows, family tragedy, and even economic instability (that is, the Panic of 1857), the Beechers looked to the preternatural.

Even though the Beecher children supported their father in his old age, they were abandoning his Calvinist faith and sometimes publicly flouting it on the way out. In *Common Sense Applied to Religion* (1857) and *Appeal to People on Behalf of their Rights as Authorized Interpreters* (1860), Catharine railed against her father's class of clergymen without completely abandoning her New England tradition.[184] She was also cultivating "a growing antipathy to male prerogatives in the 1850s."[185] Probably with good reason did the *Princeton Review* insist in 1857 that no one was more responsible for the decline of Calvinism than the Beecher children, who managed to maintain their reputation for evangelical morality even while deriding some of the most cherished evangelical ideas.[186] If not always convincing in their theories, the Beechers were well-published and prolific. In June of 1858, as Abraham Lincoln delivered his famous "House Divided" speech in Springfield, Illinois, the Beechers themselves were a family strangely united *around* their father's ideals yet *against* his brand of Calvinist religion. Toward the end of the 1850s, it is doubtful whether Lyman Beecher knew or perhaps cared about the extent of these innovations within his own family. Then again, his mind had not lost all of its acuity. And he was a "Great Reformer" himself, after all. At eighty-one years old, Lyman visited the Stowes in Andover and wished to attend one of Calvin's lectures. According to Calvin, the old revivalist "came skipping along across lots, laid his hand on top of the five-barred fence, which he cleared at a bound, and was in the lecture-room before me."[187] With death and war so uncomfortably near, and with change overtaking the nation and his own family, Lyman Beecher had not yet lost his childlike verve in his old age. While lecturing once at Plymouth, he declared, "if God said that it was *his* will that I *should* choose whether to die and go to heaven, or to begin my life over again and work once more . . . *I would enlist again in a minute!*"[188] For the eternally young Lyman Beecher, usefulness was its own reward. To work for the Lord was a privilege, not just a responsibility. Lyman's energetic presence was still the glue which tied the family together in the middle of what Henry David Thoreau called "this restless, nervous, bustling, trivial Nineteenth Century."[189]

Chapter 5

THE OLD OAK
FINALLY FELL
(1857–1870)

BY THE 1850s, Lyman Beecher's children had exchanged the traditional beliefs of New England for the Victorian culture of the Old. Puritan ideas like predestination, eternal punishment, original sin, and conversion were no longer rational or useful for society. Instead, Victorian values like social responsibility, strict personal morality, education, order, domesticity, and the art of persuasion were elevated to near-dogma, values hewn from the ethics and mores of New School Presbyterianism. While discarding the more outdated doctrines of their father's religious system, the Beechers embraced those aspects of Victorianism that were most consistent with his project of reforming and Christianizing the republic. One scholar has described Harriet's four works of New England historical fiction as "Victorian realism" with a distinctly "evangelical-dominated periphery."[1] In pursuit of a more liberal evangelicalism, the Beechers were quite at home in American Victorian society. Daniel Walker Howe explains that "in the nineteenth century, Victorian culture was shaped at least as much by liberal Protestants, who had moved beyond their strict Reformation heritage, as by orthodox evangelicals." As the children of Puritanism who admired progressive thinkers like Horace Bushnell and Ralph Waldo Emerson, the Beechers embodied the Victorian ethos of the mid-nineteenth century.

As the Beechers embraced the moral uplift of the Victorian era, they also adopted its secularization. In *Sunny Memories of Foreign Lands* (1854), a chronicle of her travels in England in 1853, Harriet delighted in a light-hearted exchange between Charles Dickens and members of the Chancery over his depiction of the clergy in his books. She wrote, "I must say I think the English are quite remarkable. Here meets the very freest handling; nothing is too sacred to be publicly shown up."[2] Reveling in a bit of sacrilege, Harriet was entranced by a culture unoffended by anticlerical fiction. Having grown up under the strict rule of Lyman Beecher, she was not allowed to speak in such irreverent terms, nor was she permitted certain worldly pleasures like Christmas. But Victorian London was not Litchfield, Connecticut. "The trip would broaden her views and give new perspectives—at times disturbing ones—on her Calvinist heritage," Nancy Koester notes.[3] Like so many of their industrialized, market-driven generation, the Beechers allowed themselves a level of indulgence they had not known as children. For example, although Charles favored total abstinence and complained about the excessive consumption of alcohol on their England trip, Harriet preferred moderation. At times, however, her moderation was not so moderate, as the daughter of the temperance champion was known to enjoy a glass or two of wine a day.[4]

In *Letters to the People on Health and Happiness* (1854), Catharine offered up a trove of Victorian advice on topics ranging from physical exercise to fresh air to social amusements. When she described parents who were given to strong drink and the potentially fatal effects upon their children, she must undoubtedly have thought of Fred Stowe: "And when the flower is cut down, the weeping parents mourn over the sacrifice offered by themselves to their own self-indulgence—to their neglect of that beneficent law, 'We that are strong ought to bear the infirmities of the weak, and not to please ourselves.'"[5] The Stowes still had many tears yet to shed over their son Fred, who was moved from Elmira to a more isolated retreat in Glen Haven due to some unsavory acquaintances he had made at the water cure.[6] Like Lyman himself, the Beechers never conducted their reforms without an eye toward reforming their children. But alcohol was not the only vice for the Stowes, whose indulgence was quickly becoming opulence. Harriet's twins—Hattie and Eliza—were warned by their mother against worldliness and the gratification of "pride and self."[7]

With greater fame and fortune, Henry was beginning to slightly modify his message of reform. He developed a taste for precious stones and was even a familiar face at Tiffany's in Manhattan. Henry Ward Beecher, the newlywed who once lived so modestly in Lawrenceburg, Indiana, had now purchased a summer home in idyllic western Massachusetts to escape the fast pace of the city.[8] Apparently, the life of the reformer did not require any extreme degree of "disinterested benevolence," at least as he saw it. In a sermon entitled "Man's True Dignity" at Plymouth Church on September 11, 1859, Henry declared, "Self is made to be the centre of individual life. Every man must first take care of his own existence. The condition of helping others is that you have power to help with." According to Henry, one needed a bit of self-love in order to love thy neighbor, a notable shift from the disinterested teachings of Samuel Hopkins that had nearly sundered Lyman's engagement to Roxana decades ago. Instead, Henry had begun to imbibe the ideas of Ralph Waldo Emerson, who encouraged his generation to practice "self-culture."[9] Still, underneath this new Victorian thinking lay the good ole Yankee moralism of his father's generation: "You are to measure yourself, not by what you are worth in your peculiar sphere of life—not by station, nor skill, nor any worldly or secular thing; but by what your moral nature makes you worth."[10]

JOHN BROWN AND HARPERS FERRY

Behind the democratic idea of "moral suasion" was the belief that sinners could change themselves instead of waiting passively for an inscrutable God to change his elect. This so-called "voluntary principle" placed a high responsibility upon individuals to exercise their own free will in coming to God and following his commands. But what if someone did *not* want to change? Moreover, what if an entire group of people refused to change? And what if their sin was exceedingly evil? How practical then was the art of moral influence? These questions went to the heart of the entire Beecher project. As Henry explained to his congregation in 1859, "Waiting for God, then, implies first doing faithfully all that in you lies, and then waiting patiently for the result."[11] One could only do what was in his or her own power; the rest was in God's hands. In some ways, Henry was preaching to himself. His marriage had grown cold. As Henry enjoyed more of the public spotlight, he spent less and less time with Eunice, who had become embittered and somewhat lonely. According to the Beecher gospel, to change someone else, individuals had to first change themselves. And change did not come easy. Further north, Fred Stowe was attempting a comeback, having completed his rehabilitation program in upstate New York. When Fred sobered up, Harriet arranged for him to attend Harvard Medical School, where her friend Oliver Wendell Holmes taught anatomy.[12] Fred's life was a continuous battle with alcohol, but he had the unconditional support of his parents.

When James, the youngest Beecher, left for the East in 1849, he too seemed like he would never change. His brawling and swearing were well-suited for life as a sailor. No amount of moral influence on the part of Lyman or Thomas could deter him from his ignoble existence. Perhaps the South China Sea could exercise its own form of "moral suasion." Five years later, it appeared as though it had. James returned from the East India trade in 1854 with some astonishing news: he now wanted to be a minister like his father. On his voyage home from China, the prodigal son declared, "Oh, I shall be a minister. That's my fate. Father will pray me into it!"[13] Once again, Lyman Beecher's prayers had drawn another son into the family business. His determination to see *all* his sons into the ministry was like a tractor beam, capable of pulling the most wandering sheep—from New Orleans to China—back to the fold. However, as usual, James blazed his own trail. After two years at Andover, where Calvin Stowe taught languages, and where he met his new wife, Ann Morse, a widow from Newburyport, Massachusetts, with one child, James accepted a call to become a missionary to oversee a seaman's bethel in Canton in Southeast China. They embarked for the East to minister to the very sailors who had once been James's lowly company. Due to an imperial conflict with Britain, James and Ann eventually relocated to Hong Kong, where they served aboard a floating chapel. The church itself was somewhat symbolic. With the best of intentions, James was doing the work of the Lord while atop a raging sea of emotional and psychological instability. In 1859, James wife's, Annie, returned to America with a form of psychosis, moving to Elmira, New York, under the care of Gleason's Sanitarium. Again, Tom served as counselor and caretaker. In a July letter to Charles, Annie credited Tom and his wife, Julia, with restoring her to sanity.[14] Nevertheless, as the Beechers knew from experience, every revival was followed by the daunting task of moral improvement. Seeking to drink away some of her sorrows, Annie quickly descended into the valley of intemperance. The old nemesis of the Beecher family had become a familiar foe.

Meanwhile, as Annie succumbed to alcoholism, the Beechers found it difficult to persuade an entire society of people to change themselves:

the South. And unlike intemperance, there was no rehabilitation strong enough to purge slavery from its people. In the South, Henry saw a culture fundamentally *opposed* to moral influence. "A system of force cannot deal with moral suasion," he insisted. "You cannot lay the foundations of a political system upon the law of Might, and then run up its towers and spires by the doctrine of Right."[15] Thus, for Henry, moral influence was the only true path to victory because it did not resort to the kind of intimidation and violence endemic to the slaveholding South. For this reason, on October 16, 1859, when an antislavery warrior by the name of John Brown stormed a federal army at Harpers Ferry, Virginia, with five Black and sixteen white crusaders, seeking to ignite a slave uprising, Henry was less than sympathetic. Leaving fourteen dead, including two of Brown's sons, the attack appeared to be as ill-conceived as it was short-lived. Brown, who had garnered something of a reputation for his hatred of slavery by fighting against proslavery forces in Kansas (his father Owen was a trustee at Oberlin), envisioned himself a kind of Old Testament warrior-judge, the kind of figure Beecher was not.

After John Brown was taken into custody by federal troops, led by one Col. Robert E. Lee, many northerners lionized him as a true American hero. Henry David Thoreau extolled Brown as "a superior man" and the "the most American of us all."[16] From Canada, where he sought refuge from enslavers, Frederick Douglass exulted that Brown "dropped an *idea*, equal to a thousand bombshells into the very Bastille of slavery."[17] From Europe, where she was vacationing for almost a year, Harriet said in 1860 that John Brown did "more than any man yet for the honor of the American name."[18] But Henry did not ascribe to him the least degree of patriotism. In fact, in a sermon delivered at Plymouth while Brown was awaiting trial in 1859, Henry jeered at the crusader. "A burning fragment struck the earth near Harpers Ferry. If the fragment of an exploding aerolite had fallen down out of the air, while the meteor swept on, it would not have been more sudden or less apparently connected either with a cause or an effect!" Deriding Brown and his band of abolitionists for their lack of courage and their "mad and feeble schemes," he scorned, "If they kill the man, it will not be so much for treason as for the disclosure of their cowardice! Let no man pray that Brown be spared. Let Virginia make him a martyr. Now, he has only blundered. His soul was noble; his work miserable."[19] Indeed, Brown was executed on December 2, but Henry's trouble had only begun.

As a people of conscience and caution, the Beechers were sometimes given to seeming contradiction. Their sense of moral superiority was only rivaled occasionally by their shrewdness, and Henry was guilty of both in 1859. The famous Brooklyn orator who had so passionately denounced slavery, staged mock auctions to emancipate slave girls, and sent rifles to "Bleeding Kansas" had gone one step too far in the eyes of many when he insisted that the "right of the slave to throw off control of his master is not abrogated." In Henry's mind, the sanctity of human free will could not be violated even among slaveholders. Free agency was sacrosanct. The solution to the crisis of slavery was persuasion and education, not coercion and violence. On this point, Henry still had more in common with Lyman Beecher than he did with John Brown. He also sounded remarkably like Lyman when he asked, "Does any man believe that this vast horde of undisciplined Africans, if set free, would have cohesive power enough to organize themselves into a government, and maintain their independence? If there be men who believe this, I am not among them." Twenty years ago, Lyman had propounded a similar thought in his defense of colonization. But Henry was arguing for nonviolent emancipation. Admonishing the sins of his own people, he then cast a spotlight upon the hypocrisy of the North: "How are the free colored people treated at the North? They are almost without education, and with but little sympathy for their ignorance. They are refused the common rights of citizenship which the whites enjoy. They cannot even ride in the cars of our city railroads."[20] Henry was playing the role of a prophet to his own people. As one might expect, his polemic made a few enemies, including Lewis Tappan and *Independent* editor Theodore Tilton, who accused Beecher of flip-flopping his views on slavery.[21] Although Henry's disdain for slavery had not subsided, it was but the beginning of his decades-long leniency toward the South.

Despite Henry's disregard for John Brown, he was still skilled at "agitation," a term of opprobrium among conservatives to describe abolitionists, radical Republicans, and other social reformers. In fact, Henry seemed to embrace the label of "agitator." In an address delivered at the Cooper Institute in February of 1860, "Woman's Influence in Politics," he argued for women's participation in public affairs. When criticized for his thoughts by Theodore Tilton, Isabella boldly responded with "Shall Women Vote? A Matrimonial Dialogue," an exchange between husband and wife on the issue of female suffrage. Contrary to her husband, Mrs. Smith contends that, because women have had life experience raising families, they are qualified for public work in a way that men are not. Isabella would continue this theme for years to come, turning Catharine's idea of self-sacrifice into suffragism. The "Matrimonial Dialogue" was also a bit of personal testimony. Isabella had experienced similar conversations with her husband, John, as he enjoyed a very public life as a lawyer in Hartford. Pushing the envelope of woman's rights, the youngest Beecher woman also had the gift of "agitation." The manner of her reform was also Victorian in nature. As Donald G. Mathews has shown, even in the South, "whereas for Christians the analogue of heaven had once been the church, it now became the home."[22] Even as the hierarchy of the American household was changing, the home itself was still a sacred space in the Beecher mind.

By the eve of the Civil War, the Beechers had earned themselves a considerable amount of moral authority in the eyes of the American public. They were hated and loved for this very reason. Whether or not their ideas were accepted, they had certainly established a reputation as proselytizers of certain evangelical values. They believed in freedom not bondage, sobriety not drunkenness, enlightenment not entertainment, and character not confessions. On one hand, the Beechers were known for their trademark personalities. When a family friend visited the Stowes in 1857 and remarked to Calvin how outgoing the children were, Calvin replied, "Yes. Beechers every one of them!"[23] As a famous family who generally spoke their minds, they had something of a collective "brand," one might say. "By their very prominence the Beechers were atypical," Marie Caskey summarizes, "even apart from the temperamental and intellectual quirks which gave rise to the term 'Beecherism.'"[24] On the other hand, aside from their eccentric personalities, it was the moral aspect of Beecherism that was so enticing or off-putting to many Americans. In Mobile, Alabama, for example, a minister complained that Henry Ward Beecher used "prayer as a vehicle through which to breathe out threatenings and slaughter against us."[25] In his view, Beecher wielded religion as a weapon. In other words, when Henry took the moral high ground, he took an offensive position. Conversely, in the North, Beecher offered a beacon of hope. Debby Applegate explains, "the main appeal of 'Beecherism' lay in its two interwoven tenets: Liberty and Sympathy, or Freedom and Love."[26] By defending these twin American ideals, the Beechers were almost destined to have an "ism" next to their name.

Therefore, for better or for worse, the Beechers were known for their principles. Just before her third trip to Europe, Harriet and other female contributors to the *Atlantic* were invited to a dinner at the Revere House. Although Harriet frequently enjoyed a glass of wine, she asked if alcohol would be served at the event. They assured her it would not.[27] Founded two years earlier by a group of New England Brahmins who wished to refine the nation, the *Atlantic* was not so refined as to silence the inner puritan inside Lyman Beecher's daughter.[28] Harriet had rejected hell, but she had not lost a strong sense of right and wrong. And just as politicians had feared his father's censure, Henry exerted his own moral authority in the political realm. At the Republican National Convention in Chicago in 1860, many of the delegates became so drunk that their debauchery elicited a reference to the pious pastor of Plymouth Church: "We are quite certain that the Reverend and holy Henry Ward Beecher would be very much shocked could he but see the enormous wickedness and dissipation going on at the assembling of his disciples."[29]

"A GREAT ANTI-SLAVERY WAR"

In the winter of 1859, the tall, rustic Illinoisan Abraham Lincoln prepared to make a speech in New York City that he believed would be the most important one of his life. Attempting to refute his rival, Stephen Douglas, on the issue of slavery in the western territories, Lincoln spent hours at the State House Library in Springfield researching the founders' views on slavery. His invitation had come from the illustrious Henry Ward Beecher, who had asked him to speak at Plymouth Church in Brooklyn. Lincoln readily accepted, eager to make his mark in the nation's largest city in the nation's most famous church. He even spent one hundred dollars on a new suit from Woods & Henckle. Needing time to prepare such a consequential address on such a significant stage, he asked Beecher that the date be pushed to February. This was no problem for Beecher, as Lincoln was a rising star in the Republican Party and the soon-to-be nominee for president. Lincoln's speech would propel him to the nomination in May. Plymouth Church had become more than a church. It was a platform for public discourse. Lincoln seized the moment. However, when he checked into the Astor Hotel in February, Lincoln was informed that the Young Men's Republican Union had taken over sponsorship of the event and moved the speech to the Cooper Institute in Manhattan.[30] The Beechers were never at the very center of antebellum politics, but they nevertheless shaped the course of American history.

It is little surprise, then, that the Beechers and their children were involved in the events leading to, during, and following the Civil War. In February of 1861, provoked by the election of Abraham Lincoln to the presidency, delegates in Montgomery, Alabama, from seven Deep South states voted to secede from the Union and establish the Confederate States of America. Lincoln was inaugurated on March 4, the very same day that the Confederacy chose its new flag. In April, the attack on Fort Sumter in Charleston, South Carolina, launched the bloodiest war in American history. In his sermon "The Battle Set in Array," Henry prepared his people for the days ahead, calling for "courage which comes from broad moral sentiment."[31] Henry struck a powerful chord in the North. According to historian James P. Byrd, it was "perhaps the most cited northern sermon after Sumter—a sermon that drew the nation's attention to the book of Exodus."[32] Meanwhile, the war interrupted Fred Stowe's first year at Harvard Medical School. After an unsuccessful attempt to become an army surgeon, Harriet's son was the first of the Beecher nephews to enlist. He joined the first company of the Massachusetts Voluntary Infantry when he was barely twenty-one years old.[33] From the classroom, Fred almost immediately plunged into battle. In July, he fought at the Battle of Bull Run (Manassas), which launched the Civil War in earnest.[34] Due in large part to his last name, Fred climbed the ranks of his company to eventually join the staff of a brigadier general.

Meanwhile, Henry Ward's eldest son, Harry, was almost twenty-one when he asked for his father's permission to join the fight. If the Beechers knew how to do one thing well, it was enlist for a cause. Henry's response left no doubt of the Beecher family's support for the Union: "If you don't, I'll disown you."[35] Henry raised three thousand dollars from Plymouth Church for his son's regiment. So supportive were the Beechers of the Union army in the early months of the war that even Thomas, who scorned the idea of emancipation, did his part to rally the troops. When the war broke out, he traveled throughout upstate New York trying to recruit badly needed soldiers for the New York regiments. Although he did not assail the evils of slavery, he preached sermons defending the Union and condemning secession.[36] This was not an uncommon position in the northern states, especially in 1861. All the Beechers rallied to the cause, albeit for different purposes. By early September of 1862, Thomas became chaplain of the 141st New York Regiment, in which he served until January 10, 1863.

Even a bloody, fratricidal war could not prevent the Beechers from attempting to intervene in their children's lives. In July of 1862, as the Stowes were in Brooklyn on business, they stopped at Henry's. During their visit, Henry caught word that Fred's company was in nearby Jersey City on its way to Washington to defend the capital from Confederate attack. Harriet and Calvin raced to New Jersey to see their son, fearing his addiction as much as any stray bullet. The military was not the safest place for a recovering alcoholic. Harriet was afraid for the "temptations and dangers of the camp and the fears that . . . obtrude of his being prisoner of barbarians or wounded and helpless."[37] As Noel Gerson notes, once they arrived at the camp, Harriet "made it her business to meet his regimental chaplain, and after assuring herself the latter was a good Christian she felt a trifle more relaxed. Her son was in safe hands."[38] But in fact Fred was headed straight for war. Soon he and his cousin Harry would join thousands of Union soldiers in Washington, DC, to face the Army of Northern Virginia, led by Robert E. Lee. Ultimately, it was Harry, not Fred, who was dismissed from his regiment due to a serious ethical infraction. "His 'crime' was hushed up, but judging by his mother's reaction, it likely took place in one of Washington's notorious bawdy houses, where booze, prostitutes, and politicians mingled freely."[39] On the battlefield, a young man could lose his life. But in the dark alleyways of Washington, he could lose his soul. With the help of Theodore Tilton, who called in a favor with Secretary of War Simon Cameron, Henry managed to secure a commission for his dissolute namesake in General McClellan's Army of the Potomac. Henry wept tears of gratitude, having salvaged a scrap of family honor. During the war, the Beechers embraced and even enhanced the sense of moral superiority that animated the North. But even a family of moral crusaders was not without its own moral failings, as Henry himself would soon discover.

As the war progressed, several of the Beechers disagreed on the precise aim of the war and the best strategy for achieving victory. At Andover, where soldiers drilled on campus and where the abolitionist spirit was especially high, Harriet believed the Civil War was a "holy war," "a sacred war," and "a great Anti-Slavery war."[40] She had grown impatient of President Lincoln's plan to free the slaves by appealing to the border states and offering them financial compensation. She was also disappointed in the "utter failure of Christian anti-slavery England" to support the North due to commercial interests in the cotton-growing South.[41] In her "Reply" to "the affectionate and Christian address of many thousands of women of Great Britain and Ireland," Harriet sought to rally the support of those women who had petitioned for liberty just years earlier.[42] Henry, on the other hand, had originally insisted that the government had no constitutional right to declare emancipation. But after a stern letter from Harriet and some public rebukes by fellow Republicans, he now supported the idea that northerners were fighting to free the enslaved.

Henry could not seem to please anyone in 1862, receiving criticism from *both* sides of the family divide. On his left, Harriet was disappointed in her brother's comments against President Lincoln's war policy in the press. To his right, Thomas chastised him for his "talk" about emancipation. The soldiers "will say, 'We ain't going to fight for the Niggers,'" Tom wrote to Henry in August. "You remember Indiana? Do you soberly think that those fighting Hoosiers would hurry to enlist for the sake of freeing the slave? Will negro hating Illinois that now gives nigh half her men to the war, consent to fight for the slaves she despises? I can answer for rural New York. The more emancipation you talk, the less recruits you can enlist."[43] For Thomas, the Civil War was not a war over slavery, but a war to recover the Union. God was punishing the North for its greed and purging northerners of their rampant materialism.[44] "For many conservatives," Eric Foner states, "the preservation of the Union was an end in itself, and to maintain it they urged that the anti-slavery agitation be abandoned. But to the radicals, the Union was a means, not an end."[45] Thomas's views about "machine-like" industrialization and the beautiful "order" of society were more in line with the Romantic beliefs of southern society. In Henry's view, however, the purpose of the Union was life, liberty, and the pursuit of happiness. This was, after all, the founders' vision for the country. By the end of 1862, with the Emancipation Proclamation forthcoming, Henry was no longer a critic of Lincoln. During his Thanksgiving sermon, Henry commended the president's cautious approach.[46]

The Beechers were busy people in the winter of 1862. Harriet was invited to a Thanksgiving dinner in Washington for "contrabands," a term given to slaves who were freed from the South during the war. Intending to see her son Fred, who was stationed just outside the capital, she made the trip with her daughter Hattie and her son Charles. Harriet also brought her half-sister Isabella, who bemoaned traveling in the entourage of "her highness."[47] Harriet enjoyed traveling with and visiting family. On her way to Washington, they stopped in Brooklyn to see Henry and Lyman and company. During their stay, Henry and Harriet arranged to meet Mary Todd Lincoln, the wife of the president. By Harriet's estimation, she was "a good hearted weak woman fat, & frank." Harriet also noted the First Lady's disdain for General McClellan, who was relieved of his command of the Army of the Potomac just days earlier.[48] McClellan, who was once labeled a "humbug" by Mrs. Lincoln, had won a key northern victory at the Battle of Antietam on September 17, the war's bloodiest day, but his refusal to heed Lincoln's instructions to "destroy the rebel army," his continued sympathy for the South, and his Democratic ambivalence toward emancipation all led to his dismissal.[49] The success at Antietam, with twenty-three thousand Union and Confederate soldiers killed or wounded in a single day, had precipitated Lincoln's plans to unveil the Emancipation Proclamation the following year. By the end of the conversation with Mrs. Lincoln, who shined as a White House hostess, Harriet was invited to Washington for tea. Harriet would confirm for herself about the Emancipation Proclamation.

When they arrived in a cold and blustery Washington, Harriet had one person on her mind: "I must see Fred."[50] Finding her battle-hardened son at Fort Runyan in Northern Virginia, they rented a room while Fred was on furlough. "Lieutenant Stowe, who had already met the enemy in combat five times, was no longer a boy, but a man," Gerson comments.[51] Before the war was over, the Army of the Potomac would suffer more combat deaths than all other Union armies combined.[52] Harriet was comforted to see Fred in once piece. She was also inspired by her visit to the barracks of the "contrabands," enjoying their very first Thanksgiving on free soil. The visit to Washington was a riveting reminder of God's blessing in the midst of so much bloodshed.

Finally, on December 2, Harriet made her now-famous visit to the White House, accompanied by Senator Henry Wilson of Massachusetts and his wife. The Beechers had never met anyone quite like Abraham Lincoln. Although Hattie and Isabella made their own noteworthy—and some-what condescending—remarks about the president's uncouth, quotidian style, it was Charles's account that has been etched into historical memory when he recalled Lincoln's introduction: "So you are the little woman who made this big war."[53] While the quote is probably apocryphal, historian David S. Reynolds admits, "The words sound like Lincoln."[54] Moreover, they illustrate the kind of reputation that would have preceded Harriet Beecher Stowe in 1862. Some scholars have speculated whether Lincoln was referring to *Uncle Tom's Cabin* the literary work or to the stage productions of the book as well.[55] Either way, "if Stowe's novel was responsible for the Civil War, so were the stage adaptations."[56] Doubtless Lincoln understood the power of Uncle Tom. According to the *Tribune*, Stowe's character had penetrated the American nation "from the great city mansion to the humblest village home."[57] Certainly, it had not missed the White House. Even before Lincoln won the presidency, he was familiar with Beecher's work and the entire Beecher clan. As a rising politician in Illinois, he was no stranger to the name of Edward Beecher, the St. Louis–area abolitionist. In 1860, Lincoln met with a family friend who reported, "He knew much about all [the members of] the talented Beecher family; showed me a well worn copy of Harriet Beecher Stowe's *Uncle Tom's Cabin*, and some clippings of Henry Ward Beecher's sermons and speeches."[58] Very few remarks have ever testified to the nation-shaping power of the Beechers more than this. And Mary Todd had attended Plymouth Church services herself in 1861, where she created a "great sensation."[59]

If indeed Lincoln knew anything about "the little woman" standing across from him, he would have also known that he and Stowe shared a good bit in common. Both had been molded by families who had ventured west, both had imbibed their father's evangelical values and ideas without necessarily adhering to his Calvinist beliefs, and both wielded those ideas in their efforts to save the republic. "There was an emotional connection between Lincoln and Harriet," argues David S. Reynolds, "their shared experience of witnessing slavery firsthand while losing close family members. In both cases, grief deepened their awareness of the horrors of slavery."[60] Over a foot taller than Stowe, the tall, gangly Illinoisan was not very different in several respects from the daughter of New England Puritanism. Similar to Uncle Tom, Lincoln would eventually die a somewhat Christlike death that galvanized the nation. By the time she left Washington, Harriet was reassured that Lincoln would sign the Emancipation Proclamation. She then wrote to her editor James Fields at the *Atlantic Monthly,* "it seems to be the opinion here that the president will stand up to his Proclamation . . . a glorious expectancy."[61] She left the capital with hope. Harriet timed the publication of her *Reply* to coincide with Lincoln's signing on January 1. The proclamation did not take effect in the border states of Missouri, Kentucky, Maryland, and Delaware, as they had never officially joined the Confederacy. Nevertheless, as Harriet summarized to the antislavery women of Britain, "The President's Proclamation simply means this: Come in, and emancipate peaceably with compensation; stay out, and I emancipate, nor will I protect you from the consequences."[62]

JAMES BEECHER: PREACHER, RECRUITER, SOLDIER

Although Harriet and Henry were the most famous Beechers, it was surprisingly the youngest Beecher who performed one of the most improbable acts of moral influence ever undertaken by any American during the war. As was his habit, he took the long road to get there. At the outset of the conflict, "the unfettered, self-determining James" returned to the United States from Hong Kong to enlist in the Union army.[63] While the ministry had softened a few of his hard edges, James was not without some resentment for the fact that none of his family except for Harriet had written to him during his sojourn in the Far East.[64] He complained to Harriet that his "only real friends are in China."[65] James never really considered Lyman's older children as his true siblings, but he still longed for a relationship with Thomas and Isabella.

Regardless, like almost all the Beecher siblings, he benefited from the patronage of his brother Henry. Through the latter's influence, he received a post as chaplain in the First Long Island Regiment, called the "Brooklyn Phalanx." As a former missionary to China, this placement seemed well-suited to James's talents and experience. However, according to his grandnephew Lyman Beecher Stowe, chaplaincy "didn't suit his ardent temperament and strong military aptitude."[66] James grew impatient and requested active duty. Since chaplains were generally not a high priority for the government, permission was granted.[67] James exceled as a soldier, eventually becoming lieutenant colonel of the 141st New York Volunteers—the very same regiment in which his brother Thomas was chaplain. The entire family swelled with pride. Thomas bragged to his father that James, boasting a new mustache, looked "more like a man than any of us."[68] During their visit to Washington to see the president, Isabella and Harriet cheered as they watched their younger brother march at the head of his regiment.[69]

While the Beecher network was effective enough to combine brothers in the very same regiment, it also came at a cost. The circumstances that arose in the 141st in late 1862 illustrate the good, the bad, and the ugly of Beecherism. When James arrived in the regiment in October, not everyone was thrilled to have another Beecher on board. Colonel Samuel G. Hathaway Jr., James's commanding officer, had accepted his appointment only under duress. Hathaway felt that Thomas had gained his brother's commission in a manner "not becoming a Christian minister."[70] In other words, James's arrival had the appearance of good old-fashioned nepotism. James was stepping into the middle of a rivalry that had developed between Thomas and Hathaway. As the son of General Samuel G. Hathaway, a former Democratic state senator and a member of Congress, the colonel was himself the product of nepotism, as were many officers in the Union and Confederate armies. He would not tolerate the scent of Beecherism in his regiment. Thomas noted that the 141st had already earned the reputation for being an "*abolition* regiment" because the chaplain (himself) was the brother of the famous Henry Ward Beecher, a known radical abolitionist. As a New York Democrat unsympathetic to abolitionism, Hathaway was embittered at the insinuation that his soldiers were fighting primarily against slavery. In New York, he wasn't alone. The majority of New Yorkers had voted for Democrat Stephen Douglas in the election of 1860.[71] Just south in New Jersey, proslavery students at Princeton had burned an effigy of Henry.[72] Oddly enough, although Thomas himself was a conservative on the issue of slavery (he opposed the Emancipation Proclamation), his loyalty to his brother was far stronger than his bond with any anti-abolitionist. "Alas that Henry Ward Beecher ever should taint the reputation of so gallant a Democrat as Col. Hathaway, and bring his regiment into disfavor!" Thomas mocked privately.[73]

But the Beechers rarely kept anything to themselves. In a stunning act of insubordination, if not treason, Thomas sent a letter to Hathaway's superiors accusing the colonel of participating in a plot to overthrow the Lincoln government! At the time of this accusation, not long after Harriet heard Mrs. Lincoln repudiating George McClellan, the sentiment that the former general, a disaffected Democrat, was defiant of Lincoln and would seek to undermine his administration was not uncommon. Indeed, McClellan *would* run against Lincoln and lose in 1864. But Thomas had mutinously severed the chain of command, and during wartime no less. As he probably knew while writing it, the letter crossed a Rubicon from which Thomas could never return. Shortly after attacking Hathaway, he resigned from the regiment to avoid scrutiny from within. Unfortunately, James became the scapegoat. Although Thomas returned to his church without repercussion (despite the reproach of locals in Elmira who frowned upon his actions), James remained in the 141st and bore the consequences of his brother's decisions. Not surprisingly, Thomas's false accusations caused James to feel isolated in the regiment. Suffering under the ire and resentment of his fellow soldiers, James grew embittered toward his brother. Feeling abandoned, he wanted Thomas to feel his pain. The words they exchanged in the aftermath of Thomas's departure would linger well after the war. Some sins could not be washed away with blood.

To make matters worse, back in Elmira, Thomas was angry with James for wanting to divorce his clinically insane wife. As Annie's condition worsened in the sanitarium, James's own psyche began to deteriorate under the weight of severe anxiety. Resorting to alcohol to drown out the hurt, he then attempted suicide by swallowing chloroform.[74] Although he survived, James could not escape his regiment, his life, or his marriage. Thomas admonished his little brother for fleeing from his duty as a husband, a gross violation of Beecher family values. Due to James's seeming infidelity, Henry's outspoken abolitionism, and his own ethical violations in the army, Thomas worried that upstate New York was beginning to turn on the Beechers. There was an "anti-Beecher Copperhead stir" afoot, beginning with resentment of Henry's sermons and intensifying with certain "innuendos" about himself. As a result, for fear of "anti-Beecher fellows," he instructed James not to make any more public statements about Annie and to stay away from Elmira.[75] The family's reputation was at stake. While Thomas issued stern rebukes, James's sister Isabella delivered a lifeline. From Connecticut, Isabella successfully persuaded Secretary of War Stanton, a friend of the Stowes and Beechers, to give James an honorable discharge and avoid being court-marshaled.[76] Annie died of delirium tremens in April of 1863. Her death had been long coming and difficult to witness. James endured the second-greatest tragedy of his life, but he also received something of a second chance in the war. When James was readmitted into the army, he was given a Herculean task: recruiting a Black regiment.

In the spring of 1863, James opened a recruiting office in New Bern, North Carolina, with the goal of enlisting Black soldiers for the war effort. He had great success, becoming the regiment chaplain of the First North Carolina Volunteers. Like his father, James knew how to enlist others in a fight. However, like his first stint in the army, James discovered that he was much more versatile than his commanding officers had first believed. He not only recruited but equipped, trained, and led the regiment.[77] Robert Gould Shaw of the Fifty-Fourth Massachusetts had led the first all-Black regiment in American history, but James was a pioneer of sorts in the Beecher family itself. While all of the Beechers (minus Thomas) were willing to fight *for* Blacks, James was the first and only Beecher to fight *with* them. In a remarkable instance of "moral suasion," after persuading freed slaves to fight for a country that considered them less than citizens, he marched next to them. On November 30, in the third battle of General Sherman's March to the Sea, the First North Carolina Volunteers fought in the Battle of Honey Hill in South Carolina, a strategic effort to break the Confederate line along the Charleston and Savannah Railroad. With the prayers and admiration of his family, James led his troops under a banner designed by his sister Harriet.[78] After the Federals suffered defeat at the hands of the Confederates, who earned one of their last victories of the war, James preached from Galatians 5:1: "Stand fast therefore in the liberty wherewith Christ hath made us free, and be not entangled again with the yoke of bondage."

As historians have shown, from the time of the American Revolution, evangelicals strongly equated spiritual freedom with political freedom, and spiritual and military warfare.[79] According to James P. Byrd, the book of Galatians offered to patriots "more clearly than any other text from the New Testament" the idea that liberty was both civil and Christian.[80] During the Civil War, evangelicals like James Beecher extended and, in some ways, intensified this tradition of explicating Galatians 5:1 as a political text.[81] James saw his work as captain and as chaplain as two sides of the same coin. He was a soldier for America *and* for the Lord. By fighting alongside Black soldiers, James understood, at least more than any other Beecher, that freedom without equality was no freedom at all. When his former soldiers took up residence on the abandoned Edisto Island after the war only to have it stripped away and returned to the original plantation owners, James strongly advocated to Senator Charles Sumner on behalf of the displaced freemen.[82] The fight for liberty had not ended on the battlefield. After the war, following his marriage to Francis "Frankie" Johnson of Guilford, Connecticut, in 1864, James reentered the ministry and even pastored his brother Thomas's church in Elmira for a time. But he continued to fight a losing battle for happiness and purpose in his own mind.

"THE OLD OAK FINALLY FELL"

At five o'clock in the morning on January 10, 1863, Lyman Beecher died at the age of eighty-seven. As Henry phrased it, "The old oak finally fell."[83] Overshadowed by his famous children, eclipsed by a civil war, and enfeebled by age, the former evangelical titan had lived out his final years on earth as a shell of his former self. In many ways, Lyman left the world similarly to the way he came into it: undersized and overlooked. But his death was as symbolic as that of any minister who had ever lived. Born nine months before the signing of the Declaration of Independence, Lyman Beecher passed nine days after the signing of the Emancipation Proclamation. For someone who devoted his entire ministry to the right exercise of human freedom, his life encompassed—and to some extent represented—America's painful struggle for liberty in its most basic sense. No public figure in the early United States heralded the Christianization of American society more than Lyman Beecher, and yet no one demonstrated more than Beecher how elastic and at times elusive that idea could be. He was, according to Vincent Harding, an eternal optimist who failed to see the world as it had become. "He had little contact with a nation that now heard an Illinois politician speak of a house divided against itself, a nation that pondered the meaning of an irrepressible conflict."[84] Forty years earlier, Lyman Beecher prophesied to his generation that the "political destiny of our nation is to be decided in the West."[85] He could never have foreseen, or perhaps comprehended, the full extent of those words.

Just days earlier, standing from a balcony in Boston Music Hall, Harriet listened to hundreds of cheering voices as the news of the Emancipation Proclamation was announced. The crowd chanted triumphantly, "Harriet Beecher Stowe, Harriet Beecher Stowe!" until she stood up and acknowledged the tribute, wiping away tears from her eyes.[86] Days later, she wept tears of a different kind. At the funeral service for her father at Plymouth Church, Dr. Leonard Bacon of Yale concluded, "This country is inhabited by saints, sinners, and Beechers."[87] Harriet remembered her last visit to see her father, the man she credited with introducing her to the antislavery cause. "Do you know that you are a very handsome old gentleman?" she asked him with a pained smile, gently stroking his head. "Tell me something new," he replied with a sly grin.[88] In his final days, Lyman had grown more senile and unaware of his surroundings. However, even at death's door, a few dying embers of Lyman's personality still burned. His so-called "fire, impulse, and Beecherism" had now passed to his children, who would venerate their father for the rest of their lives. In the Beecher family, if deceased mothers became angels, Lyman became a deity.

Buried next to his beloved friend Nathaniel William Taylor in New Haven, Lyman returned to the place where his ministry had begun. His death, like that of his mentor Timothy Dwight, represented the end of an era in American evangelicalism, when the disestablishment of state-sponsored religion was quickly replaced with the establishment of coalitional, *voluntary* religion. Lyman's children were introducing another age of American religion themselves, one far less sectarian and orthodox yet no less institutional and optimistic. Their father's death, though solemn, also came as a relief to those who had watched the slow, grinding erosion of a once ebullient mind.[89] Lyman Beecher had not ushered in the millennium as he had believed he would. But the adolescent nation was very different from the one he had inherited, thanks in large part to his efforts to "reform and purify the land."[90]

A year of turning points, 1863 was for Harriet a homecoming of sorts. After Calvin retired from Andover to begin writing his great work on the origins of the Bible, the Stowes purchased four and a half acres of land in

Hartford, Connecticut. Joining her sisters Mary and Isabella, Harriet returned to the New England town in which she had once taught at her sister Catharine's school. Soon she began supervising the construction of an eight-gabled, Gothic-style mansion on the southeastern edge of Nook Farm they would call "Oakholm." Beyond Hartford, the nation itself was also at a turning point. In July, Harriet's son Fred fought in one of the most decisive battles of the entire war: Gettysburg. Under the command of General George Meade, Fred fought alongside his cousin Robert Beecher, William's son. When Fred was struck by a bullet, Robert helped him into a nearby home at Gettysburg where a local widow and her daughter nursed him to health.[91] Somehow, even in war, Beechers still managed to find one another. During this time, Harriet and Calvin had no idea if their son was dead or alive. Although Fred survived, his wounds never fully healed. With a piece of a bullet lodged in his ear, Fred was sent to several military hospitals before eventually being sent home. "It was the worst kind of wound," explains Nancy Koester, "enough to ruin his life, yet not enough to get a discharge from the army."[92] For the rest of his life, Fred would suffer from a ringing in his ear. Another, much deeper wound was also exposed: alcohol. In the army hospital, Fred began drinking again. As one battle ended, another began again.

A week or so later, the Stowes received a letter from a chaplain that their son was "struck by a fragment of a shell, which entered his right ear" and he was "anxious that [his family] should hear from him as soon as possible."[93] To add insult to his son's injury, Calvin set off by train for Gettysburg only to be robbed at the station. He returned to Hartford with wounded pride. As for Harriet, she would soon discover the full extent of Fred's infirmities. "Harriet could accept the wound as God's will," Rugoff remarks, "but no one ever knew how she, daughter of a leader in the temperance movement, coped with the shame of having a son who was a drunkard."[94] At least for now, Fred was alive. Incredibly enough, there were in fact three Beechers at the Battle of Gettysburg who survived the most devastating conflict of the Civil War. Frederick Beecher, Charles's son, was also wounded in combat.[95] Robert E. Lee's Army of the Potomac had been turned back, losing strategic momentum they would never regain for the rest of the war. Indeed, everything was different after 1863. Just as the Civil War was never the same after Gettysburg, so the Beechers were not the same family after the death of Lyman Beecher.

LIFE AFTER LYMAN

Shortly after his son survived Gettysburg, Charles Beecher faced his own test. In Georgetown, Massachusetts, where he now ministered, a church council tried him for heresy. He was certainly not the only Beecher with heterodox beliefs or with an aversion to ecclesiastical authority. His brother Henry, who was vacationing in Europe, had become somewhat famous for his ability to hold two conflicting doctrines at once. George Marsden remarks somewhat jokingly, "Henry Ward Beecher was not a theologian. Although he was well-informed, he claimed he 'never read a book through'—presumably with the exception of those he wrote."[96] But Charles was not as shrewd as his older brother. When he questioned the doctrine of hell, as did several of his brothers and sisters, he did so quite openly. In addition to reformulating the traditional doctrine of penal substitutionary atonement, he also imbibed his brother Edward's novel theory of the preexistence of souls. The tipping point came when there was "an unhappy division in the church" because the "preaching of the pastor was not such as they desired," reported one midwestern paper.[97] In antebellum New England, bad doctrine was worrisome; bad preaching was intolerable. Nevertheless, Charles had the support of his siblings. Edward traveled all the way from Galesburg, Illinois, to advocate for his chief (and perhaps only) disciple who affirmed his unique theory. From Connecticut, Harriet was outraged at the indictment of heresy.[98] Ultimately, however, not even the Beecher name could protect Charles from a guilty verdict. Charles was not as skilled in theological argumentation nor as orthodox as his father to survive the gauntlet. The council ruled that Charles's teachings were "fundamentally erroneous" and recommended that he be dismissed. Although the smell of heterodoxy had accompanied the Beechers for decades, Charles was the first convicted heretic in the family.

If Beechers could not properly defend themselves in person, they almost always did so in print. And for Charles, the pen was mightier. Coauthored with his mentor Edward, Charles made his reply in *The Result Tested*. Protesting the ruling of the council in Massachusetts, Charles and Edward argued that the trial was essentially another strike from the Old School in their assault upon their father, Lyman Beecher. In other words, Charles was being persecuted because his last name was Beecher. Although the patriarch himself had passed away and was unable to come to the aid of his spiritual Diadochi, the Beecher children continued to frame many of their own contests in the light of their father's. Charles and Edward also tied their religious opponents to slavery. They claimed there was "a league between the rebellion in Georgetown, and the ecclesiastical copperhead-ism of New England," a sure sign that the politics of the war had colored the theological debates of the age.[99] After all, they reasoned, if the trial was purely about doctrine, why was not Edward tried for heresy as well?[100] Ultimately, Charles was vindicated in the eyes of his loyal parishioners. The majority of his church supported him through the trial, ready to withdraw fellowship from the local conference rather than lose their pastor. They also helped elect Charles to the Massachusetts legislature in 1864. (Charles was a pioneer in the Beecher family in more ways than one.) As the only one of the Lyman children to serve in government, Charles defied the traditional mold of a moral influencer. Either way, as a Beecher, he knew how to win a crowd. In all likelihood, Charles's bid for public office was motivated less by statesmanship or civic duty and more by the desire to prove that his heresy trial had been a witch hunt. Tellingly, Charles only ran for one term and was returned to good standing years later when the council's "verdict" was rescinded.[101]

In *Redeemer and Redeemed* (1864), published a year later, Charles articulated his views on the atonement and eternal judgment. (As to his brother's theory of the preexistence of souls, Charles believed Edward's argument was "unanswerable.")[102] In the preface, Charles told the story of a young man profoundly shaped by his father from his earliest days in Litchfield, Connecticut. "Everything that my father thought, I thought," he wrote; "everything he believed I believed, everything he felt I felt, everything he described I saw." Even the Bible itself sounded like Lyman. "Certain texts of Scripture are not to me, and never can be, merely verses of a written word; they are voices of my father,—voices instinct with emotion deep as eternity, incarnating themselves within me." Lyman's voice was, quite literally, the voice of God. Thus, when Charles eventually resisted the concepts of original sin and eternal punishment, his new beliefs pitted him squarely against his father, his upbringing, and his own conscience.

Charles's description of his spiritual journey from Puritan pupil to freethinking biblical rationalist is one of the most revealing pictures ever painted of the Beecher children's complicated relationship to their father:

> When my mind woke from passive receptivity to active investigation, when I was born from the womb of my father's faith to the outer sphere of independent reasoning, my mind was agitated, agonized. The faith of eternal realities was unchangeably fixed within me. The belief of the Bible as the word of God was like a part of myself. But the questions that have always fascinated earnest minds began to fascinate me. The origin of evil, the freedom of the will, and similar subjects, absorbed me, and I abandoned myself to them with the instinctive thoroughness and earnestness of my nature. They brought me to grief, but I cared not; they threw me in collision with my father, but I could not ignore them. For a time they wrecked me, temporally, and threatened shipwreck eternal, but I could not forgo them. By the mercy of God I outlived them. The time arrived when I could let them alone, and look at them from a safe distance, as I still do to this day.[103]

While Charles wrestled a bit more conscientiously (and heretically) with his father's beliefs than did his siblings, his words could very well have been written by any number of the Beecher children. Indeed, *all* the Beechers felt they had been "born in the womb" of Lyman's faith only to be thrown "in collision" with the man who raised them. In one sense, the tendency to moralize and innovate was a religious heritage bequeathed to the Beechers from the New England theological tradition dating back to the time of Jonathan Edwards. Lyman Beecher himself had continued this tradition from New Divinity theologians such as Samuel Hopkins, Timothy Dwight, and Nathaniel William Taylor. To some degree, all of these men had reconceptualized the nature of evil and the freedom of the will. Yet, in another sense, by subjecting these categories to the authority of human reason rather than *any* confession or creed, several of the Beecher children had effectively bowdlerized the New England Tradition. They were, as one historian has described Harriet Beecher Stowe, "post-Edwardsean."[104] Lyman taught his children to trust in the Scriptures, to think for themselves, and to be useful for the Lord. Ultimately, this was the *only* Beecher creed. They would follow it wherever it took them, even if it led them to reject their father's religion. As Charles confessed, "this brought me to grief." The troubled story of the entire Beecher dynasty, and to some extent the story of northern evangelicalism in the late nineteenth century, can be boiled down to this internal dialectic between conscience and reason.

Nevertheless, Lyman Beecher's children saw themselves as developing, and even elucidating, many of his ideas. For example, in the same book in which he lamented his "collision" with Lyman, Charles also quoted his father to argue against eternal judgment, an idea that Lyman clearly affirmed.[105] Curiously, he invoked his father to deny his father's beliefs. Amazingly, even Edward believed that his views were largely consistent with Lyman's.[106] Underneath all of their novel ideas and theological experimentation, George Marsden notes, was Lyman's dogged belief in the power of human reason and the potential for progress: "The aspects of his father's New England Calvinism that Henry Ward Beecher rejected were those based on 'abstract truth.' The moral government of God, God's relationship to humans, and the nature of religious experience had all been reduced to clear propositions through Common Sense and Baconian analysis."[107] With the help of Scottish Common-Sense Realism, Lyman himself had argued that human beings could trust their senses in determining the truth. His children pushed the bounds of this idea until no external religious authority could be trusted in full. When Orestes Brownson heaped burning coals upon the entire Beecher clan in 1870, he noted a common strain of rationalistic and individualistic thought: "Nothing more than the proper development and training of one's natural powers or faculties, [Beecherism] teaches, is necessary to make one an heir of the kingdom of God. This is the hobby of the feminine Beechers, and perhaps not less so of the masculine Beechers."[108] In essence, Lyman Beecher's children retooled his message of "natural ability" until humanity had no "moral inability" left. For this reason, even after the Beechers departed so decisively from Lyman's Calvinism, they continued to see themselves in the light of many of his teachings. The rest was sanctified by the ghost of Roxana. Charles's *Redeemer and Redeemed* was dedicated to his late mother, "to her who gave me birth; consecrated me to the ministry; died before I knew her; whom, next to my Redeemer, I most desire to meet in the Resurrection."[109] Although he had not changed his mind about hell, Charles had come to affirm, quite emphatically, the existence of heaven.

After Lyman's death, the Beecher children were finally released from those remaining aspects of their father's Puritanical authority that had long kept them moored to tradition rather than preference. In 1864, Harriet joined the Episcopal Church along with her twins, Hattie and Eliza. Hattie had already asked for her mother's permission to join, to which Harriet had responded, "I not only consent to your joining the Episcopal Church as you have often expressed the desire to do but I desire it so much that I will remove any obstructs in your way. I have applied for a seat in the church in town and I will sometimes go with you—always to sacrament because I find that service is more beneficial than ours."[110] Although Harriet privately regarded Episcopalian preaching as lacking in logical progression and devoid of enthusiasm, these objections finally dissolved once Lyman passed. In a symbolic gesture, Harriet was leaving the church of her father to join the church of her mother. Calvin remained a Congregationalist, and Harriet was never technically confirmed, but she did purchase a pew in Hartford's St. John's Church in April. In time, her son Fred, rehabilitating from the war and from his own addiction, also sought the communion of the Episcopal Church.[111] Like her father, Harriet believed that religion was a family affair. "To have my children with me in the fold of Christ, to unite with them in the sacrament has been the thing of all others I have longed for," Harriet wrote.[112] Eventually, she even asked her brother Charles to join her new denomination.[113] Likewise freed from her father's influence, Catharine also joined the Episcopal Church in 1864. She too was motivated by family. According to Kathryn Sklar, "Catharine had concluded that only the Episcopal church treated children decently."[114] In her view, the Episcopal doctrine of sin was much less oppressive to infants and youth. As it had throughout her life, Catharine's commitment to moral influence and her vision of education ultimately determined her religion. By the time she completed *The Religious Training of Children in the Family, the School, and the Church* (1864), a work in which she denied the idea of original sin and the Calvinist doctrine of total depravity, Catharine was a confirmed Episcopalian.

DEFENDING LINCOLN

In 1863, Henry accepted a surprise gift from his church to travel to Europe. He instantly accepted. Exhausted physically and emotionally, a leisure trip through Britain, Germany, France, Belgium, Switzerland, and Italy was a much-needed sabbatical from the most public ministry in America. However, while abroad, Henry did not keep a low profile. According to Oliver Wendell Holmes, Henry's journey through Britain was one of the greatest diplomatic accomplishments in American history. In his *Atlantic Monthly* article in January of 1864, "The Minister Plenipotentiary," Holmes boasted that Beecher had "finished a more remarkable embassy than any envoy who has represented us in Europe since Franklin pleaded the cause of the young Republic at the Court of Versailles." Although this was a bit of a stretch, the Beecher name certainly preceded him. "He was welcomed by friendly persons on the other side of the Atlantic," Holmes declared, "partly for [his] merits, partly also as 'the son of the celebrated Dr. Beecher' and 'the brother of Mrs. Beecher Stowe.'"[115] From Manchester to Glasgow to Edinburgh to Liverpool to London, Henry delivered rousing speeches to cheering crowds on a number of hot-button issues, from temperance to free speech to abolitionism.

With some encouragement from the American ambassador to England, Charles Francis Adams, Henry's primary goal was to muster British support for the North against the cotton-rich South. In Liverpool, the world's largest cotton port and "the most pro-Confederate place in the world outside the Confederacy itself," he appealed to free trade.[116] "They have said that your chief want is cotton. I deny it. Your chief want is consumers," he insisted.[117] Drawing from his days in Cincinnati, he bragged to an audience in Manchester, "I have had practice of more than twenty-five years in the presence of mobs and riots, opposing those very men whose representatives now attempt to forestall free speech." Amid shouts of "Hear!" Henry was received as America's preeminent moral influencer, a stalwart of freedom and democracy and capitalism. He did not shy away from the fanfare, although he did give credit for America's principles to the country who had birthed her. "You have been pleased to speak of me as one connected with the great cause of progress in civil and religious liberty. I covet no higher honor than to have my name joined as one among the list of that great company of noble Englishmen from whom we derived our doctrines of liberty." Even across an ocean, Henry knew how to play to a crowd. After a burst of cheers, he added, "For although I understand there is some opposition to what are called American ideas, what are these American ideas? The seed-corn we got in England."[118] Henry called for unity by appealing to history.

Touting the American founders as "abolitionists" and the Declaration of Independence as an antislavery document, Henry combined the Chase-inspired Republican ideology of political antislavery with the power and technique of the American revivalist tradition. He was an American Whitefield preaching a gospel of emancipation to the British. The pastor of Plymouth Church had come as an "envoy" of the United States, calling the president "that most true, honest, just, and conscientious magistrate, Mr. Lincoln." Once a harsh critic, Henry was now firmly in the president's corner, and he found mostly sympathetic crowds. At the mention of Lincoln's name, reported Holmes, "the audience cheered as long and loud as if they had descended from the ancient Ephesians."[119] Holmes's exaggerations aside, the United States could not have chosen a more effective and timelier ambassador on behalf of the cause of freedom. Initially his trip was just a vacation, but Beecher's "exhortation to unity" came at a critical moment in the Civil War. After failed diplomacy on the part of the Confederacy to establish a formal treaty with Britain and an unsuccessful attempt by the French to lift the Union blockade of Confederate ships, British sympathy for the South had waned. Allen Guelzo explains, "By the end of 1863, the once-bright confidence of the Confederacy that Europe would be forced by economic necessity to step in and guarantee Southern independence lay in the dust."[120] As an apostle of Lincoln to the British, Henry enjoyed soaring popularity in the same nation that had once welcomed his own sister with open arms.

Back in the United States, Thomas had also become a Lincoln convert. Despite his reservations about the Emancipation Proclamation and his reluctance to align himself with abolitionists, Thomas advocated for "Honest Ole' Abe" to his fellow New Yorkers. He even likened the president to Moses, the savior of Israel in the Old Testament, a comparison that became increasingly common after the war. In contrast to Lincoln, who embodied the principles of the founders, southerners stood against the values that had built the republic, he reasoned.[121] During the war, Thomas had become less of a firebrand and more of a family man, adopting with his wife Julia two young girls and welcoming a fourteen-year-old boy into their home. Like his brother Henry, Thomas was hostile toward the Confederacy but rather magnanimous toward Confederates. In the local prison camp in Elmira, the so-called "Andersonville of the North," Thomas preached to Confederate soldiers. At the prison, he was sometimes known for his humor. After the surrender at Appomattox Courthouse in April of 1865, Thomas concluded his sermon with a glimpse of his Beecher wit: "Now, boys, the war is over and you will soon be with your friends. When you are dismissed and return to your quarters, should you fall down in the mud, don't get up and say, 'Well damn the Yankees!'"[122]

Just as the Beechers had a hand in starting the Civil War, they also helped bring about its conclusion. With a long process of reconstruction ahead, President Lincoln selected Henry to deliver the address at Fort Sumter as the American flag was restored at the very place where the war began. General Robert Anderson, the Kentuckian who commanded the fort when it was taken in 1861, was appointed to raise the flag once again. Henry's address was symbolic for several reasons. "To put it bluntly," says Debby Applegate, "Henry Ward Beecher was one of the most hated men in the Confederacy."[123] Thus, for Beecher to proclaim the end of the Confederacy in the first official speech by a Union man on southern soil signaled both a military and moral victory for the North. "Ruin sits in the cradle of treason," he trumpeted. "Rebellion has perished. But there flies the same flag that was insulted."[124] Secondly, it was Henry Ward Beecher who had first asked Lincoln to address his own congregation in 1860. However, thanks to the Young Men's Central Republican Union, Lincoln never got the chance to wear his hundred-dollar black suit in Plymouth Church. Although he revised his address for a general political audience, his visit to New York City secured his nomination and eventual election as president.[125] In April of 1865, one might say Lincoln returned the invitation. Lincoln said, "We had better send Beecher down to deliver the address on the occasion of the raising of the flag because if it had not been for Beecher there would have been no flag to raise."[126] After galvanizing the northern public to support the Union cause and the president himself, Henry was hailed as a patriot. According to Rugoff, it marked the "high point" of Beecher's career.[127]

The pinnacle of Henry Ward's life also marked the end of President Lincoln's. On April 14, hours after Henry declared a new beginning for the nation, Lincoln was shot by a Confederate sympathizer named John Wilkes Booth on a balcony inside Ford's Theatre. He died the next day. One of the doctors who treated the president after his assassination was one Lyman

Beecher Todd, cousin of Mary Todd Lincoln, named after Henry's father. The news took several days to reach war-torn South Carolina. Off the shore of Hilton Head, where Henry and his company had stopped to enjoy the lush southern beach city of Beaufort, Senator Henry Wilson, the same man who had introduced Harriet to the president, came out of his cabin and screamed, "The president is killed!"[128] There would be no time for celebration. Describing the sense of hopelessness on the return trip to New York, Henry recalled, "Oh, the sadness of that company, and our nights' and days' voyaging back!" Victory had quickly turned to mourning. Henry's words just days earlier had been emptied of their power. "We knew nothing but this: that the President had been assassinated. All the rest was reserved for our coming into the harbor."[129] In his oration at Sumter, Henry had compared the Civil War to Israel's wandering in the wilderness for forty years after their exodus from Egypt. During this time of testing, "God would prepare Moses for emancipation," he said.[130] Henry's illustration was more apt than he ever realized. In the Bible, God delivers Israel into Canaan, but Moses himself is not permitted to enter. By the time he returned to Brooklyn, he saw the tragic irony of such a comparison. Along with scores of other preachers across the North, Beecher framed Lincoln's death in truly biblical proportions. Preaching from Deuteronomy 34 the following Sunday, he stated, "Again a great leader of the people has passed through toil, sorrow, battle, and war, and come near to the promised land of peace, into which he might not pass over. . . . he looked upon it as Moses looked upon the promised land."[131]

Abraham Lincoln was assassinated on Good Friday, the Christian holiday which celebrates the crucifixion of Jesus of Nazareth. Therefore, quite naturally, northern ministers were quick to liken Lincoln's death to the sacrificial death of Christ. In Hartford, pastor C. B. Crane at South Baptist Church was unequivocal: "Jesus Christ died for the world; Abraham Lincoln died for his country."[132] Lincoln was more than a martyr; his assassination was described in the language of atonement. A Methodist in Ohio declared that the American flag had been "made sacred by the blood of a martyred Lincoln."[133] For many clergymen, including Henry Ward Beecher, Lincoln's death was so Christlike that it served as a kind of substitute for southern wrath. Lincoln's presence in a theater was no blemish upon his sacrifice for the country. On Sunday, April 23, a week after Easter Sunday, Beecher declared, "Lincoln was slain; America was meant. The man was cast down; the government was smitten at."[134] John Wilkes Booth, the actor who murdered Lincoln with a .44 caliber pistol, indeed carried out his dramatic plot with all the wrath and rage of a southern white supremacist. In 1859, when John Brown was hanged for treason, Booth had been in the crowd, watching with great satisfaction. His hatred for abolitionists had only grown with the war. Although many Americans viewed Lincoln's death as a kind of expiation for national sins, the assassination did not achieve any semblance of peace. The North responded with a combination of lament and outrage, refusing to forgive or forget. One clergyman in New England accused his listeners, "It tells you, you have always been too lenient. You were too kind."[135]

In the wake of the tragedy, the Beechers were divided in their sentiments toward southerners. Harriet nursed a heavy resentment against the South for Lincoln's death, along with reports of southern mistreatment of Union prisoners during the war. However, in one of the few times that he did not represent the popular view, Henry called for leniency. I do not "think it wise or Christian for us to distrust the sentiments of those in the South that profess to be desirous, once again, of concord and of union," he urged his congregation in October. In Henry's view, the future of the Union depended on this single exercise of faith. "Somewhere men are to be believed and trusted, or all possibility of co-operative government is at an end."[136] Bold, forbearing, peacemaking, and optimistic, Henry Ward Beecher was never more his father's son than after Lincoln's death. He was a hopeful republican at heart. Opposing the death penalty for Jefferson Davis and assailing those who demanding Robert E. Lee's resignation from the presidency of Washington College in Virginia, his vision of reform for the nation did not include any sense of vindictiveness.[137] Harriet was more circumspect. In an 1866 letter, she asked her brother, "Do you believe that if the states you mention had been admitted at once on the simple condition of the oath of allegiance that they would have gone to work righting the negro—repealing slave laws, elevating poor whites, in short that an aristocracy would have made themselves into a democracy at once?"[138]

RECONSTRUCTION

When Andrew Johnson was nominated as Abraham Lincoln's vice president in 1864, it symbolized the Republicans' determination to reward southern leaders who had not defected to the Confederacy during the war. From the hills of Tennessee, Johnson was the lone US senator from a seceding state to remain loyal to the Union. After being appointed military governor by Lincoln, he declared for abolition in 1863. However, Johnson's true motive was less about human rights and more about his disdain for the Confederacy.[139] The original home to the Ku Klux Klan, Tennessee was not a land of abolitionists.[140] As Roger L. Hart surveys in his Reconstruction history of the state, Tennessee "suffered its own miniature civil war, with a large minority of mountain dwellers stubbornly hostile to the southern Confederacy."[141] Although he despised rebels, Johnson did not convene a new state constitutional convention until January 1865. In the eyes of most northerners, Johnson was not exactly a moral crusader. Therefore, it is somewhat surprising that Henry Ward Beecher was accused by northerners and indeed by his own congregation of being a "Johnson man." Their suspicions were not without warrant. In October of 1865, Beecher wrote to the new president, "The religious men of the north and west are rapidly growing into confidence in your patriotism, and wisdom, second only to that which they felt for Mr. Lincoln; a confidence which I am sure will increase."[142] But it didn't.

In 1866, the overwhelming majority of Congress passed a civil rights bill introduced by Senator Lyman Trumbull from Illinois. The bill guaranteed national protection for Blacks and defined further the nature of American citizenship. Under the proposed law, individuals who deprived freedmen of their rights were subject to trials in federal district courts. Officers of the courts and officials from the Freedmen's Bureau would assist in bringing suits against these individuals and prosecute their cases at the expense of the federal government. Only three Senate Republicans voted against the measure. A resolution by Thaddeus Stevens of Pennsylvania was also adopted, stipulating that no senator or representative could be admitted to the legislature until Congress declared that state entitled to representation. Despite the counsel of his cabinet to sign it, Johnson vetoed the bill. The power to confer state citizenship, he wrote, did not rest with the federal government. And citizenship was not essential to the enjoyment of rights, as he saw it. Rather than turn state judges into agents of Washington and amass an army to enforce the bill, he argued that southern states should regulate themselves. The North was apoplectic. How could former slave masters be trusted to respect the rights of their former slaves? What was the purpose of the war if southerners returned to slavery by another name? The president had "promised to be the Moses of the colored race," Frederick Douglass said, but he was really "their Pharaoh."[143] While Johnson claimed to be defending the Constitution, he managed to arouse the collective indignation of the North and establish himself as an enemy of Congress, which overrode his veto. On April 9, the civil rights bill became law. The groundwork was laid for the Fourteenth Amendment, but a war was declared with the president of the United States.

In September, Henry was invited to serve as chaplain at a convention in Cleveland, Ohio, for soldiers and sailors who were Johnson supporters. Hay fever prevented him from attending, but Henry sent a public letter in which he endorsed the convention's recommendations and criticized Radicals for impeding the process of national reconciliation. The longer that southern states were delayed in governing themselves and administering their own justice, Henry wrote, the more harm would be done to the freedmen. "The negro is part and parcel of Southern society," he reminded them. "He cannot be prosperous while it is unprospered." In the letter to the convention, Henry also demonstrated a bit of his father's blind optimism, looking past certain obstacles and moral failings in his attempt to see the good:

> We have entered a new era of liberty. The style of thought is freer and more noble. The young men of our times are regenerated. The great army has been a school, and hundreds of thousands of men are gone home to preach a truer and nobler view of human rights. All the industrial interests of society are moving with increasing wisdom toward intelligence and liberty. Everywhere, in churches, in literature, in natural science, in physical industries, in social questions, as well as in politics, the nation feels that the winter is over and a new spring hangs in the horizon and works through all the elements. In this happily changed and advanced condition of things no party of the retrograde can maintain itself. Everything marches, and parties must march.[144]

The Civil War was proof of America's evolution as a nation. With the evangelical language of the rebirth, Henry heralded the inevitable progress of the American people in virtually *all* facets of life. As the nation was still recovering from war, Henry instead pointed them to the "happily changed and advanced condition of things." Around the same time that Beecher was imbibing the ideas of Herbert Spencer, the British social thinker who coined the term "survival of the fittest," Henry promulgated a theory of America quite consistent with Spencer's "conception of gradual development."[145] To distrust their southern neighbors was, in effect, to stand in the way of that development. It was also to defy the will of the nation's Moses. As he repeated years later, Henry believed that President Lincoln had been clear before his death that a quick reconciliation was best for the country. Democracy could not be imposed by force, but by faith.

But most northerners did not feel the same way. Henry was vilified in the press and questioned in his own congregation. Horace Greeley at the *Tribune* called his words an "apostasy" and a blight upon his public record.[146] Henry rushed to his own defense, claiming he was not defending slaveholders so much as acknowledging the practicality of self-government. "Neither am I a 'Johnson man' in any received meaning of that term," he clarified to one of his concerned parishioners. "I accept that part of the policy which he favors, but with modification." In classic Beecher style, Beecher contended for a "middle course" between the president and Congress.[147] And as many Beechers knew firsthand, the "middle" could be a rather lonely place in nineteenth-century America. Henry's indomitable confidence in the future was a Beecher family trait, but not every Beecher shared his rose-colored appraisal of the situation. In one of the few instances of a Beecher publicly attacking another Beecher, Edward published a letter in the *Chicago Tribune* lambasting his brother's position. After Henry appealed to him in protest, Edward "answered with the formality of an older brother defending the honor of the family."[148] Henry seemed inextricably linked with the unpopular president. In the years leading up to the Civil War, the Beechers were as united as they had ever been, personally and politically. But in the antebellum years, they did not always see eye-to-eye on key issues.

Even when the Beechers questioned their leaders and each other, they still believed in the power of institutions. In 1866, the Equal Rights Association was formed, an organization which sought to unite Black rights and women's rights under the same banner. Henry was its first president. Organized chiefly by Theodore Tilton, the association resembled the *via media* approach of Lyman Beecher decades earlier, attempting to bring together two movements that did not always get along. Although Edward disagreed with his brother about Andrew Johnson and Reconstruction, he too was focused on the same issue. While traveling back and forth to Chicago to teach at the seminary, he drew the suspicion of conservative Presbyterians in Galesburg by accepting the presidency of a woman's suffrage convention which met in Springfield.[149]

Indeed, the war had changed the way that Edward and Henry and their siblings viewed moral reform. With religion thoroughly cured from the disease of slavery, societal transformation was more attainable than ever. The sky was the limit. They could truly change the world. Formal religion, having been used in the service of human bondage, was now more suspect than before, whereas social questions like freedom, equality, and poverty gained more attention and importance. As Molly Oshatz has observed, for Edward, the eradication of slavery was only "the beginning of a grand social project."[150] In 1865, Edward wrote in *Bibliotheca Sacra* at Andover, "We have seen the malignant power of slavery to corrupt religion and lead to apostasy. Unchristianized systems of political economy, commerce, and government, exert the same corrupting power. The leaven of the gospel has not done its work until it has leavened the whole lump. Now that God has smitten slavery unto death, he has opened the way for the redemption and sanctification of our whole social system, which was before impossible. We are therefore loudly called upon to study this problem as never before."[151] Illustrated perhaps most vividly in the Beecher family, the Civil War became for many northern evangelicals the ultimate confirmation that orthodoxy, stained by the abomination of slavery, could no longer be trusted as a reliable guide to virtuous living, and that a socially minded faith was itself the highest form of Christianity. Henry was evolving in much the same direction. In 1867, Ralph Waldo Emerson confessed, "Beecher told me, that he did not hold one of the five points of Calvinism in a way to satisfy his father." If Calvinism could not help to address the most pressing social and moral issues of the day, it must be discarded in toto. Soon Beecher would campaign to drop the concept of hell completely from the official creed of Plymouth Church, the second Beecher male (though not the last) to publicly assail the ancient doctrine.[152] For most Beechers, what had begun in the heresy trial of their father in 1835 at the hands of southern sympathizers was now complete after the victory of the North in the Civil War: the deconstruction of Calvinism.

Thomas's deconstruction, on the other hand, was a bit more precipitous. Known for conducting ecumenical services outside the church building, Tom provoked the fury of local ministers in Elmira for overlooking religious distinctions of seemingly any kind. On one occasion, when a young man asked him how to get to heaven, Thomas compared different faiths to various routes to New York City. "You can reach heaven by the Catholic church, or by the Synagogue, Universalist or Baptist, and you can even reach it through the Park Church—but, whatever you. Do, do it unto the Lord."[153] Thomas's hatred for sectarian religion, forged in the furnace of his father's heresy trials and refined by the Old School–New School debate, had evolved into a fully developed religious inclusivism unencumbered by *any* Christian belief whatsoever. The most important thing was being useful to the Lord. Twenty years earlier, when Thomas considered joining the Episcopal Church, Lyman's only counsel to him was to "be a Christian and work." This was still the essence of Thomas Beecher's religion, with a bit more emphasis on the latter than the former. When local clergymen eventually ousted Thomas from their ministerial union for his pan-denominational gatherings, local resident Samuel Clemens, aka Mark Twain, wrote sardonically to the Elmira *Advertiser:* "Happy, happy world that knows at last that a little congress of congregationless clergymen, of whom it had never heard before, have crushed a famous Beecher and reduced his audiences from fifteen hundred down to fourteen hundred and seventy-five at one fell blow!"[154] Thomas soon had the honor of officiating the wedding of Samuel Clemens and his bride, Olivia Langdon, the daughter of a wealthy coal businessman in Elmira. By suffering expulsion at the hands of local clergymen, Tom was continuing a now long-held Beecher family tradition: ecclesiastical censure with high public approval ratings.

FLORIDA SUNSHINE AND FAMILY TRAGEDY

The Beechers were always New Englanders at heart. But much had changed in New England since Lyman Beecher was born in New Haven, Connecticut, in 1775. Gone was Timothy Dwight's religious establishment and the so-called "Standing Order." Unitarianism, once a rising threat *within* Congregationalism, was now a prestigious denomination for intellectual and literary elites. Boston was no longer the seat of Puritanism, but a city brimming with European immigrants, many of whom were Catholic. Blacks were no longer slaves or fugitives, but soon-to-be citizens. In 1867, Henry and Harriet were both in the process of writing fictional works that depicted New England life, and each defended New England identity in their own unique ways. In his comedy *Norwood; Or, Village Life in New England* (1867), his first novel, Henry acknowledged the diversity of the Yankee "species" but also defended the Yankee work ethic against southerners who accused them of greed. After living in a New England village, one of Henry's characters, Tom Heywood, writes to his brother, "That's the difference between an Irishman and a Yankee; a Yankee wants his own money, an Irishman wants *yours*."[155] Being a Yankee was more than an attitude. For Henry, it was a way of life. As Henry resigned from the *Independent* and focused his talents on writing books (he received a twenty-five-thousand-dollar advance for his first), Harriet was composing a first-person story about New England life set ten years before the Revolutionary War. Eventually published under the title *Oldtown Folks*, the book was to be conceived, written, and revised before it saw print.[156]

Although the work was historical fiction, this did not prevent Harriet from envisioning a New England that embodied her own ideals. In the thirty-third chapter, the protagonist, Horace Holyoke, takes stock of the local schools: "In an age when in England schools were managed by the grossest and most brutal exercise of corporeal punishments, the schoolmasters of New England, to a great extent, had entirely dropped all resort to such barbarous measures, and carried on their schools as republics, by the sheer force of moral and intellectual influences."[157] This was Beecher preaching and pedagogy in a nutshell. Harriet traced the roots of moral influence, and to some extent the republican origins of the nation, to the New England tradition. But she was also reevaluating the New England Theology. Owing to Calvin Stowe's resignation from Andover several years earlier and his troubled relationship with Professor Edwards Amasa Park, Harriet offered a "wholly negative portrayal of Jonathan Edwards." The Edwardsean tradition had become too esoteric and metaphysical for the Stowes.[158]

From Maine to the Midwest, from New York to San Francisco, there was no region of the country to which the Beechers had not ventured. But they were not a family well-versed in southern life. Lyman had only visited Kentucky to preach at a few revivals. Harriet had crossed the river once in 1833. Charles's brief foray in New Orleans in 1838 was ended when he ran out of money and grew homesick. Henry's quick trip to South Carolina in 1865 was cut short with the news of Lincoln's assassination. Like most New Englanders, the Beechers imagined the South far more than they actually experienced it.[159] Far away was the world of Black Methodist preacher Isaac Lane, who "lived on nothing but bread, milk, and water" for sixth months in Jackson, Tennessee, following the war.[160] Still, not even Dixie could completely shut out the Beecher gospel of moral and social reform. In 1867, the Stowes purchased a thousand-acre plantation on the St. John's River south of Jacksonville, Florida. Two Connecticut farmers who had befriended their son Fred during the war had introduced them to the idea. The ten-thousand-dollar real estate venture was an investment by Harriet in at least four things: (1) her son Fred, who needed to get back on his feet after the war, (2) her writing career, which stalled in the coldest months of the year, (3) the postwar South, which needed education and moral improvement, and (4) her own state of mind. "Henry says to me the other day—My thoughts never run free till the sap begins to rise in the trees—winter months freeze me," she reported. "But I am going to take my writing desk & go down to Florida to Freds plantation where we have now a house . . . & then I doubt not I can write my three hours a day."[161] As usual, Harriet traveled with family. On her initial trip in February, she brought along her brother Charles and the wife and child of her nephew Spencer Foote, who had gone ahead with Fred in the fall. After being discharged from the army, Fred still needed a bit of supervision.

With groves of palmetto pine and orange blossoms, Harriet fell in love with the tropical landscape. "In all my foreign experience & travels I never saw such a scene," she wrote back to her family.[162] The giant, moss-draped live oaks of Jacksonville certainly seemed like a world away from the snow-covered birches of New England. Harriet stayed several months, writing, resting, and dreaming. She envisioned a place where her entire family could thrive. With Spencer's help, Fred could manage a lucrative orange grove and rehabilitate himself. Charles could become an Episcopalian priest and start a ministry. She could even start a school. The opportunities for moral influence were unlimited. Before coming to Florida, she reminded Henry that the South would never be reformed through politics, but with kindness. "As to our party, the Republicans, let them alone," she insisted, calling her brother away from the political arena. "God after all is in the vox populi. *You* have other work, Christ's work, and who can stop you there? Can the South resist our love if we love them? If we go down with food for their widows and orphans, with schools for their children and sympathy for their distresses, will they refuse us?"[163] Fueled by the moral victory of the Union, Harriet articulated a growing sentiment in the North during Reconstruction. If the South was to rebuild, it would need help. Harriet's vision for the South was not unlike Lyman's for the West forty years earlier. To improve society, one had to educate the people—whites and Blacks alike. Although southerners often begrudged the benevolent economic ventures of so-called "carpetbaggers," there can be little doubt that Harriet was a Beecher in her desire to bring moral uplift to a state that was still largely a shambolic frontier. Upon taking office in 1868, Republican governor Harrison Reed discovered there were no records of how state monies in Florida had been spent between 1848 and 1860 or immediately following the war.[164] For Harriet, the free-labor cotton plantation represented the potential for change, for Fred, for the South, and for the nation itself.

Laurel Grove was also a form of self-care. From the hydropathy of the Elmira water cure to the latest trends in diet and nutrition, the Beecher women were part of a growing therapeutic movement concerned with physical and spiritual healing. More and more Americans, particularly Yankees, were exploring the benefits of physical treatments outside of conventional medicine. There was also a religious component to health reform. In 1869, New Englander Warren Felt Evans, the first author of what became known as New Thought, promoted the advantages of a new kind of therapeutic metaphysics in his book *The Mental Cure*.[165] The verdant homestead in Jacksonville offered another salubrious outlet for Harriet to find the rest and relaxation she needed to conduct her life's work of influencing America. Although the venture in cotton failed shortly afterward due to mildew and Fred returning to drinking, the Stowes remained snowbirds for years to come. In the Victorian era, the distinction between self-care and self-indulgence was sometimes a fine line. For instance, after Fred's treatment in a mental institution in Binghamton, New York, Calvin took him on a Mediterranean voyage for the fresh air.[166]

For Harriet, as for countless Americans then and now, Florida was also an escape from reality. Life was no vacation, especially in the nineteenth century. Months after returning home from Jacksonville, Charles was greeted with the worst news of his entire life. His two youngest children, twelve-year-old Hattie and fifteen-year-old Essie, drowned while boating with their twenty-year-old cousin George, Edward's son. Charles and his wife Sarah rushed down to the pond after being told that the three had disappeared. When they saw men diving into the depths, Sarah "fell down as though dead."[167] It was to be the greatest tragedy in the history of the Beecher family, but not the last for Charles. Although his son Frederick had survived the slaughter of Gettysburg and had healed from his injuries, he remained in the army. In 1868, he was killed in a skirmish with the Cheyenne in what is now Colorado. The battle was later labeled "the Battle of Beecher Island."[168] For Harriet, on the other hand, her son Fred was proof that the toll of the war could not be counted in mere body totals. On her way back to Jacksonville with her son Charley, she stopped in Charleston, where she heard a heroic story about a Union colonel named Robert Beecher—her nephew, William's son—who saved an elderly woman from a band of looters. The woman's son, a former Confederate soldier and Presbyterian divinity school student, had likewise been fighting in the belief that he was on the side of God.[169] Stories such as these drove Harriet further away from traditional evangelical religion and closer toward the therapeutic religion of the age.

With the war behind them, the Beecher women now turned their attention back to the household. But this issue was no less important for the republic. In fact, the mission was the same: reforming America. By elevating the lives of women, the Beecher sisters believed they were strengthening the family *and* the nation. As Nancy Hardesty has noted in her work on revivalism and feminism, "The Moral Reform movement gave pious, middle-class women permission, and in fact motivation, to move outside the home." But it provided more than a chance to publish and be heard. "It offered more than twenty thousand women a significant work to do in ushering in the millennium. Most significantly, however, it functioned somewhat as modern consciousness-raising groups do, to attune women to the injustice oppressing them and to allow them avenues to give vent to the anger that such consciousness engenders."[170] While they had never been full-blown Finneyites like their deceased brother George, and although they came to blows with radical leaders like Angelina Grimké, the Beecher sisters were part of this great movement from moral reform to women's rights. The same evangelical impulse that took aim at intemperance and slavery now turned its millennial gaze upon the inequality of women. The benevolent empire "blossomed" into the woman's movement in the soil of reformist thought.[171] In many ways, the Union victory in the Civil War cemented this perfectionist movement to sanctify America of injustice, but some were slower to join the cause than others. Not every abolitionist was a woman's crusader. As they had with abolition, the Beechers joined the women's rights movement gradually, with extreme caution, and on their own terms.

In 1868, after helping to publish Calvin's *The Origin and History of the Books of the Bible,* Harriet launched a new periodical called *Hearth and Home.*[172] She was juggling quite a few projects designed to promote the health of the family. Harriet and her sister Catharine were also collaborating on a new book, *The American Woman's Home* (1869). For almost an entire year Catharine lived with the Stowes in their modest residence that was part of Hartford's famous literary colony, Nook Farm.[173] During this time, Catharine began thinking about reopening the Hartford Female Seminary. Isabella was also busy. In late 1868, she published "A Mother's Letters to a Daughter on Woman Suffrage" in *Putnam's Monthly.* Once again contending that women have a unique capacity for government due to their responsibilities in the home, Isabella also argued that men could confer voting rights to women without any loss of honor or reputation.[174] Isabella illustrated her point by appealing to multiple members of her own family. The most competent mother, the mother told her daughter, was "like your Aunt E., [who] has helped six stout boys and four of their quick-witted sisters all the way from babyhood up to manhood and womanhood, with a wisdom and gentleness and patience that have been the wonder of all beholders." This was clearly a reference to Aunt Esther, the matron of the Beecher family. Isabella also referred to her brother James, who was suspicious of women's rights, when she later added,

> Her youngest boy, the privileged, saucy one of the crowd, has just attained his majority, we will say, and declaims in her hearing on the

incompetence of women to vote—the superiority of the masculine element in politics, and the danger to society if women were not carefully
guarded from contact with its rougher elements—and I seem to see
her quiet smile and slightly curling lip, while in memory she runs back
to the years when said stripling gathered all he knew of laws, country,
home, heaven, and earth, at her knee—and as for soiling contacts, oh!
My son, who taught you to avoid these, and first put it into your curly
little head, that evil communications corrupt good manners, and that
"a man cannot *touch* pitch, except he be defiled."[175]

Isabella's point was simple: without mothers, her brother James could
not have arrived at such ideas and principles. But for the care of maternal figures, there would be no learning at all. In her view, James's argument was self-defeating. Motherhood was the supreme form of moral
influence because it was the most formative in human development. Isabella's lampooning of her "privileged, saucy" brother was a first for the
Beecher clan, revealing that the last Beecher sister was not the same kind
of "public woman" as her older sisters. Things had changed since Catharine
drew fondly from her upbringing to promote proper domestic economy.
Isabella did not always look upon the home of her youth with the same
rose-colored lens. As demonstrated by the exchange between Edward and
Henry in the *Chicago Tribune*, since Lyman Beecher's death, the Beechers
were not above publicly criticizing their own siblings to make a point. Isabella was also a bit resentful of her older sisters' fame. *A Mother's Letter* was
published without the author's name because Isabella wanted the essay to
"make its own way, than be helped by my Beecher name."[176]

    While blazing her own trail, Isabella was also following Henry. Unlike
James and Thomas, her full siblings, her half-brother in Brooklyn likewise
believed that women should have the right to vote. It was not simply their
right but their duty to do so. The latter was the more important value in
the Beecher mind. The Beechers still preferred the republican language
of "duty" rather than the more liberal concept of "rights." The former was
about what the individual owed to society; the latter was about what society
owed to the individual. Throwing his energies into the "woman question,"
in 1869 Henry became the first president of the American Woman Suffrage Association (AWSA), centered in Boston with the likes of Julia Ward

Howe, Thomas Wentworth Higginson, Lucy Stone, and others. In contrast to the more radical New York wing of the movement led by Elizabeth Cady Stanton and Susan B. Anthony (called the National Woman Suffrage Association), the AWSA was a more conservative answer to a very liberal question. According to Barbara W. White, even Isabella was "definitely on the conservative side" of the split.[177] As they had been on the question of abolition, the Beechers were always on the progressive side of women's rights, but never on the fringe. Also in 1869, Harriet published her controversial *Lady Byron Vindicated*, a defense of the disgraced wife of Lord Byron, a well-known British Romantic poet that Harriet had once admired.[178] By publicly airing the dirty laundry of a well-known figure, Harriet had established a dangerous precedent.[179] Ironically, at the same time that the Beechers were committing themselves so exhaustively to the question of women, Henry was more than likely having an affair with Elizabeth Tilton, the wife of the *Independent* editor in New York. Beginning in October and lasting for the next year and a half, Henry would engage in an illicit relationship that would cost him his reputation, his legacy, and relationships within his own family.

Chapter 6

THE WOMAN
(OR WOMEN) QUESTION
(1870–1878)

AT THE BEGINNING of the 1870s, the Beechers were unquestionably one of the most famous families in America. As durable and outspoken as their father, they showed no signs of slowing down. Invited by the American Literary Bureau of Boston to do a series of public readings of her works, sixty-year-old Harriet, now a grandmother, began a lecture tour across New England in the spring of 1872. A year later, she took on the entire Midwest.[1] In Brooklyn, preaching to larger audiences than any other pastor in the nation, Henry was arguably better-known than his sister. He had become, as one historian has called him, "the first popular leader" of American liberal Protestantism, developing and legitimizing a movement that was previously relegated to academicians and cultural elites.[2]

Across the state, Thomas had steadily amassed a fan base of his own. In a *New York Times* article in July of 1871, "A New Beecher Church," Mark Twain applauded the construction of Thomas's new church building, which was renamed "Park Church." According to Twain, who later wrote *Tom Sawyer* in Elmira, the Beecher name was its own trademark. Other churches may identify as Baptist or Methodist or Presbyterian, "but when a Beecher projects a church, that edifice is necessarily going to be something entirely fresh and original. It is not going to be like any other church in the world; marked with as peculiar and striking an individuality as a Beecher himself," he observed with amusement. The church would certainly have "a deal more Beecher in it" than any creed or confession, Twain wrote somewhat prophetically. "Consequently, to call it a Congregationalist Church would not give half an idea of the thing. There is only one word broad enough and deep enough to take in the whole affair and express it clearly, luminously

and concisely, and that is *Beecher*."[3] Twain was right about the Beecher pa-
nache. Park Church enjoyed such resounding success with so many community service programs and outdoor ministries that Thomas later called
it "an experiment in Christian socialism," leading one historian to identify Beecher as a forerunner to the Social Gospel movement decades later.[4]

At the height of their popularity, the Beechers were also closer to one
another than they had been since their days in Cincinnati. Beginning in
the 1870s, all four of the Beecher sisters lived in Hartford. On Nook Farm,
where they lived near the Stowes, Isabella and John hosted Mark Twain
and his new wife, Olivia Langdon, a friend of the Hookers. In 1871, Edward
left Galesburg, Illinois, and returned east one last time. His son George,
disabled with rheumatism, needed care in New York. After serving for two
years as assistant editor of the *Christian Union*, where he wrote frequently
on God and society, he bought a house on Macon Street in Brooklyn and
joined Plymouth Church. Retiring from public life, he became a counselor
to his brother Henry.

As for Charles, he quit his post in Georgetown in 1870 and moved to
the Florida Panhandle to commence a new kind of moral influence: public education in the Reconstruction South. With the recommendation of
Harriet, he served for two years as state superintendent of public schools
in Newport, Florida. Picked by the Republican-appointed administration,
Charles was part of a wave of "redeemer" governments established in the
postbellum South to bring stability and moral uplift to a fractured and dis-
paraged region. Still motivated by his racist beliefs, Tom was encouraged
but not necessarily hopeful to see his brother help the Black community, for
he believed that the postwar South was ruled by "venal whites" and "ignorant blacks" who were "pandering to the passions and flattering the childish
expectations of the colored men."[5] When James made the swampy journey
to Tallahassee to visit Charles in the winter of 1871, his efforts at moral
influence were likewise colored by racism. On January 19, he wrote in his
journal, "Frank and I wanted to make ourselves useful as well as ornamen-
tal, by teaching some of the darkies the art of writing. There will be some
six or seven in the class." After doing so well teaching his "darky S. School,"
James soon discovered that he had been volunteered for another task. "To
our surprise and disgust [Charles] announced in church that there would
be a bible class formed under the guidance of Frank and myself, which was

to say the least a rather peculiar proceeding, as nothing had been said to us."[6] Sometimes moral influence could feel a tad bit like coercion. As one of the most passionate of Beechers, Charles knew how to throw himself into a cause. Like Harriet, he fell in love with the tropical climate. He lived in a small home surrounded by orange, fig, and pecan trees on a two-and-a-half-acre farm with pomegranates, bananas, dates, peaches, and a grapevine. Charles also conducted experiments with potato plants. (When James visited in 1871, he hunted for deer, ducks, woodpeckers, and even alligators.)[7] Harriet wrote her brother in Florida, "I never knew such altogether perfect weather. It is enough to make a saint out of the toughest old Calvinist that ever set his face as a flint. How do you think New England theology would have fared if our fathers had been landed here instead of on Plymouth Rock?"[8] Florida offered a refuge from cold weather and cold religion.

Unfortunately, Charles's tenure as superintendent did not bear as much fruit as his garden. After being deemed "unsound," he returned to New England after two years.[9] In the final chapter of his life, Charles kept steady communication with his brothers and sisters, visiting both Hartford and New York. He maintained, along with Henry, a "deeper respect not to say reverence for Edward, than for any living man."[10] Aside from William, who retired in 1870 and moved to Chicago to live with his daughters, no Beecher was deprived of meaningful relationships with at least one or two other siblings. After years of sore relations, Thomas and James vacationed together in the Catskill Mountains of New York, where James eventually bought land and built a house on another Beecher namesake: Beecher Lake.[11] Wherever the Beechers went, they left their mark. And they usually went together.

THE BEECHER-TILTON AFFAIR

With meteoric celebrity and closer proximity to one another, the family became embroiled in a perfect storm of controversy when Henry, the most public Beecher, was accused of adultery in 1871. The scandal not only pitted the children of Roxana Foote against those of Harriet Porter, but it exposed deep-seated ideological divisions in the family on the issue of women's rights. The four-year imbroglio that ensued was the closest thing to a civil war ever waged by Lyman Beecher's children. And like the Civil War itself, some wounds never fully healed.

As editor of the *Independent* and the Brooklyn-based *Union,* Theodore Tilton was a friend and admirer of Henry Ward Beecher. Before the war, primarily on the momentum of Beecher's soaring popularity, the *Independent* became one of the most formidable and widely read abolitionist newspapers in the country. Although the newspaper was founded by prominent New York merchant Henry C. Bowen and edited by respected Congregationalist ministers, Henry was the main attraction. The biggest draw was Beecher's sermons, transcribed by Theodore Tilton. After the depression of 1857 delivered a financial blow to the paper and forced a wedge between Bowen and his editors, Henry took over as editor-in-chief in 1861. During the war, the *Independent* became even more Beecher-centric, serving as Henry's primary organ of communication through the war years and further establishing him as America's most eminent religious luminary. At his side was Theodore Tilton, who essentially ran the paper as managing editor. He also attended Plymouth Church. Riding the heels of Beecher's success, the starstruck Tilton addressed his friend, pastor, and mentor as "my Dear Bishop" in their correspondence. He later reflected that "I loved that man as well as I ever loved a woman."[12] When Henry returned from his highly publicized speaking tour in England in 1863, Tilton's allegiance to Beecher had increased and so had Tilton's influence. Even with Henry as editor-in-chief, Tilton now controlled the *Independent,* was well-connected in Radical Republican and antislavery circles, and even had a friend in the White House. With a servile appreciation for the man who had sparked his career, Tilton confessed to Beecher at war's end: "By you I was baptized; by you married; you are my minister, teacher, father, brother, friend, companion. The debt I owe you I can never repay."[13] But Tilton's adulation soon turned into animosity.

When Henry supported the Johnson administration after the war, Tilton denounced his former hero as a traitor, claiming Beecher had done more harm to the republic than any American other than Johnson himself.[14] A year later, Henry stepped down from his editorial role due in part to Tilton's skepticism about the Bible. At the same time, Edward and other midwestern ministers attacked Tilton at the *Independent* for his un-Christian beliefs, accusing him of pantheism.[15] Tilton's politics were becoming just as radical as his theology, as he became a sharp critic of then-presidential candidate Ulysses S. Grant, whom Beecher supported. Nevertheless, Henry was making himself at home in the Tilton residence.

As the president of a radical women's suffrage group, Tilton offered an avenue by which Henry could shake hands and exchange ideas with the more progressive leaders of the women's rights movement, who were based in New York. According to Rugoff, "The leading suffragists were frequent visitors at the Tilton salon and Henry became familiar with all of them." By the fall of 1870, "Tilton's was the second home of Mr. Beecher."[16] Evidently it was a bit too cozy.

In some ways, Theodore Tilton's wife, Elizabeth, had become estranged to her husband for the same reason that Eunice Beecher had become estranged to hers: both men were frequently not at home. Theodore spent considerable time away on the lecture circuit, as did Henry. Tilton's purportedly sexual relationship with women's rights activist Laura Curtis Ballard was the subject of some gossip within their coterie of friends. In addition to his doubts about biblical religion, Theodore also held comparatively milder views on women's rights than his wife, creating more intellectual, emotional, and physical distance between the two. During this time, Elizabeth (or "Lib" to her friends) developed an emotional relationship with Henry, who had conducted the funeral for their son Paul when the latter died of cholera two years prior. After a while, Elizabeth and Henry became more than friends. Religion slowly turned to coquettish romance. Once Elizabeth humorously referred to herself, Theodore, and the pastor of Plymouth Church as a "trinity."[17]

As Elizabeth and Henry grew more intimate, they were also imbibing the progressive thought of many in the women's rights movement. The most influential upon Elizabeth was the flamboyant and vituperative feminist Victoria Woodhull, who made Theodore Tilton—and most Victorian Americans—rather uncomfortable with her idea of "free love." Rounding the lecture circuit with a sickly Civil War veteran named Colonel John H. Blood, Woodhull would shout to a stunned audience, "There stands my lover, but when I cease to love him, I shall leave him!" Along with her sister, Tennessee Claflin, who was a traveling fortune teller and healer, Woodhull was a spiritualist who claimed the power to talk to the dead. Together, the two purported charlatans broke the mold for nineteenth-century feminism. As one columnist at the *New Yorker* described them a century later, "The two sisters were not beautiful, actually, but they had the dash and verve that a later generation came to call sex appeal." Donning masculine jackets along with skirts that boldly stopped at their shoe tops, the busty pair wore their hair short and curly and sported ties and Alpine hats.[18] The dandified duo also ran a paper called *Woodhull & Claflin's Weekly* that touted the slogan, "Progress! Free Thought! Untrammeled Lives!" Known simply as "the Woodhull," Victoria was an audacious and polarizing figure.

As Henry was pushing the bounds of his relationship with Elizabeth Tilton, his sisters were preaching against free love and the destruction of the family. On June 9, 1870, Harriet wrote a letter to the *Woman's Journal,* the organ of the American Woman Suffrage Association, warning readers against the dangerous idea of free love.[19] Victoria Woodhull was not named, but she was certainly implied. Harriet also used the power of fiction. When she published *My Wife and I* (1871), Woodhull was satirized under the fictional name "Audacia Dangyereyes."[20] Speaking in Boston, Catharine proclaimed her support for the right of women to "happiness and usefulness" and to equal value with men but chided the leaders of the women's suffrage movement for thinking that a vote would solve the injustices of women. The answer to oppressive patriarchy was not suffrage or the end of monogamous marriages, but advanced education and economic independence. While women were called to be good housewives, they did not simply need to be "educated to be somebody's wife," she argued. Catharine's grandniece, Charlotte Perkins Gilman, would make a similar argument in one of the most influential feminist treatises of the entire nineteenth century, *Woman and Economics.*[21] The following year, Catharine and Harriet advertised a summer institute that included health courses for women, offering a more holistic, pro-family alternative to the more libertine ideology of "free love." (Or as Thomas put it, "free lust.")[22] Although the sisters did not receive enough inquiries to get the project off the ground, they both supported the emerging women's club movement as a means to elevate women. Drawing from the Beecher playbook of moral influence, Catharine and Harriet still preferred voluntary groups to the crass political theater and ballyhoo of the extreme left.[23]

However, not every Beecher sister was averse to Victoria Woodhull's brand of radical feminism. By 1870, Isabella was already sympathetic with Woodhull's irreverent style and many of her ideas about the dangers of male-only authority. In 1871, she drew up a "Declaration and Pledge of the Women of the United States Concerning their Right to . . . the Elective

Franchise." After collecting thousands of signatures for the petition, Isabella was invited to testify before the Senate Judiciary Committee, where Charles Sumner praised her presentation as "able, lucid and powerful."[24] Isabella was not the first or even the second Beecher sister to draw up a petition for a cause, but she was not as interested in achieving her reforms through the traditional channels of moral influence. For Isabella, Washington would always be the primary artery of social change, not the church or the classroom or the club room. As the wife of a lawyer, she was more familiar with the courthouse than the meetinghouse. Consequently, when Henry was accused of exerting his own form of "moral influence" upon Elizabeth Tilton, Isabella did not side with his congregation or her own family.

In October of 1868, Ulysses S. Grant was running for president. Chosen to speak at an election rally in New York, Henry praised the Civil War general as a hero of the American people and as someone he deeply admired. In the audience that day was Elizabeth Tilton, who was more impressed with Henry than with the future president. She was smitten and probably infatuated with the pastor of Plymouth Church, one of the most famous men in America. According to suffragist Susan B. Anthony, in her diary that day Elizabeth recorded the roaring applause after Henry's speech and called October 10 a "A Day Memorable."[25] What exactly she meant by these words became the subject of controversy for the next four or five years. As Theodore Tilton testified at Beecher's trial, Henry and Elizabeth began their affair on October 10, 1868. Whatever transpired for the next fifteen months, it was not until July 3 of 1870 that Mrs. Tilton made a full confession to her husband about the alleged affair. By Tilton's initial account, Henry persuaded her that their "high religious love" did not need to be sanctified by marriage, suggesting that Henry's Darwinian appraisal of the human condition had imbued his view of relationships as well. Love had somehow evolved beyond the limits of marriage to something more sacred and divine. According to Tilton, Henry convinced her that their sexual intercourse was not sinful because it fulfilled "a greater love" that he could not find at home.[26] Initially, Theodore Tilton kept the affair to himself. But not for long.

HENRY'S THEORY OF MORAL EVOLUTION

In the year prior to the affair, in a Thanksgiving sermon, "The Family as an American Institution," Henry preached one of the most revealing messages he would ever deliver on the state of men, women, sexuality, and marriage. The sermon was filled with the usual Beecher themes. Preaching to an auditorium filled mostly with New Englanders, he asked, "who are they that build colleges? Who are they that found academies? Who are they that beautify villages? . . . Who are they whose states have, in the worst times, the best credit? It is the Yankees." For Henry Ward Beecher, as for Lyman before him, the template for national prosperity was found in the New England way, beginning with the home. Suggesting that "the frost-line marks the realm of republicanism," Beecher argued that Yankees were more successful because they were more family-centric, a model confirmed in his own upbringing. In his view, "true republican commonwealths grow out of the power which is generated only in the Christian household." Without the building blocks of strong families, there could be no human flourishing. "The civilizing centre of modern America must be home and the family," he urged upon his congregation.

But Henry's vision of the home was anything but Puritan. Despite his pride in New England, Beecher found one glaring weakness: "the old Puritan prejudice against pleasure."[27] Just as Henry faulted New Yorkers for their hedonism, so he chastised Yankees for their "asceticism." Deprived of secular entertainments for years under the strong hand of his father, Henry insisted that life was meant to be enjoyed. Foreshadowing social critic H. L. Mencken's remark that Puritanism is "the haunting fear that someone, somewhere, may be happy," Beecher believed that the children of Puritanism needed to live a little. That included women. Traditionally, the Puritans had suppressed women, but no longer. "The world's history has traveled in one direction," Beecher declared. "Woman began at zero, and has, through the ages, slowly unfolded and risen. Each age has protested against growth as *unsexing* women. There has been nothing that men have been so afraid as *unsexing* women." But Beecher was not afraid to properly "sex" the other sex. Heralding a new dawn of women, Beecher preached that female liberty and power were part of America's "destiny" and that,

"in the new years that are coming, a nobler womanhood will give to us nobler households."[28] Borrowing his father's millennial view of history and his
language of "destiny," Henry was applying a Darwinian lens to society, education, and even gender. Convinced that women had started at "zero," he
believed they were evolving into a "nobler" form of themselves, something
human history had never seen.

In fact, almost *all* the Beecher men were arriving at similar views about
human development. Helping to establish the Elmira Academy of Sciences
with his friend Charles Samuel Farrar, Thomas corresponded with Charles
Darwin in the wake of his *Origin of Species* (1859). Thomas also exchanged
letters with Thomas Henry Huxley, the English biologist dubbed "Darwin's
bulldog" for his staunch advocacy of Darwin's theory of evolution by natural
selection.[29] In 1869, Huxley coined the term "agnostic" to describe his own
attitude about ultimate things, instead putting his faith in "the constancy
of the order of nature."[30] The agnosticism of men like Huxley and Herbert
Spencer troubled Thomas, who was concerned that "men of science" were
far outpacing clergymen in American society.[31] Horace Bushnell, Thomas's
spiritual mentor, had once called naturalism a "new infidelity."[32] Nevertheless, Darwinism appeared to explain the natural world in a coherent,
understandable way, offering a model for rational inquiry by which all scientific claims could be tested. As the Anglican paper *Guardian* declared in
1866, Darwin's theory of evolution "was everywhere in the ascendant," and
this was true on both sides of the Atlantic.[33]

The Beechers experienced what one scholar has called the "Victorian
crisis of faith" in the late nineteenth century, seeking to reconcile religion
with the new science.[34] As the Beecher brothers considered how this scientific revolution pertained to God and humanity, they consulted one another. In 1867, when Edward visited Henry in Brooklyn from Illinois, the
two shared a long walk in the woods, chatting about Herbert Spencer and
his ideas about "the survival of the fittest."[35] While Edward was a bit more
reluctant to dispense with a sinful "Fall" of humanity, Henry appeared to
drink the new science whole. According to William McLoughlin, "Spen-
cerian science and Liberal Protestantism walked hand in hand down the
aisle of Plymouth Church."[36] Henry also surrounded himself with like-
minded intellectuals. His friend Robert G. Ingersoll, a New York lawyer
nicknamed "the Great Agnostic," was one of Thomas Huxley's staunchest

American supporters.[37] Unlike Darwin himself, Henry Ward Beecher fully subscribed to the idea that evolution applied to human beings. In a sermon in February of 1873, at the height of the sex scandal, he preached a sermon, "Through Fear to Love," wherein he promoted a theory of *moral* evolution. "Human life begins in fear, and ends in love, working all the way up on a scale through a variety of modification," he exposited from 1 John 4:18.[38] According to Henry, this was not just true of civilization, but of human beings themselves. Love was more than a command or an emotion; it was the highest form of humanity. Combined with the culture of "free love" that swirled around the New York wing of the women's rights movement, Henry's belief in moral evolution assuaged his guilty conscience between 1868 and 1870 during his adulterous relationship with Elizabeth Tilton.

A SEX SCANDAL

Theodore Tilton did not see Henry Ward Beecher's romantic love as the pinnacle of human development. In his opinion, it was rank hypocrisy. How could a man who preached on the importance of the family violate the sanctity of marriage? Henry C. Bowen, editor of the *Independent*, had warned Tilton for several years of Beecher's mistresses, but Theodore was inclined to believe the best about his idol. Finally, after months of sitting on the news of his wife's infidelity, Theodore told Elizabeth Cady Stanton and Laura Curtis Ballard about the affair over dinner. When he came home, a quarrel broke out between himself and Elizabeth, touching off a strange series of events. In December of 1870, under no small amount of duress, Elizabeth retracted her original confession. Apparently, she and Henry had *not* indulged in sexual intercourse. A few hours later, however, she retracted her retraction. The truth was buried somewhere underneath these statements, each one less reliable than the one before.

To make matters more confusing, on December 23, 1870, Theodore Tilton's mother-in-law wrote a scathing letter to Henry Bowen accusing Tilton of being a womanizer and a drunk. With an already strained relationship with Tilton, Bowen confronted his editor. Adding to the morass of false motives and half-truths, Theodore then convinced his boss that it was in fact Beecher, not he, who was guilty of seduction. For a moment, Bowen and Tilton were united in their opposition to Beecher. But the moment was short-lived. Demanding that Beecher resign from Plymouth and leave Brooklyn, Tilton placed his bold letter in the hands of Bowen, who would take the message to Plymouth Church. However, Bowen was not a faithful messenger. Instead of delivering Tilton's letter, Bowen surreptitiously brokered a deal with Beecher. Attempting to gain the patronage of the Grant administration and the commercial interests in the J. B. Ford syndicate, Bowen assured Henry that he would fire Tilton as editor of the *Independent* and the *Brooklyn Daily Union* in exchange for Beecher's good word with the new president. Sent as an emissary for Tilton, Bowen had switched teams. This kind of backdoor horse-trading was New York politics at its finest. At a party on New Year's Eve, Bowen informed Beecher that he had fired Theodore Tilton.

To become a full-blown sex scandal, the affair needed the power of the press, and Elizabeth Cady Stanton lit the match when she told Victoria Woodhull about the situation in the spring of 1871. Woodhull could not let such a delicious tale of power and deception go untold. After all, she was nursing a grudge against the Beechers. In a letter to Henry, she divulged her pain at being the object of Harriet's and Catharine's scorn. "Two of your sisters have gone out of their way to assail my character and purposes, both by the means of the public press, and by numerous private letters written to various persons with whom they seek to injure me, and thus to defeat the political ends at which I aim. You doubtless know that it is within my power to strike back," she warned.[39] It was not just Henry but the Beecher name that Woodhull evidently despised. On May 20, she doubled down on her threat when she penned an open letter in the *New York World* magazine, announcing her "absolute right" to confront male hypocrisy. "I know of one man, a public teacher of eminence, who lives in concubinage with the wife of another public teacher of almost equal eminence. All three concur in denouncing offenses against morality. . . . I shall make it my business to analyze some of these lives, and will take my chances in the matter of libel suits."[40] It was fairly obvious to whom she was referring. Sparking the rumor mill in New York City, Brooklyn was awash in gossip. Hiding from his parishioners and from the press, Beecher spent almost the entire summer isolated at his farm in Peekskill. According to Debby Applegate, "His mood on vacation was almost manic."[41] America's most famous man had retreated from public life. America's Demosthenes was rendered silent.

On November 2, 1872, Woodhull finally made good on her threat, publishing an exposé of the affair in *Woodhull and Claflin's Weekly* entitled "THE BEECHER-TILTON SCANDAL CASE: The Detailed Statement of the Whole Matter by Mrs. Woodhull." Although even Theodore Tilton confessed that some of Woodhull's claims in the article were a bit outlandish, she succeeded in staining one of the most polished images in the United States. Woodhull could not resist publicizing Beecher's indiscretions because they were committed by someone who made a habit of policing morality in the public square. The Beecher sisters had criticized her freely in the press, and Henry had enforced his own moral code from the pulpit. Woodhull was simply returning the favor.

The news of Henry's affair also ignited a firestorm of controversy in the Beecher family itself, and lines were drawn quickly. With a mixture of shock and disgust, Roxana Foote's children rushed to Henry's defense. In Harriet's eyes, her little brother was the victim of hucksters trying to make a name for themselves at his expense. Seeing Woodhull's exposé as an attention-seeking vendetta against the Beecher family, Harriet and Catharine never doubted Henry's innocence for a second. Now in his new role as theologian-in-residence at Plymouth Church, Edward naturally sided with Henry. According to Charles Beecher, who likewise rallied behind his brother, Edward "stood like a rock before Henry when Slander assailed him."[42] However, Isabella was not as trusting. By the fall of 1871, she defended her fellow spiritualist Victoria Woodhull as a "PROPHETESS" and "MY DARLING QUEEN."[43] As a result, she was immediately alienated from her family. Harriet was shocked at her sister's fawning over Woodhull. Furthermore, as Barbara White explains, "Isabella was doing the unthinkable in championing the women who had accused her brother."[44] Although Thomas did not support women's suffrage and was certainly no follower of Victoria Woodhull, he too suspected that the accusations against Henry had substance. As a result, he and Isabella wrote back and forth and spoke frequently about the matter over the next few years. In the aftermath of the Woodhull exposé, Isabella wrote matter-of-factly to her brother:

> The blow has fallen, and I hope you are better prepared for it than you might have been but for our interview. I wrote H. a single line last week thus, "Can I help you?" and here is his reply, "If you still believe in that

woman [Woodhull] you cannot help me. . . . I tread the falsehoods into the dust from whence they spring, and go on my way rejoicing. . . . I trust you give neither countenance nor credence to the abominable coinage that has been put afloat. The specks of truth are mere spangles upon a garment of falsehood."[45]

Isabella then remarked to Thomas, "So far as I can see it is he who has dragged the dear child into the slough—and left her there."[46] With every denial, Henry only roused the indignation of his half-sister. The primary issue for Isabella was the abuse of power. The "dear child" Elizabeth Tilton had been "dragged" into fornicating with her famous brother and now could not defend herself from public scrutiny due to his own vanity and pride. The entire ordeal was proof that men used their authority to suppress women.

Meanwhile, Isabella's siblings could only see the megalomania of Victoria Woodhull, who was running for president under the newly formed Equal Rights Party. She appeared to be using Henry to promote her own platform and her own godless ideology of "free love." When Isabella insisted to Edward that Henry should confess his sin for his own salvation, Edward replied defiantly, "if he is guilty, confession will not save him. He will fall in all the Christian world, as [did] Lucifer son of the morning. . . . His own people will not forgive him." Jesus Christ, he noted, "condemns divorce except for one cause, and denounces even looking at a woman to lust after her as adultery. Mrs. Woodhull's movement will sink in perdition all who indorse it." In short, if Henry was guilty, Victoria Woodhull was guiltier. But Edward concluded, "I fully believe he is innocent and pure . . . and I do not believe that God would thus sustain a liar, a hypocrite and a libertine, and he is all that if he is guilty."[47] Isabella was disappointed that the intellectual and moral leader of the family could err so grievously on such an all-important matter. Edward's response left her in "astonishment."[48]

CHOOSING SIDES

Combined with the effects of age and tragedy, Henry's affair exacted its toll upon every member of the family. The year 1872 was Henry's twenty-fifth anniversary at Plymouth Church, but the scandal overshadowed everything. Instead of a celebration, pressure mounted on the church to open an investigation. As one might expect, "Beecher was a wreck."[49] At Yale Divinity School, Henry was chosen as the first Lyman Beecher Lecturer in a prestigious lectureship that continues to this day. One could argue that during his three-year tenure as lecturer (1872–75), Henry experienced the height of his cultural influence at the very same time that it was beginning to slip away. In Hartford, after selling their Oakholm mansion due to its location in a deteriorating part of town, the Stowes purchased a home on Forrest Street on Nook Farm. But their real home was in Florida. Between 1866 and 1884, Harriet and Calvin spent almost six months a year in Mandarin. Harriet called the homestead her "calm isle of Patmos," after the island where John the Evangelist was marooned in the book of Revelation.[50] Like John, Harriet's pen was active. From her orange-laden veranda overlooking the St. John's River, Harriet wrote to Charles about their new house on Forrest Street. "we have bought a pretty cottage there, near to Belle, and shall spend the summer there."[51] Still, while Harriet was physically closer to her baby sister, the two seemed farther apart than they had ever been. Isabella was not even allowed in the Stowe home. In fact, by 1873, only Catharine continued to speak to Isabella.[52] At various opportune times in their careers, the Beechers had cast their lots with radical revivalists and abolitionists, but never at the expense of their own family. In their view, Isabella was sacrificing Henry on the altar of womanist extremism. The price was high.

Although a bit more apprehensive, Harriet did share an interest with her little sister in spiritualism. In the fall of 1870, Harriet wrote a series of articles on the subject for the *Christian Union*, identifying spiritualism as an authentic religious movement grounded in the "communion of the saints." As Nancy Koester notes, Harriet's interest in supernatural communication was attached to her disillusionment with traditional religion: "If people thought the Church could not help them, they turned to spiritualism."[53] Harriet's longing to speak to her deceased children only increased after the loss of her son Fred. After a visit to Charleston, the beleaguered Fred Stowe announced in the summer of 1871 that he was joining the crew of a merchant ship on a voyage around Cape Horn to San Francisco. It would be the last time he ever spoke to his family. After the journey around South America, Fred was last seen by his fellow sailors trying to buy liquor in the streets of San Francisco. He was never seen again. The Stowes searched for their son for years. "I never forget my boy," Harriet quaked.[54] But their search was in vain. Fred would never come home and would never be buried with the rest of the family, a painful fact for Harriet. With a mixture of courage and decadence, Fred Stowe embodied the very best and worst of the Beecher family. As the son of a famous author and seminary professor, he was afforded nearly every opportunity that one could be given to a child in the nineteenth century. But his end was as ignominious as his life. Ultimately, he was a missing person on the other side of the country, a rather grim reminder for a family of temperance advocates that one could never flee from one's problems.

The personal and the political were never more interwoven than in 1872 and 1873, when Henry's affair became a sort of Rorschach test in the family for woman's rights. Those who stood in Henry's corner generally supported women's suffrage, but with qualifications. Still as prolific as any Beecher, Catharine wrote *Woman's Profession as Mother and Educator with Views in Opposition to Woman Suffrage* (1872). Although in favor of women's suffrage, she believed that women should be allowed to vote only if they had accumulated personal wealth and were on tax rolls. Economic independence was the key to elevating women, not universal voting rights.[55] In her lengthy dedication "to the Ministers of Religion in the United States," Catharine first leveraged her father and brothers. "As the daughter and sister of nine ministers of Jesus Christ you will allow me to address you," she pontificated. Catharine next took aim at the woman's movement, which she believed was destroying the American family (and hers): "This *woman movement* is one which is uniting by co-operating influences, all the antagonisms that are warring on the family state. Spiritualism, free-love, free divorce, the vicious indulgences consequent on unregulated civilization, the worldliness which tempts men and woman to avoid *large* families, often by sinful methods, thus making the ignorant masses the chief supply of the future majorities; and most powerful of all, the feeble constitution and poor health of women, causing them to dread maternity as—what it is fast becoming—an accumulation of mental and bodily tortures."[56]

The more the American social landscape changed in the late nineteenth century, the more Catharine Beecher appeared to stay the same. Since her literary debates with Angelina Grimké in the 1830s, Catharine had continually argued for a more nuanced position for woman's rights, straddling the line between the conventional and the radical. Although Catharine now supported a conditional women's suffrage, her message of woman's health, education, and prosperity had little changed. She believed that "women teachers of our common schools" would shape the next generation. Like her father, Catharine was always reforming, but never revolutionizing. Victoria Woodhull's botched campaign for president in 1872 only vindicated Catharine's belief in the goodness of male hierarchy. After listing several reasons why women's suffragists were in error, Catharine appealed to moral influence:

> The final objection to universal woman suffrage is that there is a safer, surer, and more speedy method at command which would secure all the benefits aimed at without any of these dangers. This method is based on the general principle that in seeking either favors or rights it is a wise policy to assume the good character and good intentions of those who have the power to give or withhold. The law-making power is now in the hands of men, and the advocates of women suffrage practically say, "you men are so selfish and unjust that you cannot be trusted with the interests of your wives, daughters, and sisters; therefore give them the law-making power that they may take care of themselves." As a mere matter of policy, to say nothing of justice, how much wiser it would be to assume that men are ready and willing to change unjust laws and customs whenever the better way is made clear and then to ask to have all evils that laws can remedy removed.[57]   ·

By assuming that men were willing to change on their own if given the opportunity, and that lawmakers could be persuaded toward a "better way" without being compelled against their will, Catharine was perpetuating a classic Beecher belief, no different from Lyman's view of westerners or Henry's view of southerners. This was the so-called "voluntary principle" from the early republic in late-nineteenth-century form. With a very Beecheresque optimism in the "good intentions" of human beings, Catharine was applying a bit of moral suasion to the issue of women's rights. She even outlined practical ways to achieve this end. For example, instead of simply circulating newspapers, why not enlist the influence of clergymen? Was the church to be treated as a foe and not a friend of the cause? Catharine's plea was somewhat surprising. As Barbara White humorously asks, "Did she momentarily forget she had spent the past twenty years attacking the clergy in her writings?"[58] In Catharine's mind, the only thing more frightening than clerical hypocrisy was a world completely devoid of religion.

For Isabella, raising her voice in Washington was the "better way." After Catharine signed a widely circulated petition *against* suffrage, Isabella rallied the forces of women's rights at the nation's capital. At a convention in Washington, DC, in 1872, thousands of women campaigned for the so-called "New Departure," the idea that the naturalized "persons" and "citizens" stipulated in the Fourteenth and Fifteenth amendments included women as much as it did Black men. From the fruit of the abolitionist movement sprouted the seeds of women's suffrage. At the convention, Isabella reported on the work of her National Woman Suffrage and Educational Committee, which had recommended that women attempt to register to vote in every election. Contending that "men and women should pour out money like water" to advocate for female suffrage, Isabella believed that every family in the United States should be sent a copy of the Declaration of Independence and the Constitution, "together with an argument on the fair interpretation of these documents."[59] The solution to injustice was not to dispense with the American dream but to renew it. Isabella was very much her father's daughter in her devotion to the sanctity of the founders' vision for the country. Apparently, she also acted like a Beecher. Elizabeth Cady Stanton resented Isabella's ego, commenting, "The Beecher conceit surpasses understanding."[60] Beecherism was hard to stomach at times. Nevertheless, at the convention, Stanton coauthored a resolution with Susan B. Anthony and Isabella demanding that Congress pass legislation paving the way for women to vote under the Fourteenth and Fifteenth amendments. Although it was eventually turned down by Congress, the memorial was eventually presented to the Judiciary Committee. Isabella also appealed to the White House. In a letter to President Grant, she pleaded for a presidential proclamation directing electors to admit women to the polls, adding that the First Lady, Julia Grant, had the power to imitate the biblical Esther and intercede for the people.[61]

For Isabella, social and moral change would not come through ecclesial authority, but through *executive* authority. Henry's hypocrisy only made her question further the divinity of the church. The only real source of truth was the Bible itself. Her brother Thomas, although a minister, was arriving at similar conclusions. In *Our Seven Churches* (1870), compiled from a series of lectures and dedicated to Horace Bushnell, Thomas made the most radical defense of ecumenical Christianity ever made by a Beecher. He charged, "As a book of ecclesiastical regulations the Bible is a failure. As a repast for saints the Bible is a marvelous success."[62] Christians would never agree on denominations and doctrine, he argued. The only point of Christianity was to try to do the will of the Lord and to love thy neighbor. "It is a blessed thing to be gathered into any church," Thomas declared. "It is a cursed thing, having been gathered in, to blaspheme the dwelling-place of other saints."[63] Thomas was disgusted by the religious balkanization of the age. The Beecher deconstruction of ecclesial authority was in full swing, exacerbated by the division they witnessed among God's people. What mattered most was working hard and improving the lives of those around them. Thomas believed in uplifting his community, but even he had his limitations. Joking about his wife Julia's support for the women's temperance movement, he confessed, "I'm passing thro' one of the periodic persecutions which afflict Julia so much—There's a temperance revival here. And there's ale in my cellar."[64] Ironically, Thomas later ran for the Prohibition Party.

ANOTHER BEECHER ON TRIAL

As pressure mounted and rumors amplified, the pastor of Plymouth Church prepared his letter of resignation. But he never resigned. Isabella wrote many times to Henry in 1872 and 1873, warning him against the sins of infidelity and duplicity. "I can endure no longer," Isabella wrote indignantly to her brother. "I must see you and persuade you to write a paper which I will read, going alone to your pulpit, and taking sole charge of the services." This was a bold demand, but then again Isabella conceived of herself as a kind of American prophetess. Writing as one "commissioned from on high," she ordered, "Do not fail me, I pray you; meet me at noon on Friday as you hope to meet your own mother in heaven." The brother and sister met in person on multiple occasions, but any attempts at exoneration or reconciliation were to no avail. Henry would not admit guilt. For all his impassioned pleas for sisterly support, there was no confession of adultery. Isabella remained thoroughly unconvinced of his innocence. As Isabella explained once to Henry, she was always open to the truth: "I had come to see that human laws were an impertinence, but could get no further, though I could see glimpses of a possible new science of life that at present was revolting to my feelings and my judgment; that I should keep myself open to conviction, however . . . and as fast as I *knew* the truth I should stand by it, with no attempt at concealment."[65] Ironically, Isabella was prosecuting her brother in a very Beecher fashion. Once convinced of the truth (Beechers could never ignore a "new science"), she pursued it with full conviction. In this case, the truth was not on Henry's side, she charged.

Despite some warm exchanges in their correspondence, relations between Isabella and Henry eventually became so icy that Isabella joked that Eunice would probably kill her if she had the opportunity. The result was more of a cold war than a civil war, and Isabella relied upon the only Beecher in her corner, Thomas, with whom she shared letters from both Victoria Woodhull and Henry. In a letter to Isabella, Thomas replied, "Of the two, Woodhull is my hero, and Henry my coward, *as at present advised.* I return the papers. You cannot help Henry. You must be true to Woodhull."[66] The entire ordeal was a lose-lose situation for all parties involved. In Hartford, Isabella was exiled from her social group for her support of Victoria Woodhull. Even Mark Twain had begun to distance himself from the Hookers. Evidently, no one in Nook Farm took Woodhull seriously. In Brooklyn, Henry stationed Harriet in the front pew at church in case Isabella showed up and decided to publicly confront her brother in front of his congregation! Harriet, who was now comparing women's rights extremists to French Revolutionaries, was still shocked that Isabella would throw in her lot with "The Woodhull."[67] With matching martyr complexes, both Beechers—Henry and Isabella—relied upon their favorite siblings for moral support.

Of course, Henry's real enemy was the press. After publishing a "True Story" of the scandal and a "Letter To a Complaining Friend" in order to clear his own name and divert attention to Beecher's sins, Theodore Tilton had his wife Elizabeth sign a mini-confession: "In July, 1870, prompted by my duty, I informed my husband that Rev. H. W. Beecher, my friend and pastor, had solicited me to be a wife to him, together with all that this implies."[68] While the words themselves had shock value, Elizabeth Tilton's credibility was suspect. Obsessed with exacting revenge upon his pastor, Theodore threatened to publicize Beecher's "Letter of Contrition" that he had written to the Tiltons months earlier. Although the letter was not quite a confession of guilt, Beecher was ready to submit his letter of resignation if Tilton went forward with his plan. His public image was cracking under the weight of tabloid journalism. But Henry could not sit on his hands. After receiving word that wealthy New York businessmen were demanding that Victoria Woodhull turn over any letters that would incriminate him, Beecher decided to defend himself in the press, calling the accusations of infidelity "grossly untrue" and "utterly false."[69] The statement did little to change the minds of those who had already decided that Beecher was a wolf in sheep's clothing. When Susan B. Anthony read the statement, she raged, "when God shall take up his old plan of punishing *liars*—there will be a good many people struck dead in Gotham and its suburbs."[70] Despite his previous attempts to play both sides of the women's movement, Henry Ward Beecher no longer enjoyed an ounce of cachet in the radical wing of women's rights. Finally, on October 31, 1873, Plymouth Church stood by Beecher, excommunicating Tilton for "slandering" their pastor. By a vote of 210 to 13, the decision was unequivocal: Henry Ward Beecher was still beloved by most of his own congregation.

If Lyman Beecher was the heart of the family and Roxana its soul, Harriet remained the central nervous system. Even in a family crisis, she managed to maintain relationships with almost all of her siblings (minus Isabella, who lived down the street). In a dynamic and gregarious family such as the Beechers, Harriet was the most dynamic and gregarious. She was alone in her unique ability to forge connections with brothers and sisters of all ages and across great distances. For example, the eldest of the clan, William, was now the only Beecher who resided permanently in the West, living near his children in Chicago. In addition to his geographical remoteness, William had also been the least successful of the Beechers. Battling dyspepsia and thorny congregations for his entire career, he was given the unfortunate nickname "The Unlucky" for good reason. As Lyman Beecher Stowe recounted with a somewhat rose-colored lens of his uncle, "William Beecher's life illustrated how dangerous were the Beecher family traits. He had the same courage, the same honesty, the same humor and the same missionary zeal, but in his case they served only to insure his being constantly harried and persecuted."[71] But not even William could elude Harriet's friendly company. When she made her speaking tour through the West in 1873, she worked her way through Pennsylvania, New York, Michigan, Indiana, Kentucky, Ohio, *and* Illinois. During her stop in Chicago, where her audiences had grown significantly larger, "Uncle William drove them around the city so that they could see how splendidly it had been rebuilt after the Great Fire."[72]

Also noteworthy is that Harriet stayed with Thomas in Elmira as she passed through New York, proving that not even family drama and Thomas's support for Isabella prevented Harriet from seeing her half-brother (and Elmira's water cure). During her tour through Ohio, Harriet also visited Walnut Hills, escorted by Sarah Beecher's son, George, her nephew.[73] Riding around Cincinnati with the namesake of her fallen brother was a bittersweet reminder of her former life in Ohio, where she witnessed death and suffering like few New Englanders ever would, and where she would take up her life's calling of speaking for the voiceless. Harriet's sense of history and heritage brought her home to the place where she became Harriet Beecher Stowe. Over two decades after the publication of *Uncle Tom's Cabin* and over a decade after the Emancipation Proclamation, Walnut Hills represented the arduous progress of the nation and the Beecher family itself. Although her pen changed the course of American history, Harriet's greatest contribution to the Stowe family was her willingness to stay in touch with distant members of the family, whether in Chicago or on the Florida Panhandle. In the Beecher dynasty, this was a significant step toward some sense of family unity after Lyman's death. In times of change, Harriet's epistolary correspondence and personal visits to her brothers and sisters provided the ligaments and sinews to a family in flux. However, after the midwestern tour, the sixty-two-year-old was completely exhausted. Eventually, after making an appearance in Washington, DC, Harriet headed south to Mandarin. She never lectured again.

Conversely, as Harriet became the connective tissue of the Beecher family, Isabella felt like an island. In fact, at various times, she felt alienated from almost everyone in her life. Even her beloved husband felt so unsettled by her involvement in the Beecher-Tilton affair that he fled to Europe even though Isabella told him she could not make the trip. In 1873, being concerned about Isabella's association with Victoria Woodhull, he wrote to his wife from Florence, Italy, about how to protect her reputation.[74] He preferred to have his wife portrayed as someone who was trying to be a positive influence upon Woodhull rather than someone who was blindly following her. In the highest, most educated circles of New England, Woodhull was a pariah. John was afraid that his wife had become a kind of political *and* religious disciple of Woodhull in the public eye. Branded by her sisters as a "she-devil," Woodhull had cost Isabella more than a few relationships. She was now ostracized by most of her family, most of her Hartford community, and to a lesser extent by her husband. As Francis D. Moulton later testified, Isabella was even prevented from carrying out her threats against her brother because Theodore Tilton threatened to "reveal" that she had committed adultery with a senator while in Washington![75] Wherever the spirit of "free love" was welcomed, accusations of adultery were never far behind. Finding camaraderie with her fellow women's activists, Isabella attended a Woman's Congress in October of 1873 with the likes of Sarah Grimké, Julia Ward Howe, Elizabeth Cady Stanton, Mary Livermore, and Lucy Stone. Susan B. Anthony chafed that she did not get an invitation while Isabella and Stanton, "the two *greatest Woodhull sinners*," received letters.[76]

Theodore Tilton was disfellowshipped from Plymouth Church, but Henry was by no means in the clear. In October, a special committee at Plymouth opened an investigation into the charges of adultery brought by Tilton. Not surprisingly, he was absolved from any wrongdoing. Nevertheless, the controversy went far too deep and involved far too many people to go away completely. The following summer, a second investigation was opened. The new accuser was Frank Moulton, a mutual friend of Tilton and Beecher. By 1874, the entire affair had taken on a life of its own as Beecher found himself at the center of a highly publicized sex scandal that was eroding his reputation. Harriet called the ensuing trial a "national event" akin to the "assassination of Lincoln."[77] Henry Ward Beecher, the most famous pastor in America and the leading religious voice for women's rights, was tried by his own church for having an affair with a fellow activist who attended Plymouth. Had there ever been a juicier, more contemptible, more captivating spectacle in the history of the church? In the words of historian Barbara White, "The trial immediately became a media event comparable to the affair of President Clinton in the 1990s."[78] Accusations of public figures committing adultery had existed in the United States since fellow New Yorker Alexander Hamilton's affair with Maria Reynolds in the 1790s. However, the combination of religion, women's rights, and the name Beecher made the trial in July irresistible and virtually unprecedented in America.

As usual, Harriet came to the aid of her little brother. During the second trial, she stayed for three weeks with Henry and Eunice in their home. Eunice was not the most hospitable host, as her resentment for Harriet still burned since their earliest days in Ohio. But the friction with Harriet was nothing comparable to her disdain for Isabella. In August, Henry was found innocent of the charges against him. When the verdict was read, the crowd erupted in celebration. America's preeminent pastor was vindicated, at least by his followers. Beecher would continue to wield public influence for years to come, but never from the same moral high ground he once occupied. Elizabeth Cady Stanton called the trial a "holocaust of womanhood."[79]

THE FUTURE OF WOMANHOOD

While Beecher was fighting for his career, his sisters were fighting for the cause of women. Isabella, Harriet, and Catharine all wrote books on the subject of women in 1874, but each with her own focus. Following the Woman's Congress, Isabella penned her first and only work, *Womanhood: Its Sanctities and Fidelities*. Published during Henry's sex scandal, the book cemented Hooker's reputation as a "free lover." Still, in typically paradoxical style for a Beecher, the book was both progressive and conservative in its social outlook. While including a provocative section on sex-education reform for boys, Isabella also contended vociferously against the licensing of prostitutes. Hooker was concerned with advancing society *and* protecting it from things like vice and disease. All in all, the work was poorly titled but well written.[80] Isabella did not have the same knack for writing as her two older sisters, but she could certainly write with purpose. There was still work to be done on behalf of women's rights. In 1874, the U.S. Supreme Court decided against the New Departure in *Minor v. Happersett*, judging that female citizenship did not automatically grant women the right to vote. Suffragists were outraged.

Catharine, on the other hand, was defending her legacy as a reformer of women's education in *Educational Reminiscences and Suggestions* (1874). From her founding of the Hartford Seminary to the American Woman Educational Association, Catharine touted her professional résumé and beat the same drum of America's salvation through higher learning for women. Like a revivalist sermon, her book concluded with an exhortation and a decision to be made. Her penultimate chapter was "American Women: Will You Save Your Country?" By warning against the extremes of the French Revolution, heralding education as the sole means of establishing intelligence and virtue, and holding up religion as the only remedy for public morality, Catharine Beecher was trumpeting the same message her father had preached in the Ohio Valley decades earlier. She was still trying to "save" America, the very mission Lyman had invited her to fulfill when she was in Hartford all those years ago. Now, from the same city, at the same school, she still believed in his vision for the nation. While conceding that taxpaying women should be allowed to vote, she emphasized traditional family values more than ever: "The most important and influential of all our educational institutions is that of the family, in which the housekeeper and mother is the chief minister, with her kitchen, nursery and school assistants."[81] Women, specifically mothers, held the key to the nation's future.

Catharine never relinquished her deep appreciation for her childhood and never stopped idealizing her parents. According to Kathryn Sklar, it might have been a bit too much, for "although she did full justice to Lyman's role in her upbringing, she slightly exaggerated her debt to 'certain traits in [her] mother's character and their influence on [her] early training.'"[82] Catharine was the only one of Roxana's children to continue speaking to Isabella during the trial, perhaps because she saw that America's women and America's families could ill afford to be divided in a generation of change. "When our country was on the brink of disunion and destruction," she recalled with gusto, "the women of our country *organized* to perform their part of the self-sacrificing labor involved, and they did it wisely and well. No less dangers are now impending from the inroads of ignorance and vice threatening speedy ruin."[83] Like her father, Catharine was making a clarion call to Americans to face down the next deadliest foe imperiling the nation. Time was of the essence—again.

In 1874, Harriet was also calling American women to embrace a particular vision of themselves. But she was looking backward, not forward.

Her book *Woman in Sacred History: A Series of Sketches* featured vignettes, illustrations, poems, and commentary of women throughout the Bible for the purpose of demonstrating "the development of that high ideal of woman which we find in modern Christian countries."[84] In some ways, Harriet subscribed to her own semi-Darwinian view of womanhood. On one hand, she believed that the earliest women of the Bible had "reigned as queens of the interior," and she praised them for their "monogamic affection" in a polygamous culture. (There was no license for "free love" in the Old Testament.) The women of biblical history were not unrefined cavewomen with crude manners and morals, but exemplary figures to be imitated. On the other hand, with the advent of the "Christian Era," Jesus Christ had "brought, in still higher degree, salvation to women."[85] By embracing the saving gospel and obeying the principles of the Bible, women could attain a level of moral and spiritual apotheosis, the "high ideal" of womanhood. In many ways, Harriet had committed her life to lifting up the nation to a more excellent version of itself—even in Mandarin. In 1874, she was invited by the governor of Florida to a reception honoring northerners who had helped in the Reconstruction of the state. To some, Harriet was a self-interested carpetbagger. To others, she was a selfless reformer.

Henry's acquittal by his church left Catharine and Harriet with a sense of relief, Isabella with consternation, and Henry with a public blemish that he could never entirely remove. When Henry traveled to Richmond, Virginia, a few years later for a series of lectures, a local doctor distributed leaflets protesting his arrival. Since the 1850s, Beecher had become accustomed to the usual southern insults thrown in his direction. But a new designation was added to the typical list of diatribes. Dr. George W. Bagby called Beecher a "liar, coward, sneak, libertine, hypocrite, adulterer . . . one unbroken mass of meanness and of sin . . . the wonder and shame of mankind."[86] Henry, the son of a Puritan preacher, now wore a scarlet letter. Surprisingly, even though the Virginia legislature voted informally not to attend Beecher's lecture, Henry still managed to attract a packed house for two hours.[87] He might have been an adulterer, but he was still a Beecher.

The outcome of Henry's trial left Isabella with a kind of scarlet letter of her own. Unfaithful to her own family and yoked with the leprous name of Woodhull, Isabella bore the reproach of her Hartford neighbors. In the summer of 1874, it seemed like too much. Seeking to avoid more insinuation and controversy, Isabella and John escaped the New England rumor mill by traveling to Europe and staying for a year and a half. John was still a bit annoyed with his wife for praising Victoria Woodhull in a newsletter of the National Woman Suffrage Association, but another trip to Europe was a chance to spend time together and reconnect.[88] There was much to talk about. In November, their daughter Mary shocked the family by giving birth to twins. Isabella never had an exceptional relationship with her sons-in-law due to her exceedingly low view of men, but she was a doting grandmother. During this time, Isabella dallied once again with the practice of spiritualism. For many, like her sister Harriet, spiritualism was an attempt to heal from the wounds of the past. In a post–Civil War generation, the memory of the dead was always nearby. However, for Isabella, communing with the deceased was more of an escape from the present. As Nancy Koester surveys, "Some people saw spiritualism as a new form of science. After all, if unseen forces like electricity, magnetic fields, and radio waves were being harnessed, why not try to understand and use unseen forces in the spirit world?"[89] From phrenology to water cures, Beechers could never ignore an emerging pseudo-science, no matter how questionable it might seem.

SURVIVAL OF THE FITTEST

Henry Ward Beecher was nothing if not adaptable. From his lectures in the 1820s on phrenology in rural Massachusetts to his revivals in the Midwest in the 1830s and 1840s to his progressivist sermons in the nation's largest church in Brooklyn, Beecher could be all things to all people. His lecture tour in the South in the 1880s would indeed solidify his reputation as the most dynamic speaker in America. But the Tilton scandal had taken its toll upon his mind and to some extent his confidence. Isabella was even worried about her brother's psychological state during the trial, suggesting that he might commit suicide.[90] So when Theodore Tilton issued a complaint to the Brooklyn City Court against his former pastor for the loss of his "comfort, society, aid, and assistance of his sad wife" and for "great distress in body and mind," Beecher's anxiety and nervousness only increased. Lyman Beecher had endured two ecclesial trials, and so had Henry. Like father, like son. But on January 11, 1875, in City Court, Henry faced a *civil* trial, a first for the Beecher family. For allegedly alienating him from his wife and destroying their marriage, Tilton demanded a hundred thousand dollars in damages from Beecher.[91] Adding to the drama, the courtroom was packed with reporters and celebrities. Henry complained that the newspapers devoted more space to the trial than they did the Civil War.[92] To pay for his team of six lawyers, Henry had support from his church. Members of Plymouth Church raised $100,000 for his legal expenses, demonstrating the power and wealth of his Brooklyn congregation. Henry's chief counselor during the trial was William Maxwell Evarts, who would eventually become secretary of state under Rutherford B. Hayes, elected president of the United States just two years later. In some ways, after twenty-eight years, Plymouth Church had become a mirror of their pastor and their pastor his church: willing to stand on principle and leverage influence. The trial itself revealed little that had not already been made known in the papers. As a result, Beecher was easily exonerated. Tilton, on the other hand, was financially ruined and his credibility shattered.

By the end of the trial, the Beecher family was still standing. But it walked with a slight limp. Henry resumed his career as a lecturer, but his moral influence was not quite as "moral" as it once had been. As the *Tribune* stated on October 5, "Ten thousand immoral and obscene novels could not have done the harm which this case has done, in teaching the science of wrong to thousands of quick-witted and curious boys and girls."[93] Although Beecher had survived the trial, the optics were bad. Henry Ward Beecher had begun his public career by speaking authoritatively to the next generation of Americans in his *Lectures to Young Men*. Now, it was not so apparent that he could do so any longer, having been part of such an ignoble series of events. Beecher had always played to the ideas and feelings of middle-class Americans, and after the trial he was more populistic than ever. His most popular lecture on the circuit was entitled "Reign of the Common People," a lecture he delivered in the North *and* the South. As usual, Beecher drew thousands. Moreover, for the first time, African Americans could attend his speeches with greater ease. The Civil Rights Act of 1875 guaranteed all citizens access to places like theaters, public schools, churches, and cemeteries.

Back at home, the sex scandal did not improve Henry's marriage. Eunice's distrust for her husband only worsened after listening to all of Henry's dirty laundry aired before the American public. One can only imagine the conversations at the Beecher residence following all three trials, each seemingly nastier than the other. Eunice alienated herself from all the Beechers, still resenting Harriet for having a level of intimacy with her husband that she never had. The two sisters-in-law never got along well.[94] Likewise, Harriet was also at odds with Isabella. Even though they lived so close for six months out of the year, the two were still not on speaking terms. Isabella's betrayal of Henry was not easily forgiven, and her self-proclaimed psychic and prophetic powers made it difficult for Harriet (and much of Nook Farm) to take her seriously.[95] While Harriet was willing to speak *to* the dead, Isabella seemed to speak *for* them. Underneath almost every conflict in the Beecher family lay a spiritual component.

While Harriet and Isabella continued their cold war, Catharine finally took up permanent residence with her half-brother Thomas in Elmira, New York. Now almost seventy-seven years old, the eldest Beecher was not as independent as she had been for most of her wayfaring career. She needed a place to live out the final chapter of her incredibly productive life, as she still aimed to continue writing. Thankfully, like Harriet, Thomas had the gift of hospitality. So, apparently, did Juliet. When Thomas asked his wife if they might be able to provide a final home for Catharine, Julia replied, "I think there are worse afflictions in the world than the care of an old Christian woman who has at least tried to do good all her life and needs someone's kind attentions till the Lord calls her home."[96] With a water cure to relax and a local women's college where she could devote her talents, Elmira was an ideal place for such a restless personality as Catharine Beecher. "I am relieved and glad to think of you at home at last with Brother Tom," Harriet wrote affectionately to her sister. "Too many years have passed over your head for you to be wandering like a trunk without a label."[97] In the final season of her life, after devoting her career to the art of domesticity, Catharine, the one Beecher who never married or had children, found a home.

Fittingly, in the last year of her life, the founder of home economics also helped mend the Beecher family itself. In the summer of 1877, as she was visiting Harriet and Calvin in Hartford, Catharine invited Isabella over to play croquet. Two years after Henry's trial, Isabella was still not allowed inside the Stowe house, but croquet is played outdoors. While the two sisters caught up on each other's lives, Isabella confided to Catharine that the Hookers were experiencing hard times financially. After the game of croquet, Catharine later relayed this unfortunate piece of information to Harriet, who felt sorry for her little sister. No matter how grievous Isabella's sins, she had suffered enough. In the Bible, the command to love thy neighbor did not come with conditions. With Catharine as mediator, Harriet sent a cash gift to her sister, signaling that it was time to reconcile and leave the past behind.[98] Although the two sisters would never see eye-to-eye about Henry's guilt or innocence in the Tilton affair, Isabella received Harriet's donation with thankfulness. The Beechers were known for their unwavering sense of right and wrong, but they could also be very forgiving people. Harriet and Isabella remained close friends for the rest of their lives. This was perhaps Catharine's final lesson in domestic education.

A year after arriving in Elmira to stay with Thomas, Catharine died of a stroke in her sleep on May 12, 1878. In many ways, her spirit endured powerfully in her two sisters. After the Connecticut legislature passed a bill in 1877 giving property rights to women, a bill that the Hookers had presented since 1870, Isabella spent the rest of her life campaigning for women's suffrage. Like her older sister, she believed that women should have a voice, and she routinely made her voice heard on behalf of a cause that she believed would save America. Whereas Catharine had begun her reformist career on behalf of the Cherokee, Harriet likewise took up the cause of Native Americans in the latter half of her career. In April of 1877, she published a two-part essay in the *Christian Union* on "The Indians of St. Augustine," protesting the slaughter of Native Americans in Florida.[99] She also threw her time and resources to educating this group imprisoned in her adopted state. In an April 8, 1877, letter to Col. James W. Forsyth, a Lieutenant Richard Henry Pratt of Fort Marion wrote: "Mrs. H. B. Stowe, recently here, was so much interested in the advancement the younger men have made, and in their disposition to learn, that she is making an effort towards giving some of them privileges of education at Amherst Agricultural School, with Govt. aid, if that can be obtained, and if not, there by private means if the Govt. will allow it. To satisfy her inquiries I submitted the question and found that twenty-three, of the most promising, would elect to remain east for education, rather than go home, if such an alternative was offered."[100] For every cause into which they threw themselves,

Harriet and Isabella proved that they were as determined and unyielding as the eldest Beecher sister and even as the chief Beecher himself. America had rapidly transformed since 1829 and 1830, when Catharine was gathering petitions with the help of her father for the Cherokee against Andrew Jackson. But the United States was still very much a nation of reform. The Beechers were still some of the leading catalysts in that most American of endeavors.

Chapter 7

A FAMILY LIKE OURS
(1878-1907)

AT CATHARINE'S FUNERAL in Elmira in 1878, the Beechers were still picking up the pieces from Henry's affair with Elizabeth Tilton. Plagued by a lingering sex scandal, the typically genial Henry had aged beyond his years. His long brown hair was beginning to reveal hints of gray. Mary and Isabella made the trip down from Hartford—separately. They were not on speaking terms. There could be no "fellowship" between the two, Mary chided, unless Isabella confessed that Henry was innocent. Even as they grieved together over the loss of their sister, there was no truce on the horizon. Likewise, after some hurtful remarks by Charles about Henry's affair, Isabella decided never to visit her older brother again. The Beechers were growing further apart. A disappointing absence at the funeral was Harriet, who could not attend because she was in Mandarin. The famous writer of New England fiction was basically a Floridian. While Harriet had reconciled with Isabella, a "coolness" remained between herself and Thomas.[1] Although a well-known pastor himself and something of a small celebrity in western New York, Tom bristled at having to still play second fiddle to his adulterous brother. One Sunday when he filled in for Henry at Plymouth Church, he announced defiantly, "All those who came here to worship Henry Ward Beecher may now leave—all who came to worship God may remain." Bringing his own brand of Beecherism to the Plymouth pulpit, Tom did little to hide the large chip on his shoulder. He later confessed that being the son of Lyman Beecher and the brother of Henry Ward Beecher was the greatest "misfortune" of his life.[2]

The funeral service was also a painful reminder that the family was divided along maternal lines. Although Catharine had corresponded with Isabella during Henry's trials, she did not bother to mention her half-sister in any of her final letters or papers. The omission spoke volumes. Isabella was reminded yet again that she did not share in the special bond between Roxana's daughters.[3] The difference between the nostalgic unity of Lyman's funeral and the seething disunity of Catharine's funeral was dramatic and palpable. Henry's affair had tinged the entire family with varying degrees of hostility and unfriendliness.

With a talent for masking pain with humor, Tom described what it was like to be a Beecher toward the end of the nineteenth century:

> How, I wonder, . . . could an outsider know what a family like ours feels like? . . . We are all marooned in a constant changing of allegiances, fierce defiance, and unyielding loyalty, a dreadful grinding on the nervous system. Especially when we gather . . . with all the spouses and rowdy kin, it is an endless bumping into Time. At the table . . . I exchange a glance with sister Catharine, for we both have seen sister Isabella shoot the butter straight into her lap, then daintly dribble nectar on her bosom, and fairly die with the honor of being confined in a single, human, female form.[4]

The Beechers were acutely aware of just how much baggage they brought to the family table. According to Thomas, it was increasingly difficult to reconcile the various "allegiances" and causes within their tribe. In a sense, Beecherism had been balkanized. Suffering with bouts of depression, Thomas struggled his entire life to embrace his family. Now, with the loss of Catharine, it seemed there was even less tying them together.

The funeral service was held at Tom's newly constructed church in Elmira, built for a congregation that had multiplied significantly during his tenure. Filled with calisthenic courses, boys' clubs, dancing classes, Sunday schools, and a theater, Park Church was a testament to Beecher innovation and reform. Making almost no real distinction between churches and denominations, Catholic or Unitarian or otherwise, Tom fulfilled his father's vision of becoming a socially minded pastor but abandoned his father's stricter version of Christianity. Placing a high premium on individual freedom and the power of healthy decision-making, the Beechers were nearly as dedicated to moral influence as their father had been, but their definition of "free agency" was a bit more, well, free. For example, Henry was still a vocal proponent for temperance, continuing his father's primary legacy. However, in 1878, Henry also advocated against the so-called "Blue Laws" in the suburbs of New York which prohibited the sale of alcohol on Sundays.[5] If New Yorkers were to advance the cause of temperance, they would do it by moral suasion and not by state law.

Presiding over the service was Edward, who once again reformulated his view of human progress. After obliterating the doctrine of creation in *The Conflict of Ages* (1853), Edward was now rethinking the traditional concept of hell. Exchanging the idea of eternal punishment for universal restoration, Edward's *History of Opinions on the Scriptural Doctrine of Retribution* (1878) posited that hell was just a fiery pit stop on the way to glory. Rewriting the very doctrine which had featured so prominently in his father's preaching, Edwards's book would likely have been dismissed by Lyman as another "little theological hencoop." Although hell was a more relevant topic in the nineteenth century than the preexistence of souls, Elizabeth Cady Stanton was probably right when she quipped that Edward dealt in "theological antiquities."[6] No matter how eccentric their views, as the Beechers aged and buried their own, they thought more about the life to come. Catharine's funeral was yet another reminder of the inevitability of death. But there was no question that dear Catharine, the most useful of all her siblings, was now in paradise with Lyman and Roxana. After all, hardly a Beecher remained who believed in the alternative to heaven.

HARRIET AND CHARLEY

In 1878, Harriet published her last novel, *Poganuc People*. She had never intended to write another serial, as the book was originally composed for a Christmas brochure. But as she became engrossed in her reminiscences about her New England childhood, Harriet could not put down her pen. On the St. John's River, under the hot Florida sun and to the sound of rustling palm leaves, Stowe grew more nostalgic than ever. The first chapter of the book begins in "a large, roomy, clean New England kitchen of some sixty years ago," almost exactly as she remembered (or envisioned) her Litchfield upbringing.[7] Ever immortalized in Harriet's mind, Lyman appears in the novel in the character of Dr. Cushing, the local preacher. In many ways, *Poganuc People* was evidence that Harriet was uneasy with the direction of the world and wished to return to a simpler time. The episode with Henry and Elizabeth Tilton had left her somewhat jaded and not as optimistic about certain aspects of society. After publication, she wrote to her friend Oliver Wendell Holmes Sr., "It is an extremely quiet story for these sensational days, when heaven and earth seem to be racked for a thrill; but as I get old I do love to think of these quiet, simple times, when there was not a poor person in the parish, and the changing glories of the year were the only spectacle."[8] Harriet may have slightly misjudged the innocence of Lyman's generation. According to Joan Hedrick, the book "exhibited flashes of nativism that was so closely bound up with Lyman Beecher's evangelical mission."[9] Nevertheless, *Poganuc People* sold well. For Stowe, the pen was always mightier.

The year 1878 was also memorable for Harriet's son, Charles E. Stowe. Returning from his theological studies in Bonn, Germany, "Charley" took his first pastorate in Saco, Maine, just forty miles down the coast from where he was born and where his mother penned *Uncle Tom's Cabin* in Brunswick. As a Congregationalist minister, the twenty-eight-year-old Charley was finally entering the family business. The Congregationalist Church was a bit less orthodox since his grandfather pastored in New England almost a century earlier, and Charley was somewhat representative of that generational shift.[10] His graduation from Harvard in 1875 set him on a much less evangelical path than the one at Yale. Originally attending his grandfather's alma mater for his theological training, Charley chose instead to study in Europe, a decision that Harriet "always regretted."[11]

In many ways, Charley's road to the ministry was typical for a Beecher. As a rebellious son in a religious family who was frequently disciplined at school, he had run off to sea like his uncle James (and like his uncle Henry had dreamed before being convinced otherwise by Lyman). In the hopes of one day becoming a ship captain, Charley embraced a sailor's life. But he was not cut out for the high seas. Eventually, he became homesick or seasick or both. Once he returned from his Atlantic voyage, he informed his parents that he wanted to go into the ministry.[12] For Harriet, who did not lack for achievements and awards, there was perhaps no greater honor in her lifetime than to consecrate her son in service to the Lord. "I cannot describe to you the ardor with which I desire & pray that you may become a minister after Christ's own heart," she melted, reminding her son of his "peculiar history" as Lyman Beecher's grandson and Calvin Stowe's son. He was following in his family's illustrious footsteps. (His son Lyman Beecher Stowe eventually authored *Saints, Sinners, and Beechers* in 1934, the first attempt to chronicle the family history.) Surely, Harriet noted, the ministry had been "bequeathed" to her son as a "sacred trust by their prayers and consecration." Like the sons of Aaron in the Old Testament, two generations of Beechers had passed their sacred profession onto a third.[13]

However, Harriet's son also inherited another family trait: reform. Just as the past generation of Beechers had innovated upon the traditions of their father, so Charley was almost destined to push the bounds of his family's beliefs—or reject them entirely. For starters, the young parson was not impressed with his uncle Henry's "liberal orthodoxy." In a letter to his mother, Charley scrutinized the "slovenly inconsistencies" and "dishonesty" of his uncle in Brooklyn. If Henry did not actually hold to Congregational tenets of the faith, how could he remain a Congregationalist in good conscience? For reasons both intellectual and moral, Charley did not respect his uncle. Reading her son's critiques of her brother might have made Harriet feel a bit conflicted—and defensive. After all, Harriet had become Henry's bulldog in her later years and shared his aversion to theological systems. Although an Episcopalian, she was probably not too far from Henry on several matters. She urged her son to follow Christ, not doctrines *about* Christ.[14]

In the Beecher dynasty of pastors, as in much of the nineteenth century, history often took an ironic turn. All of Lyman's sons eventually denied or deconstructed parts of his faith, from creation to original sin to predestination to conversion to holiness (that is, drinking, slavery) to divine judgment. There were few aspects of Lyman's belief system that were not amended by his children in some way. This was the nature of Beecherism, *semper reformanda*. Nevertheless, while sisters Catharine and Harriet had joined the Episcopal Church and several of their brothers had been accused of heresy (and another convicted), no Beecher had ever jettisoned historic orthodox Christianity entirely. But Charley Stowe was contemplating a newer, more modern, more enlightened faith. The grandson of the great Unitarian fighter Lyman Beecher was considering Unitarianism. This New England–based denomination, which denied that God was both three *and* one, appealed to the young theologian because of its emphasis upon human reason. Some of the supernatural and seemingly contradictory elements of the Bible did not seem rational to the young Beecher. The news was a gobstopper to Harriet, who was frozen in utter disbelief when she held her son's letter in her hands. How had it come to this? In the house of Lyman Beecher, there were numerous enemies of Christianity, but only two represented complete apostasy from the faith: Catholics and Unitarians. Charley might as well have announced that he was entering the priesthood! Although Harriet embraced a more accepting, tolerant form of Christianity than she did as a child, the possibility that her son would actually *become* a Unitarian was horrifying. "I protest with all the energy of my heart & soul against your joining the camp of the Unitarians," she pleaded. Harriet did not deny that there were "good soldiers & servants of Christ" in the Unitarian camp, but the denomination itself was devoid of the life and communion and mystery of the gospel and, most of all, the roots to an ancient faith that she had come to appreciate so dearly.[15]

Had Charley simply admired some of the Transcendentalists and their attention to intuition and social reform, it might have been another matter. Uncle Henry, after all, had been shaped by the ideas of Ralph Waldo Emerson. Part of the "Secret Six" who supported John Brown's war against slavery, Theodore Parker had been a radical abolitionist before the Civil War. Margaret Fuller's *Woman in the Nineteenth Century* (1845) had offered the first in-depth treatment of women's rights in the United States.[16] However, the mainstream Unitarianism of Harvard and urban New England, epitomized by scholars like Andrews Norton, was not a romantic religion but a reasonable one. Becoming increasingly rationalistic after the war, Unitarianism, though more socially engaged, represented exactly the kind of strict intellectualism that Harriet had left in the Presbyterian Church. Unitarianism was simply dogmatism by another name, in her opinion.

In some respects, Charley had much in common with his legendary grandfather. Both men were New Englanders to the hilt. As scions of the New England Theology, both were convinced that the Bible was a rational book. At the end of his life, after expressing his gratitude to Jonathan Edwards and his disciples for bringing "many truths out of relative obscurity," Lyman maintained, "If I understand my own mode of philosophizing, it is the Baconian. Facts and the Bible are the extent of my philosophy."[17] Beecher was committed to the inductive method of scientific reasoning laid out by the English philosopher Francis Bacon, trusting that simple empirical observation could lead a person to the truth. Trained in the scientific inquiry of the German mediating theologians, Charles E. Stowe was no less confident in the power of human reason. The difference was that Charley no longer held the same evangelical priorities as his revivalist grandfather. If the Bible seemed to conflict with human reason, it was the former, not the latter, which was held in question.

The irony could not have been lost upon Harriet. In the end, her son Fred succumbed to the very intemperance to which her father devoted his life trying to end, and her son Charley imbibed the same Unitarianism that Lyman fought ceaselessly against. She had lost the first Charley at eighteen months to cholera. She would not lose the second to a cold and lifeless religion. By the 1880s, German romantic and intuitional thought had already permeated the thought of Congregationalist theologians like Edwards Amasa Park at Andover. However, by the turn of the century, seventy years after Lyman Beecher joked to his son Edward at Andover about "German infidelity," Edwards Amasa Park was something of a dinosaur for trying to preserve some sense of the old order against German higher criticism.[18] (In another piece of poetic irony, Andover Seminary was subsumed into Harvard Divinity School in 1906.) As one historian has summarized, "Edwards Amasa Park was the last American theologian of significance to identify consciously with Jonathan Edwards."[19] The Beecher family was a microcosm of this larger transformation of New England religion in the nineteenth century. Charley Stowe did not become a Unitarian (at least in denomination), but like any New England theologian worth his salt, he was not beholden to any creeds or confessions.

As the world turned, Harriet Beecher Stowe remained an unstoppable force in American literary culture. While her sister Isabella was struggling to make ends meet, keeping house again on Forest Street to pay bills, Harriet was publishing widely read books and attending parties in her honor hosted by New England elites.[20] In 1882, she received one of the greatest recognitions of her life. For her seventieth birthday (actually her seventy-first), Houghton Mifflin Company, the publishers of the *Atlantic Monthly,* threw Stowe a garden party at the home of the former governor of Massachusetts, a friend of Harriet's. The lavish party was a who's who of Massachusetts high society. About two hundred notable guests—doctors and lawyers, authors, clergymen, and college presidents—attended the event under a festive tent, "Under the Elms."[21] The mayor of Boston was also there to celebrate the life of one of America's most famous writers. Henry Oscar Houghton, former mayor of Cambridge, claimed that *Uncle Tom's Cabin* "began by being a prophecy, and is now history."[22] Illustrating the angst of slavery like few novels ever could, the enormously popular book was now a chronicle of America's struggle for freedom. Stowe had changed the flow of human history and become part of it. She had also created something of an American legend. Across the North, and especially in New England, the august character of Uncle Tom had become synonymous with integrity and manliness. In Boston, one stage production a few years later described the actor who played Uncle Tom as giving the character "a personation of quiet dignity."[23] For a nation still attempting to answer questions about the individual and society, Uncle Tom was republicanism personified.

In addition to the glitz of the outdoor ceremony, there was glamor. John Greenleaf Whittier and Oliver Wendell Holmes Sr. both feted Harriet with poems in her honor. Since the Beechers were one of the most famous families in America, it was not surprising that brothers Henry and Edward each gave speeches. The air was filled with so much cheer and celebration that, for a brief moment, the Beechers almost forgot about their sour relations. Although Henry and Eunice made sure to avoid Isabella, Mary finally reconciled with her sister. The cold war in Hartford was over. Two months later, Mary Beecher Perkins made a visit to the Hookers. Just as Catharine had found a way to bring Harriet and Isabella back together, so Harriet now paid it forward to Mary and Isabella. The garden party was indeed the zenith of Harriet's notoriety in popular America, symbolizing not only her accolades as a writer but her contributions to social and moral reform. Not surprisingly, Harriet seized the moment to promote her latest cause, speaking about the freedmen in Mandarin and the opportunities presented in the new America. Stowe "had come to see herself as an ambassador for the freed slaves."[24] Florida had opened for Harriet an entirely new way of thinking about education and the potential for improving humanity. In the fall of 1882, after leaving early for Florida, the Stowes tried their hand at a new form of moral influence: they planted a church. Growing out of informal Bible studies led by Calvin Stowe in their home, the Mandarin Church of Our Savior was dedicated. Harriet donated land for the building project and helped oversee the construction. The new Episcopal minister, C. M.

Sturgess, was "perfect" for the job, according to Harriet.[25] The church combined high church and evangelical sensibilities, much like the marriage of Lyman Beecher and Roxana Foote.

As historian Barbara White has observed, despite their vastly different lives, Harriet and Isabella had very similar families. In the early 1880s, both women took care of their ailing husbands; each had daughters that were frequently the source of anxiety for their mothers; and both had exemplary, loyal sons who made their parents proud. Although they were worlds apart on certain issues, not least of which were Henry and women's rights, "their psychology was much the same."[26] Their families also became intertwined. When Calvin fell ill to Bright's disease, his doctor in Hartford was Ned Hooker, Isabella's son, with whom Isabella and John lived during the winter. Calvin's health was indeed failing. The winter months of 1883 and 1884 were the Stowes' last in Florida.

RUM, ROMANISM, AND REBELLION

The explosive industrial growth in late-nineteenth-century urban America widened the gap between wealth and poverty, and nowhere more than in New York. In the so-called "Gilded Age" (a term coined by Hartford resident Mark Twain), Tom preached often against the extravagance of the American middle and upper classes. At Park Church, he delivered scathing rebukes to businessmen and politicians for their greed and corruption.[27] Concern for the poor had been a mainstay in his ministry since arriving in Elmira. On July 4 of 1886, after the Chicago Haymarket riots in which labor demonstrators were bombed, Tom expressed his disgust at the rapacity of corporate power: "The United States are rapidly ripening into a highly organized and energetic Plutocracy!" He cried out, "The man or class or corporation that manipulates and administers upon money and credit, is the 19th century ruler or king. Behold your king, people!"[28] At Plymouth, Henry was less iconoclastic, but still attentive to the widespread poverty in Brooklyn. In the suburbs of Manhattan, it was hard to miss. With a burst of conviction, he interrogated his congregation:

> Where do all the poor go that are at the bottom of our cities, crawling like vermin and worms in and out of the crevices of palaces, and in

dens and dungeons in abject poverty? What becomes of them? Where do they come from, and where do they go to? What becomes of those whose education is neglected? What becomes of the great under-mass of mankind everywhere? I love the noble and the cultured; I have the most fastidious sense of the ethical and the aesthetic qualities in society; I rejoice in all that is resilient and beautiful; there is in my heart a leaping sensibility to all these things; but, after all, it is those who are low and degraded that are heaviest on my mind.[29]

Of all the social and moral causes in the 1880s, there was none more pressing than poverty. Even during the Civil War, southerners had sought to justify their treatment of slaves by pointing to abuses against factory laborers in the North. The issue of poverty was therefore very political, and not always easy to navigate. For example, even though Henry spoke often about hard work and helping the needy, he opposed the rise of labor unions, a decision unpopular with many.[30] Many unions were composed of Irish Catholics, a group which did not engender much love on Beecher's part for their alleged intemperance and anti-republicanism. In Elmira, Thomas's contempt for the Democratic Party aligned with these same prejudices.

For Henry, the biblical command to consider the poor did not preclude fraternizing with the well-to-do. In fact, one often served the other. In 1882, he was one of the speakers at Delmonico's in New York for a special dinner in honor of evolutionist Herbert Spencer during his three-month tour of America. Covered extensively in the next morning's newspapers, the dinner included prominent names like steel titan Andrew Carnegie. Like Beecher, Carnegie had shed the Calvinism of his youth in favor of a more sanguine estimation of the human condition. With Spencer's help, Carnegie "got rid of theology and the supernatural [and] found the truth of evolution."[31] Also at the event were journalists E. L. Godkin and Charles A. Dana; telegraph mogul Cyrus Field; current and future U.S. senators Carl Schurz, Chauncey Depew, and Elihu Root; New York City mayor Abraham Hewitt; congressman Perry Belmont; artist Albert Bierstadt; and sociologists William Graham Sumner and Lester Ward. With such an impressive guest list, one can begin to see how evolutionary theory involved much more than science. Beecher was attracted to the idea of natural selection not just because it seemed logical, but because it was quite fashionable among the most enlightened figures in New York. The headwinds of American culture never passed by a Beecher unawares. By aligning himself with the name of Herbert Spencer, Henry was able to adroitly position himself alongside the most influential and noteworthy citizens of the United States.

Henry did not approve of Spencer's agnosticism but nevertheless welcomed his ideas about history, society, and humanity. At the dinner, he did not sound like a man standing on the fence. Beecher stated, "Apes came down from the same starting-point with us, working towards bone and muscle, and men came down on the other side, working towards nerve and brain." Noting that some did not share this belief, Henry quipped, "I would just as life have descended from a monkey as from anything else if I had descended far enough."[32] The room erupted in laughter. The son of Lyman Beecher could always work a crowd. Henry may have been the "Spokesman for a middle-class America," but he neared the end of his career speaking to *all* classes.

In an age of dramatic social polarization, the idea of evolution helped Beecher to square his message of social reform with his refined lifestyle. Wealthy sinners did not need to "repent" of their inherent selfishness but rather to unlock their potential and develop into a more benevolent people. The problem was not gaining wealth or influence; it was refusing to share the wealth or influence the poor. For Beecher, the kingdom of God was measured in societal progress. "The measure of civilization and of Christianity in the community must be taken where the mass of its population reside," Beecher preached. "Now, the question of the times is 'What is the condition of the great laboring mass, the thousand to one, that earn their daily bread, and that eat their bread by the sweat of their brow? Is their condition ample, large?' No, it is not. . . . We know that it is necessary that there should be struggle, conflict, fighting, in life, in order that the fruit of the Spirit may be wrought out in men."[33] Just as men and women had evolved from an ape-like ancestor, so the "great laboring mass" was evolving into a higher form of itself—morally, intellectually, and economically. Calling himself a "cordial Christian evolutionist," Henry confessed to his friend Dr. Kinnard, "I would not agree by any means with all of Spencer, nor all of Huxley, Tyndall and their school. They are agnostic. I am not— emphatically. But I am an evolutionist and that strikes at the root of all medieval and orthodox modern theology. Men have not fallen as a race. Men have come up."[34]

However, not all of Henry's brothers shared his optimistic appraisal of humankind. Charles became increasingly skeptical of evolution. Now settled back in Georgetown in the home of their daughter Mary Noyes, Charles wrote to his brother in 1884, "I inferred from some remarks you made when I last saw you, that you had some slight differences of opinion in matters theologic from me and Edward. . . . We think man a fallen being, you think him a risen being,—but that need not prevent our writing letters to each other. . . . It seems to me that a belief in the fall of man may be tolerated in this era of liberty and liberality."[35] Amazingly, for a family characterized by its lack of attention to "matters theologic," the Beechers gave considerable discussion to that very subject. When one brother visited another, it was apparently not uncommon for the topic of original sin to arise. Raised in the art of salon-style dinner-table discussion, the Beechers continued this tradition for decades. Not unexpectedly, there were disagreements. Whereas Henry would not brook the notion of "fallen" human beings, Edward and his disciple Charles believed that the first man and woman had, in one life or another, rebelled against God and lowered themselves in their sin. Unanimously rejecting the Calvinist doctrine of total depravity, the Beechers were united in their optimistic belief in the *trajectory* of humanity but not of one mind on the exact *source* of humanity's problems. Nevertheless, of all their various disputes, the Beechers never suffered serious division over doctrine. Like his older brother Henry, Charles was an astute surveyor of the times, noting the "era of liberty and liberality" in which they lived. Indeed, the Beechers played a significant part in shaping this period of tolerance in America. For Charles, his relationship to his brother was more important than intellectual victory over the doctrine of sin. If the weakness of Beecherism was its lack of theological clarity, one of its strengths was its charity.

Still, Henry was irritated. He wrote back to Charles with the aggravated tone of a big brother, "I am annoyed that you go back to Adam for an adequate supply of sin to furnish the needs of the world. About here, we can have it fresh, first class, too, manufactured on the spot. . . . The fact is Adam's sin is like stale yeast, not fit to rise."[36] In short, the doctrine of original sin was not adequate to explain the world as it appeared to Henry Ward Beecher. Why quibble about a primeval sin when there were millions of individual sins permeating the world at this very moment? Adam's supposed "fall" from grace was not only unbiblical, argued Henry, it was irrelevant. While theologians dissected one prehistoric sin, people were making their own choices. One century earlier, during the New Divinity debates, a young Lyman Beecher had grappled with this exact issue. For New Englanders, it was still a vexing question: why was there so much sin in the world? Henry had more important matters to tend to, like helping people to love as Christ did. After all, this was the "highest" form of Christianity: "In all sobriety—just now among thinking unchurchly men, and among many ministers, the choice is between Evolution and Infidelity. I prefer the former. The whole force of organized religion has been directed to *Fear and Conscience*. In a low and barbarous condition this works well. It is time that as much *power* upon the soul should be developed from the higher religious sentiments, hope, trust, faith, Love, as from its basilar powers."[37] Choosing to look forward and not backward, upward and not downward, Henry believed that the more positive aspects of Christianity were the most effective for godly living. While Milton Rugoff has argued that this line of thinking foreshadowed New York pastor Norman Vincent Peale's *The Power of Positive Thinking* (1952), Beecher would have certainly contended that true Christianity had less to do with the mind and more to do with the posture of the heart.[38]

However, Henry had a personal reason not to emphasize themes like judgment and conscience. Over a decade since the Tilton affair, he was still repairing his tarnished image as an adulterer. In 1884, Henry decided once again to change with a changing America. In the presidential election, New York governor Grover Cleveland faced off against James G. Blaine of Maine. The election presented a dilemma. Although Blaine was a Republican, Cleveland was a New Yorker. Since the creation of the Republican Party and especially since the presidency of Ulysses S. Grant, Henry had been staunchly in the Republican corner. Along with friends like Mark Twain, Beecher stumped for Republican candidate James A. Garfield during the campaign of 1880.[39] But much had changed in four years. In 1881, Garfield was assassinated, leaving Vice President Chester Arthur at the helm. When Cleveland first announced his bid for the presidency, Beecher was opposed for numerous reasons. During the election, Republicans (like Thomas Beecher) mocked the Democratic Party for its "Rum, Romanism, and Rebellion." These antecedents of the party comprised three of the most suspect things in the Beecher mind: intemperance, Catholicism, and southerners. On the eve of the election, it certainly did not seem as if Cleveland would gain the support of New York's most famous pastor. The governor was also unpopular among New York workingmen, another potential obstacle for someone like Beecher, who coveted popular support.[40]

Perhaps the biggest roadblock in Beecher's mind was the widely circulated stories about Cleveland's saloon days in Buffalo, where he first got his start. Buffalo newspapers had also published tales about Cleveland fathering an illegitimate son with a local widow. The dark-horse candidate was not exactly a shining beacon of moral purity. The issues at stake in the 1884 election were significant: lingering prejudices from the Civil War, the pensions of war veterans, Catholicism, anti-British sentiment, nativism, and prohibition. All of these were relevant for Beecher as a pastor and public figure.[41] However, in 1884, Henry reversed his course. Instead of supporting the Republican, Beecher backed the fornicating, saloon-dwelling, southern-sympathizing, Catholic-supported Democrat. His reasons had little to do with fiscal policy or national unity. Instead, when Beecher saw a man chased by unfair accusations of infidelity, he saw himself. He compared rumors about Cleveland to the "venomous lies" in his own sex scandal with Elizabeth Tilton. In theory, Beecher was rooting for a Democrat for the good of the country. In reality, he was also rooting for himself. According to Debby Applegate, "Even to casual observers it seemed that Henry was using the Cleveland campaign to vindicate his own past. His argument was much like the one he'd used in 1866 in advocating leniency toward the South, indeed, toward all sinners."[42] Cleveland's victory in 1885 was thus a good omen that Beecher could make a comeback in the public eye. After all, Christianity was about moving forward, not backward. Also in 1885, Henry published *Evolution and Religion* in which he largely denied the divine inspiration of the Bible, boasting that "divine revelation, interpreted by Evolution, will in my judgment free the Sacred Scriptures from fictitious pretensions made by men, from clouds of misconceptions, and give to us the book as a clear shining light, instead of an orb veiled by false claims and worn-out philosophies."[43]

In Maine, although he was not fond of his uncle Henry, Charley Stowe had come to similar conclusions about the Bible. During his first several years in Saco, Charley's parishioners did not sit well with his more liberal beliefs. (His decision to serve wine instead of great juice for the Lord's Supper was also controversial.)[44] Harriet was still concerned about her son's foray into Unitarianism. But this did not keep a Beecher mother from trying to guide (or goad) her son in the right direction. Most likely arranged by Harriet, in 1885 Charley was ordained as pastor of Windsor Avenue Congregational Church in the Beecher stronghold of Hartford, a congregation that accepted his more progressive views. Harriet and Calvin used the sale of their Florida property to buy their son a home. The move also afforded Harriet's son the opportunity to work on her biography. As his aunts and uncles had done for their own father, Charley began preparing an autobiographical work for his mother, a project that Harriet had been planning for some time, organizing letters and papers. Catharine's death had spurred her to consider her own legacy. Always drawn to her siblings, Harriet used the endeavor to reconnect with her family. In a letter to Isabella in January of 1885, Harriet reported joyfully, "I think more of my brothers and sisters than I ever have done before have written to all and got replies from all but Henry. Your letter is a comfort to me."[45] As the world changed, so did the Beechers. Although the Bible may have lost something of its divinity, family was still sacrosanct.

THE PROGRESS OF DEATH

The Beechers were nearly incapable of conceiving of a life that did not gradually improve in some way. Therefore, even death was subject to the law of increasing spiritual returns. As Thomas once told his church in 1872, "Death is necessary to life. It is an orderly and useful step in the great procession of life."[46] For Lyman Beecher and *all* of his children, things like suffering and loss were firmly under the moral government of God, who worked all things for a greater purpose. Everything happened for a reason. Spiritualism was also consistent with this belief in the goodness of divine providence. When Isabella first encountered spiritualism at the water cure in Elmira in the 1840s, she discovered a religion that was both empowering to women and optimistic about the grave. When a loved one died, they were not gone to a transcendent world. Instead, their spirit lingered on to encourage the living. Mary Todd Lincoln, for example, was purported to have brought mediums into the White House.[47] For women who had lost children, like Mrs. Lincoln, spiritualism was a link to those who had been lost and a ray of hope for the grieving.

As a late convert to spiritualism, Isabella embraced her new faith with a sense of authority and creativity that made some of her friends and neighbors uncomfortable. Calling it "The New Wildcat Religion," Mark Twain compared spiritualism to the Methodist camp meetings and Campbellite revivals of old. ("You never heard of a Presbyterian going crazy on religion," he joked.)[48] Like a team of evangelists, both Isabella and John gave "parlor talks" on how to commune with the dead. Isabella's sisters, however, were a bit more cautious. Harriet was generally suspicious of mediums, although she was open to communicating with the deceased. When she was alive, Catharine had also been skeptical. On one occasion, one of the famous Fox sisters claimed they had seen a vision of Lyman Beecher kneeling before Catharine, offering a rose as a symbol of her purity. But Catharine didn't buy it. She scoffed with a bit of condescension: "Such nonsense! When my father never in his life praised me, although he used to say that I was the best boy he had."[49] Catharine knew her father better than that. The real Lyman Beecher would never have been so affectionate. Interestingly, Catharine did not have any deceased children and thus did not exhibit the same affinities toward spiritualism. Aside from Isabella, the Beecher who demonstrated the most interest in spiritualism was Charles. After the death of three of his children, he yearned to speak with his loved ones. Nevertheless, whether through the more *en vogue* religion of spiritualism or through the more traditional Puritan belief in God's sovereignty over the world, the Beechers clung to the idea that God works all things for good—even in death.

In 1886 and 1887, the Beechers' optimism in the face of death was put to the test like never before. On January 20, Isabella lost her daughter Mary at the age of twenty-nine to tuberculosis. After Mary's death, both Isabella and John contacted her on the other side. As Barbara White notes, "It was a great comfort to have Mary coming back for a chat about the spirit world."[50] Months later, an even greater shock wave was sent through the family when James Beecher shot himself on August 25 while at the Gleason Water Cure. The news was devastating to Isabella and especially Tom, his closest brother and friend. Toward the end of his life, after pastoring two different churches in New York, James had sought help for his mental suffering in an asylum in Middletown, New York, before eventually finding refuge in Elmira near his brother. Henry had offered him the pulpit at Plymouth Church after he retired, but it was too much for a tortured mind and a soul that preferred the outdoors. Although most of the Beecher siblings were never as close to James as was Tom, the tragedy of James Beecher's life filled everyone with deep sorrow and was a reminder that yet *another* Beecher had taken his own life. James shot himself in the mouth with a rifle, just like George had in 1843.

Having attempted to kill himself years earlier, James suffered from depression, the same melancholy that had once afflicted Lyman and that now blanketed most of his children in one form or another. Ironically, for a family with unflinching confidence in the world, the Beechers' immediate view of the world was sometimes dark. With its victories and valleys, James's existence embodied the conflict of the Beecher family and indeed the nation itself. He had run away, but he had come back and become a war hero. He had rebelled against his father, but he had fulfilled his father's prophecy of becoming a minister. He had failed as a husband and brother, but he had helped others, from sailors to Black soldiers. James Beecher was the most enigmatic Beecher but a Beecher nonetheless, driven by a sense of public service and the greater good. Adding more heartbreak to a dreadful situation was James's death in the very place that had become a place of rest and salubrious treatment for his brothers and sisters. Elmira would never be the same place to the Beechers.

For Harriet, 1886 and 1887 changed everything. The family she had worked so diligently to keep together was now succumbing to the one destructive force on earth that could never be reformed by a voluntary group: death. In August, she was barely able to mourn her brother's suicide because her husband of fifty years had died three days earlier in their home in Hartford. Calvin Stowe, the renowned Bible scholar and sidekick to America's most famous author, was buried in the same cemetery in Andover where they had buried young Henry. Months later, Harriet suffered another crippling loss. After losing her best friend, her brother Henry suffered a stroke in March and died a few days later. He was seventy-three. Although no longer a major force in American public life, Henry was still incredibly popular. On the Sunday after Beecher died, famed Boston Episcopal preacher Phillips Brooks closed the sermon with these words: "I know that you are all thinking as I speak of the great soul that has passed away, of the great preacher, for he was the greatest preacher in America, and the greatest preacher means the greatest power in the land." Brooks added, "surely no man had greater love of truth or love of souls than Henry Ward Beecher." Henry was honored by fifty thousand mourners who waited in line for hours to view his casket. His legacy, like his life, was complicated. Beecher family friend Mark Twain fought back tears while listening to the funeral sermon by Nook Farm minister Joseph Twichell, later writing to Twichell, "What a pity that so insignificant a matter as the chastity or un-chastity of an Elizabeth Tilton could clip the locks of this Samson and make him as other men, in the estimation of a nation of Lilliputians creeping and climbing about his shoe-soles."[51]

Fueled more by emotions than by his intellect, Henry Ward Beecher left behind a legacy of open-mindedness and love for neighbor. Well-known New York City pulpiteer Harry Emerson Fosdick, who was consistently compared to Beecher throughout his career for his eloquence and theolog-ical liberalism, lauded the Brooklyn preacher for his courage to "challenge the orthodox religion of his day." However, after years of evading the issue of infidelity, Beecher's open-mindedness was perceived by many as mere people-pleasing and his love for neighbor as self-preservation. Henry also left behind a complicated legacy in the Beecher family. After the funeral, Eunice received the rest of the Beechers into the home, but Isabella was barred from the door. Waiting to be let in, Isabella walked around outside before eventually returning to Hartford. (Thankfully, she later communed with the deceased Henry, who was more than willing to let bygones be bygones.)[52] Offering no pardon for sins even after her husband was gone, Eunice called her sister-in-law "the griffin."[53] Some wounds would never be healed. Henry's claims of innocence had never been enough for Isabella, and Isabella's appeals for peace would never be enough for his widow. While Lyman's daughters had made amends, it was little surprise that Eu-nice, known for her general unpleasantness, withheld mercy. Among the Beecher men, not all was forgiven. Tom still nursed a quiet grudge against his brother and former "hero."[54] As the family boarded the hearse on its way to the grave site, Tom refused to join the carriage, demurring, "I'm not going to traipse all over Brooklyn behind a corpse."[55] For a brother he could barely honor in life, Tom mustered very little in death.

Just a few months later, Harriet lost another piece of herself. In Au-gust, her daughter Georgiana, or "Georgie," died at the age of forty-four. Years earlier, Georgie and her husband, Rev. Henry Freeman Allen, had welcomed a son. After childbirth, doctors prescribed morphine to dull the pain, and Georgie became addicted. Through several grinding seasons of highs and lows, she finally died of septicemia. More than any of her sisters, Harriet knew the bitter taste of losing a child. Of her seven children with Calvin, only three survived. Samuel Charles, her "sunshine child," had died of cholera. Henry had drowned at eighteen. Fred had disappeared in California. Now Georgie passed before her mother. With all of these tragedies, Harriet found a source of comfort in the one person she had avoided for years: Isabella. The two visited one another and reminisced at Nook Farm, determined to spend such fleeting days with family. Of course, Harriet was not the only Beecher to experience the departure of a child to the eternal realm. Of all Lyman's children, none had lost more children than Edward. Only two of their eleven children survived. Not surprisingly, he too dabbled in spiritualism and attended seances with Isabella and her husband. Death was never the end for the Beechers.

At the age of eighty-six, even after the eldest Beecher brother, William, passed away in June, Edward was still pastoring a church at Parkville in New York. Devoted to the work of the ministry, he was as indestructible as his father. Coming home one night from a church meeting, Edward fell from a platform at a train station, and his leg was crushed. Nevertheless, he continued to walk with an artificial leg and a cane. Also like his father, his mind gave out before his body. In his last few years, Edward became senile and was helped by his wife, Isabella. "He thinks every day is Sunday," she wrote. "He wonders why we do not go to church."[56] Nothing could keep a Beecher away from the house of the Lord. Edward's legacy was carried on by his brother and loyal disciple Charles, who composed his autobiography, *Life of Edward Beecher.* Living in Georgetown in the home of one of his daughters, Charles wrote a friend that he did not think the book would ever see print in his "lifetime—if ever."[57] It did not. The work was never published, but Charles had once again memorialized another Beecher, continuing a well-established tradition in the family. In the fall of 1889, Charley finished his mother's autobiography, *Life of Harriet Beecher Stowe: Compiled from Her Letters and Journals.* In the work, Harriet paid homage to her father and patriarch, describing Lyman as "so true an image of the Heavenly Father."[58] Shortly after the publication of *Life of Harriet Beecher Stowe,* as if her final mission had been completed in securing her legacy, the most famous Beecher had a stroke, ending her public life.

In many ways, like the Ohio Valley decades earlier, death became another frontier for the remaining Beechers. Even after Margaretta Fox confessed in 1888 that she had produced the "spirit rappings" that launched the spiritualist movement, Isabella and John Hooker, who celebrated fifty years of marriage in 1891, remained faithful spiritualists for the rest of their lives. Her brother Tom pushed the conventional boundaries of death and funeral rites even further. By the 1890s, Tom advocated for cremation as opposed to the traditional in-ground burial. Holding a radical position for his time, Tom defended suicide as an acceptable end-of-life option for Christians in certain cases.[59] As Tom honored the dead in sanctuaries, so Isabella lectured on the dead at conferences. For twenty-five dollars a speech, she delivered talks on spiritualism and her other favorite topic: women's rights.[60]

At the International Council of Women in the spring of 1888, Isabella spoke on "The Constitutional Rights of the Women of the United States," still convinced that the U.S. Constitution, rightly interpreted, guaranteed women the right to vote. Like her father, Isabella was gifted at bringing groups together, convening fifty-three organizations at the fortieth anniversary of the Seneca Falls Convention. Hooker was also present in 1890 in Washington, DC, when the AWSA and NWSA, the two largest women's rights groups in America, combined to form the NAWSA, the National American Woman Suffrage Association. Like the other Beechers, Isabella was a bridge-builder for reform. By Milton Rugoff's estimation, "The progress from Catharine Beecher's early campaigns for women's education and financial independence to Isabella's work for women's rights, and thence to Charlotte's efforts to live as a liberated woman in the 1890s, is perhaps the most striking example of the persistence in the Beecher family of commitment to a social ideal."[61] After one hundred years, the Beechers were still passing on the family trade of reform.

In 1865, Edward Beecher supplied perhaps the best articulation of the Beecher project when he defined the purpose of the church in "The Scriptural Philosophy of Congregationalism and of Councils." In Edwards's view, the primary goal of Christianity is "to bring civil government, the state, commerce, political economy, the arts and sciences, and the schools, under the influence of God, so as to pervade them with the influence of his law and the gospel, and thus to make them a harmonious and consistent part of his kingdom."[62] With an emphasis upon the "influence" of law, gospel, and God, Edward's mission statement was nothing less than Lyman's Beecher's vision of the world. Every single Beecher believed in the societal breadth of that vision. However, the concepts of law, gospel, and God had been transformed. In Isabella's "Confession of Faith," penned toward the end of her life, she stated her belief, "In the God of the Hebrew and the Christian, the Buddhist and the Mahometan alike we may recognize the all-wise, tender, brooding Mother Spirit of the Universe, under whose providential discipline, called evolution by the scientist, and foreordination and decrees by the theologian, all souls shall at last reach their culmination."[63] Isabella Beecher Hooker's vision of Christianity was as comprehensive and optimistic as any Beecher had ever dared to dream. However, what she meant by Christianity would have been unrecognizable to anyone from her father's generation. What remained was moral influence.

In 1895, the same year that Edward Beecher passed, Isabella presented a marble bust of her sister Harriet to the Hartford Public Library. The sculpture was a testament to the longevity of Harriet Beecher Stowe's sterling career and her place in the pantheon of New England literary greats. That Isabella presented the bust was also symbolic. Once an enemy in the Stowe home, the last Beecher was now helping to immortalize her famous sister. On July 1 of 1896, Harriet passed away. She was buried in Andover cemetery between Calvin and Henry. When Harriet passed, the life of the family passed with her. The greatest of Lyman Beecher's house was neither a man nor a pastor. But she could preach. By the power of her pen, she spoke profoundly to the American people *and* to her very own family. Without Harriet, the Beechers would have been a very different group of people at the end of the nineteenth century. She became, in many ways, the parson of the family, encouraging, counseling, reproving, warning, and exhorting those in her flock. In one of America's most eclectic families, Harriet was a bridge-builder to the bridge-builders and a preacher to the preachers.

In a remarkable coincidence four years later, on March 4, 1900, Thomas Beecher died on the same day as his sister Mary. Having completed his *Life of Edward Beecher,* Charles died one month later. Only Isabella remained of the Beecher family. Fittingly, in a final act of Beecherism, she composed a magazine article in 1905 entitled "The Last of the Beechers."[64] The title alone was enough to demonstrate that the Beechers had become something of an American institution, even at the dawn of the twentieth century. Isabella died two years later. In her spacious dining room on Nook Farm, celebrated in *Connecticut Magazine,* two legacies came together over one table. On the south end, portraits and photographs of John Hooker's famous family hung on the wall, including a leather-bound notebook of the Rev. Thomas Hooker, John's ancestor, the founder of Connecticut Colony. On the north end, along with a prestigious award from a suffrage association and a drawing by her sister Catharine, were shelves of published books by the renowned Beecher family. In the middle of the room, by itself, was an oil portrait of the Rev. Lyman Beecher, still exerting his influence upon one of America's most influential families.[65]

Notes

INTRODUCTION

1. "Call to Philadelphia," in *Autobiography of Lyman Beecher, Vol. II*, ed. Cross, 100.

2. H. B. Stowe, "Reminiscences," in *Autobiography of Lyman Beecher, Vol. II*, ed. Cross, 86.

3. L. Beecher, *Six Sermons on the Nature, Occasions, Signs, Evils, and Remedy of Intemperance*, 68.

4. Philadelphia was the birthplace of the A.M.E. Church. Richard Allen, the founder of "Mother Bethel" church in Philadelphia, was named to A.M.E. bishop in 1816. "With roughly fourteen hundred congregants by 1816, Bethel Church was a bastion of black power" (Newman, *Freedom's Prophet*, 170).

5. "Dr. Beecher to William. Within Point Judith, June 5, 1830," in *Autobiography of Lyman Beecher, Vol. II*, ed. Cross, 165–66.

6. Sklar, *Catharine Beecher*, 99.

7. Marsden, *The Evangelical Mind and the New School Presbyterian Experience*, 20.

8. Marty, *Pilgrims in Their Own Land*, 234.

9. Harding, *A Certain Magnificence*, 232. Organizing broad coalitions of like-minded evangelicals for social and moral causes was Lyman Beecher's primary contribution to the American evangelical tradition. For example, the Federal Council of Churches (FCC), an ecumenical association of thirty-two denominations, was established in 1908 to combat child labor, poverty, intemperance, and other vices brought on by industrialization. It was supported by President Woodrow Wilson (1913–1921), a socially minded, idealistic Presbyterian (and son of a seminary professor) similar in some ways to Lyman Beecher. (See Hankins, *Woodrow Wilson*.) On the other side of the fundamentalist divide was William Jennings Bryan, a silver-tongued Presbyterian and "an innate optimist" with a Beecherian faith in the American people. Although a politician, Bryan preached to churches like a revivalist, and like Beecher, Bryan was a man of his time who objected to the ideologies of his age (that is, evolution) on *moral* grounds (Larson, *Summer for the Gods*, 197, 198, 145). Organizing the World's Christian Fundamentals Association in 1919 and working tirelessly for the outlawing of liquor, Minnesota Baptist William Bell Riley was also a Beecherian figure who once called modernism "the new infidelity" (*God Hath Spoken*, 27). Beecher's blueprint for societal change (and sometimes a bit of his personality) was inherited by his evangelical descendants.

10. White, *The Beecher Sisters*, 235.

11. "Dr. Beecher to Catharine. Boston, June 8, 1830," in *Autobiography of Lyman Beecher, Vol. II*, ed. Cross, 167–68.

12. Howe, *What Hath God Wrought*.

13. "Dr. Skinner to Dr. Beecher. March 16, 1830," in *Autobiography of Lyman Beecher, Vol. II*, ed. Cross, 163.

14. L. Beecher, *A Plea for the West*, 9–10.

15. Alexander Campbell, in *A Debate on the Roman Catholic Religion between Alexander Campbell and Rt. Rev. John B. Purcell*, 331. Also see Butler, *Standing Against the Whirlwind*, 112–14.

16. See Sweeney, *Nathaniel Taylor, New Haven Theology, and the Legacy of Jonathan Edwards*.

17. "Dr. Porter's Letter," in *Autobiography of Lyman Beecher, Vol. II*, ed. Cross, 122–23.

18. "Dr. Beecher's Reply. Boston, June, 1829," in *Autobiography of Lyman Beecher, Vol. II*, ed. Cross, 128.

19. "Dr. Beecher to William. Boston, February 10, 1830," in *Autobiography of Lyman Beecher, Vol. II*, ed. Cross, 162.

20. "Dr. Beecher to William. Boston, November 1, 1830," in *Autobiography of Lyman Beecher, Vol. II*, ed. Cross, 176.

21. Lyman Beecher, "Extract from an Address to the Bowdoin Street Church and Society, July 5, 1832," in *Autobiography of Lyman Beecher, Vol. II*, ed. Cross, 205–6.

22. Rugoff, *The Beechers*, 112.

23. "From a letter by George," in *Autobiography of Lyman Beecher, Vol. II*, ed. Cross, 209.

24. Henry, *Unvanquished Puritan*, 25.

25. Rugoff, *The Beechers*, 82.

26. H. B. Stowe, *Men of Our Times*, 535.

27. Merideth, *The Politics of the Universe*, 27–28.

28. C. Beecher, *Educational Reminiscences and Suggestions*, 73–74.

29. H. B. Stowe, *The Minister's Wooing*, xvi.

30. "Dr. Beecher to Catharine. Boston, June 8, 1830," in *Autobiography of Lyman Beecher, Vol. II*, ed. Cross, 167.

31. Henry, *Unvanquished Puritan*, 9.

32. Charles Beecher to Henry Ward Beecher, April 12, 1857, Beecher Family Papers, Beinecke Library, Yale University, box 7, folder 305, MS 71, ser. 1.

33. Howe, *The Political Culture of the American Whigs*, 150–51.

34. In L. B. Stowe, "The First of the Beechers," 209.

35. Hibben, *Henry Ward Beecher*, 104.

36. Noll, *America's God*, 427.

37. Rugoff, *The Beechers*, 392.

38. In *The Autobiography of Charles H. Spurgeon, Compiled from His Diary, Letters, and Records, Vol. IV: 1878–1892*, ed. Susannah Spurgeon, 58.

39. In 1934, Lyman Beecher Stowe named his book *Saints, Sinners, and Beechers* from this quote by Bacon.

40. Rugoff, *The Beechers*, 404, 421, 450.

41. Isabella Beecher Hooker to Robert Allen, April 1, 1868, microfiche 38, *The Isabella Beecher Hooker Project,* ed. Margolis.

42. For instance, Rugoff calls Andover Seminary a "center of Old School dogma" (*The Beechers,* 71). In fact, this is not entirely true. Andover was founded by traditional and Edwardsean Calvinists alike and actually became a bulwark of New School thought. Rugoff also suggests that George's suicide was due to Lyman's Calvinist religion, which has no evidence to support it (203–4). On another occasion, Rugoff argues, "Beecher himself was full of hope, not because he shared the American optimism about what earthly man could accomplish but because he believed so implicitly that Christ's universal reign was imminent and the ultimate reality was salvation" (32). This is also not accurate, as it was widely known that Lyman Beecher believed in the "natural ability" of the sinner and was even put on trial for his particularly high view of human potential. Rugoff seems to belie his own theological leanings when he concludes, "It was the kind of vanity and pride—sinful pride, as the religious would say—that crusaders of every sort are often guilty of" (297). This is quite a generic and biased statement to make about a person who was often praised for his love of his children. Not surprisingly, all of this colors Rugoff's view of the Beecher family ties. For instance, after noting Thomas's mention of "long, long discussions" at the family table, Rugoff dismisses this as "theological indoctrination and debate imposed unsparingly on young minds" (139). It would seem that any kind of theological conversation or religious training is chalked up as "indoctrination" in Rugoff's mind. Surely a better balance of Lyman Beecher's parental strengths and weaknesses can be struck.

43. Ingersoll, *The Works of Robert G. Ingersoll, Volume XII,* 419–24.

44. Rugoff, *The Beechers,* 296.

45. A more ambivalent and accurate commentary of the father-son relationship comes from Debby Applegate when she concludes, "Lyman Beecher was the polestar of Henry's childhood, a loving, heroic figure who stood only slightly below God himself in the boy's eyes. Yet, like the Lord of the Old Testament, Lyman often seemed capricious in the way in which he wielded his great power" (*The Most Famous Man in America,* 34).

46. Applegate, *The Most Famous Man in America,* 156.

47. In her recent history of xenophobia, Erika Lee posits, "Beecher was a leading commander in the nineteenth-century Protestant Crusade that connected America's anti-Catholic and xenophobic traditions for the first time." She also submits, "it was Lyman Beecher's 1835 book *A Plea for the West* that best connected America's older tradition of anti-Catholicism with the newer one of xenophobia" (*America for Americans,* 47, 49).

48. H. B. Stowe, *Oldtown Folks,* 1.

49. L. B. Stowe, *Saints, Sinners, and Beechers.*

50. Caskey, *Chariot of Fire.*

51. See Gerson, *Harriet Beecher Stowe;* Hedrick, *Harriet Beecher Stowe;* Kilpack, *All That Makes Life Bright.*

52. Edward Farwell Hayward's *Lyman Beecher,* written in 1904, is a relatively brief account of his life and work.

53. Barbara M. Cross, "Editor's Introduction," in *Autobiography of Lyman Beecher, Vol. I,* ed. Cross, xxvii.

54. Henry, *Unvanquished Puritan;* Fraser, *Pedagogue for God's Kingdom.*

55. Harding, *A Certain Magnificence.*

56. Hedrick. *Harriet Beecher Stowe;* White, *The Beecher Sisters;* Applegate, *The Most Famous Man in America;* Koester, *Harriet Beecher Stowe.*

57. Sklar, *Catharine Beecher,* 99.

58. Sklar, *Catharine Beecher,* 177, 203.

59. C. Beecher, *Treatise on Domestic Economy,* 255–56.

60. Sklar, *Catharine Beecher,* 10.

61. Sklar, *Catharine Beecher,* 38.

62. White, *The Beecher Sisters,* 162.

63. Unlike her Puritan brother-in-law, Aunt Harriet was not a Congregationalist. Like her deceased sister Roxana, Harriet had been raised in the Episcopal Church. Aunt Harriet's Old World faith caused a degree of friction in the Beecher home after she helped care for the children after Roxana's death. She catechized young Harriet in the Anglican Catechism, not in the Westminster Shorter Catechism. In her heart of hearts, Harriet did not consider Lyman an ordained minister, even walking past his church on Sundays in Litchfield, Connecticut in order to attend a much smaller Episcopal church.

64. Caskey, *Chariot of Fire,* 32. Among the books in George Beecher's library is a Greek New Testament signed by Lyman Beecher in 1823, presumably gifted to his young son. This small collection is housed at the Harriet Beecher Stowe Center.

65. Campbell, *Tempest-Tossed,* 29.

66. Dr. Beecher to Dr. Plummer, 1836, in *Autobiography of Lyman Beecher, Vol. I,* ed. Cross, 293. Also see Harding, *A Certain Magnificence,* 18.

67. W. C. Beecher and S. Scoville, *A Biography of Rev. Henry Ward Beecher,* 138.

68. Catharine Beecher, "Household Recollections," in *Autobiography of Lyman Beecher, Vol. I,* ed. Cross, 149.

69. L. Beecher, *The Remedy for Duelling,* 3, 36.

70. See McDonald, "Edward Beecher and the Anti-Slavery Movement in Illinois," 9–35. Just a year before, Catharine had published her *Essay on Slavery and Abolitionism with Reference to the Duty of American Females* (1837). However, Catharine did not take the abolitionist position. Instead, she argued for colonization.

71. E. Beecher, *A Narrative of Riots at Alton,* 124, 136.

72. E. Beecher, *A Narrative of Riots at Alton,* 123, 136. Leo P. Hirrel argues that scholars who hold to an "optimist interpretation" of New School reform have "failed to appreciate how deeply the New School feared human depravity" (*Children of Wrath,* 5).

73. Rugoff, *The Beechers,* 101.

74. According to Molly Oshatz, "Antebellum antislavery Protestants, including Francis Wayland, Leonard Bacon, Edward Beecher, and William Ellery Channing, became the inadvertent pioneers of liberal Protestantism" (*Slavery and Sin,* 4).

75. Sklar, *Catharine Beecher,* xiii.

76. Foster, *An Errand of Mercy,* vii.

77. *Journals and Miscellaneous Notebooks of Ralph Waldo Emerson,* ed. Allardt, vol. 15: 72.

78. Lewis, "Foreword," in Hibben, *Henry Ward Beecher,* vii.

79. H. W. Beecher, *The Independent*, May 11, 1850.

80. In 1862, Harriet's daughter Hattie requested to join the Episcopal Church. Harriet not only gave her blessing but applied for a seat in the church herself (Gerson, *Harriet Beecher Stowe*, 149–50).

81. Gerson, *Harriet Beecher Stowe*, 35.

82. L. B. Stowe, *Saints, Sinners, and Beechers*, 149.

83. Marsden, *The Evangelical Mind and the New School Presbyterian Experience*, 20.

84. Wilson, *Christian Register*, February 11, 1832.

85. "Mrs. Stowe and *Dred*."

86. "Mrs. Stowe and *Dred*."

87. In Oliver, *Critical Companion to Walt Whitman*, 262.

88. Applegate, *The Most Famous Man in America*, 4.

89. Clemens, "The Character of Man," *Autobiography of Mark Twain, Volume 1*, ed. Smith, 314–15.

90. "Getting a divorce," Elizabeth Cady Stanton to Susan B. Anthony, June 27, 1870, in *Elizabeth Cady Stanton as Revealed in Her Letters, Diary and Reminiscences*, ed. Stanton and Blatch, vol. 2: 127.

91. Rugoff, *The Beechers*, 168.

92. White, *The Beecher Sisters*, 202.

93. Merideth, *The Politics of the Universe*, 37.

94. Gura, *American Transcendentalism*, 9.

95. Mesmerism, founded by German physician Franz Anton Mesmer (1734–1815), was also called animal magnetism and was the precursor to hypnosis.

96. Brownson, "Beecherism and Its Tendencies," 436.

97. According to Applegate, "Beecher was very much a *Christian* Transcendentalist—in many ways less of a theological than a stylistic distinction" (*The Most Famous Man in America*, 274).

98. Brownson, "Beecherism and Its Tendencies," 446.

99. James Chaplin Beecher, "Tuesday, Jan. 10, 1871," Beecher Family Papers, Beinecke Library, Yale University, box 72, folder 31, MS 71, ser. 3, p. 6.

100. Henry, *Unvanquished Puritan*, 9.

101. See Kidd, "Where Did the Term 'Post-Millennial' Come From?"

102. Lowell Mason, in *Autobiography of Lyman Beecher, Vol. II*, ed. Cross, 112.

103. White, *The Beecher Sisters*, 209.

104. Henry Ward, circular letter, in *Autobiography of Lyman Beecher, Vol. II*, ed. Cross, 311; George, circular letter, in *Autobiography of Lyman Beecher, Vol. II*, ed. Cross, 312.

105. Catharine to Edward, Litchfield, July 1822, in *Autobiography of Lyman Beecher, Vol. I*, ed. Cross, 358–59.

106. In her biography of Harriet Beecher Stowe, Joan D. Hedrick explains, "In one respect, Roxana represented a wider circle than the son of the blacksmith. The Episcopal, novel-reading daughter of the well-traveled Foote family was quite a prize, in secular terms, for a humble evangelical minister—one might well ask what Lyman Beecher thought he was doing in such worldly company" (*Harriet Beecher Stowe*, 9).

107. Catharine to Dr. Beecher, Franklin, New Year's Day 1823, in *Autobiography of Lyman Beecher, Vol. I*, ed. Cross, 369.

108. White, *The Beecher Sisters*, 233.

109. Koester, *Harriet Beecher Stowe*, 195.

110. Charles Beecher to Henry Ward Beecher, April 12, 1857, Beecher Family Papers, Beinecke Library, Yale University, box 7, folder 305, MS 71, ser. 1.

111. "From Mrs. H. B. Stowe," in *Autobiography of Lyman Beecher, Vol. I*, ed. Cross, 390.

112. Mrs. H. B. Stowe, "Early Remembrances," in *Autobiography of Lyman Beecher, Vol. I*, ed. Cross, 395; Mrs. H. B. Stowe, "Reminiscences," in *Autobiography of Lyman Beecher, Vol. II*, ed. Cross, 83, 87–88.

113. Mrs. H. B. Stowe, "Reminiscences," in *Autobiography of Lyman Beecher, Vol. II*, ed. Cross, 84; H. B. Stowe, "Early Remembrances," in *Autobiography of Lyman Beecher, Vol. I*, ed. Cross, 392.

114. C. Beecher, *Treatise on Domestic Economy*, 36.

115. Sklar, *Catharine Beecher*, 84.

116. Douglas, "Introduction," in H. B. Stowe, *Uncle Tom's Cabin*, 13.

117. H. B. Stowe, *Uncle Tom's Cabin*, 83–84.

118. White, *The Beecher Sisters*, 142.

119. White, *The Beecher Sisters*, 136.

120. Clark, *Henry Ward Beecher*, 84, 190.

121. Johnson, *A Shopkeeper's Millennium*, 9. Johnson also notes that Beecher "rivals [Charles] Finney as the era's most prominent evangelist" (5).

122. "Dr. Beecher to Edward, January 5, 1824," in *Autobiography of Lyman Beecher, Vol. I*, ed. Cross, 407.

123. Dr. Beecher, circular letter, in *Autobiography of Lyman Beecher, Vol. II*, ed. Cross, 312.

124. Mark A. Noll has noted "the unusual convergence of republicanism and Christianity in the American founding," identifying a so-called "Christian republicanism" that dominated and even molded the church. "American Christians," Noll insists, "despite substantial conflict among themselves, took for granted a fundamental compatibility between orthodox Protestant religion and republican principles of government. Most English-speaking Protestants outside the United States did not" (*America's God*, 54, 57, 73–92).

125. L. Beecher, "The Republican Elements of the Old Testament," in *Beecher's Works, Vol. 1*, 187.

126. L. Beecher, *Six Sermons on the Nature, Occasions, Signs, Evils, and Remedy of Intemperance*, 56.

127. Mell, *Slavery*, 15n1.

128. Harriet wrote to her brother Henry after the publication of *Uncle Tom's Cabin*, "if there is a holy cause it is that of Liberty!" (Harriet Beecher Stowe, "My Dear Brother," Andover, February 1 [no year, most likely 1852], Beecher Family Papers, Beinecke Library, Yale University, box 44, folder 1932, MS 71, ser. 1).

129. Koester, *Harriet Beecher Stowe*, 188.

130. Sections of the previous paragraph were taken from Todd, "Evangelicals, Justice, and the Civil War," 207–23.

131. As David Bebbington has outlined in his landmark book, *Evangelicalism in Modern Britain* (1989), four defining characteristics of evangelicals are activism, biblicism, conversionism, and crucicentrism. For a people so focused upon the cross of Jesus Christ and called to express their faith in public life (like the Beechers), justice became a moral and theological category by which crucicentrism (divine justice) and activism (human justice) intersected in the evangelical mind.

132. Henry Ward Beecher, "Abraham Lincoln," in *Patriotic Addresses in America and England*, ed. Howard, 711.

133. What Ronald Walters said in 1997 of Lyman Beecher and Charles Finney could be said of the Beecher family itself: "Beecher's generation softened Calvinism still further and Finney, nominally a Presbyterian, overthrew it" (*American Reformers*, 27).

1. A NEW ENGLAND "ESTABLISHMENT" (1823–1832)

1. Rugoff, *The Beechers*, 16.

2. L. Beecher, *The Remedy for Duelling*, 34.

3. Henry, *Unvanquished Puritan*, 94.

4. "Dr. Beecher to Catharine, Boston, June 8, 1830," in *Autobiography of Lyman Beecher, Vol. II*, ed. Cross, 167–68. Lyman probably meant the Mississippi *and* Ohio river valleys.

5. Ch. Beecher, "The Life of Edward Beecher," 3.

6. C. Beecher, *The Biographical Remains of Rev. George Beecher*, 11.

7. Paul, *Indivisible*, 170.

8. White, *The Beecher Sisters*, 24.

9. Sklar, *Catharine Beecher*, 52.

10. Sklar, *Catharine Beecher*, 60.

11. "Dr. Beecher to Edward, January 5, 1824," in *Autobiography of Lyman Beecher, Vol. I*, ed. Cross, 407.

12. Lyman Beecher, "Downfall of the Standing Order," in *Autobiography of Lyman Beecher, Vol. I*, ed. Cross, 252–53.

13. "Dr. Beecher to the Children (At Hartford), July, 1823," in *Autobiography of Lyman Beecher, Vol. I*, ed. Cross, 405.

14. Sam Haselby frames Timothy Dwight as something of a transitionary figure: "Dwight served as a bridge between establishment Protestantism and the missionary organizations. He inspired, and guided, many young men into missionary work" (*The Origins of American Religious Nationalism*, 89).

15. Sassi, *A Republic of Righteousness*, 173–74, 281.

16. L. Beecher, *Six Sermons on the Nature, Occasions, Signs, Evils, and Remedy of Intemperance*, 70.

17. "Dr. Beecher to the Children (at Hartford), September 1, 1823," in *Autobiography of Lyman Beecher, Vol. I*, ed. Cross, 405.

18. Catharine to Edward, July 18, 1824," in *Autobiography of Lyman Beecher, Vol. II*, ed. Cross, 7–8.

19. Sklar, *Catharine Beecher*, 94.

20. "Dr. Beecher to Catharine, September 8, 1826," in *Autobiography of Lyman Beecher, Vol. II*, ed. Cross, 49.

21. Ch. Beecher, "The Life of Edward Beecher," 36; L. Beecher, *The Bible a Code of Laws*.

22. "Dr. Beecher to Edward, September 5, 1826," in *Autobiography of Lyman Beecher, Vol. II*, ed. Cross, 48.

23. Merideth, *The Politics of the Universe*, 36.

24. Seigel, "A Passionate Missionary to the West," 327.

25. Henry, *Unvanquished Puritan*, 21.

26. Sklar, *Catharine Beecher*, 67.

27. For an excellent treatment of this concept, see Dreisbach, *Thomas Jefferson and the Wall of Separation Between Church and State*, 9–24.

28. Merideth, *The Politics of the Universe*, 49–51.

29. L. B. Stowe, *Saints Sinners and Beechers*, 152.

30. In the article, Catharine concluded, "A lady should study, not to *shine* but to *act*" ("Female Education," 221). See Burstyn, "Catharine Beecher and the Education of American Women," 386–403.

31. In C. Beecher, *Educational Reminiscences and Suggestions*, 73–74.

32. Edwards, *Freedom of the Will*, 146–47.

33. William Beecher to George Beecher, February 17, 1825, Acquisitions, Harriet Beecher Stowe Center.

34. According to Mark Noll, Beecher's mentor Timothy Dwight was the chief developer of the trope of moral government (*America's God*, 290–91); L. Beecher, *The Faith Once Delivered to the Saints*, 3.

35. L. Beecher, *The Bible a Code of Laws*, 5.

36. L. Beecher, "Resources of the Adversary, and Means of Their Destruction," 415.

37. Hedrick, *Harriet Beecher Stowe*, 60.

38. Schweiger, *A Literate South*, 85.

39. "Dr. Beecher to Catharine, June 30, 1826," in *Autobiography of Lyman Beecher, Vol. II*, ed. Cross, 44.

40. Sklar, *Catharine Beecher*, 95.

41. George Beecher to Edward Beecher, October 19, 1829, Acquisitions, Harriet Beecher Stowe Center.

42. Gerson, *Harriet Beecher Stowe*, 27.

43. Sklar, *Catharine Beecher*, 98.

44. C. Beecher, *Educational Reminiscences and Suggestions*, 62.

45. Howe, *What Hath God Wrought*, 349–51.

46. Koester, *Harriet Beecher Stowe*, 50–51.

47. White, *The Beecher Sisters*, 10.

48. Edwards's first public step, *A Narrative of Riots at Alton*, would become an important part of the abolitionist movement because it immortalized Elijah Lovejoy, an editor and fellow Presbyterian minister, after his death at the hands of a proslavery mob in Alton, Illinois. Lovejoy was remembered as an abolitionist hero into the twentieth century. In his work *Up from Slavery* (1901), Booker T. Washington explains, "From the time that Garrison, Lovejoy,

and others began to agitate for freedom, the slaves throughout the South kept in close touch with the progress of the movement" (4).

49. Sklar, *Catharine Beecher*, xiii.

50. "Dr. Beecher to Catharine, Boston, June 8, 1830," in *Autobiography of Lyman Beecher, Vol. II*, ed. Cross, 168.

51. "Dr. Beecher to Edward, July, 1826," in *Autobiography of Lyman Beecher, Vol. II*, ed. Cross, 46.

52. "Mrs. Beecher to. Edward, June 25, 1826," in *Autobiography of Lyman Beecher, Vol. II*, ed. Cross, 43.

53. "Dr. Beecher to Edward, September 5, 1826," in *Autobiography of Lyman Beecher, Vol. II*, ed. Cross, 48.

54. "Dr. Beecher to Dr. Wisner, 1825," in *Autobiography of Lyman Beecher, Vol. II*, ed. Cross, 11.

55. Applegate, *The Most Famous Man in America*, 58.

56. Amasa Walker, in *Autobiography of Lyman Beecher, Vol. II*, ed. Cross, 110.

57. Mrs. H. B. Stowe, "Reminiscences," in *Autobiography of Lyman Beecher, Vol. II*, ed. Cross, 81.

58. See Henry, *Unvanquished Puritan*, 137.

59. Gross, *The Transcendentalists and Their World*, 409.

60. Budiansky, *Oliver Wendell Holmes*, 38.

61. Applegate, *The Most Famous Man in America*, 52.

62. L. Beecher, "The Faith Once Delivered to the Saints," in *Sermons Delivered on Various Occasions, in Beecher's Works, Vol. II*, 409.

63. H. W. Beecher, "William Ellery Channing," in *Lectures and Orations*, ed. Hillis, 160.

64. In December of 1827, Lyman reported to the editor of the *Christian Spectator*, "we have advanced now to a point in which I am well convinced that we must have the aid of a local magazine. The mass of mind which is now awake to investigate and feel, and to receive impressions such as those will make who most frequently approach it, renders the pulpit unequal, and a new means of enlightening and forming public sentiment indispensable" (*Autobiography of Lyman Beecher, Vol. II*, ed. Cross, 91).

65. H. B. Stowe, "Reminiscences," in *Autobiography of Lyman Beecher, Vol. II*, ed. Cross, 82.

66. H. B. Stowe, *Oldtown Folks*, 9.

67. Marsden, *Religion and American Culture*, 55.

68. Chinard, *Honest John Adams*, 11; Wood, *Friends Divided*, 27–28.

69. Whitefield, *George Whitefield's Journals (1737–1741)*, October 5, 1740, ed. David, 144.

70. Howe, *The Unitarian Conscience*, 8.

71. See Sassi, *A Republic of Righteousness*.

72. L. Beecher, "The Faith Once Delivered to the Saints," 410.

73. Voluntarism is the principle of relying upon voluntary action, rather than legal enforcement, to support the welfare of society. In Lyman's case, voluntary societies included the Temperance Society, Bible Society, and other agencies.

74. Porterfield, *Conceived in Doubt*, 205.

75. Carwardine, *Evangelicals and Politics in Antebellum America*, 37.

76. Applegate, *The Most Famous Man in America*, 73.

77. Anti-Trinitarianism directly shaped the theological institutions of the early republic. The first graduate school in American history, Andover Theological Seminary, was established in 1807 by both Edwardsean and traditional Congregationalists in response to Unitarian Henry Ware's appointment to the Hollis Chair of Divinity at liberal Harvard in 1805. Just seven years after the founding of Andover, Princeton Theological Seminary opened its doors with a similar Trinitarian consciousness. In its founding document, *The Plan*, academic, theological, and spiritual expectations are listed for the students, including an ability to defend the doctrine of the Trinity.

78. Quote in Hibben, *Henry Ward Beecher*, 35–36. Hibben adds, "It was the day of the Webster-Hayne debate in the Senate, and feeling against the South ran high in New England. It was scarcely as yet an open question of slavery; and even had it been, Lyman Beecher would have been relatively unaffected. He was opposed to slavery, as were the majority of New England clergymen; but it was not to his mind an evil comparable to Unitarianism or the growth of the Roman Catholic church in America" (36).

79. Applegate, *The Most Famous Man in America*, 60.

80. W. C. Beecher and S. Scoville, *A Biography of Rev. Henry Ward Beecher*, 102–3.

81. H. W. Beecher, *Eulogy on General Grant*, 17.

82. Howard, *Henry Ward Beecher*, 30.

83. In W. C. Beecher and S. Scoville, *A Biography of Rev. Henry Ward Beecher*, 119.

84. Dorrien, *The Making of American Liberal Theology*, 183.

85. Lanier, "Henry Ward Beecher: A Lecture Tour of Georgia," 335.

86. In W. C. Beecher and S. Scoville, *A Biography of Rev. Henry Ward Beecher*, 114–15.

87. In W. C. Beecher and S. Scoville, *A Biography of Rev. Henry Ward Beecher*, 118.

88. In W. C. Beecher and S. Scoville, *A Biography of Rev. Henry Ward Beecher*, 79.

89. In a similar vein, Joan Hedrick observes of Harriet's *The Minister's Wooing* (1859), "men make theological systems—abstractly—but women, Stowe suggests, must deal with the emotional reality behind them" (*Harriet Beecher Stowe*, 279).

90. Glenn, *Thomas K. Beecher*, xii, 3.

91. Bratt, "From Revival to Romance," in *Antirevivalism in Antebellum America*, ed. Bratt, 192.

92. Clark, *Henry Ward Beecher*, 18.

93. Applegate, *The Most Famous Man in America*, 56.

94. Howard, *Henry Ward Beecher*, 26.

95. "Mrs. Beecher to Catharine, February 26, 1827," in *Autobiography of Lyman Beecher, Vol. II*, ed. Cross, 65.

96. Rugoff, *The Beechers*, 75.

97. Hambrick-Stowe, *Charles G. Finney and the Spirit of American Evangelicalism*, 69–70; L. Beecher, "Resources of the Adversary, and Means of Their Destruction," 417.

98. Rugoff, *The Beechers*, 78.

99. Pinheiro, *Missionaries of Republicanism*, 27.

100. L. Beecher, *A Plea for the West*, 95–96.

101. Tocqueville, *Democracy in America*, 323.

102. Merideth, *The Politics of the Universe,* 7.

103. Hirrel, *Children of Wrath,* 102.

104. E. Beecher, *Papal Conspiracy Exposed,* 152.

105. William G. McLoughlin analyzed: "As a young preacher in Indianapolis in 1840, mouthing his father's Calvinistic theology and attacking Roman Catholics, Beecher was certainly a reactionary. As an old and respected pastor in the wealthy New York suburb of Brooklyn Heights in 1885, he was, as one historian has said, 'the summit of complacency' and social conservatism" (*The Meaning of Henry Ward Beecher,* 9).

106. L. Beecher, *Six Sermons on the Nature, Occasions, Signs, Evils, and Remedy of Intemperance,* 26.

107. L. Beecher, *The Gospel According to Paul,* 8.

108. Dr. Beecher to William, Boston, September 3, 1830, in *Autobiography of Lyman Beecher, Vol. II,* ed. Cross, 169.

109. L. Beecher, *The Memory of Our Fathers,* 11.

110. Applegate, *The Most Famous Man in America,* 86.

111. Applegate, *The Most Famous Man in America,* 86, 111.

112. Amasa Walker, in *Autobiography of Lyman Beecher, Vol. II,* ed. Cross, 109–10.

113. Sassi, *A Republic of Righteousness,* 194.

114. Merideth, *The Politics of the Universe,* 85–86.

115. Garrison, *Address at Park Street Church,* 8–9.

116. Garrison, *Address at Park Street Church,* 10–11.

117. Merideth, *The Politics of the Universe,* 76.

118. Merideth, *The Politics of the Universe,* 77–78.

119. New Englanders had also shaped the religion of the South. For an excellent treatment of this diaspora from New England, see Najar, *Evangelizing the South.*

120. "Catharine to Harriet, Cincinnati, April 17, 1832," in *Autobiography of Lyman Beecher, Vol. II,* ed. Cross, 200–01.

121. Lyman Beecher, in *Autobiography of Lyman Beecher, Vol. II,* ed. Cross, 212.

2. THE WILD, WELD WEST (1832–1837)

1. Hurt, *The Ohio Frontier,* 348.

2. Maulden, *The Federalist Frontier,* 3–11, 154–55. See Sellers, *The Market Revolution.*

3. Trollope, *Domestic Manners of the Americans, Vol. I,* 54, 60.

4. The real estate bubble would eventually burst in the Panic of 1837.

5. Allen, *The Life and Services of Rev. Lyman Beecher as President and Professor of Theology in Lane Seminary,* 5.

6. Harding, *A Certain Magnificence,* 310.

7. Cartwright, *The Backwoods Preacher,* 208.

8. "January 23, 1832," in *Autobiography of Lyman Beecher, Vol. II,* ed. Cross, 188.

9. J. L. Tracy to Theodore Dwight Weld, Lexington, KY, to Oneida Institute, November 24, 1831, quoted in Abzug, *Passionate Liberator,* 74.

10. Morris, *Oberlin, Hotbed of Abolitionism*, 5.

11. "Dr. Beecher to Catharine. Boston, July 8, 1830," in *Autobiography of Lyman Beecher, Vol. II*, ed. Cross, 169.

12. "Harriet to Mrs. P——, October 6, 1832," in *Autobiography of Lyman Beecher, Vol. II*, ed. Cross, 207.

13. Goodin, "Cincinnati—Its Destiny," 306. Also see Glaab, "Visions of Metropolis," 24–25.

14. "Philadelphia, February 16th, 1832," in *Autobiography of Lyman Beecher, Vol. II*, ed. Cross, 189.

15. Koester, *Harriet Beecher Stowe*, 59.

16. H. Beecher and C. Beecher, *Primary Geography for Children*, 106, 108.

17. Trollope, *Domestic Manners of the Americans, Vol. I*, 54.

18. Henry Clay, "Speech of Mr. Clay, of Kentucky, in the Senate of the United States, February 5 and 6, 1850," 127. See Delbanco, *The War Before the War*, 303.

19. Alexis de Tocqueville to his mother, December 6, 1831, in Zunz, ed., *Alexis de Tocqueville and Gustave de Beaumont in America*, 184.

20. Sklar, *Catharine Beecher*, 108.

21. Gray, *The Confessions of Nat Turner*, 5. Patrick H. Breen comments that Turner's "attempt to compare his impending execution to Jesus's only made it harder for Southampton's whites to see him as anything other than completely deluded" (*The Land Shall Be Deluged in Blood*, 145–46).

22. See Thompson, "Lyman Beecher's Long Road to Conservative Abolitionism," 89–109.

23. "Anti-Slavery Imbroglio," in *Autobiography of Lyman Beecher, Vol. II*, ed. Cross, 242.

24. Harding, *A Certain Magnificence*, 376.

25. "Walnut Hills," in *Autobiography of Lyman Beecher, Vol. II*, ed. Cross, 230–31.

26. The Beechers did not actually move into the home at Walnut Hills until the spring of 1833.

27. Harding, *A Certain Magnificence*, 334.

28. Rugoff, *The Beechers*, 286. Raines, *Silent Cavalry*, 161.

29. White, *The Beecher Sisters*, 14.

30. Historian Sam Haselby has called the Plan of Union a "no-competition agreement for the souls of frontier settlers" (*The Origins of American Religious Nationalism*, 7). Also see Porterfield, *Conceived in Doubt*, 94–95.

31. By the 1820s, the Presbyterian Church had in fact succeeded in making some distinctions between the churches in western regions. See Rohrer, *Keepers of the Covenant*, 13.

32. Harding, *A Certain Magnificence*, 512.

33. "Skirmishing," in *Autobiography of Lyman Beecher, Vol. II*, ed. Cross, 215.

34. In a letter from Batavia, George recollects, "After discussing both sides of the question, about an hour, it was unanimously agreed, that I ought to take a year for studying. The reasons are these. My course of education in college, was interrupted by ill health, both sophomore and junior years, so that I was obliged to leave during the summers. In the vacation of the first term of the senior year, I lost the use of my eye, and this rendered study impossible for two years; during which time, to a great degree, I lost my habits of mental discipline" (C. Beecher, *The Biographical Remains of Rev. George Beecher*, 37–38).

35. C. Beecher, *The Biographical Remains of Rev. George Beecher*, 33–34.

36. Harding, *A Certain Magnificence*, 338.

37. Lyman Beecher to Ezra Stiles Ely, January 20, 1829, in Ezra Stiles Ely to Andrew Jackson, January 28, 1829, *The Papers of Andrew Jackson, Digital Edition*, ed. Feller, 7. I am indebted to my friend Daniel N. Gullotta for this reference.

38. Isaac Appleton Jewett to Joseph Willard, Cincinnati, October 25, 1832, in Dunn, ed., "Cincinnati Is a Delightful Place: Letters of a Law Clerk, 1831–34," 270.

39. Gerson, *Harriet Beecher Stowe*, 36.

40. Gerson, *Harriet Beecher Stowe*, 35.

41. Thomas K. Beecher, "My Brother Henry," in *Notable Sermons, Vol. I*, 5. Thomas also found Edward somewhat uninteresting, once calling his brother "Edward the nondescript" in a letter to his sister Harriet in 1846 (Thomas Beecher to Harriet Beecher Stowe, Philadelphia, July 30, 1846, box 1: A-102, M-45, 37, Beecher-Stowe Family Papers, 1798–1956).

42. Glenn, *Thomas K. Beecher*, 3.

43. Sklar, *Catharine Beecher*, 110, 112.

44. Applegate, *The Most Famous Man in America*, 124.

45. McPherson, "Antebellum Southern Exceptionalism," 430.

46. Stahr, *Salmon P. Chase*, 10–12, 51, 57.

47. Koester, *Harriet Beecher Stowe*, 62.

48. Sklar, *Catharine Beecher*, 112.

49. Sklar, *Catharine Beecher*, 110.

50. Abzug, *Passionate Liberator*, 52. Abzug explains, "The conversion also marked a choice between the religious sensibility of his real father and that of Finney, in a sense his spiritual father" (50).

51. T. D. Weld, "My dear father in Christ," Fabius [NY], April 22, 1828, in *New York's Burned-Over District: A Documentary History*, ed. McBride and Dorsey, 148.

52. Marsden, *The Evangelical Mind and the New School Presbyterian Experience*, 93.

53. See Cross, *The Burned-Over District*.

54. Abzug, *Passionate Liberator*, 66.

55. Hardesty, *Your Daughters Shall Prophesy*, 111.

56. Abzug, *Passionate Liberator*, 86, 95.

57. Harding, *A Certain Magnificence*, 341.

58. Harding, *A Certain Magnificence*, 290.

59. "Anti-Slavery Imbroglio," in *Autobiography of Lyman Beecher, Vol. II*, ed. Cross, 241.

60. Glenn, *Thomas K. Beecher*, 5–6: In February 1834, Weld began series of revivalist meetings at Lane that converted seventy-five of one hundred students to abolitionism.

61. In 1845, after receiving a silver pitcher from local Black leaders in Cincinnati for his work defending fugitive slaves, Salmon P. Chase delivered a speech in which he argued that this law was unconstitutional. Walter Stahr summarizes: "Chase insisted that the 1831 state statue denying Black children the right to attend Ohio's public schools was contrary to the state constitution, which promised public school education for 'every grade, without any distinction or preference whatever.' Likewise, he condemned the Ohio law that prohibited Blacks from testifying in court., saying that 'almost all humane and benevolent people' opposed this form of exclusion'" (*Salmon P. Chase*, 105).

62. Masur, *Until Justice Be Done*, 91.

63. Taylor, *American Republics*, 243.

64. Harding, *A Certain Magnificence*, 351–52.

65. Dorrien, *The Making of American Liberal Theology*, 218.

66. One anonymous Cincinnatian actually coined the term "Weldite" for *Buck's Theological Dictionary*, providing a lengthy definition which excoriated Weld's followers. (See Bowman and Brown, "Reverend Buck's Theological Dictionary and the Struggle to Define American Evangelicalism, 1802–1851," 441–73.)

67. Merideth, *The Politics of the Universe*, 88.

68. Caskey, *Chariot of Fire*, 31.

69. Masur, *Until Justice Be Done*, 92.

70. The introduction to Weld's *American Slavery as It Is* (1839), opens with a lawyerlike exhortation: "Reader, you are empannelled as a juror to try a plain case and bring in an honest verdict" (7).

71. Harding, *A Certain Magnificence*, 295.

72. Strong, "The Exodus of Students from Lane Seminary to Oberlin in 1834," 4–5.

73. Beecher declined to debate students at Lane ("Anti-Slavery Imbroglio," in *Autobiography of Lyman Beecher, Vol. II*, ed. Cross, 243).

74. Harding, *A Certain Magnificence*, 358.

75. Charles Stuart was one of the most influential figures in Weld's life and in his development on the issue of slavery (Charles Stuart to Theodore Dwight Weld, Apulia, New York, August 5, 1834, in *Letters of Theodore Dwight Weld, Angelina Grimké Weld, and Sarah Grimké, Vol. I*, ed. Barnes and Dumond, 165).

76. Morris, *Oberlin, Hotbed of Abolitionism*, 25.

77. "Lane Seminary," *Vermont Chronicle*, November 7, 1834, 3.

78. "Anti-Slavery Imbroglio," in *Autobiography of Lyman Beecher, Vol. II*, ed. Cross, 245.

79. "Anti-Slavery Imbroglio," in *Autobiography of Lyman Beecher, Vol. II*, ed. Cross, 248.

80. Mahan, *Autobiography*, 177–78.

81. Abzug, *Passionate Liberator*, 112.

82. Abzug, *Passionate Liberator*, 111.

83. Strong, "The Exodus of Students from Lane Seminary to Oberlin in 1834," 6.

84. Henry, *Unvanquished Puritan*, 198.

85. Harding, *A Certain Magnificence*, 372.

86. Glenn, *Thomas K. Beecher*, 6.

87. Robinson, *The Death of Adam*, 137.

88. In Perry, *Lift Up Thy Voice*, 106, 133.

89. Merideth, *The Politics of the Universe*, 87–89.

90. See Minkema and Stout, "The Edwardsean Tradition and the Antislavery Debate, 1740–1865," 47–74.

91. Johnson, *William Lloyd Garrison and His Times*, 177–78.

92. Ch. Beecher, "The Life of Edward Beecher," 120.

93. The episode had an especially profound impact upon young Thomas. See Glenn, *Thomas K. Beecher*, 6.

94. Merideth, *The Politics of the Universe*, 90.

95. "Dr. Beecher to William. Seminary, July 15, 1835," in *Autobiography of Lyman Beecher, Vol. II*, ed. Cross, 259–69.

96. Abzug, *Passionate Liberator*, 129.

97. "Skirmishing," in *Autobiography of Lyman Beecher, Vol. II*, ed. Cross, 217.

98. Vincent Harding notes that Lyman was aware of George's attraction to these meetings, and "it could not fail to affect him for he sensed there were real dangers in the radical way" (*A Certain Magnificence*, 351).

99. Merideth, *The Politics of the Universe*, 87.

100. Lauck, *The Good Country*, 38.

101. E. Beecher. "The Nature, Importance, and Means of Eminent Holiness Throughout the Church."

102. Merideth, *The Politics of the Universe*, 92.

103. E. Beecher. "The Nature, Importance, and Means of Eminent Holiness Throughout the Church."

104. E. Beecher. "The Nature, Importance, and Means of Eminent Holiness Throughout the Church."

105. Robert Merideth contends, "No doubt Beecher had Garrison in mind as he wrote that last passage" (*The Politics of the Universe*, 93).

106. Merideth, *The Politics of the Universe*, 95.

107. "Anti-Slavery Imbroglio," in *Autobiography of Lyman Beecher, Vol. II*, ed. Cross, 246.

108. Later entitled "Uncle Sam's Emancipation," the piece was originally published as "Immediate Emancipation: A Sketch" in the *New-York Evangelist*, January 2, 1845.

109. Hooker, "The Last of the Beechers," 288.

110. Nancy Koester notes, "Beecher was so deeply wounded that Harriet must have felt his distress" (*Harriet Beecher Stowe*, 69).

111. H. B. Stowe, *Men of Our Times*, 252.

112. Sklar, *Catharine Beecher*, 113.

113. Burstyn, "Catharine Beecher and the Education of American Women," 395.

114. L. Beecher, *A Plea for the West*, 92. Eight years earlier, Episcopal bishop Philander Chase published his own *A Plea for the West* (1827) with many of the same themes, but without Beecher's anti-Catholicism.

115. Wilson also appealed to the General Assembly, but Lyman did not have to appear physically before a tribunal.

116. "The Trial," in *Autobiography of Lyman Beecher, Vol. II*, ed. Cross, 269.

117. Marsden, *The Evangelical Mind and the New School Presbyterian Experience*, 97.

118. Bennet Tyler wrote, "Had it not been for his connection with these men (i.e. Taylor and Finney), and the fact that he was supposed to sympathize with them in their theological views, [Beecher] never would have been the object of such jealousy and suspicion" ("Perils," in *Autobiography of Lyman Beecher, Vol. II*, ed. Cross, 284–85).

119. Goen, *Broken Churches, Broken Nation*, 5.

120. Theodore Dwight Weld to William Lloyd Garrison, Hartford, CT, January 2, 1833, quoted in Davis, *Inhuman Bondage*, 273.

121. "The Trial," in *Autobiography of Lyman Beecher, Vol. II*, ed. Cross, 266.

122. Hooker, "The Last of the Beechers," 289.

123. Koester, *Harriet Beecher Stowe,* 70.

124. "The Trial," in *Autobiography of Lyman Beecher, Vol. II,* ed. Cross, 269.

125. Clark, *Henry Ward Beecher,* 36.

126. C. Beecher, *Letters on the Difficulties of Religion,* 344–45.

127. Sklar, *Catharine Beecher,* 125.

128. "The Trial," in *Autobiography of Lyman Beecher, Vol. II,* ed. Cross, 267–68.

129. "The Trial," in *Autobiography of Lyman Beecher, Vol. II,* ed. Cross, 265.

130. Rugoff, *The Beechers,* 160–61.

131. In a letter to Lyman on August 30, 1835, Edward wrote, "As far as I am concerned, though I never was with her as with my own mother, and though I could never feel for her that peculiar attachment for a mother which can, as I suppose, be felt but once, yet my feelings toward her were those of unmingled respect and affection . . . and I look forward with joyful anticipations to the time when I shall join her and my own dear mother in heaven" (in *Autobiography of Lyman Beecher, Vol. II,* ed. Cross, 276–77).

132. Thomas K. Beecher to Isabella Beecher Hooker, January 26, 1842, Joseph K. Hooker Collection, Harriet Beecher Stowe Center.

133. "A Family Meeting," in *Autobiography of Lyman Beecher, Vol. II,* ed. Cross, 273.

134. Applegate, *The Most Famous Man in America,* 124; Rugoff, *The Beechers,* 162.

135. The synod had also demanded that Beecher put his views in writing. The result was his *Views in Theology.*

136. *Cincinnati Journal,* May 19, 1836.

137. Harding, *A Certain Magnificence,* 408.

138. Porterfield, *Conceived in Doubt,* 54–55.

139. Peck, *Forty Years of Pioneer Life,* 106.

140. Whitney R. Cross defines "ultraism" as "An amorphous thing in an intellectual sense, it can scarcely be considered a system of belief. It is better described as a combination of activities, personalities, and attitudes creating a condition of society which could foster experimental doctrines" (*The Burned-Over District,* 173).

141. George Beecher, in C. Beecher, *The Biographical Remains of Rev. George Beecher,* 16.

142. Applegate, *The Most Famous Man in America,* 130.

143. *Cincinnati Journal,* July 11, 1836.

144. Koester, *Harriet Beecher Stowe,* 77.

145. Applegate, *The Most Famous Man in America,* 130.

146. Koester, *Harriet Beecher Stowe,* 78.

147. Foner, *Free Soil, Free Labor, Free Men,* 74.

148. Birney, "Ohio Threatened," 3.

149. Koester, *Harriet Beecher Stowe,* 78.

150. Applegate, *The Most Famous Man in America,* 131.

151. Koester, *Harriet Beecher Stowe,* 78.

152. C. E. Stowe and L. B. Stowe, *Harriet Beecher Stowe,* 105.

153. Rugoff, *The Beechers,* 371.

154. Merideth, *The Politics of the Universe,* 96.

155. Merideth, *The Politics of the Universe*, 101.

156. Koester, *Harriet Beecher Stowe*, 93.

157. Sklar, *Catharine Beecher*, 130.

158. Rugoff, *The Beechers*, 225.

159. L. Beecher, *Views in Theology*, 19.

3. NEW SCHOOL KIDS (1837–1847)

1. Allen C.Guelzo, "Charles Hodge's Antislavery Moment," in *Charles Hodge Revisited: A Critical Appraisal of His Life and Work*, ed. Stewart and Moorhead, 304.

2. Lewis Tappan led a walkout in the AASS over this issue in 1840, forming the American and Foreign Anti-Slavery Society.

3. Angelina Grimké Weld to Theodore Dwight Weld and J. G. Whittier, in *The Letters of Theodore Weld, Angelina Grimké Weld and Sarah M. Grimké, 1822–1844* (New York: Da Capo Press, 1970), 431–32.

4. Howe, *The Political Culture of the American Whigs*, 54.

5. Meyers and Walker, *The Reverse Underground Railroad in Ohio*, 54.

6. Clark, *Henry Ward Beecher*, 38.

7. C. Beecher, *Essay on Slavery and Abolitionism with Reference to the Duty of American Females*, 21, 23–24. According to Kathryn Sklar, "Only Edward Beecher's courageous *Narrative of the Riots at Alton* broke through the family's hesitancy and firmly declared sympathy for the abolitionists in 1837" (*Catharine Beecher*, 133).

8. E. Beecher, "The Nature, Importance, and Means of Eminent Holiness Throughout the Church."

9. "Family History," in *Autobiography of Lyman Beecher, Vol. II*, ed. Cross, 310.

10. C. Beecher, *Biographical Remains of George Beecher*, 18.

11. "Family History," in *Autobiography of Lyman Beecher, Vol. II*, ed. Cross, 309–11.

12. In C. Beecher, *Biographical Remains of George Beecher*, 149–50.

13. Cross, *The Burned-Over District*, 251.

14. Merideth, *The Politics of the Universe*, 96.

15. "Perils," in *Autobiography of Lyman Beecher, Vol. II*, ed. Cross, 307.

16. Applegate, *The Most Famous Man in America*, 88.

17. Henry Ward Beecher to Chauncey Howard, March 20, 1835, Acquisitions, Harriet Beecher Stowe Center.

18. Applegate, *The Most Famous Man in America*, 129.

19. Catharine believed that Ohio should imitate the "good education of the Yankees," to the disdain of people like Cincinnati elites such as Edward King (Sklar, *Catharine Beecher*, 120).

20. Sklar, *Catharine Beecher*, 139.

21. Lyman Beecher, in "Correspondence, 1837–1838," in *Autobiography of Lyman Beecher, Vol. II*, ed. Cross, 316.

22. "Correspondence, 1837–1838," in *Autobiography of Lyman Beecher, Vol. II*, ed. Cross, 317.

23. L. Beecher, *A Plea for the West*, 45.

24. See Bell, *Degrees of Equality*.

25. Merideth, *The Politics of the Universe*, 81.

26. Miller, *Arguing about Slavery*, 39.

27. "Revolution," in *Autobiography of Lyman Beecher, Vol. II*, ed. Cross, 322.

28. For an examination of this New Divinity hallmark, see Todd, *The Moral Governmental Theory of Atonement*. Mark Noll has observed, "the more directly Presbyterians promoted revival, the more they identified self-consciously with Edwards and his lineage. Likewise, the more fully Presbyterians internalized the republican (and then later the democratic) political culture of the United States, the more closely they were aligned not with Edwards but with the theological line stretching in New England from Timothy Dwight to Lyman Beecher and Nathaniel W. Taylor" ("Jonathan Edwards, Edwardsian Theologies, and the Presbyterians," in *After Jonathan Edwards*, ed. Crisp and Sweeney, 179).

29. Marsden, *The Evangelical Mind and the New School Presbyterian Experience*, 93, 97.

30. For a look into Edwards's influence on proslavery theologians, see Todd, *Southern Edwardseans*.

31. E. Beecher, *A Narrative of Riots at Alton*, 20.

32. Lucas, "Eighteenth- and Nineteenth-Century Presbyterianism in North America," in *The Oxford Handbook of Presbyterianism*, ed. Smith and Kemeny, 60.

33. "Revolution," in *Autobiography of Lyman Beecher, Vol. II*, ed. Cross, 323.

34. *Register of Debates in Congress*, 24th Congress, 2nd Session (Washington: Gales and Seaton, 1837), 721–22.

35. See Thornwell, *The Rights and Duties of Masters*.

36. Elder, *Calhoun*, 339–40.

37. Thanks to Robert Elder for his helpful email on this subject.

38. "Revolution," in *Autobiography of Lyman Beecher, Vol. II*, ed. Cross, 323.

39. Front matter in Merideth, *The Politics of the Universe*.

40. "Consequences," in *Autobiography of Lyman Beecher, Vol. II*, ed. Cross, 327.

41. Glenn, *Thomas K. Beecher*, 8; Applegate, *The Most Famous Man in America*, 129. Thomas later had misgivings about the authenticity of this conversion.

42. Hedrick, *Harriet Beecher Stowe*, 117.

43. In Kentucky, Henry Clay was also conciliatory (Klotter, *Henry Clay*, 206).

44. E. Beecher, *A Narrative of Riots at Alton*, 22.

45. Ch. Beecher, "The Life of Edward Beecher," 37.

46. E. Beecher, *A Narrative of Riots at Alton*, 22

47. E. Beecher, *A Narrative of Riots at Alton*, 24.

48. Merideth, *The Politics of the Universe*, 96, 98.

49. The "Butternut" region was populated by many transplants from the upper South. According to James McPherson, "They remained rural, southern, and localist in their orientation, hostile toward 'Yankees' of New England heritage who settled the northern portions of these states made accessible by the Erie Canal after 1825" (*Battle Cry of Freedom*, 31.)

50. E. Beecher, *A Narrative of Riots at Alton*, 38–39.

51. E. Beecher, *A Narrative of Riots at Alton*, 44.

52. E. Beecher, *A Narrative of Riots at Alton*, 88.

53. E. Beecher, *A Narrative of Riots at Alton*, 47.

54. Peck, *Forty Years of Pioneer Life*, 276.

55. Schneider, "Lincoln's Lyceum Speech as a Model of Democratic Rhetoric," 511. Schneider concludes, "Lincoln refrains from condemning the Alton rioters because he knows that a condemnation will not change his listeners' minds" (512).

56. In Muelder, *Theodore Dwight Weld and the American Anti-Slavery Society*, 120.

57. E. Beecher, *A Narrative of Riots at Alton*, 5.

58. Dillon, *Elijah P. Lovejoy*, 181.

59. Merideth, *The Politics of the Universe*, 96.

60. Merideth, *The Politics of the Universe*, 101.

61. E. Beecher, *A Narrative of Riots at Alton*, 157.

62. L. Beecher, *A Reformation of Moral Practical and Indispensable*, 13.

63. H. W. Beecher, *Christian Union*, December 6, 1871.

64. Applegate, *The Most Famous Man in America*, 189.

65. Applegate, *The Most Famous Man in America*, 156.

66. Flint, *Recollections of the Last Ten Years*, 114.

67. Hatch, *The Democratization of American Christianity*.

68. White, *The Beecher Sisters*, 21, 25, 27.

69. White, *The Beecher Sisters*, 23.

70. "Consequences," in *Autobiography of Lyman Beecher, Vol. II*, ed. Cross, 329.

71. *The Limits of Sisterhood*, ed. Boydston, Kelley, and Margolis, 100.

72. Isabella Beecher Hooker to John Hooker, February 7, 1841, microfiche 1, *The Isabella Beecher Hooker Project*, ed. Margolis.

73. "The Lost Found," in *Autobiography of Lyman Beecher, Vol. II*, ed. Cross, 350.

74. Sklar, *Catharine Beecher*, 145.

75. Sklar, *Catharine Beecher*, 135.

76. Seigel, "A Passionate Missionary to the West," 329.

77. Charles Beecher, in "The Lost Found," in *Autobiography of Lyman Beecher, Vol. II*, ed. Cross, 351.

78. Larsen, *John Stuart Mill*, 27.

79. "The Lost Found," in *Autobiography of Lyman Beecher, Vol. II*, ed. Cross, 351–53.

80. Henry, *Unvanquished Puritan*, 23.

81. Glenn, *Thomas K. Beecher*, 9.

82. "Correspondence, 1840–42," in *Autobiography of Lyman Beecher, Vol. II*, ed. Cross, 335.

83. "Correspondence, 1840–42," in *Autobiography of Lyman Beecher, Vol. II*, ed. Cross, 335–36.

84. Sklar, *Catharine Beecher*, 120.

85. "Correspondence, 1840–42," in *Autobiography of Lyman Beecher, Vol. II*, ed. Cross, 335.

86. "Revolution," in *Autobiography of Lyman Beecher, Vol. II*, ed. Cross, 321.

87. Applegate, *The Most Famous Man in America*, 187.

88. Muelder, *Theodore Dwight Weld and the American Anti-Slavery Society*, 98.

89. Ramage and Watkins, *Kentucky Rising*, 273. In his magisterial work *Religion in the Old South*, Donald G. Mathews states, "The weakness of the southern Evangelical antislavery movement was obvious. It could never acquire a broad social base from which to operate" (76).

90. Applegate, *The Most Famous Man in America*, 186.

91. Applegate, *The Most Famous Man in America*, 174.

92. Applegate, *The Most Famous Man in America*, 187.

93. Gerson, *Harriet Beecher Stowe*, 55.

94. Rugoff, *The Beechers*, 284.

95. *The Limits of Sisterhood*, ed. Boydston, Kelley, and Margolis, 341; H. B. Stowe, "The Drunkard Reclaimed."

96. Harry L. Watson states, "In reality, William Henry Harrison did not live in a log cabin, and he probably drank very little hard cider, but no matter. The characteristic dwelling and beverage of the frontier were both glorified by Whig papers and celebrated from uncounted platforms and parade grounds until they came to symbolize the new popular appeal of the Whig Party" (*Liberty and Power*, 215).

97. Stahr, *Salmon P. Chase*, 74–75.

98. Applegate, *The Most Famous Man in America*, 148.

99. White, *The Beecher Sisters*, 43–44.

100. C. Beecher, *Treatise on Domestic Economy*, 324.

101. Henry, *Unvanquished Puritan*, 22.

102. C. Beecher, *Treatise on Domestic Economy*, 43.

103. C. Beecher, *Treatise on Domestic Economy*, 41.

104. Kerber, "The Republican Mother," 187–205.

105. C. Beecher, *Treatise on Domestic Economy*, 25.

106. C. Beecher, *Treatise on Domestic Economy*, 38.

107. Rugoff, *The Beechers*, 61.

108. C. Beecher, *Treatise on Domestic Economy*, 33, 34, 26.

109. C. Beecher, *Treatise on Domestic Economy*, 159.

110. Rugoff, *The Beechers*, 183.

111. Thomas K. Beecher to Isabella Beecher Hooker, October 4, 1842, Joseph K. Hooker Collection, Harriet Beecher Stowe Center.

112. Applegate, *The Most Famous Man in America*, 174.

113. Thomas K. Beecher to Isabella Beecher Hooker, January 9, 1843, Joseph K. Hooker Collection, Harriet Beecher Stowe Center.

114. Applegate, *The Most Famous Man in America*, 177.

115. Dorrien, *The Making of American Liberal Theology*, 189.

116. "Western Colleges," in *Autobiography of Lyman Beecher, Vol. II*, ed. Cross, 343.

117. Harding, *A Certain Magnificence*, 447.

118. Harding, *A Certain Magnificence*, 449.

119. Seigel, "A Passionate Missionary to the West," 329.

120. Seigel, "A Passionate Missionary to the West," 332.

121. Indeed, one could argue that evangelicals kept making their "Plea for the West" long after Lyman's death. Pushing further west, Americans adopted Beecher's formula for social and

moral change. From the oil patches of Texas to the bustling port cities of California, evangelical activists during the Progressive Era addressed the social ills of urbanization and industrialization with the "two-headed gospel of revival and reform" (Dochuk, *Anointed with Oil,* 119).

122. *Ladies' Home Journal* 9, no. 2 (1892): 5.

123. "Georgie" passed away in 1846 after contracting a fever. In a letter to Henry in 1842, George reported the progress of his "orchard," complete with cherries, pears, and apples (George Beecher to Henry Ward Beecher, April 5, 1842, Acquisitions, Harriet Beecher Stowe Center).

124. "Correspondence, 1845," in *Autobiography of Lyman Beecher, Vol. II,* ed. Cross, 371.

125. "The Broken Link," in *Autobiography of Lyman Beecher, Vol. II,* ed. Cross, 346.

126. Harding, *A Certain Magnificence,* 448.

127. C. Beecher, *The Biographical Remains of Rev. George Beecher,* 6–7.

128. Caskey, *Chariot of Fire,* 134.

129. See Riddle, "Discovery of Henry Ward Beecher," 854–57.

130. "Western Colleges," in *Autobiography of Lyman Beecher, Vol. II,* ed. Cross, 343.

131. Rugoff, *The Beechers,* 268.

132. H. W. Beecher, *Lectures to Young Men,* 150.

133. Merideth, *The Politics of the Universe,* 85; H. W. Beecher, *Lectures to Young Men,* 148.

134. C. Beecher, *Evils Suffered by American Women,* 5.

135. C. Beecher, *Evils Suffered by American Women,* 11.

136. C. Beecher: *The Duty of American Women,* 64.

137. Hedrick, *Harriet Beecher Stowe,* 170–71.

138. Flexner and Fitzpatrick, *Century of Struggle,* 31.

139. C. Beecher, *An Address to the Protestant Clergy,* 21.

140. Caskey, *Chariot of Fire,* xi–xii.

141. One such example is Yellin and Van Horne, eds., *The Abolitionist Sisterhood.*

142. C. Beecher, *The Duty of American Women,* 32, 30.

143. Bell, *Degrees of Equality,* ix, 5, 25, 27.

144. Stahr, *Salmon P. Chase,* 95, 113–15.

145. See Meyers and Walker, *The Reverse Underground Railroad in Ohio.*

146. Seigel, "A Passionate Missionary to the West," 352.

147. H. B. Stowe, "Immediate Emancipation," 1.

148. Hedrick, *Harriet Beecher Stowe,* 172.

149. In *Radicals: Audacious Writings by American Women, Vol. 1: 1830–1930,* ed. Stabel and Turpin, 189.

150. Hedrick, *Harriet Beecher Stowe,* 172.

151. Harriet Beecher Stowe to George Beecher, February 20 [1830?], Acquisitions, Harriet Beecher Stowe Center.

152. Abraham Lincoln, *Congressional Globe,* December 22, 1847, 64–65.

153. Lepore, *These Truths,* 243.

154. "Correspondence, 1840–42," in *Autobiography of Lyman Beecher, Vol. II,* ed. Cross, 340.

155. Rugoff, *The Beechers,* 21.

156. Sklar, *Catharine Beecher,* 178–79.

157. Sklar, *Catharine Beecher,* 178, 203.

158. "Autumn Leaves," in *Autobiography of Lyman Beecher, Vol. II,* ed. Cross, 380–81.

159. "Autumn Leaves," in *Autobiography of Lyman Beecher, Vol. II,* ed. Cross, 381.

160. "Autumn Leaves," in *Autobiography of Lyman Beecher, Vol. II,* ed. Cross, 380.

161. "Autumn Leaves," in *Autobiography of Lyman Beecher, Vol. II,* ed. Cross, 380.

162. L. B. Stowe, *Saints, Sinners, and Beechers,* 45–46.

4. SHALL WE COMPROMISE? (1847–1857)

1. The first railroad car of the Madison and Indianapolis Railroad rolled into the city on October 1, 1847. Debby Applegate aptly summarizes: "Reverend Beecher boarded the first train to leave Indianapolis. Henry went West with the age of the steamboat and left as it passed into the age of the railroad" (*The Most Famous Man in America,* 197).

2. Rugoff, *The Beechers,* 369.

3. Sklar, *Catharine Beecher,* 177, 180.

4. Channing, *Self-Culture,* 80.

5. Miller's followers called him "Father Miller" while his critics dubbed him "Prophet Miller" (Rowe, *God's Strange Work,* xix).

6. E. Beecher, *The Conflict of Ages,* 14.

7. Charles Beecher to Harriet Beecher Stowe, May 1, 1848, box 1, A-102: M-45, 29, Beecher-Stowe Family Papers, 1798–1956.

8. "Correspondence, 1847–1851," in *Autobiography of Lyman Beecher, Vol. II,* ed. Cross, 403.

9. "Correspondence, 1847–1851," in *Autobiography of Lyman Beecher, Vol. II,* ed. Cross, 404.

10. Arguing for a "pervasive, driving fear of dissolution" that motivated Americans during this era of history, historian Alan Taylor has called "manifest destiny" the "most misleading phrase ever offered to explain American expansion" (*American Republics,* xxiv).

11. Quoted in Kammen, *A Machine That Would Go of Itself,* 97–100.

12. That Brooklyn would have its own religious culture is not surprising. According to Charles Sellers, the emerging American middle-class had a moral impulse. "The so-called middle-class was constituted not by mode and relations of production but by ideology. . . . A numerous and dispersed bourgeoisie of small-scale enterprisers pushed both themselves and their workers to staggering effort by mythologizing class as a moral category" (*The Market Revolution,* 237).

13. Reynolds, *Walt Whitman's America,* 35; Clark, *Henry Ward Beecher,* 76.

14. Applegate, *The Most Famous Man in America,* 4.

15. Reynolds, *Walt Whitman's America,* 255.

16. Rugoff, *The Beechers,* 370.

17. Reynolds, *Walt Whitman's America,* 172.

18. Reynolds, *Walt Whitman's America,* 256.

19. Dorrien, *The Making of American Liberal Theology,* 191–92.

20. According to Richard Hofstadter, "Finney was gifted with a big voice and a flair for pulpit drama. But his greatest physical asset was his intense, fixating, electrifying, madly prophetic eyes, the most impressive eyes—except perhaps for John C. Calhoun's—in the portrait gallery of nineteenth-century America" (*Anti-Intellectualism in American Life,* 92).

21. Hambrick-Stowe, *Charles G. Finney and the Spirit of American Evangelicalism*, 161–64.

22. Applegate, *The Most Famous Man in America*, 214.

23. Edwards Amasa Park to Dr. Amasa Walker, May 29, 1857, Harvard Archives, in Clark, *Henry Ward Beecher*, 134.

24. Reynolds, *Walt Whitman's America*, 173.

25. Applegate, *The Most Famous Man in America*, 273.

26. Dorrien, *The Making of American Liberal Theology*, 192.

27. McLoughlin, *The Meaning of Henry Ward Beecher*, 26–27.

28. H. W. Beecher, *Sermons by Henry Ward Beecher, Plymouth Church, Brooklyn, Vol. II*, 367.

29. "The Lost Found," in *Autobiography of Lyman Beecher, Vol. II*, ed. Cross, 359.

30. Seigel, "A Passionate Missionary to the West," 339, 343.

31. Ch. Beecher, *The Bible a Sufficient Creed*, 25.

32. Rugoff, *The Beechers*, 198.

33. Seigel, "A Passionate Missionary to the West," 350.

34. Ch. Beecher, *The Bible a Sufficient Creed*, 26.

35. Ch. Beecher, *The Bible a Sufficient Creed*, 41.

36. Merideth, *The Politics of the Universe*, 131.

37. Thomas K. Beecher to Lyman Beecher, n.d. (before 1850), White Collection, Harriet Beecher Stowe Center. According to Myra Glenn, "Internal evidence suggests that Thomas Beecher wrote this letter in the late fall or winter of 1846" (*Thomas K. Beecher*, 188n37).

38. Glenn, *Thomas K. Beecher*, 19.

39. Glenn, *Thomas K. Beecher*, 33.

40. Mullin, *The Puritan as Yankee*, 4.

41. White, *The Beecher Sisters*, 62.

42. Bushnell, *Christian Nurture*, 22.

43. Glenn, *Thomas K. Beecher*, 37.

44. Mullin argues, "*Christian Nurture* should be seen not only as the beginning of the Christian education movement in the United States, but also as a work Bushnell used to further his notion of a comprehensive Christianity. Reuniting the children of the Puritans, and bringing together the orthodox emphasis on piety and the Unitarian concern with character, was one of his goals" (*The Puritan as Yankee*, 126).

45. Bushnell, *Christian Nurture*, 92.

46. Mullin, *The Puritan as Yankee*, 64.

47. Mullin, *The Puritan as Yankee*, 164.

48. Glenn, *Thomas K. Beecher*, 37.

49. Caskey, *Chariot of Fire*, 17.

50. Nathan Lord to Lyman Beecher, June 6, 1845, box 1, A-102: M-45, 36, Beecher-Stowe Family Papers, 1798–1956.

51. Glenn, *Thomas K. Beecher*, 29.

52. Harriet Beecher Stowe to Charles Edward Stowe, October 3, 1877, box 4: A-102, M-45, 192, Beecher-Stowe Family Papers, 1798–1956.

53. "Correspondence, 1847–1851," in *Autobiography of Lyman Beecher, Vol. II*, ed. Cross, 404–5.

54. Glenn, *Thomas K. Beecher*, 29.

55. Thomas K. Beecher to Lyman Beecher, August 11 and 12, 1846, White Collection, Harriet Beecher Stowe Center.

56. Sklar, *Catharine Beecher*, 183, 217. In 1849 she issued an entire circular explaining her reasons for the break with Slade.

57. Glenn, *Thomas K. Beecher*, 34–35.

58. Isabella Beecher Hooker to John Hooker, July 18, 1852, microfiche 11, *The Isabella Beecher Hooker Project*, ed. Margolis.

59. Rugoff, *The Beechers*, 292, 451.

60. Isabella Beecher Hooker to John Hooker, July 18, 1852, microfiche 11, *The Isabella Beecher Hooker Project*, ed. Margolis.

61. Glenn, *Thomas K. Beecher*, 164, 166.

62. "Correspondence, 1847–1851," in *Autobiography of Lyman Beecher, Vol. II*, ed. Cross, 405.

63. Seigel, "A Passionate Missionary to the West," 345.

64. Rugoff, *The Beechers*, 371.

65. In his book *Who Is an Evangelical? The History of a Movement in Crisis* (2019), Thomas S. Kidd explains, "By the eve of the Civil War, America had come as close numerically to being a 'Christian nation' as it had ever been, at least in terms of numbers" (38).

66. Klotter, *Henry Clay*, 316. For an examination of other ministers' response to the Hamilton-Burr duel, see Todd, "American Prophets," 563–75.

67. Stout, *American Aristocrats*, 226.

68. *New York Tribune*, March 3, 1848, in Klotter, *Henry Clay*, 360.

69. Ramage and Watkins, *Kentucky Rising*, 45.

70. Stout, *American Aristocrats*, 208.

71. Wilentz, *The Rise of American Democracy*, 637.

72. Ramage and Watkins, *Kentucky Rising*, 44.

73. Reynolds, *Abe*, 328.

74. Koester, *Harriet Beecher Stowe*, 104.

75. Hedrick, *Harriet Beecher Stowe*, 193.

76. Howe, *The Political Culture of the American Whigs*, 204–7.

77. *The Independent*, February 21, 1850.

78. H. W. Beecher, "The Fugitive Slave Bill at Its Work," 10.

79. Chesebrough, *"No Sorrow Like Our Sorrow,"* xi.

80. Reynolds, *Walt Whitman's America*, 173.

81. Hedrick, *Harriet Beecher Stowe*, 203; Rugoff, *The Beechers*, 249.

82. John Greenleaf Whittier's poem "Ichabod" reflected his thoughts about the Fugitive Slave Law of 1850.

83. Rugoff, *The Beechers*, 317.

84. "The Slave-Law and the Union," 10.

85. Harriet Beecher Stowe to "Dear Sister" [Catharine Beecher], n.d., [1850 or 1851], quoted in Hedrick, *Harriet Beecher Stowe*, 204.

86. Harriet Beecher Stowe to Henry Ward Beecher, February 1, 1851, quoted in Hedrick, *Harriet Beecher Stowe*, 205. Also see Brophy, "'Over and above," 457.

87. Henson, *The Life of Josiah Henson.*

88. Koester, *Harriet Beecher Stowe*, 111.

89. See Merrill, "'May She Read Liberty in Your Eyes?'" 127–44.

90. Dorrien, *The Making of American Liberal Theology*, 195.

91. Ch. Stowe, *Life of Harriet Beecher Stowe*, 145.

92. Henry Stowe and Harriet Beecher Stowe to Calvin Stowe, December 1850, Acquisitions, Harriet Beecher Stowe Center.

93. Harriet Beecher Stowe to Calvin Stowe, after December 27, 1850, Acquisitions, Harriet Beecher Stowe Center.

94. Ch. Beecher, *The Duty of Disobedience to Wicked Laws.*

95. Rugoff, *The Beechers*, 408.

96. Seigel, "A Passionate Missionary to the West," 346.

97. White, *The Beecher Sisters*, 67.

98. Catharine Beecher to Mary Beecher Perkins, September 27, 1851, Beecher Family Papers, Beinecke Library, Yale University, box 2, folder 105, MS 71, ser. 1. Also see Kirkham, *The Building of Uncle Tom's Cabin*, 127.

99. Sklar, *Catharine Beecher*, 219.

100. Sklar, *Catharine Beecher*, 234.

101. Melville, *Moby-Dick*, 43.

102. In Illinois, Wheaton College was founded by Rev. Jonathan Blanchard, a graduate of Lane Seminary in 1828 under Lyman Beecher.

103. "Return to Boston," in *Autobiography of Lyman Beecher, Vol. II,* ed. Cross, 408.

104. Hedrick, *Harriet Beecher Stowe*, 222.

105. Koester, *Harriet Beecher Stowe*, 143.

106. H. B. Stowe, *Uncle Tom's Cabin*, 42. Clint Smith writes, "Abraham Lincoln himself may have read the book, at a crucial turning point in the Civil War: Records indicate that the 16th president checked it out from the Library of Congress on June 16, 1862, and returned it on July 29. Those 43 days correspond with the period during which Lincoln drafted the Emancipation Proclamation" ("The Man Who Became Uncle Tom," 98).

107. Stowe, *Uncle Tom's Cabin*, 252.

108. Stowe, *Uncle Tom's Cabin*, 518.

109. Stowe, *Uncle Tom's Cabin*, 169.

110. Stowe, *Uncle Tom's Cabin*, 385.

111. Stowe, *Uncle Tom's Cabin*, 500–501.

112. Douglas, *The Feminization of American Culture*, 241.

113. Gates, "Foreword," in Spingarn, *Uncle Tom*, xii.

114. See Vollaro, "Lincoln, Stowe, and the 'Little Woman / Great War' Story," 18–34.

115. Spingarn, *Uncle Tom*, 10–11.

116. Spingarn, *Uncle Tom*, 5.

117. Fredrickson, *The Black Image in the White Mind;* Baldwin, *Everybody's Protest Novel.*

118. H. B. Stowe, "Uncle Tom's Cabin; or, Life among the Lowly."

119. In White, *The Beecher Sisters*, 54.

120. Schweiger, *A Literate South*, 193.

121. "More Uncle Tom Material."

122. *"Parson Brownlow's Opinion of Harriet Beecher Stowe."*

123. "Mrs. Stowe and *Dred.*"

124. Sklar, *Catharine Beecher,* 186.

125. Sklar, *Catharine Beecher,* 217.

126. E. Beecher, *The Conflict of Ages,* 552.

127. Merideth, *The Politics of the Universe,* 153.

128. Merideth, *The Politics of the Universe,* 127.

129. E. Beecher, *The Conflict of Ages,* 188.

130. King, Review of *The Conflict,* 34–35.

131. With Edward's untenable view of the preexistence of souls, Princeton theologian Charles Hodge believed that *The Conflict of Ages* actually supported the Old School side (Review of *The Conflict,* 96–97). For other examples of reviews, see Merideth, *The Politics of the Universe,* 150–52.

132. "Mrs. Stowe and *Dred.*"

133. L. B. Stowe, *Saints, Sinners, and Beechers,* 149.

134. For example, see Clark, *Henry Ward Beecher,* 136.

135. Glenn, *Thomas K. Beecher,* 57–59.

136. Excerpts from this public lecture can be found in Thomas Beecher's scrapbooks (1853–1910) at the Harriet Beecher Stowe Center.

137. Glenn, *Thomas K. Beecher,* 59.

138. Glenn, *Thomas K. Beecher,* 83, 85.

139. Thomas K. Beecher to Jervis Langdon and Church Brethren, September 18, 1854, reprinted in L. B. Stowe, *Saints, Sinners, and Beechers,* 359–61; Taylor, *A History of the Park Church,* 37.

140. Hedrick, *Harriet Beecher Stowe,* 251.

141. These four criteria are often called the "Bebbington Quadrilateral," although Bebbington's criteria have been frequently critiqued. See Bebbington's *Evangelicalism in Modern Britain.*

142. Quoted in Koester, *Harriet Beecher Stowe,* 188.

143. Merideth, *The Politics of the Universe,* 131.

144. Blight, *Frederick Douglass,* 222.

145. Blight, *Frederick Douglass,* 217.

146. Koester, *We Will Be Free,* 111, 132.

147. Hedrick, *Harriet Beecher Stowe,* 252.

148. Applegate, *The Most Famous Man in America,* 214.

149. Hedrick, *Harriet Beecher Stowe,* 252.

150. Lepore, *These Truths,* 265–66.

151. Seigel, "A Passionate Missionary to the West," 354.

152. Carwardine, *Evangelicals and Politics in Antebellum America,* 238.

153. Hedrick, *Harriet Beecher Stowe,* 256–57.

154. Glenn, *Thomas K. Beecher,* 94.

155. Foner, *Free Soil, Free Labor, Free Men,* 54.

156. Applegate, *The Most Famous Man in America,* title page.

157. Applegate, *The Most Famous Man in America*, 281.

158. Hibben, "Author's Preface," *Henry Ward Beecher*, xiii.

159. Applegate, *The Most Famous Man in America*, 339.

160. McLoughlin, *The Meaning of Henry Ward Beecher*, 7.

161. Ch. Beecher, *The God of the Bible Against Slavery*, 2.

162. Koester, *Harriet Beecher Stowe*, 201, 204.

163. "The Last of Earth," in *Autobiography of Lyman Beecher, Vol. II*, ed. Cross, 414. The trustees of Lane gave Lyman a parting sum of $3,800. Lyman's old friends in Boston also gave him a life annuity of $500. Lyman was also supported by some of his children (413).

164. Rugoff, *The Beechers*, 294.

165. Rugoff, *The Beechers*, 405.

166. Lauck, *The Good Country*, 91, 132.

167. L. B. Stowe, *Saints Sinners and Beechers*, 150.

168. Rugoff, *The Beechers*, 451.

169. Rugoff, *The Beechers*, 405.

170. Charles Beecher to Henry Ward Beecher, April 12, 1857, Beecher Family Papers, Beinecke Library, Yale University, box 7, folder 305, MS 71, ser. 1.

171. Thomas K. Beecher to Calvin Stowe, February 14, 1857, Acquisitions, Harriet Beecher Stowe Center.

172. Thomas K. Beecher to Calvin Stowe, February 14, 1857, Acquisitions, Harriet Beecher Stowe Center.

173. Sklar, *Catharine Beecher*, 239.

174. Stowe, *The Minister's Wooing*, 215.

175. Gordon, *John Calvin's Institutes of the Christian Religion*, 110.

176. H. B. Stowe, *The Minister's Wooing*, 24.

177. White, *The Beecher Sisters*, 64. Sojourner Truth and her eight-year-old grandson James visited the Stowes in Andover for a few days in 1853. Harriet based one of the fictional characters in her second antislavery novel, *Dred, a Tale of the Great Dismal Swamp* (1856) on Sojourner Truth (Koester, *We Will Be Free*, 117).

178. Adams, "Family Influences on 'The Minister's Wooing' and 'Oldtown Folks,'" 28.

179. Buell, *New England Literary Culture*, 267.

180. Schantz, *Awaiting the Heavenly Country*.

181. See Seeman, *Speaking with the Dead in Early America*. Although unorthodox in its beliefs, spiritualism was not the first religion in America to feature communication with the dead. The teachings of Swedish theologian Emanuel Swedenborg (1688–1772) included the ability to correspond with souls long since passed. Swedenborgian communities emerged across the United States.

182. Hedrick, *Harriet Beecher Stowe*, 274. Even Charles, who originally critiqued spiritualism as unbiblical in *A Review of the "Spiritual Manifestations,"* eventually developed his own unique view. James, however, was skeptical of spiritualism.

183. Rugoff, *The Beechers*, 416.

184. According to Sklar, "Although she seemed an innovator, Catharine actually endorsed as much as she rejected of the New England tradition" (*Catharine Beecher*, 245).

185. Sklar, *Catharine Beecher*, 211.

186. *The Biblical Repository and Princeton Review*, October 1857.

187. "Return to Boston," in *Autobiography of Lyman Beecher, Vol. II*, ed. Cross, 412.

188. "The Last of Earth," in *Autobiography of Lyman Beecher, Vol. II*, ed. Cross, 414.

189. Thoreau, *Walden*, 435.

5. THE OLD OAK FINALLY FELL (1857–1870)

1. Buell, *New England Literary Culture*, 261.

2. H. B. Stowe, *Sunny Memories of Foreign Lands*, 103. See *Harriet Beecher Stowe in Europe*, ed. Van Why and French. Also see *Transatlantic Stowe*, ed. Kohn, Meer, and Todd.

3. Koester, *Harriet Beecher Stowe*, 155.

4. Koester, *Harriet Beecher Stowe*, 159.

5. C. Beecher, *Letters to the People on Health and Happiness*, 173.

6. Rugoff, *The Beechers*, 351.

7. Harriet Beecher Stowe, "My Dear Girls," Ascension Sunday, June 1, 1862, box 3: A-102, M-45, 115, Beecher-Stowe Family Papers, 1798–1956.

8. Rugoff, *The Beechers*, 380.

9. See Lysaker, *Emerson and Self-Culture*.

10. H. W. Beecher, "Man's True Dignity," in *Sermons by the Rev. Henry Ward Beecher, Vol. 1*, 26, 28.

11. H. W. Beecher, "Waiting for the Lord," in *Sermons by the Rev. Henry Ward Beecher, Vol. 1*, 74.

12. Rugoff, *The Beechers*, 351.

13. Rugoff, *The Beechers*, 452.

14. Annie Beecher to Charles Beecher, July 8, 1859, Joseph K. Hooker Collection, Harriet Beecher Stowe Center.

15. H. W. Beecher, "On Which Side Is Peace?" in *Patriotic Addresses in America and England*, ed. Howard, 197.

16. Byrd, *A Holy Baptism of Fire and Blood*, 38.

17. Blight, *Frederick Douglass*, 311.

18. Reynolds, *Mightier Than the Sword*, 303.

19. H. W. Beecher, "The Nation's Duty to Slavery," in *Patriotic Addresses in America and England*, ed. Howard, 204, 207.

20. Beecher, "The Nation's Duty to Slavery," 214, 215, 216.

21. Applegate, *The Most Famous Man in America*, 314–15.

22. Mathews, *Religion in the Old South*, 101.

23. Rugoff, *The Beechers*, 348.

24. Caskey, *Chariot of Fire*, xi.

25. Byrd, *A Holy Baptism of Fire and Blood*, 87–88.

26. Applegate, *The Most Famous Man in America*, 291.

27. White, *The Beecher Sisters*, 73.

28. Hedrick, *Harriet Beecher Stowe*, 288.

29. Achorn, *The Lincoln Miracle,* 268.

30. Achorn, *The Lincoln Miracle,* 137.

31. H. W. Beecher, "The Battle Set in Array," in *Freedom and War,* 84–110.

32. Byrd, *A Holy Baptism of Fire and Blood,* 60.

33. Gerson, *Harriet Beecher Stowe,* 154.

34. Guelzo, *Fateful Lightning,* 156.

35. Rugoff, *The Beechers,* 389.

36. Glenn, *Thomas K. Beecher,* 101.

37. Rugoff, *The Beechers,* 352.

38. Gerson, *Harriet Beecher Stowe,* 157.

39. Applegate, *The Most Famous Man in America,* 330.

40. H. B. Stowe, "The Holy War," 1; "Letter from Andover," 1.

41. Koester, *Harriet Beecher Stowe,* 235.

42. H. B. Stowe, *A Reply to "The Affectionate and Christian Address of Many Thousands of Women of Great Britain and Ireland. . . ."*

43. Thomas Beecher to Henry Ward Beecher, August 30, 1862, Beecher Family Papers, Beinecke Library, Yale University, box 8, folder 331, MS 71, ser. 1.

44. Glenn, *Thomas K. Beecher,* 105, 122.

45. Foner, *Free Soil, Free Labor, Free Men,* 141.

46. Applegate, *The Most Famous Man in America,* 331.

47. Isabella Beecher Hooker to Mary Hooker, November 19, 1862, microfiche 25, *The Isabella Beecher Hooker Project,* ed. Margolis.

48. Koester, *Harriet Beecher Stowe,* 241. See Burlingame, *An American Marriage,* 229.

49. McPherson, *Battle Cry of Freedom,* 559; Reynolds, *Abe,* 604.

50. Harriet Beecher Stowe to Hatty Stowe, November 4, 1862, box 3: A-102, M-45, 119, Beecher-Stowe Family Papers, 1798–1956.

51. Gerson, *Harriet Beecher Stowe,* 161.

52. McPherson, *Battle Cry of Freedom,* 472.

53. The quote first emerged in C. E. Stowe and L. B. Stowe, *Harriet Beecher Stowe,* 203.

54. Reynolds, *Abe,* 326.

55. Wesley Morris, "Music," in Hannah-Jones, *The 1619 Project,* 370.

56. Spingarn, *Uncle Tom,* 87.

57. Quoted in Spingarn, *Uncle Tom,* 77.

58. Reynolds, *Abe,* 326.

59. Burlingame, *An American Marriage,* 133.

60. Reynolds, *Abe,* 327.

61. Hedrick, *Harriet Beecher Stowe,* 305.

62. H. B. Stowe, *A Reply to "The Affectionate and Christian Address of Many Thousands of Women of Great Britain and Ireland . . . ,"* 46.

63. Henry, *Unvanquished Puritan,* 273.

64. Henry, *Unvanquished Puritan,* 272.

65. James Beecher to Harriet Beecher Stowe, January 27, 1862, box 1: A-102, M-45, 32, Beecher-Stowe Family Papers, 1798–1956.

66. L. B. Stowe, *Saints, Sinners, and Beechers,* 385.

67. Byrd, *A Holy Baptism of Fire and Blood,* 73.

68. Thomas K. Beecher to Lyman and Lydia Beecher, November 9, 1862, White Collection, Harriet Beecher Stowe Center.

69. Rugoff, *The Beechers,* 455.

70. John W. Dininny to Isabella Beecher Hooker, March 23, 1863, White Collection, Harriet Beecher Stowe Center.

71. Steinmetz, *American Rascal,* 28.

72. Poland, *America's Good Terrorist,* 251.

73. In Glenn, *Thomas K. Beecher,* 109.

74. Glenn, *Thomas K. Beecher,* 113.

75. Thomas K. Beecher to James Beecher, March 25, 1863, Joseph K. Hooker Collection, Harriet Beecher Stowe Center.

76. Glenn, *Thomas K. Beecher,* 113.

77. Rugoff, *The Beechers,* 457.

78. Applegate, *The Most Famous Man in America,* 9.

79. Kidd, *God of Liberty,* 59.

80. Byrd, *Sacred Scripture, Sacred War,* 133.

81. James P. Byrd explains, "the Civil War forged an alliance between spiritual and military warfare—just as the Revolutionary War had. In both wars, preachers called on a militant Christ for inspiration in military as well as spiritual struggles" (*A Holy Baptism of Fire and Blood,* 76–77).

82. Beecher's regiment eventually disbanded in June of 1866.

83. Quoted in Wilson, *Crusader in Crinoline,* 491.

84. Harding, *A Certain Magnificence,* 470.

85. L. Beecher, *A Plea for the West,* 11.

86. Hedrick, *Harriet Beecher Stowe,* 306.

87. Bacon, "Obsequies of Rev. Dr. Lyman Beecher," 5.

88. "The Last of Earth," in *Autobiography of Lyman Beecher, Vol. II,* ed. Cross, 416.

89. Caskey, *Chariot of Fire,* 192.

90. L. Beecher, *Six Sermons on the Nature, Occasions, Signs, Evils, and Remedy of Intemperance,* 93.

91. Koester, *Harriet Beecher Stowe,* 247.

92. Koester, *Harriet Beecher Stowe,* 252.

93. C. E. Stowe and L. B. Stowe, *Harriet Beecher Stowe,* 205.

94. Rugoff, *The Beechers,* 358.

95. Rugoff, *The Beechers,* 358.

96. Marsden, *Fundamentalism and American Culture,* 223.

97. "Trial of Rev. Charles Beecher for Heresy."

98. Koester, *Harriet Beecher Stowe,* 249.

99. Ch. Beecher and E. Beecher, *The Result Tested,* 23.

100. Merideth, *Politics of the Universe,* 221.

101. Merideth, *Politics of the Universe,* 224.

102. Ch. Beecher, *Redeemer and Redeemed,* ix.

103. Ch. Beecher, *Redeemer and Redeemed*, vii.

104. Buell, *New England Literary Culture*, 269.

105. Ch. Beecher, *Redeemer and Redeemed*, 287.

106. "Conclusion," in *Autobiography of Lyman Beecher, Vol. II*, ed. Cross, 435–38.

107. Marsden, *Fundamentalism and American Culture*, 23.

108. Brownson, "Beecherism and Its Tendencies," 441.

109. Ch. Beecher, *Redeemer and Redeemed*, dedication page.

110. Gerson, *Harriet Beecher Stowe*, 149–50; Koester, *Harriet Beecher Stowe*, 256.

111. Caskey, *Chariot of Fire*, 193.

112. Caskey, *Chariot of Fire*, 191.

113. Rugoff, *The Beechers*, 415.

114. Sklar, *Catharine Beecher*, 260.

115. Holmes, "The Minister Plenipotentiary."

116. Beckert, *Empire of Cotton*, 260.

117. H. W. Beecher, "Speech in the Philharmonic Hall, Liverpool, October 16, 1863," in *Patriotic Addresses in America and England*, ed. Howard, 522.

118. H. W. Beecher, *England and America*, 8.

119. Holmes, "The Minister Plenipotentiary."

120. Guelzo, *Fateful Lightning*, 298.

121. Glenn, *Thomas K. Beecher*, 120.

122. Cited in Holmes, *The Elmira Prison Camp*, 320–21.

123. Applegate, *The Most Famous Man in America*, 5.

124. H. W. Beecher, *Presentation Memorial to Working Men*, 12.

125. Donald, *Lincoln*, 237–38.

126. Emanuel Hertz to William C. Beecher, December 20, 1926, Beecher Family Papers, Beinecke Library, Yale University, box 2, folder 81, MS 71, ser. 1.

127. Rugoff, *The Beechers*, 394.

128. Applegate, *The Most Famous Man in America*, 17.

129. H. W. Beecher, *The Independent*, May 11, 1865.

130. H. W. Beecher, *Presentation Memorial to Working Men*, 16.

131. Chesebrough, *"No Sorrow Like Our Sorrow,"* 36.

132. Crane, *Sermon on the Occasion of the Death of President Lincoln*, 6.

133. Salisbury, *Sermon; Preached at West Alexandria, Ohio, April 30th, 1865*, 11.

134. H. W. Beecher, "Abraham Lincoln," in *Patriotic Addresses in America and England*, ed. Howard, 708–9.

135. Chesebrough, *"No Sorrow Like Our Sorrow,"* 63.

136. H. W. Beecher, "Conditions of a Restored Union," in *Patriotic Addresses in America and England*, ed. Howard, 716–17.

137. Applegate, *The Most Famous Man in America*, 358; McLoughlin, *The Meaning of Henry Ward Beecher*, 223.

138. Harriet Beecher Stowe to Henry Ward Beecher, October 8, 1866, typed transcript, box 44, folder 1932, MS 71, series 1, Beecher Family Papers, Beinecke Library, Yale University.

139. Foner, *A Short History of Reconstruction*, 20.

140. Guelzo, *Reconstruction*, 64–65.

141. Hart, *Redeemers, Bourbons, & Populists*, 1.

142. Henry Ward Beecher to Andrew Johnson, October 23, 1865, *The Papers of Andrew Johnson, Vol. 9*, ed. Graf et al., 269. See Levine, *The Failed Promise*, 72–74.

143. Blight, *Frederick Douglass*, 482–83.

144. H. W. Beecher, "Letter to the Convention," in *Patriotic Addresses in America and England*, ed. Howard, 739–40.

145. Applegate, *The Most Famous Man in America*, 355.

146. Rugoff, *The Beechers*, 396.

147. H. W. Beecher, "Letter to a Parishioner," in *Patriotic Addresses in America and England*, ed. Howard, 742–43.

148. Rugoff, *The Beechers*, 396.

149. L. B. Stowe, *Saints, Sinners, and Beechers*, 150.

150. Oshatz, *Slavery and Sin*, 130.

151. E. Beecher, "The Scriptural Philosophy of Congregationalism and of Councils," 312.

152. Applegate, *The Most Famous Man in America*, 355.

153. Rugoff, *The Beechers*, 449.

154. Rugoff, *The Beechers*, 450.

155. H. W. Beecher, *Norwood*, 286.

156. Hedrick, *Harriet Beecher Stowe*, 332.

157. H. B. Stowe, *Oldtown Folks*, 383.

158. Adams, "Family Influences on 'The Minister's Wooing' and 'Oldtown Folks,'" 46.

159. See Najar, *Evangelizing the South*.

160. Isaac Lane, "From Slave to Preacher among the Freemen," in *African American Religious History: A Documentary Witness*, ed. Sernett, 248.

161. Hedrick, *Harriet Beecher Stowe*, 331.

162. Harriet Beecher Stowe to Calvin Stowe and children, March 10, 1867, box 2: A-102, M-45, 85, Beecher-Stowe Family Papers, 1798–1956.

163. Koester, *Harriet Beecher Stowe*, 263.

164. Foner, *A Short History of Reconstruction*, 164.

165. See Evans, *The Mental Cure*.

166. Koester, *Harriet Beecher Stowe*, 265–66.

167. Rugoff, *The Beechers*, 414.

168. Bloomfield and Behncke, *Custer*, 237.

169. Rugoff, *The Beechers*, 363.

170. Hardesty, *Your Daughters Shall Prophesy*, 126.

171. Hardesty, *Your Daughters Shall Prophesy*, 127.

172. H. B. Stowe, "Greeting from Mrs. Stowe," 8.

173. Sklar, *Catharine Beecher*, 263.

174. White, *The Beecher Sisters*, 128.

175. Hooker, *A Mother's Letter to a Daughter on Woman Suffrage*, 3–4.

176. Isabella Beecher Hooker to Robert Allen, April 1, 1868, microfiche 38, *The Isabella Beecher Hooker Project*, ed. Margolis.

177. White, *The Beecher Sisters*, 136.

178. H. B. Stowe, *Lady Byron Vindicated*.

179. White, *The Beecher Sisters*, 228.

6. THE WOMAN (OR WOMEN) QUESTION (1870–1878)

1. Hedrick, *Harriet Beecher Stowe*, 383, 386. Her first grandchild, Georgiana's son Freeman Allen, was baptized in the Episcopal Church in 1870.

2. Dorrien, *The Making of American Liberal Theology*, 180–81.

3. Twain, "A New Beecher Church," 6.

4. Glenn, *Thomas K. Beecher*, 148, 156, 159, 160.

5. "A Review," *Elmira Daily Gazette*, March 5, 1877, clipping in Thomas Beecher Scrapbook, no. 3, p. 12, White Collection, Harriet Beecher Stowe Center.

6. James Chaplin Beecher, "Thursday, Jan. 19, 1871," Beecher Family Papers, box 72, folder 31, MS 71, ser. 3, pp. 13, 15, Beinecke Library, Yale University.

7. James Chaplin Beecher, "Friday, Jan. 20, 1871," Beecher Family Papers, box 72, folder 31, MS 71, ser. 3, p. 15, Beinecke Library, Yale University.

8. C. E. Stowe and L. B. Stowe, *Harriet Beecher Stowe*, 406.

9. Rugoff, *The Beechers*, 517, 519, 520.

10. Merideth, *The Politics of the Universe*, 226, 228.

11. Glenn, *Thomas K. Beecher*, 171.

12. Dorrien, *The Making of American Liberal Theology*, 201; Marshall, *The True History of the Beecher Scandal*, 113.

13. Theodore Tilton to Henry Ward Beecher, November 30, 1865, quoted in W. C. Beecher and S. Scoville, *A Biography of Rev. Henry Ward Beecher*, 489.

14. Editorial, *The Independent*, September 6, 1866, 1.

15. Rugoff, *The Beechers*, 400.

16. Rugoff, *The Beechers*, 472, 475.

17. Rugoff, *The Beechers*, 474.

18. Shaplen, "The Beecher-Tilton Affair."

19. Hedrick, *Harriet Beecher Stowe*, 373.

20. H. B. Stowe, *My Wife and I*, 257, 269.

21. Sklar, *Catharine Beecher*, 267.

22. Glenn, *Thomas K. Beecher*, 140.

23. White, *The Beecher Sisters*, 185.

24. Rugoff, *The Beechers*, 570.

25. Rugoff, *The Beechers*, 475.

26. Marshall, *The True History of the Beecher Scandal*, 116.

27. H. W. Beecher, "The Family as an American Institution," in *The Original Plymouth Pulpit: Sermons of Henry Ward Beecher, Vol. 1*, 425, 428.

28. H. W. Beecher, "The Family as an American Institution," 429, 430.

29. Glenn, *Thomas K. Beecher*, 155.

30. Huxley, *Collected Essays* 4: 47.

31. Glenn, *Thomas K. Beecher*, 155.

32. Bushnell, *Nature and the Supernatural*, 16–18.

33. Desmond and Moore, *Darwin*, 536.

34. D. H. Meyer, "American Intellectuals and the Victorian Crisis of Faith," in *Victorian America*, ed. Howe, 61.

35. Merideth, *The Politics of the Universe*, 227.

36. McLoughlin, *The Meaning of Henry Ward Beecher*, 250.

37. D. H. Meyer, "American Intellectuals and the Victorian Crisis of Faith," 63.

38. H. W. Beecher, "Through Fear to Love," in *The Sermons of Henry Ward Beecher, Vol. 9*, 453.

39. Quoted in *The Great Brooklyn Romance: All the Documents in the Famous Beecher-Tilton Case*, 268.

40. Quoted in Gabriel, *Notorious Victoria*, 111.

41. Applegate, *The Most Famous Man in America*, 415.

42. Merideth, *The Politics of the Universe*, 229.

43. Campbell, *Tempest-Tossed*, 115.

44. White, *The Beecher Sisters*, 214.

45. Quoted in Doyle, "*The Romance of Plymouth Church*," 508.

46. Quoted in Doyle, "*The Romance of Plymouth Church*," 509.

47. Rugoff, *The Beechers*, 490.

48. Isabella Beecher to Edward Beecher, Hartford, CT, January 16, 1873, in Merideth, *The Politics of the Universe*, 229.

49. Applegate, *The Most Famous Man in America*, 417.

50. Eacker, "Gender in Paradise," 501.

51. C. E. Stowe and L. B. Stowe, *Harriet Beecher Stowe*, 406.

52. White, *The Beecher Sisters*, 213.

53. Koester, *Harriet Beecher Stowe*, 296.

54. Thulesius, *Harriet Beecher Stowe in Florida*, 76.

55. Sklar, *Catharine Beecher*, 266.

56. C. Beecher, *Woman's Profession as Mother and Educator*, dedication page.

57. C. Beecher, *Woman's Profession as Mother and Educator*, 197–98.

58. White, *The Beecher Sisters*, 185.

59. *History of Woman Suffrage, Vol 2: 1861–1876*, ed. Stanton, Anthony, and Gage, 497.

60. "Getting a divorce," Elizabeth Cady Stanton to Susan B. Anthony, June 27, 1870, in *Elizabeth Cady Stanton as Revealed in Her Letters, Diary and Reminiscences*, ed. Stanton and Blatch, vol. 2: 127.

61. White, *The Beecher Sisters*, 193.

62. T. K. Beecher, *Our Seven Churches*, 128. According to Rugoff, *Our Seven Churches* was "a mind-opening little book and perhaps Thomas Beecher's most precious legacy. It would have astonished and confounded Lyman Beecher" (*The Beechers*, 557).

63. T. K. Beecher, *Our Seven Churches*, 141.

64. Thomas K. Beecher to Ella Wolcott, 24 January 1865, Acquisitions, Harriet Beecher Stowe Center.

65. Rugoff, *The Beechers*, 577–78.

66. Rugoff, *The Beechers*, 560.

67. H. B. Stowe, *My Wife and I*, 264.

68. Marshall, *The True History of the Beecher Scandal,* 559.

69. Marshall, *The True History of the Beecher Scandal,* 329.

70. *The Selected Papers of Elizabeth Cady Stanton & Susan B. Anthony, Volume 2: Against an Aristocracy of Sex, 1866 to 1873,* ed. Gordon, 618.

71. L. B. Stowe, *Saints, Sinners, and Beechers,* 143.

72. Hedrick, *Harriet Beecher Stowe,* 386.

73. Hedrick, *Harriet Beecher Stowe,* 387.

74. Rugoff, *The Beechers,* 578.

75. "Isabella Beecher, the Eccentric."

76. Susan B. Anthony to Isabella Beecher Hooker, October 13, 1873, microfiche 118, *The Isabella Beecher Hooker Project,* ed. Margolis.

77. Koester, *Harriet Beecher Stowe,* 288.

78. White, *The Beecher Sisters,* 227.

79. Stanton, *Chicago Tribune,* September 18, 1874.

80. Hooker, *Womanhood.*

81. C. Beecher, *Educational Reminiscences and Suggestions,* 241–42.

82. Sklar, *Catharine Beecher,* 270.

83. C. Beecher, *Educational Reminiscences and Suggestions,* 264–65.

84. H. B. Stowe, *Woman in Sacred History,* 17.

85. H. B. Stowe, *Woman in Sacred History,* 20, 298.

86. Bagby, "Will Beecher Draw?" (Chapel Hill, 1877), George W. Bagby Papers, Southern Historical Collection.

87. Lanier, "Henry Ward Beecher: A Lecture Tour of Georgia," 340.

88. White, *The Beecher Sisters,* 219.

89. Koester, *Harriet Beecher Stowe,* 294.

90. White, *The Beecher Sisters,* 211.

91. Shaplen, "The Beecher-Tilton Affair."

92. See Shaplen, *Free Love & Heavenly Sinners.*

93. Marshall, *The True History of the Beecher Scandal,* 609.

94. White, *The Beecher Sisters,* 209.

95. Koester, *Harriet Beecher Sisters,* 307.

96. Julia Beecher to Olivia Langdon, April 28, 1877, Langdon Collection, Harriet Beecher Stowe Center.

97. Hedrick, *Harriet Beecher Stowe,* 390.

98. Koester, *Harriet Beecher Stowe,* 307.

99. H. B. Stowe, "The Indians at St. Augustine," 345, 372.

100. Hayes, "The Experiment at Fort Marion," 13–14.

7. A FAMILY LIKE OURS (1878–1907)

1. Rugoff, *The Beechers,* 547, 586.

2. Drummond, *The Story of American Protestantism,* 375.

3. White, *The Beecher Sisters,* 259.

4. Elmira-area historian Nelda Holton attributed this quote to Beecher but provided no source or date for it. See her "Thomas K. Beecher," April 25, 1981, typescript, p. 1, Chemung County Historical Society, Elmira, New York.

5. McLoughlin, *The Meaning of Henry Ward Beecher*, 172.

6. *The Selected Papers of Elizabeth Cady Stanton and Susan B. Anthony, Vol. III: National Protection for National Citizens, 1873 to 1880*, ed. Gordon, 106.

7. H. B. Stowe, *Poganuc People*, 1.

8. "Introductory Note," in H. B. Stowe, *Poganuc People*, vii.

9. Hedrick, *Harriet Beecher Stowe*, 393.

10. According to Annette G. Aubert, "A strong grasp of the relationship between Protestant nineteenth-century America and Germany is essential to understanding the distinct intellectual forces at work during this period in the United States. Theological similarities should not be viewed as coincidental, but as examples of the direct influence of German theologians on their American counterparts" (*The German Roots of Nineteenth-Century American Theology*, 6–7).

11. Koester, *Harriet Beecher Stowe*, 310.

12. Koester, *Harriet Beecher Stowe*, 308.

13. Harriet Beecher Stowe to Charles Stowe, October 3, 1877, box 4: A-102, M-45, 192, Beecher-Stowe Family Papers, 1798–1956.

14. Harriet Beecher Stowe to Charles Stowe, October 3, 1877.

15. Harriet Beecher Stowe to Charles Stowe, October 3, 1877.

16. Gura, *American Transcendentalism*, 171–72.

17. "Correspondence, 1830," in *Autobiography of Lyman Beecher, Vol. I*, ed. Cross, 175.

18. "Dr. Beecher to Edward at Andover, Middletown, January, 1825," in *Autobiography of Lyman Beecher, Vol. I*, ed. Cross, 10.

19. Phillips, *Edwards Amasa Park*, 218.

20. White, *The Beecher Sisters*, 268.

21. Hedrick, *Harriet Beecher Stowe*, 394.

22. Anonymous, "The Birthday Garden Party to Harriet Beecher Stowe," 1882, in Susan Belasco, ed., *Stowe in Her Own Time*, 202.

23. "Amusements," *Boston Daily Globe*, June 19, 1888.

24. White, *The Beecher Sisters*, 274.

25. *Life and Letters of Harriet Beecher Stowe*, ed. Annie Fields, 387. See Foster and Foster, *Beechers, Stowes, and Yankee Strangers*.

26. White, *The Beecher Sisters*, 266.

27. Glenn, *Thomas K. Beecher*, 164.

28. Glenn, *Thomas K. Beecher*, 168.

29. H. W. Beecher, "Divine Love," in *Plymouth Pulpit: Sermons Preached in Plymouth Church, Brooklyn (September 1874–March 1875)*, 373.

30. Rugoff, *The Beechers*, 505.

31. Nasaw, *Andrew Carnegie*, 226–27.

32. H. W. Beecher, *Lectures and Orations*, ed. Hillis, 318, 323.

33. H. W. Beecher, "Foundation Work," in *Plymouth Pulpit: Sermons Preached in Plymouth Church, Brooklyn (September 1874–March 1875)*, 309.

34. Paxton, *Henry Ward Beecher*, 340.

35. Rugoff, *The Beechers*, 522–23.

36. Rugoff, *The Beechers*, 522.

37. Rugoff, *The Beechers*, 522.

38. Rugoff, *The Beechers*, 522.

39. Goodyear, *President Garfield*, 389.

40. Merrill, *Bourbon Leader*, 65.

41. Merrill, *Bourbon Leader*, 61–62, 66–67.

42. Applegate, *The Most Famous Man in America*, 463.

43. H. W. Beecher, "The Inspiration of the Bible," in *Evolution and Religion, Part 1*, 56.

44. Koester, *Harriet Beecher Stowe*, 309.

45. *The Limits of Sisterhood*, ed. Boydston, Kelley, and Margolis, 355.

46. T. K. Beecher, "The Fear of Death," *Elmira Daily Gazette*, March 9, 1872. A clipping of this sermon can be found in Thomas Beecher's scrapbooks (1853–1910) in the White Collection at the Harriet Beecher Stowe Center.

47. Baker, *Mary Todd Lincoln*, 220; Apkarian-Russell, *Washington's Haunted Past*, 45.

48. Twain, "The New Wildcat Religion."

49. Sklar, *Catharine Beecher*, 272.

50. White, *The Beecher Sisters*, 279.

51. *Life and Letters of Phillips Brooks, Vol. III*, ed. Allen. Mark Twain to Joseph Twichell, March 14, 1887, Joseph Twichell's Journal, vol. 5: 121, Joseph Hopkins Twichell Papers.

52. Fosdick, "Christian Faith—Fantasy or Truth?" 32. Also see Miller, *Harry Emerson Fosdick*, 100, 109, 110. White, *The Beecher Sisters*, 281.

53. Applegate, *The Most Famous Man in America*, 467–68.

54. T. K. Beecher, "My Brother Henry," in *Notable Sermons, Vol. I*, 7.

55. T. K. Beecher, "My Brother Henry," 13–14.

56. Rugoff, *The Beechers*, 518.

57. Merideth, *The Politics of the Universe*, 224.

58. C. E. Stowe and L. B. Stowe, *Harriet Beecher Stowe*, 509.

59. Glenn, *Thomas K. Beecher*, 163.

60. White, *The Beecher Sisters*, 296.

61. Rugoff, *The Beechers*, 593.

62. Merideth, *The Politics of the Universe*, 230.

63. I. B. Hooker, "Confession of Faith," 305.

64. I. B. Hooker, "The Last of the Beechers," 286.

65. I. B. Hooker, "Home Life of Isabella Beecher Hooker," 301.

Bibliography

PRIMARY SOURCES

Manuscript Collections

Beinecke Library, Yale University
    Beecher Family Papers.
    Joseph Hopkins Twichell Papers.
Schlesinger Library, Radcliffe Institute, Harvard University
    Beecher-Stowe Family Papers, 1798–1956.
Southern Historical Collection, University of North Carolina Library
    George W. Bagby Papers.
Harriet Beecher Stowe Center, Hartford, CT
    Acquisitions.
    Joseph K. Hooker Collection.
    Langdon Collection.
    White Collection.
University of Virginia
    The Papers of Andrew Jackson, Digital Edition, ed. Daniel Feller. Charlottes-
        ville, 2015.

Newspaper and Magazine Articles

"Amusements." *Boston Daily Globe,* June 19, 1888.
Bacon, Leonard. "Obsequies of Rev. Dr. Lyman Beecher." *New York Times,* Janu-
    ary 15, 1863, 5.
Beecher, Henry Ward. *Christian Union,* December 6, 1871.
——. "The Fugitive Slave Bill at Its Work." *The Independent,* January 16, 1851, 10.
——. *The Independent,* May 11, 1850.
Beecher, Thomas K. The Fear of Death." *Elmira Daily Gazette,* March 9, 1872.
Biblical Repository and Princeton Review, October 1857.

Birney, James. "Ohio Threatened." *The Philanthropist*, December 18, 1838, 3.

Cincinnati Journal, May 19, 1836.

Editorial. *The Independent*, September 6, 1866, 1.

Hodge, Charles. Review of *The Conflict*. *Princeton Review* 26 (January 1854): 96–97.

Holmes, Oliver Wendell. "The Minister Plenipotentiary." *The Atlantic*, January 1864.

Hooker, Isabella Beecher. "Confession of Faith." *Connecticut Magazine* 9 (Spring 1905): 305.

———. "Home Life of Isabella Beecher Hooker." *Connecticut Magazine* 9 (Spring 1905).

———. "The Last of the Beechers: Memories on My Eighty-Third Birthday." *Connecticut Magazine* 9 (Spring 1905).

"Isabella Beecher, the Eccentric." *Hartford Courant*, August 26, 2001. www.courant. com/2001/08/26/isabella-beecher-the-eccentric.

King, Thomas Starr. Review of *The Conflict*. *Universalist Quarterly and General Review* 11 (January 1854): 34–35.

Ladies' Home Journal 9, no. 2 (1892): 5.

"Lane Seminary." *Vermont Chronicle*, November 7, 1834.

"More Uncle Tom Material." *Little Rock* (AR) *True Democrat*, January 25, 1853. utc. iath.virginia.edu/proslav/prar183at.html.

"Mrs. Stowe and *Dred*." *Southern Literary Messenger*. October 1858. In *"Uncle Tom's Cabin" and American Culture*, ed. Stephen Railton. utc.iath.virginia.edu/proslav/prar24jt.html.

New York Evangelist, March 22, 1834.

New York Tribune, March 3, 1848.

"Parson Brownlow's Opinion of Harriet Beecher Stowe." *Little Rock* (AR) *State Gazette & Democrat*. August 5, 1853. utc.iath.virginia.edu/proslav/prar179ct.html.

"A Review." *Elmira Daily Gazette*, March 5, 1877.

Riddle, Alfred G. "Discovery of Henry Ward Beecher." *Magazine of Western History* 5 (1887): 854–57.

"The Slave-Law and the Union." *The Independent*, January 16, 1851, 10.

Stanton, Elizabeth Cady. *Chicago Tribune*, September 18, 1874.

Stowe, Harriet Beecher. "The Drunkard Reclaimed." *New York Evangelist*, November 30–December 7, 1839.

———. "Greeting from Mrs. Stowe." *Hearth and Home*, December 26, 1868, 8.

———. "The Holy War." *The Independent*, May 9, 1861, 1.

———. "Immediate Emancipation: A Sketch." *New-York Evangelist*, January 2, 1845, 1.

———. "The Indians at St. Augustine." *Christian Union*, April 18 and 25, 345, 372.

———. "Letter from Andover: The Times, the British People, the Havelock Grays, the Andover Company." *The Independent*, June 20, 1861, 1.

Stowe, Lyman Beecher. "The First of the Beechers." *The Atlantic*, August 1933.

"Trial of Rev. Charles Beecher for Heresy." *Michigan Argus*, July 24, 1863.

Twain, Mark. "A New Beecher Church." *New York Times*, July 23, 1871, 6.

———. "The New Wildcat Religion." *The Golden Era* March 4, 1866. www.twain-quotes.com/Era/18660304.html.

Wilson, Joshua. *Christian Register*, February 11, 1832.

Other Published Primary Sources

Abzug, Robert H. *Passionate Liberator: Theodore Dwight Weld and the Dilemma of Reform*. New York: Oxford University Press, 1980.

Allardt, Linda, ed. *Journals and Miscellaneous Notebooks of Ralph Waldo Emerson, vol. 15*. Cambridge, MA: Harvard University Press, 1982.

Barnes, Gilbert H., and Dwight L. Dumond, eds. *Letters of Theodore Dwight Weld, Angelina Grimké Weld, and Sarah Grimké, Vol. I*. Gloucester: Peter Smith, 1964.

Beecher, Catharine E. *An Address to the Protestant Clergy of the United States*. New York: Harper & Brothers, 1846.

———. *An Appeal to the People in Behalf of Their Rights as Authorized Interpreters of the Bible*. New York: Harper & Brothers, 1860.

———. *The Biographical Remains of Rev. George Beecher*. New York: Leavitt, Trow and Co. 1844.

———. "Circular Addressed to the Benevolent Ladies of the U. States," December 25, 1829. In Theda Purdue and Michael D. Green, eds., *The Cherokee Removal: A Brief History with Documents*, 2nd ed. Boston: Bedford, 2005. 111–14.

———. *Common Sense Applied to Religion; Or, The Bible and the People*. New York: Harper & Brothers, 1857.

———. *The Duty of American Women to their Country*. New York: Harper & Brothers, 1845.

———. *Educational Reminiscences and Suggestions*. New York: J. B. Ford and Co., 1874.

———. *Essay on Education of Female Teachers*. New York: Van Nostrand & Dwight, 1835.

———. *Essay on Slavery and Abolitionism with Reference to the Duty of American Females*. Philadelphia: Henry Perkins, 1837.

———. *Evils Suffered by American Women and American Children: The Causes and the Remedy*. New York: Harper & Brothers, 1846.

——. "Female Education." *American Journal of Education* 2, no. 4–5 (1829): 221.

——. *Letters on the Difficulties of Religion.* Hartford, CT: Belknap & Hamersley, 1836.

——. *Letters to the People on Health and Happiness.* New York: Harper & Brothers, 1855.

——. *The Religious Training of Children in the Family, the School, and the Church.* New York: Harper & Brothers, 1864.

——. *A Treatise on Domestic Economy.* New York: Harper & Brothers, 1848.

——. *Woman's Profession as Mother and Educator with Views in Opposition to Woman Suffrage.* Philadelphia: Geo. Maclean, 1872.

——, and Harriet B. Stowe. *The American Woman's Home: Principles of Domestic Science.* New York: J. B. Ford & Co., 1869.

Beecher, Charles. *The Bible a Sufficient Creed.* Boston: J. V. Himes, 1846.

——. *The Duty of Disobedience to Wicked Laws: A Sermon on the Fugitive Slave Law.* New York: John A. Gray, 1851.

——. *The God of the Bible Against Slavery.* New York: American Anti-Slavery Society, 1855.

——. "The Life of Edward Beecher." Unpublished manuscript, 543 pages. Edward Beecher Collection, Illinois College Schewe Library.

——. *Redeemer and Redeemed: An Investigation of the Atonement and of Eternal Judgment.* Boston: Lee and Shepard, 1864.

——, and Edward Beecher. *The Result Tested: A Review of the Proceedings of a Council at Georgetown, Massachusetts, August 15, 16, and 22, 1863.* Boston: Wright & Porter, 1863.

——. *A Review of the "Spiritual Manifestations."* New York: G. B. Putnam & Co., 1853.

Beecher, Edward. *The Conflict of Ages; or The Great Debate on the Moral Relations of God and Man.* Boston: Phillips, Sampson, & Co., 1853.

——. *History of Opinions on the Scriptural Doctrine of Retribution.* New York: D. Appleton and Co., 1878.

——. *A Narrative of Riots at Alton: In Connection with the Death of Rev. Elijah P. Lovejoy.* Alton, IL: George Holton, 1838.

——. "The Nature, Importance, and Means of Eminent Holiness Throughout the Church." December 31, 1835. From *Teaching American History.* teachingamericanhistory.org/document/eminent-holiness-throughout-the-church/.

——. *Papal Conspiracy Exposed, and Protestantism Defended, in the Light of Reason, History and Scripture.* Boston: Stearns & Co., 1855.

——. "The Scriptural Philosophy of Congregationalism and of Councils." *Bibliotheca Sacra* 22 (April 1865): 284–315.

Beecher, Harriet, and Catharine Beecher. *Primary Geography for Children, on an Improved Plan: with eleven maps and numerous engravings.* Cincinnati: Corey and Fairbank, 1833.

Beecher, Henry Ward. *England and America: Speech of Henry Ward Beecher at the Free-Trade Hall, Manchester, October 9, 1863.* Boston: James Redpath, 1863.

——. *Eulogy on General Grant.* New York: Jenkins & McCowan, 1885.

——. *Evolution and Religion, Part 1.* Boston: Pilgrim Press, 1885.

——. *Freedom and War: Discourses on Topics Suggested by the Times.* Boston: Ticknor and Fields, 1863.

——. *Lectures to Young Men and Various Important Subjects.* New York: John B. Alden, 1890.

——. *Norwood; Or, Village Life in New England.* New York: Charles Scribner & Co., 1868.

——. *The Original Plymouth Pulpit: Sermons of Henry Ward Beecher, Vol. 1: September, 1868 to March, 1869.* New York: Fords, Howard & Hulbert, 1893.

——. *Plymouth Pulpit: Sermons Preached in Plymouth Church, Brooklyn (September 1874–March 1875).* New York: Fords, Howard, & Hulbert, 1892.

——. *Presentation Memorial to Working Men: Oration at the Raising of "The Old Flag" at Sumter; and Sermon on the Oath of Abraham Lincoln, President of the United States.* Manchester, UK: Alexander Ireland and Co., 1865.

——. *Sermons by Henry Ward Beecher, Plymouth Church, Brooklyn, Vol. II.* New York: Harper & Brothers, 1869.

——. *Sermons by the Rev. Henry Ward Beecher, Vol. 1.* London: J. Heaton & Son, 1859.

——. *The Sermons of Henry Ward Beecher, Vol. 9: September, 1872 to March, 1873.* New York: J. B. Ford & Co., 1874.

——. "William Ellery Channing." In *Lectures and Orations,* ed. Newell Dwight Hillis. New York: Fleming H. Revell Co., 1913.

Beecher, Lyman. *The Bible a Code of Laws.* Andover, MA: Flagg, 1818.

——. *The Faith Once Delivered to the Saints: A Sermon, Delivered at Worcester, Mass. Oct. 15, 1823, at the Ordination of the Rev. Loammi Ives Hoadly.* Boston: Crocker and Brewster, 1824.

——. *The Gospel According to Paul: A Sermon Delivered Sept. 17, 1828, at the Installation of the Rev. Bennet Tyler, D.D. as Pastor of the Second Congregational Church in Portland, Maine.* Boston: T. R. Marvin, 1829.

——. *The Memory of Our Fathers: A Sermon Delivered at Plymouth.* Boston: T. R. Marvin, 1828.

——. *A Plea for the West.* Cincinnati: Truman & Smith, 1835.

——. *A Reformation of Moral Practical and Indispensable: A Sermon Delivered at New-Haven on the Evening of October 27, 1812.* Andover, MA: Flagg and Gould, 1814.

———. *The Remedy for Duelling.* New York: J. Seymour, 1809.

———. "The Republican Elements of the Old Testament." In *Beecher's Works, Vol. 1: Lectures on Political Atheism.* Boston: John P. Jewett & Co., 1852.

———. "Resources of the Adversary, and Means of Their Destruction." In *Sermons, Delivered on Various Occasions,* in *Beecher's Works, Vol. II.* Boston: John P. Jewett & Co., 1852.

———. *Six Sermons on the Nature, Occasions, Signs, Evils, and Remedy of Intemperance.* New York: American Tract Society, 1827.

———. *Views in Theology.* Cincinnati: Truman and Smith, 1836.

Beecher, Thomas K. *Notable Sermons, Vol. I.* Elmira: Osborne Press, 1914.

———. *Our Seven Churches.* New York: J. B. Ford & Co., 1870.

———. Scrapbooks (1853–1910). White Collection. Harriet Beecher Stowe Center. Hartford, CT.

———. Typescript. Chemung County Historical Society, Elmira, New York.

Beecher, William Constantine, and Samuel Scoville. *A Biography of Rev. Henry Ward Beecher.* New York: Charles L. Webster & Co., 1888.

Brooks, Phillips. In *Life and Letters of Phillips Brooks, Vol. III.,* ed. Alexander V. G. Allen. New York: E. P. Dutton and Co., 190.

Brownson, Henry F. ed. *The Works of Orestes A. Brownson, Vol. III.* Detroit: Thorndike Nourse, 1883.

Brownson, Orestes Augustus. "Beecherism and Its Tendencies." *Catholic World* 12, no. 70 (January 1871): 433–50.

Bushnell, Horace. *Christian Nurture.* New York: Scribner, Armstrong, & Co., 1876.

———. *Nature and the Supernatural, as Together Constituting One System of God.* New York: Scribner, 1858.

Campbell, Alexander, and John B. Purcell. *A Debate on the Roman Catholic Religion between Alexander Campbell and Rt. Rev. John B. Purcell.* New York: Benziger Brothers, 1837.

Cartwright, Peter. *The Backwoods Preacher: The Autobiography of Peter Cartwright.* London: Alexander Heylin, 1858.

Channing, William E. *Self-Culture: An Address Introductory to the Franklin Lectures.* Boston: Dutton and Wentworth, 1838.

Clay, Henry. "Speech of Mr. Clay, of Kentucky, in the Senate of the United States, February 5 and 6, 1850." *Appendix to the Congressional Globe* 1 (February 6, 1850): 127.

Crane, C. B. *Sermon on the Occasion of the Death of President Lincoln.* Hartford, CT: Press of Case, Lockwood and Co., 1865.

Cross, Barbara M. ed. *The Autobiography of Lyman Beecher, Vols. 1–2.* Cambridge, MA: Harvard University Press, 1961.

Edwards, Jonathan. *Freedom of the Will.* In *The Works of Jonathan Edwards,* vol. 1: *Freedom of the Will,* ed. Paul Ramsey. New Haven, CT: Yale University Press, 2009.

Evans, W. F. *The Mental Cure, Illustrating the Influence of the Mind on the Body, Both in Health and in Disease, and the Psychological Method of Treatment.* Boston: Colby and Rich, 1884.

Flint, Timothy. *Recollections of the Last Ten Years, Passed in Occasional Residences and Journeyings in the Valley of the Mississippi, from Pittsburg and the Missouri to the Gulf of Mexico, and from Florida to the Spanish Frontier.* Boston: Cummins, Hilliard, and Co., 1826.

Fosdick, Harry Emerson. "Christian Faith—Fantasy or Truth?" In *Living Under Tension: Sermons on Christianity Today.* New York: Harper & Brothers, 1941.

Garrison, William Lloyd. *Garrison's First Anti-Slavery Address in Boston: Address at Park Street Church, Boston, July 4, 1829.* Boston: Directors of the Old South Work, 1907.

Gordon, Ann. ed. *The Selected Papers of Elizabeth Cady Stanton and Susan B. Anthony, Volume II: Against an Aristocracy of Sex 1866–1873.* New Brunswick: Rutgers University Press, 2000.

Graf, Leroy P., et al. *The Papers of Andrew Johnson. Vol. 9.* Knoxville: University of Tennessee Press, 1991.

Gray, Thomas R. *The Confessions of Nat Turner, the Leader of the Late Insurrection in Southampton, VA.* Baltimore, 1831.

Henson, Josiah. *The Life of Josiah Henson, Formerly a Slave, Now an Inhabitant of Canada.* Boston: Arthur D. Phelps, 1849.

Hooker, Isabella Beecher. *"A Mother's Letter to a Daughter on Woman Suffrage." Putnam's Monthly, November and December, 1868.*

———. *Womanhood: Its Sanctities and Fidelities.* Boston: Lee and Shephard, 1873.

Howard, John R. ed. *Patriotic Addresses in America and England, from 1850 to 1885, on Slavery, the Civil War, and the Development of Civil Liberty in the United States.* New York: Fords, Howard, & Hulbert, 1891.

Huxley, Thomas Henry. *Collected Essays.* New York: Greenwood, 1968.

Ingersoll, Robert G. *The Works of Robert G. Ingersoll, Volume XII.* New York: Cosimo Classics, 2009.

Lincoln, Abraham. "Resolutions." *Congressional Globe,* December 22. Washington, DC: Blair & Rives, 1847. 64–65.

Mahan, Asa. *Autobiography: Intellectual, Moral, and Spiritual.* London: T. Woolmer, 1882.

Mell, P. H. *Slavery, A Treatise, Showing That Slavery Is Neither a Moral, Political, Nor Social Evil*. Penfield, GA: Benj. Brantly, 1844.

Melville, Herman. *Moby-Dick; or, The Whale*. 1851. Rpt. New York: Penguin Books, 1992.

Peck, John Mason. *Forty Years of Pioneer Life: Memoir of John Mason Peck, D.D.*, ed. Rufus Babcock. Philadelphia: American Baptist Publication Society, 1864.

Riley, William Bell. *God Hath Spoken*. Philadelphia: Bible Conference Committee, 1919.

Salisbury, S. *Sermon; Preached at West Alexandria, Ohio, April 30th, 1865*. Eaton, OH: Eaton Weekly Register, 1865.

Sernett, Milton C. ed. *African American Religious History: A Documentary Witness*. Durham, NC: Duke University Press, 1999.

Smith, Harriet Elinor, ed. *Autobiography of Mark Twain, Volume 1*. Berkeley: University of California Press, 2010.

Spurgeon, Susannah. ed. *The Autobiography of Charles H. Spurgeon, Compiled from His Diary, Letters, and Records, Vol. IV: 1878-1892*. Philadelphia: American Baptist Publication Society, 1892.

Stanton, Theodore, and Harriet Stanton Blatch, eds. *Elizabeth Cady Stanton as Revealed in Her Letters, Diary and Reminiscences. Vol. 2*. New York: Harper & Brothers, 1922.

Stowe, Calvin E. *The Origin and History of the Books of the Bible, Both the Canonical and the Apocryphal, Designed to Show What the Bible Is Not, What It Is, and How to Use It*. Hartford, CT: Hartford Publishing Co., 1868.

Stowe, Charles Edward. *Life of Harriet Beecher Stowe: Compiled from Her Letters and Journals*. Boston: Houghton, Mifflin and Co., 1889.

Stowe, Charles Edward, and Lyman Beecher Stowe. *Harriet Beecher Stowe: The Story of Her Life*. Boston: Houghton Mifflin Co., 1911.

Stowe, Harriet Beecher. *Dred; A Tale of the Great Dismal Swamp*. Boston: Phillips, Sampson and Co., 1856.

——. *Lady Byron Vindicated: A History of the Byron Controversy, From Its Beginning in 1816 to the Present Time*. Boston: Fields, Osgood, & Co., 1870.

——. *Men of Our Times*. Hartford, CT: Hartford Publishing Co., 1868.

——. *The Minister's Wooing*. New York: Penguin Books, 1999.

——. *My Wife and I*. New York: J. B. Ford & Co., 1871.

——. *Oldtown Folks*. Montreal: Dawson Brothers, 1869.

——. *Poganuc People: Their Loves and Lives, and Pink and White Tyranny: A Society Novel*. Boston: Houghton, Mifflin and Co., 1896.

——. *A Reply to "The Affectionate and Christian Address of Many Thousands of Women of Great Britain and Ireland, to their Sisters, the Women of the United States of America."* London: Sampson Low, Son, and Co., 1863.

———. *Sunny Memories of Foreign Lands.* London: George Vickers, Angel Court, Strand, 1854.

———. "Uncle Tom's Cabin; or, Life among the Lowly." *The Liberator,* March 26, 1852. In *"Uncle Tom's Cabin" and American Culture,* ed. Stephen Railton. utc. iath.virginia.edu.

———. *Uncle Tom's Cabin, or, Life Among the Lowly.* Ed. Ann Douglas. New York: Penguin Books, 1986.

———. *Woman in Sacred History: A Series of Sketches.* Boston: J. B. Ford and Co., 1873.

Stowe, Lyman Beecher. *Saints, Sinners and Beechers.* Indianapolis: Bobbs-Merrill Co., 1934.

Strong, Sydney. "The Exodus of Students from Lane Seminary to Oberlin in 1834." *Papers of the Ohio Church History Society* 4 (1893): 1–16.

Thoreau, Henry D. *Walden; or, Life in the Woods.* 1854. Rpt. New York: Thomas Y. Crowell & Co., 1910.

Thornwell, J. H. *The Rights and Duties of Masters.* Charleston, SC: Steam-Power Press of Walker & James, 1850.

Tocqueville, Alexis de. *Democracy in America.* Trans. Henry Reeve. New York: D. Appleton and Co., 1899.

Trollope, Frances. *Domestic Manners of the Americans, Vol. I.* London: Whittaker, Treacher, & Co., 1832.

Van Why, Joseph S., and Earl French, eds. *Harriet Beecher Stowe in Europe: The Journal of Charles Beecher.* Hartford, CT: Stowe-Day Foundation, 1986.

Washington, Booker T. *Up From Slavery.* 1901. Rpt. New York: Dover Publications, 1995.

Weld, Timothy Dwight. ed. *American Slavery as It Is: Testimony of a Thousand Witnesses.* New York: American Anti-Slavery Society, 1839.

Whitefield, George. *George Whitefield's Journals (1737–1741).* Ed. William V. David. Edinburgh: Banner of Truth Trust, 1986.

Whittier, John Greenleaf. "Ichabod." In *The Poetical Works of John Greenleaf Whittier,* vol. 4. Boston: Houghton, Mifflin and Co., 1892. 61–62.

Zunz, Oliver. ed. *Alexis de Tocqueville and Gustave de Beaumont in America: Their Friendship and Their Travels.* Charlottesville: University of Virginia Press, 2011.

SECONDARY SOURCES

Achorn, Edward. *The Lincoln Miracle: Inside the Republican Convention That Changed History.* New York: Atlantic Monthly Press, 2023.

Adams, Kimberly VanEsveld. "Family Influences on 'The Minister's Wooing' and 'Oldtown Folks': Henry Ward Beecher and Calvin Stowe." *Religion & Literature* 38, no. 4 (Winter 2006): 27–61.

Allen, D. Howe. *The Life and Services of Rev. Lyman Beecher as President and Professor of Theology in Lane Seminary.* Cincinnati: Johnson, Stephens & Co., 1863.

Apkarian-Russell, Pamela E. *Washington's Haunted Past: Capital Ghosts of America.* Charleston, SC: Arcadia Publishing, 2006.

Applegate, Debby. *The Most Famous Man in America: The Biography of Henry Ward Beecher.* New York: Doubleday, 2006.

Aubert, Annette G. *The German Roots of Nineteenth-Century American Theology.* New York: Oxford University Press, 2013.

Austen, Lucy S. R. *Elisabeth Elliot: A Life.* Wheaton: Crossway, 2023.

Baker, Jean H. *Mary Todd Lincoln: A Biography.* New York: W. W. Norton & Co., 1989.

Baldwin, James. *Everybody's Protest Novel.* Durham, NC: Duke University Press, 1955.

Bebbington, David W. *Evangelicalism in Modern Britain: A History from the 1730s to the 1980s.* Abingdon, UK: Routledge, 1989.

Beckert, Sven. *Empire of Cotton: A Global History.* New York: Vintage Books, 2014.

Belasco, Susan, ed., *Stowe in Her Own Time: A Biographical Chronicle of Her Life, Drawn from Recollections, Interviews, and Memoirs by Family, Friends, and Associates.* Iowa City: University of Iowa Press, 2009.

Bell, John Frederick. *Degrees of Equality: Abolitionist Colleges and the Politics of Race.* Baton Rouge: Louisiana State University Press, 2022.

Blight, David W. *Frederick Douglass: Prophet of Freedom.* New York: Simon & Schuster, 2018.

Bloomfield, Gary L., and Ted Behncke. *Custer: From the Civil War's Boy General to the Battle of the Little Bighorn.* Philadelphia: Casemate, 2020.

Bowman, Matthew, and Samuel Brown. "Reverend Buck's Theological Dictionary and the Struggle to Define American Evangelicalism, 1802–1851." *Journal of the Early Republic* 29, no. 3 (Fall 2009): 441–73.

Boydston, Jeanne, Mary Kelley, and Anne Margolis, eds. *The Limits of Sisterhood: The Beecher Sisters on Women's Rights and Woman's Sphere.* Chapel Hill: University of North Carolina Press, 1988.

Bratt. James D. ed. *Antirevivalism in Antebellum America: A Collection of Religious Voices.* New Brunswick, NJ: Rutgers University Press, 2006.

Breen, Patrick H. *The Land Shall Be Deluged in Blood: A New History of the Nat Turner Revolt.* New York: Oxford University Press, 2015.

Brophy, Alfred L. "'Over and above . . . There Broods a Portentous Shadow,—The Shadow of Law': Harriet Beecher Stowe's Critique of Slave Law in 'Uncle Tom's Cabin.'" *Journal of Law and Religion* 12, no. 2 (1995–96): 457–506.

Budiansky, Stephen. *Oliver Wendell Holmes: A Life in War, Law, and Ideas.* New York: W. W. Norton & Co., 2019.

Buell, Lawrence. *New England Literary Culture: From Revolution through Renaissance.* Cambridge, UK: Cambridge University Press, 1986.

Burlingame, Michael. *An American Marriage: The Untold Story of Abraham Lincoln and Mary Todd.* New York: Pegasus Books, 2021.

Burstyn, Joan N. "Catharine Beecher and the Education of American Women." *New England Quarterly* 47, no. 3 (1974): 386–403.

Butler, Diana Hochstedt. *Standing Against the Whirlwind: Evangelical Episcopalians in Nineteenth-Century America.* New York: Oxford University Press, 1995.

Byrd, James P. *A Holy Baptism of Fire and Blood: The Bible and the American Civil War.* New York: Oxford University Press, 2021.

———. *Sacred Scripture, Sacred War: The Bible and the American Revolution.* New York: Oxford University Press, 2013.

Campbell, Susan. *Tempest-Tossed: The Spirit of Isabella Beecher Hooker.* Middletown, CT: Wesleyan University Press, 2014.

Carwardine, Richard J. *Evangelicals and Politics in Antebellum America.* New Haven, CT: Yale University Press, 1993.

Caskey, Marie. *Chariot of Fire: Religion and the Beecher Family.* New Haven, CT: Yale University Press, 1978.

Chesebrough, David B. *"No Sorrow Like Our Sorrow": Northern Protestant Ministers and the Assassination of Lincoln.* Kent, OH: Kent State University Press, 1994.

Chinard, Gilbert. *Honest John Adams.* Boston: Little, Brown, and Co., 1964.

Clark, Clifford E. Jr. *Henry Ward Beecher: Spokesman for a Middle-Class America.* Urbana: University of Illinois Press, 1978.

Crisp, Oliver D., and Douglas A. Sweeney, eds. *After Jonathan Edwards: The Courses of the New England Theology.* New York: Oxford University Press, 2012.

Cross, Whitney R. *The Burned-Over District: The Social and Intellectual History of Enthusiastic Religion in Western New York, 1800–1850.* New York: Harper & Row, 1965.

Davis, David Brion. *Inhuman Bondage: The Rise and Fall of Slavery in the New World.* New York: Oxford University Press, 2006.

Delbanco, Andrew. *The War Before the War: Fugitive Slaves and the Struggle for America's Soul from the Revolution to the Civil War.* New York: Penguin Books, 2018.

Desmond, Adrian, and James Moore. *Darwin: The Life of a Tormented Evolutionist.* New York: W. W. Norton & Co., 1994.

Dillon, Merton L. *Elijah P. Lovejoy.* Urbana: University of Illinois Press, 1961.

Dochuk, Darren. *Anointed with Oil: How Christianity and Crude Made Modern America.* New York: Basic Books, 2019.

Donald, David Herbert. *Lincoln.* New York: Simon & Schuster, 1995.

Dorrien, Gary. *The Making of American Liberal Theology: Imagining Progressive Religion, 1805-1900.* Louisville, KY: Westminster John Knox, 2001.

Douglas, Ann. *The Feminization of American Culture.* New York: Doubleday, 1988.

Doyle, J. E. P. *"The Romance of Plymouth Church."* Not published.

Dreisbach, Daniel. *Thomas Jefferson and the Wall of Separation Between Church and State.* New York: New York University Press, 2002.

Drummond, Andrew Landale. *The Story of American Protestantism.* Boston: Beacon Press, 1950.

Dunn, James Taylor, ed. "Cincinnati Is a Delightful Place: Letters of a Law Clerk, 1831-34." *Bulletin of the Historical and Philosophical Society of Ohio* 10 (October 1952): 256-77.

Eacker, Susan A. "Gender in Paradise: Harriet Beecher Stowe and Postbellum Prose on Florida." *Journal of Southern History* 64, no. 3 (August 1998): 495-512.

Elder, Robert. *Calhoun: American Heretic.* New York: Basic Books, 2021.

Fields, Annie, ed. *Life and Letters of Harriet Beecher Stowe.* Boston: Houghton, Mifflin, and Co., 1897.

Flexner, Eleanor, and Ellen Fitzpatrick. *Century of Struggle: The Woman's Rights Movement in the United States.* Cambridge, MA: Harvard University Press, 1996.

Foner, Eric. *Free Soil, Free Labor, Free Men: The Ideology of the Republican Party before the Civil War.* New York: Oxford University Press, 1970.

———. *A Short History of Reconstruction, 1863-1877.* New York: HarperCollins, 2014.

Foster, Charles I. *An Errand of Mercy: The Evangelical United Front, 1790-1837.* Chapel Hill: University of North Carolina Press, 1960.

Foster, John T. Jr., and Sarah Whitmer Foster. *Beechers, Stowes, and Yankee Strangers: The Transformation of Florida.* Gainesville: University Press of Florida, 1999.

Fraser, James W. *Pedagogue for God's Kingdom: Lyman Beecher and the Second Great Awakening.* Lanham, MD: University Press of America, 1975.

Fredrickson, George. *The Black Image in the White Mind.* Middletown, CT: Wesleyan University Press, 1987.

Gabriel, Mary. *Notorious Victoria: The Uncensored Life of Victoria Woodhull—*

Visionary, Suffragist, and First Woman to Run for President. Chapel Hill, NC: Algonquin Books, 1998.

Gerson, Noel B. *Harriet Beecher Stowe.* New York: Praeger Publishers, 1976.

Glaab, Charles N. "Visions of Metropolis: William Gilpin and Theories of City Growth in the American West." *Wisconsin Magazine of History* 45, no. l (Autumn 1961): 21–31.

Glenn, Myra C. *Thomas K. Beecher: Minister to a Changing America, 1824–1900.* Westport, CT: Greenwood Press, 1996.

Goen, C. C. *Broken Churches, Broken Nation: Denominational Schisms and the Coming of the Civil War.* Macon, GA: Mercer University Press, 1985.

Goodin, S. H. "Cincinnati—Its Destiny." In *Sketches and Statistics of Cincinnati in 1851,* ed. Charles Cist, 306–20. Cincinnati, 1851.

Goodyear, C. W. *President Garfield: From Radical to Unifier.* New York: Simon & Schuster, 2023.

Gordon, Bruce. *John Calvin's Institutes of the Christian Religion: A Biography.* Princeton, NJ: Princeton University Press, 2016.

The Great Brooklyn Romance: All the Documents in the Famous Beecher-Tilton Case, Unabridged. New York: J. H. Paxon, 1874.

Gross, Robert A. *The Transcendentalists and Their World.* New York: Farrar, Straus and Giroux, 2021.

Guelzo, Allen C. *Fateful Lightning: A New History of the Civil War and Reconstruction.* New York: Oxford University Press, 2012.

———. *Reconstruction: A Concise History.* New York: Oxford University Press, 2018.

Gura, Philip F. *American Transcendentalism: A History.* New York: Hill & Wang, 2008.

Hambrick-Stowe, Charles E. *Charles G. Finney and the Spirit of American Evangelicalism.* Grand Rapids, MI: Eerdmans, 1996.

Hankins, Barry. *Woodrow Wilson: Ruling Elder, Spiritual President.* New York: Oxford University Press, 2016.

Hannah-Jones, Nikole. *The 1619 Project: A New Origin Story.* London: One World, 2021.

Hardesty, Nancy A. *Your Daughters Shall Prophesy: Revivalism and Feminism in the Age of Finney.* Brooklyn: Carlson Publishing, 1991.

Harding, Vincent. *A Certain Magnificence: Lyman Beecher and the Transformation of American Protestantism, 1775–1863.* Brooklyn: Carlson Publishing, 1991.

Hart, Roger L. *Redeemers, Bourbons, & Populists: Tennessee 1870–1896.* Baton Rouge: Louisiana State University Press, 1975.

Haselby, Sam. *The Origins of American Religious Nationalism.* New York: Oxford University Press, 2015.

Hatch, Nathan O. *The Democratization of American Christianity*. New Haven, CT: Yale University Press, 1991.

Hayes, Sarah Kathryn Pitcher. "The Experiment at Fort Marion: Richard Henry Pratt's Recreation of Penitential Regimes at the Old Fort and Its Influence on American Indian Education." *Journal of Florida Studies* 1, no. 7 (2018): 1–22.

Hayward, Edward F. *Lyman Beecher*. Boston: Pilgrim Press, 1904.

Hedrick, Joan D. *Harriet Beecher Stowe: A Life*. New York: Oxford University Press, 1994.

Henry, Stuart C. *Unvanquished Puritan: A Portrait of Lyman Beecher*. Grand Rapids, MI: Eerdmans, 1973.

Hibben, Paxton. *Henry Ward Beecher: An American Portrait*. New York: Press of the Readers Club, 1927.

Hirrel, Leo P. *Children of Wrath: New School Calvinism and Antebellum Reform*. Lexington: University Press of Kentucky, 1998.

Hofstadter, Richard. *Anti-Intellectualism in American Life*. New York: Vintage Books, 1963.

Holmes, Clay W. *The Elmira Prison Camp*. New York: G. P. Putnam's Sons, 1912.

Howard, John R. *Henry Ward Beecher: A Study of His Personality, Career, and Influence in Public Affairs*. London: Brentano's, 1891.

Howe, Daniel Walker. *The Political Culture of the American Whigs*. Chicago: University of Chicago Press, 1979.

———. *The Unitarian Conscience: Harvard Moral Philosophy, 1805–1861*. Middletown, CT: Wesleyan University Press, 1988.

———. *What Hath God Wrought: The Transformation of America, 1815–1848*. New York: Oxford University Press, 2007.

———. ed. *Victorian America*. Philadelphia: University of Pennsylvania Press, 1976.

Hurt, R. Douglas. *The Ohio Frontier: Crucible of the Old Northwest, 1720–1830*. Bloomington: Indiana University Press, 1998.

Johnson, Oliver. *William Lloyd Garrison and His Times*. Boston: Houghton, Mifflin and Co., 1881.

Johnson, Paul E. *A Shopkeeper's Millennium: Society and Revivals in Rochester, New York, 1815–1837*. New York: Hill and Wang, 2004.

Kammen, Michael. *A Machine That Would Go of Itself: The Constitution in American Culture*. New York: Routledge, 2017.

Kerber, Linda. "The Republican Mother: Women and the Enlightenment—An American Perspective." *American Quarterly* 28, no. 2 (Summer 1976): 187–205.

Kidd, Thomas. *God of Liberty: A Religious History of the American Revolution*. New York: Basic Books, 2010.

———. "Where Did the Term 'Post-Millennial' Come From?" *The Gospel Coali-*

tion, October 3, 2016. www.thegospelcoalition.org/blogs/evangelical-history
/where-did-the-term-post-millennial-come-from/.

———. *Who Is an Evangelical? The History of a Movement in Crisis.* New Haven, CT: Yale University Press, 2019.

Kilpack, Josi S. *All That Makes Life Bright: The Life and Love of Harriet Beecher Stowe.* Salt Lake City: Shadow Mountain Publishing, 2017.

Kirkham, E. Bruce. *The Building of Uncle Tom's Cabin.* Knoxville: University of Tennessee Press, 1977.

Klotter, James C. *Henry Clay: The Man Who Would Be President.* New York: Oxford University Press, 2015.

Koester, Nancy. *Harriet Beecher Stowe: A Spiritual Life.* Grand Rapids, MI: Eerdmans, 2014.

———. *We Will Be Free: The Life and Faith of Sojourner Truth.* Grand Rapids, MI: Eerdmans, 2023.

Kohn, Denise, Sarah Meer, and Emily B. Todd, eds. *Transatlantic Stowe: Harriet Beecher Stowe and European Culture.* Iowa City: University of Iowa Press, 2006.

Lanier, Doris. "Henry Ward Beecher: A Lecture Tour of Georgia in 1883." *Georgia Historical Quarterly* 68, no. 3 (Fall 1984): 334–55.

Larsen, Timothy. *John Stuart Mill: A Secular Life.* New York: Oxford University Press, 2018.

Larson, Edward J. *Summer for the Gods: The Scopes Trial and America's Continuing Debate Over Science and Religion.* New York: Basic Books, 2006.

Lauck, Jon K. *The Good Country: A History of the American Midwest, 1800–1900.* Norman: University of Oklahoma Press, 2022.

Lee, Erika. *America for Americans: A History of Xenophobia in the United States.* New York: Basic Books, 2019.

Lepore, Jill. *These Truths: A History of the United States.* New York: W. W. Norton & Co., 2018.

Levine, Robert S. *The Failed Promise: Reconstruction, Frederick Douglass, and the Impeachment of Andrew Johnson.* New York: W. W. Norton & Co., 2021.

Lysaker, John T. *Emerson and Self-Culture.* Bloomington: Indiana University Press, 2008.

Margolis, Anne Throne, ed. *The Isabella Beecher Hooker Project: A Microfiche Edition of Her Papers.* Millwood: KTO Microform, 1979.

Marsden, George M. *The Evangelical Mind and the New School Presbyterian Experience: A Case Study of Thought and Theology in Nineteenth-Century America.* Eugene, OR: Wipf & Stock, 2003.

———. *Fundamentalism and American Culture*, 2nd ed. New York: Oxford University Press, 2006.

———. *Religion and American Culture: A Brief History.* 3rd ed. Grand Rapids, MI: Eerdmans, 2018.

Marshall, Charles F. *The True History of the Beecher Scandal.* Philadelphia: National Publishing Co., 1874.

Marty, Martin E. *Pilgrims in Their Own Land: 500 Years of Religion in America.* New York: Penguin Books, 1984.

Masur, Kate. *Until Justice Be Done: America's First Civil Rights Movement, from the Revolution to Reconstruction.* New York: W. W. Norton & Co., 2021.

Mathews, Donald G. *Religion in the Old South.* Chicago: University of Chicago Press, 1977.

Maulden, Kristopher. *The Federalist Frontier: Settler Politics in the Old Northwest, 1783–1840.* Columbia: University of Missouri Press, 2019.

McBride, Spencer W., and Jennifer Hull Dorsey, eds. *New York's Burned-Over District: A Documentary History.* Ithaca, NY: Cornell University Press, 2023.

McDonald, Jeanne Gillespie. "Edward Beecher and the Anti-Slavery Movement in Illinois." *Journal of the Illinois State Historical Society* 105, no. 1 (Spring 2012): 9–35.

McLoughlin, William G. *The Meaning of Henry Ward Beecher: An Essay on the Shifting Values of Mid-Victorian America, 1840–1870.* New York: Alfred A. Knopf, 1970.

McPherson, James M. "Antebellum Southern Exceptionalism: A New Look at an Old Question." *Civil War History* 50, no. 4 (December 2004): 418–33.

———. *Battle Cry of Freedom: The Civil War Era.* New York: Oxford University Press, 1988.

Merideth, Robert. *The Politics of the Universe: Edward Beecher, Abolition, and Orthodoxy.* Nashville: Vanderbilt University Press, 1968.

Merrill, Horace Samuel. *Bourbon Leader: Grover Cleveland and the Democratic Party.* Boston: Little, Brown and Co., 1957.

Merrill, Lisa. "'May She Read Liberty in Your Eyes?' Beecher, Boucicault and the Representation and Display of Antebellum Women's Racially Indeterminate Bodies." *Journal of Dramatic Theory and Criticism* 26, no. 2 (Spring 2012): 127–44.

Meyers, David, and Elise Meyers Walker. *The Reverse Underground Railroad in Ohio.* Cheltenham, UK: History Press, 2022.

Miller, Robert Moats. *Harry Emerson Fosdick: Preacher, Pastor, Prophet.* New York: Oxford University Press, 1985.

Miller, William Lee. *Arguing about Slavery.* New York: Alfred A. Knopf, 1996.

Minkema, Kenneth P., and Harry S. Stout. "The Edwardsean Tradition and the Antislavery Debate, 1740–1865." *Journal of American History.* 92, no. 1 (June 2005): 47–74.

Morris, J. Brent. *Oberlin, Hotbed of Abolitionism: College, Community, and the Fight for Freedom and Equality in Antebellum America.* Chapel Hill: University of North Carolina Press, 2014.

Muelder, Owen W. *Theodore Dwight Weld and the American Anti-Slavery Society.* Jefferson: McFarland & Co., 2011.

Mullin, Robert Bruce. *The Puritan as Yankee: A Life of Horace Bushnell.* Grand Rapids, MI: Eerdmans, 2002.

Najar, Monica. *Evangelizing the South: A Social History of Church and State in Early America.* New York: Oxford University Press, 2008.

Nasaw, David. *Andrew Carnegie.* New York: Penguin Books, 2007.

Newman, Henry S. *Freedom's Prophet: Bishop Richard Allen, the AME Church, and the Black Founding Fathers.* New York: New York University Press, 2008.

Noll, Mark A. *America's God: From Jonathan Edwards to Abraham Lincoln.* New York: Oxford University Press, 2002.

Oliver, Charles M. *Critical Companion to Walt Whitman: A Literary Reference to His Life and Work.* New York: Facts on File, 2006.

Oshatz, Molly. *Slavery and Sin: The Fight against Slavery and the Rise of Liberal Protestantism.* New York: Oxford University Press, 2012.

Paul, Joel Richard. *Indivisible: Daniel Webster and the Birth of American Nationalism.* New York: Riverhead Books, 2022.

Perry, Mark. *Lift Up Thy Voice: The Sarah and Angelina Grimké Family's Journey from Slaveholders to Civil Rights Leaders.* New York: Penguin Books, 2001.

Phillips, Charles W. *Edwards Amasa Park: The Last Edwardsean.* Gottingen: Vandenhoeck & Ruprecht, 2018.

Pinheiro, John C. *Missionaries of Republicanism: A Religious History of the Mexican-American War.* New York: Oxford University Press, 2014.

Poland, Charles P. Jr. *America's Good Terrorist: John Brown and the Harpers Ferry Raid.* Philadelphia: Casemate, 2020.

Porterfield, Amanda. *Conceived in Doubt: Religion and Politics in the New American Nation.* Chicago: University of Chicago Press, 2012.

Raines, Howell. *Silent Cavalry: How Union Soldiers From Alabama Helped Sherman Burn Atlanta—And Then Got Written Out of History.* New York: Crown Publishing, 2023.

Ramage, James A., and Andrea S. Watkins. *Kentucky Rising: Democracy, Slavery, and Culture from the Early Republic to the Civil War.* Lexington: University Press of Kentucky, 2011.

Reynolds, David S. *Abe: Abraham Lincoln in His Times.* New York: Penguin Books, 2021.

———. *Mightier Than the Sword: Uncle Tom's Cabin and the Battle for America.* New York: W. W. Norton & Co., 2012.

——. *Walt Whitman's America: A Cultural Biography*. New York: Knopf, 1995.

Robinson, Marilynne. *The Death of Adam: Essays on Modern Thought*. New York: Picador, 2005.

Rohrer, James R. *Keepers of the Covenant: Frontier Missions and the Decline of Congregationalism, 1774–1818*. New York: Oxford University Press, 1995.

Rowe, David L. *God's Strange Work: William Miller and the End of the World*. Grand Rapids, MI: Eerdmans Publishing, 2008.

Rugoff, Milton. *The Beechers: An American Family in the Nineteenth Century*. New York: Harper Collins, 1981.

Sassi, Jonathan D. *A Republic of Righteousness: The Public Christianity of the Post-Revolutionary New England Clergy*. New York: Oxford University Press, 2001.

Schantz, Mark S *Awaiting the Heavenly Country: The Civil War and America's Culture of Death*. Ithaca, NY: Cornell University Press, 2008.

Schneider, Thomas E. "Lincoln's Lyceum Speech as a Model of Democratic Rhetoric." *History of Political Thought* 32, no. 3 (Autumn 2011): 499–522.

Schweiger, Beth Barton. *A Literate South: Reading before Emancipation*. New Haven, CT: Yale University Press, 2019.

Seeman, Erik R. *Speaking with the Dead in Early America*. Philadelphia: University of Pennsylvania Press, 2019.

Seigel, Peggy. "A Passionate Missionary to the West: Charles Beecher in Fort Wayne, Indiana, 1844–1850." *Indiana Magazine of History* 106, no. 4 (2010): 325–55.

Sellers, Charles. *The Market Revolution: Jacksonian America, 1815-1846*. New York: Oxford University Press, 1991.

Shaplen, Robert. "The Beecher-Tilton Affair: He was the pastor of a fashionable Brooklyn church—and a ladies' man." *New Yorker*, June 4, 1954.

——. *Free Love & Heavenly Sinners: True Story of One of America's Greatest Scandals*. New York: Consul Books, 1954.

Sklar, Kathryn Kish. *Catharine Beecher: A Study in American Domesticity*. New York: W. W. Norton & Co., 1973.

Smith, Clint. "The Man Who Became Uncle Tom." *The Atlantic* 332, no. 3 (October 2023): 96–104.

Smith, Gary Scott, and P. C. Kemeny, eds. *The Oxford Handbook of Presbyterianism*. New York: Oxford University Press, 2019.

Spingarn, Adena. *Uncle Tom: From Martyr to Traitor*. Stanford, CA: Stanford University Press, 2018.

Stabel, Meredith, and Zachary Turpin, eds. *Radicals: Audacious Writings by American Women, Vol. 1: 1830-1930*. Iowa City: University of Iowa Press, 2021.

Stahr, Walter. *Salmon P. Chase: Lincoln's Vital Rival*. New York: Simon & Schuster, 2021.

Stanton, Elizabeth Cady, Susan B. Anthony, and Matilda Joslyn Gage, eds. *History of Woman Suffrage, Vol 2: 1861–1876*. Rochester, NY: Susan B. Anthony, 1887.

Steinmetz, Greg. *American Rascal: How Jay Gould Built Wall Street's Biggest Fortune*. New York: Simon & Schuster, 2022.

Stewart, John W., and James H. Moorhead, eds. *Charles Hodge Revisited: A Critical Appraisal of His Life and Work*. Grand Rapids, MI: Eerdmans Publishing, 2002.

Stout, Harry S. *American Aristocrats: A Family, a Fortune, and the Making of American Capitalism*. New York: Basic Books, 2017.

Sweeney, Douglas A. *Nathaniel Taylor, New Haven Theology, and the Legacy of Jonathan Edwards*. New York: Oxford University Press, 2003.

Taylor, Alan. *American Republics: A Continental History of the United States, 1783–1850*. New York: W. W. Norton & Co., 2021.

Taylor, Eva. *A History of the Park Church, 1846–1971*. Rev. ed. Elmira, NY: Park Church, 1971.

Thompson, J. Earl, Jr. "Lyman Beecher's Long Road to Conservative Abolitionism." *Church History* 42, no. 1 (March 1973): 89–109.

Thulesius, Olav. *Harriet Beecher Stowe in Florida, 1867 to 1884*. Jefferson, NC: McFarland Publishing, 2001.

Todd, Obbie Tyler. "American Prophets: Federalist Clergy's Response to the Hamilton-Burr Duel of 1804." *Themelios* 45, no. 1 (2020): 563–75.

———. "Evangelicals, Justice, and the Civil War." *Journal of the Evangelical Theological Society* 65, no. 2 (2022): 207–23.

———. *The Moral Governmental Theory of Atonement: Re-Envisioning Penal Substitution*. Eugene, OR: Cascade Books, 2021.

———. *Southern Edwardseans: The Southern Baptist Legacy of Jonathan Edwards*. Göttingen: Vandenhoeck & Ruprecht, 2022.

Vollaro, Daniel R. "Lincoln, Stowe, and the 'Little Woman / Great War' Story: The Making, and Breaking, of a Great American Anecdote." *Journal of the Abraham Lincoln Association* 30, no. 1 (Winter 2009): 18–34.

Wacker, Grant. *America's Pastor: Billy Graham and the Shaping of a Nation*. Cambridge, MA: Harvard University Press, 2014.

Walters, Ronald G. *American Reformers, 1815–1860*. 2nd ed. New York: Hill and Wang, 1997.

Watson, Harry L. *Liberty and Power: The Politics of Jacksonian America*. New York: Hill and Wang, 2006.

White, Barbara A. *The Beecher Sisters*. New Haven, CT: Yale University Press, 2003.

Wilentz, Sean. *The Rise of American Democracy: Jefferson to Lincoln*. New York: W. W. Norton & Co., 2005.

Wilson, Forrest. *Crusader in Crinoline: The Life of Harriet Beecher Stowe.* New York: J. B. Lippincott, 1941.

Wood, Gordon S. *Friends Divided: John Adams and Thomas Jefferson.* New York; Penguin Press, 2017.

Yellin, Jean Fagan, and John C. Van Horne, eds. *The Abolitionist Sisterhood: Women's Political Culture in Antebellum America.* Ithaca, NY: Cornell University Press, 1994.

Index

abolitionism, 16, 32, 42, 49, 56, 62, 70, 71–77, 80, 117–18, 127, 135, 147, 150, 158, 193; "abolition regiment," 198; anti-abolitionists, 105, 108, 115–18, 148, 160, 172; conservative abolitionism, 63, 90, 126–28; divisions within, 173–74; evolution of, 161–62; and Kansas-Nebraska controversy, 177; and western newspapers, 88–89, 115–18; and women issue, 105–6, 138–39

Adams, Charles Francis, 209

Adams, John, 46, 87

adventism, 145

agnosticism, 234, 266

African American suffrage, 151

Alien and Sedition Acts, 87

Allan, William, 72

Allen, Georgiana May Stowe, 273–74

American Revolution, 8, 105, 200

Amherst College, 4, 48–49, 51, 108

Anderson, Charles, 160

Anderson, Robert, 211

Andover Theological Seminary, 5, 6, 48, 60, 91, 111, 120, 149, 165, 187, 219; and drilling of soldiers, 193; and German Romantic thought, 262

Anglican Catechism, 282n63

Anthony, Susan B., 16, 225, 232, 242, 245, 247

Arminianism, 1

Atlantic Monthly, 191, 197

Bacon, Francis, 261

Bacon, Leonard, 10, 202

Bailey, Gamaliel, 89, 164

Baptists, 17, 47, 87, 218, 226

Barnes, Albert, 111

Bebbington Quadrilateral, 285n131, 304n141

Beecher, Catharine, 2, 3, 5, 8, 9, 13, 16, 27, 29, 37, 57; as a contradictory woman, 168; death of, 254, 256–58; domestic values of, 25, 26, 27–28, 129–31, 254; education of, 14, 25, 32, 34–35, 39, 41, 58, 69, 81–82, 137–38, 154–55, 168, 249; health and well-being of, 185; helps Harriet in writing *Uncle Tom's Cabin*, 164; honors father and mother, 249; in Florida, 227–28; joins Episcopal Church, 208; living with Thomas, 253; mediates between Harriet and Isabella, 239, 249, 253–54; missionary teachers and, 91, 138, 141, 144, 155, 164, 241; organizes family reunion in 1856, 178; revivalist-style message of, 249; and siblings, 35, 39, 61, 134, 148, 231; skeptical of spiritualism, 271; and slavery, 106, 122; and suffrage, 240–42; and theology, 17, 25, 32, 34, 82–84, 122, 136–37, 151, 168; and women's rights, 106, 136, 168, 240–41, 249; writing career of, 68, 106, 136–37, 185, 249, 253

Beecher, Charles, 8, 17, 22, 26, 68, 114; composes Lyman's autobiography, 179–80; death of, 276; as disciple of Edward, 170, 179, 204, 228, 276; and drowning of daughters, 222; and Fugitive Slave Law, 163–64; heresy trial of, 204–5; and job termination, 164; and Kansas-Nebraska controversy, 175; ministry of, 133, 155; and music, 27, 132–33, 164; and New Orleans,